WHO IS FOURIER?

A Mathematical Adventure

Transnational College of LEX

Translated by Alan Gleason

Language Research Foundation

BOSTON

Published by:
Language Research Foundation, 68 Leonard Street, Belmont, MA 02178

©Language Research Foundation 1995

First Published 1995

Library of Congress Catalog Card Number:94-79684

ISBN 0-9643504-0-8

Printed in the United States of America   10 9 8 7 6 5 4 3 2 1

Acknowledgments

Writing and producing the original version and the translation of this book has involved many people. It gives us great pleasure to acknowledge those people who have taken time to help and advise us with our projects.

English Version

Dr. Yoichiro Nambu(Ph.D.), Elementary Particle Physics at E. Fermi Institute, University of Chicago

Ms. Mayumi Morimoto, Statistics/Probability, Department of Mathematics (Ph.D. Program), Boston University

Japanese Language Services, Boston

Dr. Jerry Lemieux, BSEE, MSEE, PhDEE(MIT)

Advisors to the original Japanese Version

Mr. Genpei Akasegawa, Artist and Writer and Photographer

Dr. Jiro Ohta, Cell Biology, President of Ochanomizu Women University

Mr. Tan Sakakibara, Automatic Control Engineering, Director of LEX Institute

Dr. Hiroshi Shimizu, Biological complexity and information, The "Ba" Research Institute, Kanazawa Institute of Technology & International Media Foundation

Mr. Yusuke Tsukahara, Technical Research Institute in Toppan Printing Co.

Ms. Yao Nakano, Senior Fellow in LEX Institute

Dr. Teru Hayashi, Control and System Engineering, Professor emer. of Tokyo Institute of Technology / Professor of Toin University of Yokohama

Dr. Toyoo Maeda, Metallurgist, IHI Research Institute Vice Director

Dr. Junichi Miida, Nuclear Engineering, Japan Atomic Energy Research Institute(1956-1981) Deputy Director / Nuclear Science and Engineering, OECD Nuclear Energy Agency, Paris.(1976-1979) Deputy Director

Dr. Shigeyuki Minami, Electromagnetism, Osaka City University

Dr. Kazuo Yamazaki, Theoretical Physics, Professor emer. of Kyoto University / Professor of Kobegakuin University

Dr. Keiko Nakamura, Biohistory, Biohistory Research Hall Deputy Director General / Professor of Waseda University

Dr. Takao Saito, Space Physics, Professor emer. of Tohoku University

Hippo Family Club Members, who joined in the Fourier Family at Tokyo, Nagoya and Osaka

Cover

Fourier illustration from, *Portraits et Historire des HommesUtiles, Collection de Cinquante Portraits,* (Société Montyon et Franklin, 1839-1840) in Boston Public Library.

FOREWORD TO THE ENGLISH-LANGUAGE EDITION

Fourier mathematics is a powerful means of analyzing phenomena, such as light, sound, vibrations, and heat conduction, that take the form of waves. Sound can be defined as waves of pressure that vibrate the air and are thereby transmitted. Words uttered by human beings are of course a kind of sound, and therefore can be described as waves. A sustained vocal sound, such as a vowel, consists of repetitions of the same wave pattern. Fourier formulas come in very handy when we wish to analyze the structure of these sounds.

From the first stages of its production, the original book was never intended to be sold in regular bookstores. It was conceived and written for the purpose of relating the experiences of the students of the Transnational College of LEX to as many Hippo Family Club members as possible. Those experiences included many surprise discoveries and emotional moments encountered on their adventure into the field of Fourier mathematics. To us, the members of Hippo are the same as relatives. This book was meant for the rest of our family. That the book was produced by amateurs is evident in its appearance. It does not look like a typical "book". In addition to the lack of consistency between chapters and the jagged letters produced by our word processor, the use of jokes and foreign words which could only be understood by Hippo members lined the pages.

The students were divided into groups and each group studied a different aspect of Fourier. The first drafts for each chapter were written by the most mathematically inexperienced first year students of each group. Watching them develop an understanding of the subject and begin to use its jargon bonded everyone together. There were many emotional moments in this process which could never have been seen in a gathering of mathematicians. Every student in the group explained in detail how they came to understand each step. They methodically explored the individual concepts. This book is as much about the process of learning as it is about Fourier mathematics. That may explain why readers are able to readily understand the methods employed.

At first, the students took up the study of Fourier mathematics simply to obtain some basic knowledge to help in their analysis of the voice. But the deeper they plunged in their study of the phenomena of sound, the more they realized that this mathematics and its formulas were a bona fide language for describing these phenomena. The familiar trigonometric functions sine and cosine; differentiation for finding the velocity or acceleration of a moving object; integration for finding the distance moved by an object; the imaginary number i, so useful in calculations; the base e of natural logarithms, which has a special significance in differentiation and integration; vectors, which have both magnitude and direction; and Maclaurin's expansion, which allows the conversion of any expression into a single format. All of these concepts, which are normally learnt about separately when studying physics or mathematics, appear on-stage together in the drama of Fourier's wave analysis.

We, the student authors, made absolutely no efforts to advertise the book to the public. Its popularity spread by word of mouth. Now, that same word has led to the publication of the English language edition and its sale in the United States. Thinking back about a book that began with the printing of only 700 copies and now has sold over 60,000 copies, and seeing how far it has come makes us inexpressibly happy.

We have also been blessed with the chance to have the English version checked for technical errors by Dr. Yoichiro Nambu of the University of Chicago, a world renowned researcher in elementary particle physics, and a number of other prominent scholars. However, any errors in this work are completely our responsibility. Thanks to this book we have met many people and will treasure those ties. We look forward to encountering the many new readers of this book someday in the future.

January 1995
Transnational College of LEX

CONTENTS

INTRODUCTION TO THE ENGLISH-LANGUAGE EDITION

"Behind the chaos lurks a simple order"

Nature appears chaotic and ever-changing. But behind the eternal fluctuation of natural phenomena lurks an immutable order. This natural order of things is very simple. Seasons repeat, progressing from spring to summer to fall to winter, then back to spring again. Water falls from the sky as rain, flows from high places to low, evaporates, rises to form clouds, then falls to the earth as rain again. Nature is constantly recreating itself, but always in accordance with a set of clear, concise natural laws. This is the concept underlying the ancient Chinese text *I Ching*, or Book of Changes.

Since time immemorial human beings have been asking themselves, "What is nature, and what is my place in the natural order?" We continue to ask the same questions today. But we have discovered a language that allows us to precisely describe, to some degree at least, the order that underlies the vicissitudes of nature. That language is what we call natural science.

There is a broad range of possible meanings in an expression as simple as "You're crazy!" Depending on the speaker and the situation, it could mean "You're an interesting character," "You're really cute," or even "You're a complete idiot!" This broad fluctuation in meaning is what makes everyday language so richly expressive. However, broad ambiguity becomes a liability when we try to use language to describe the order behind the fluctuation. For this purpose we have a language made up of words with a narrow range of meaning — clear, unambiguous words. That language is mathematics. The clarity and brevity of mathematics were critical to the success of the new science of quantum mechanics as well. One of the pioneers of quantum mechanics, Dr. Werner Heisenberg, was heard to have repeatedly told his students the following:

"Use ordinary, everyday language when you analyze or debate a concept. When the image that emerges becomes so clear that anyone can understand it, that is the time to start thinking of an applicable formula for it." Of course, first you must have a full command of the language of mathematics in order to do this.

Mathematics is nothing less than a powerful language devised by human beings for the purpose of describing natural phenomena.

The purpose of the Transnational College of LEX (TCL) is to provide a venue for the scientific study of languages and of the human beings that speak those languages.

The crucible for all research conducted by LEX is the Hippo Family Club, of which every student at the College is a member (see Note). The Hippo Family Club provides its members with the opportunity to acquire multiple languages by a natural method. When the Club was founded in 1981, its Japanese-speaking members started out by simultaneously learning English, Korean and Spanish. By 1988, when this book was written, the list had grown to include German, French and Chinese, for a total of seven languages. Russian and Italian were added in 1990, and Malaysian and Thai in 1991. Thus Hippo members now practice speaking eleven languages at the same time. At first glance this may seem unrealistic from the standpoint of conventional thinking. But the number of languages is insignificant. What the Hippo experience has done is radically alter the way people view languages, and with it the way they comprehend them.

An infant raised in an environment that exposes him to a spoken language will, in time, learn to speak that language on his own. This is an absolute given, perhaps even a defining characteristic of human beings. If a child is exposed to a new linguistic environment at any point up to about five or six years of age, it will only be a matter of months or a year before he can speak the new language as well. We have all noticed that people who come to Japan from places like Africa or India, where many languages are spoken, seem to pick Japanese up almost instantly. This is true of adults as well as children. If the language is spoken by human beings somewhere, it can be acquired naturally by anyone.

"Language spoken by human beings" may sound redundant, but it is a key point. For all of their superficial differences, languages share the common definition of being spoken by humans. They share certain characteristics precisely because they are all a form of human language.

Consider another kind of language, or form of self-expression, if you will — music. However strange the melody or rhythm might be, people intuitively recognize it as music, made by human beings just like themselves. Just as people from multilingual environments are quick to learn new languages, people already familiar with a variety of melodies and rhythms learn new musical forms with ease.

In multilingual regions of the world, that is, regions not dominated by one or even two languages, people are constantly exposed to speech that may be unfamiliar to them. People who grow up in such an environment are instinctively curious about new languages. To them, it is perfectly natural to want to figure out and understand what the unfamiliar words mean. By contrast, people raised in regions where one language dominates tend to write off foreign tongues as something beyond their comprehension. They unconsciously shut their ears to new sounds.

"How did you learn to speak Korean so well? You sound just like a native!"

Hippo Family Club member Mrs. Ogura was overjoyed when her homestay guest from Korea, Mrs. Kim complimented her in this manner. This is what Mrs. Ogura later told her fellow club members:

"When Mrs. Kim said I sounded just like a native Korean, I guess that meant she thought my pronunciation was perfect. But I've never once studied how to pronounce Korean! When I first listened to the Hippo language tapes, I would just hum the sounds I heard as if they were a song. Gradually I was able to distinguish individual sounds, and then I got to the point where I could mimic them. Even now, if someone told me to enunciate the vowels and consonants of Korean one at a time, I probably couldn't do it!"

"There are still so many Korean words whose meanings I don't exactly know. A year ago, I could only repeat most of the sounds I heard on the Korean tapes without knowing what any of them meant. When I met some Korean friends back then, I would speak to them in their language even when I wasn't sure of the meaning of the words I was using. But they understood! I was so happy! From then on I spoke Korean as often as I could, and gradually I figured out what the different phrases meant. The more I used them, the clearer they became."

"Now, if I really sounded just like a native to Mrs. Kim, that means my grammar must have been correct too. But I've never studied Korean grammar either..."

"During the one week she stayed with us, Mrs. Kim kept drawing Korean sounds out of my mouth like a magician pulling rabbits from a hat. At some point, what were at first just sounds to me turned into words I could understand. And even more mysteriously, I found that Mrs. Kim could utter a Korean word or expression I'd never heard before, and after hearing it only once or twice, I'd start using it too, without even thinking about it! Once I'd used a phrase myself, I felt I understood not only its basic meaning, but its more subtle nuances as well. It was as if I'd somehow acquired a magic box in my head for catching and storing Korean. Even after Mrs. Kim left, I could still hear in my head the sounds of the Korean we spoke together."

Listening to Mrs. Ogura tell her story was like hearing a little child describe her first encounter with language. Indeed, it was a glimpse of the child that lives on inside every adult.

We take it for granted that a baby in a natural environment where language is spoken will acquire that language on his own. But what are the characteristics and conditions that define this environment, this learning process? These are questions that need to be answered.

If we take Mrs. Ogura's experience and apply it to the way a baby learns a language, we can interpret it in the following way: All human languages, despite their superficial differences in sound and structure, share an elegant and universal order. The set of sounds that make up the Korean language has its own distinctively Korean melodies and rhythms. But Korean is a human language. Consequently any human should be able to speak Korean. If you repeatedly listen to it and try speaking it, you will be able to distinguish and mimic smaller and smaller components of what started out as just a vaguely Korean-like sound to you. Among the sounds that make up human language, there is none that the human ear cannot, through repeated listening, eventually isolate from the whole and identify as a discrete sound. And once you have identified a sound, learning how to reproduce it with your own mouth will come easily. If the sound is part of a natural language, it should not require any undue effort, such as muscle strain or the like, to reproduce. It is the same with music; if you listen to any song often enough, you will eventually be able to sing it. The individual sounds that make up a language are never separate from that language; they are always embedded within it. You cannot simply string a bunch of discrete sounds together and hope to make sense. The whole is always greater than the sum of its parts.

If our analysis is correct, then the pronunciation drills of conventional foreign language study reflect a woeful misunderstanding of the natural process of human cognition. Rather, they appear to be an unnatural, artificial form of pronunciation exercise. How can you form your mouth in the right shape to produce a sound that you haven't or can't even *hear* yet? Whatever language you acquire, you must first start by listening to the whole. As you gradually break this down into ever-smaller parts, pronunciation will come naturally.

Meaning is created when sounds of a language initiate an anticipated response. So the sounds of a language by their very nature must have meaning. Yet at the start of the language learning process, we may articulate sounds without knowing what they mean. Babies provide a good example of this. Adults however, may even be met with surprise or ridicule, with others asking, "Do you actually know what you're saying?" The temptation is to run to the dictionary for help...But babies don't use dictionaries! The meanings to be found in dictionaries are obviously derivative, secondary to the primary meaning a baby understands.

Without a dictionary, we have no choice but to guess at a word's meaning and try it out in conversation. If we aren't understood, then we guess and try again. Oh, the joy when we're understood! This is the natural way for human beings to learn any language. We unconsciously attempt to find connections between the sounds of language and the environment in which we hear them. In time, we acquire the urge to try speaking those sounds ourselves.

Out of the mouths of two- and three-year-old toddlers fly expressions that sometimes astonish grown-ups. The child may not actually understand what he's saying, but if he tries it out and it gets the proper response, he begins to acquire a hazy sense of the meaning of the sound.

Suppose we were to ask this infant, "Do you understand the meaning of everything you are saying? He would undoubtedly answer, "No...what's meaning?" If we continued to ask, "Are the words you are now using the sum total of everything you can say?" He would undoubtedly reply, "Absolutely not! There are plenty of sounds I possess that will come forth from my mouth when the situations arise."

By the time he turns three years of age, words will be pouring forth from his mouth.

Mrs. Ogura elaborates from the perspective of an adult: "In language, there is no such thing as a meaningless sound. When you try using an unfamiliar sound or phrase, you're just taking a guess at its meaning. If it meets with a good response, that gives you an inkling, at least, of what it means. So you try using it again. But 'taking a guess' is actually an unconscious process. It's as if the environment or situation, the context in which you're using the language, draws the phrase out of you. This is possible because you already have the sound itself inside you. If you learn a language by this natural process, you won't find yourself uttering sounds that are just meaningless imitations of language."

Like the process by which we master the sounds of language, the process by which we discover their meaning begins with a vague, overall impression. From there we move forward little by little, fitting pieces into the puzzle until a clear picture emerges from the connections we have established between these sounds and their environment. Indeed, this is the function languages are supposed to fulfill for human beings, both young and old, that exist in a world of language.

Humanity did not recognize that there were rules we subsequently called grammar until after it had invented letters, and had begun to write down the language that until then had existed only in speech. Only when words could be written and read over and over again could people have noticed that language has its own remarkable order. It must have been a shocking discovery, that the words we speak so unthinkingly adhere to a strict set of rules. These rules were not consciously invented by us. Somehow, humanity, which we can perhaps define as a phenomenon of nature that speaks language, created language with a structure ideally suited to the cognitive

circular argument

capabilities bestowed upon our species by nature. Once our ancestors discovered the rules of so called 'classical' grammar and defined them, they must have had a notion that languages concealed an even deeper, more subtle structure. When people — even a child or an adult who knows nothing of grammar — learn language by the natural process, they basically do not make mistakes. Indeed, most of us are blissfully ignorant of the rules of our mother tongue. When we write something in our native language, all we have to do is first try speaking the words, and a suitable expression spontaneously emerges from within the natural flow of sounds and language.

When we acquire a language by natural means, we do not learn to read or write until we have reached a certain stage in our verbal development. We can only create letters once we have speech. This is because the written letters themselves do not convey the sounds of language. Depending on the written word prematurely tends to make us view language from a distance. First we must feel comfortable with the spoken word. Then, when the time is right, we are ready to work with letters.

We have suggested that an order common to all human language lies behind the apparently random sounds of different spoken languages. Surely a similar order can be found in the seemingly disparate grammars of all languages. Grammar, the structure of the patterns we detect in the repetition of sounds in every language, must share certain universal traits as well.

Today's concept of grammar resembles the approach to natural science in the days of classical biology, every part is classified and isolated from the organism as a whole. Likening grammatical structure to the human skeletal form, modern grammar isolates and names each bone or joint, then sets about assembling the adult human skeleton like so many building blocks. This is how contemporary grammarians regard language. But this is not how language is put together. The entire skeleton already lies latent in the structure of a single fertilized egg. As the embryo grows, so do the various parts, together forming a whole which eventually grows into an adult.

Unlike modern grammar, modern biology has long since moved beyond the confines of natural science's classic building block approach. In such fields as molecular biology, scientists are now beginning to seek universal definitions that will answer such questions as "What is life?" and "What does it mean to be alive?"

Hippo Family Club members today speak of creating a fertile environment for acquiring languages. We call it a "language place (言語場)." The language place is created by the people that participate in this "place." Consider a newborn baby. We tend to think of the infant as an incomplete person, an empty vessel yet to be filled, but this is far from the truth. A new language place immediately arises around a newborn child. The mother tries to discern the meaning of her baby's every glance, gesture, murmur or cry. And these sounds and expressions do have meaning; they are already a form of language. Human languages can be defined as a means of being able to create and carry meaning.

From the day the baby is born, he becomes an active and central participant in the new language place. The adults around him find themselves making adoring, richly expressive utterances they would never use if the baby were not there. The baby draws this language from the mouths of the adults, all the while actively taking in their facial expressions and gestures, and of course the sounds they make. The baby murmurs these sounds to himself, instinctively seeking out the meaning of the speech he hears, and eventually finding it. In this sense, babies are all very talkative participants in this language place.

This language place cannot exist by itself, but only as the creation of the people who engage in it. The place is built by the cooperative process of people seeking, finding and creating language together. Many Hippo members participate in club activities as entire families. The family unit is, after all, the first and closest language place available to people.

Five-year-old Taro moved with his family from Japan to the United States when his father was transferred overseas by his employer. On his first visit to the neighborhood park, Taro met an American boy who was playing and shouting in a totally unfamiliar language. Another Japanese boy who had arrived in America a year or so earlier was shouting back in the same strange tongue. Young Hanako, who had been in the country three or four months, was also playing with the boys and saying something too. The park provided no beginner's lessons, no instructors. There was nothing for Taro to do but jump in and start playing with the other children. In a short time, he too would be a central member of this language place. Within a year he would become a fluent speaker of the dominant language of this place. A language place is created by the participation of people in real life, everyday activities.

When our colleague Mrs. Ogura began speaking Korean with her friend Mrs. Kim, it was not because Mrs. Kim was setting an example for her. Rather, it was because her visit provided the opportunity for Hippo club members to form a new language place with Mrs. Kim at its center. In the process of creating that place, the Korean that had only been a set of sounds to Mrs. Ogura formed a link with her environment and began to flow freely from her mouth.

Not everyone who participates in Hippo club activities starts speaking new languages this quickly. Some find the process easier than others. The reason for this has gradually become clear, however. Those who immediately try to speak the sounds they hear, just as a baby does, improve rapidly. The ones who make little progress are those who succumb to an adult's self-consciousness and are afraid they will make mistakes or sound foolish. It is important to be surrounded by kindred spirits who will listen attentively to the sounds you make. Conversely, it is listening to the sounds *they* make that stimulates your own speech. We acquire our language from others around us.

A three-year-old child is capable of understanding and saying just about anything. All the words he has learned at this point were picked up from the people around him. Using the sounds he was given, he goes on to create his own unique world with them. The ability to speak a language occurs as a result of living in a rich language place.

The Hippo language group is unique. It ranges from first-day newcomers to veterans who have been members for over ten years and speak a number of languages quite well. The continuing practice of Hippo group participants is simple: to produce as fertile and creative a language place as possible together. It must be a place grounded in everyday reality where multiple languages fly through the air unrestrained. This is the natural learning environment for languages that we seek.

Choosing to work on ten or more languages at the same time in the Hippo Family Club activity has proven to be an excellent strategy. It effectively prevents anyone from actually *studying* the languages. If you study only one or two languages, you tend to become distracted by the superficial differences among them. With three or more languages, people unconsciously become aware of the similarities rather than the differences.

Those participants in the Hippo experiment who have become proficient in a number of languages all say more or less the same thing: "Languages may appear different, but they're ultimately the same. Now, when I hear a new language, it's as if I've gotten a head start from all the other languages I've learned. The new ones come easier and easier. In fact, I can't wait to learn more."

There are many human languages. From the outside they appear completely different, both phonetically and grammatically, but at their core they are the same. This is what babies have been telling us from the beginning and now adults are beginning to realize it too.

We label as "foreign" those languages we approach from the outside. Those we learn from the inside, by the natural method, we call our mother tongue. This is what we meant when we said at the beginning that the Hippo experience radically alters the way we understand languages. The practical, real-life approach to language employed by Hippo makes every language our mother tongue.

As the Hippo Family Club language learning process has evolved, so has the research conducted by TCL.

It all began when we were discussing the sounds that make up a language. Suddenly someone said, "I wonder what the ideal distribution of the five Japanese vowels would be?" (The Japanese vowels are AH, EE, UU, EH, and OH.) "Ideal distribution" means the placement of vowels that would most clearly distinguish them from one another, that is, make them easy for people to tell apart. We tentatively concluded that the ideal distribution would take the form of a regular pentagon. The reasoning was that a pentagon represents the most balanced configuration of five vowels placed as far apart from each other as possible. That was as far as our discussion went at the time. To paraphrase Dr. Heisenberg, we were using everyday language to try to come up with a clear image of order in language.

Then one day, a member of another Hippo group came rushing in to announce breathlessly, "There's a way we can see the sounds of language with our own eyes!" See the sounds of language? How? As a series of complex waves it turns out. If sounds could be viewed as waveforms, that meant they could be measured as physical quantities. Someone else announced that they had heard of a type of mathematics that analyzed waves of this sort, something called Fourier analysis. From this point there was no stopping the TCL students.

"Math is a language for accurately describing nature, isn't it? Let's just treat it like any other language and add it to our Hippo multilingual activity list!"

Most of the TCL students had given up on mathematics when they were in middle school or high school. But now they were Hippo club members, comfortable with the Hippo process, which was to start learning a new language by listening to the language tapes over and over. Applying this same principle to the language of math, they started reading mathematics books over and over, turning the pages even when they didn't understand a word on them. And just as the sounds of a new language start to flow from a person's mouth as soon as his or her ear becomes used to them, the TCL students started to chat about math as they began to familiarize themselves with the new concepts. If when having tried to explain a concept to others, they were unable to follow your explanation well enough to understand it themselves, it meant your own understanding was still incomplete. It meant you were still speaking the math equivalent of baby talk. It took less than a year before everyone was speaking the language of math, or to be specific, Fourier analysis. The fruit of our labors is this book — *WHO IS FOURIER? A Mathematical Adventure.*

Once again, let us paraphrase the words of Heisenberg: "Use simple, everyday language when you present an argument, and when the image becomes so clear that anyone can understand it, that is the time to start thinking of an applicable formula to express your concept."

At long last we were ready to put our newly acquired mathematical language, Fourier analysis, to the test. We began analyzing data on the five Japanese vowels, AH-EE-UU-EH-OH, as spoken by many different individuals (see Chapter Four). No two people's voices displayed the same vowel distribution, yet a very clear pattern began to emerge. We tried adding up the individual data and taking an average, increasing the number of subjects from five to ten, to twenty and more. As we randomly added and averaged more and more data, the average distribution of the five Japanese vowels began to assume a graceful symmetry. It was very close to the pentagon we had predicted in the first place! Behind the variation in individual values, there indeed lay a simple and elegant order. This was our first glimpse of the natural structure of the sounds of language. We knew we had barely scratched the surface of the phenomenon of vowels. But we also knew our quest was headed in the right direction.

Our discovery about vowels suggests that the consonants of Japanese can also be described as physical quantities, and that we will find an elegant symmetry among them as well. We can also predict that if this symmetry exists among the sounds of Japanese, it must be found in other languages as well.

But what happens when we introduce the indeterminate quantity of "meaning" to the equation? Suddenly the development of a comprehensive description of the order in natural languages seems more problematic. Yet the formation of meaning is an integral part of the formation of language. We cannot ignore the importance of the role played by sounds as an expression of meaning.

The TCL researchers have only just begun to address this question in their effort to develop a scientific approach to the understanding of language and the human beings that speak those languages.

January 1995
Transnational College of LEX

Note: Hippo Family Club Activities

The Hippo Family Club engages in activities that promote the natural mastery of eleven languages simultaneously — Japanese, English, Korean, Spanish, German, French, Chinese, Russian, Italian, Malaysian and Thai. The club uses tapes of songs from around the world as well as stories told in all eleven languages. Club members listen to these tapes as they go about their daily business. Some play the tapes at home like so much background music, while others listen to them through headphones while commuting.

Hippo members are of all ages, from babies to elderly grandmothers and grandfathers. It is not uncommon for entire families to participate; in fact, it is actively encouraged as the ideal form of membership.

Members meet once or twice a week in regional groups known as Hippo Families. Group interaction resembles that which takes place in an open space or park, with many languages flying through the air at once. As in a park setting, there is no curriculum nor classes held at these group meetings. Instead, we sing and dance and try speaking the new languages we are acquiring every chance we get. New members, even adults, sing or hum the words just as a baby would. Currently we have six hundred such groups in Japan, with a total of over 25,000 members. Hippo Families also get together at large gatherings of several groups, as well as at special meetings and camps for teens, singles, parents and so on.

There are no teachers in the Hippo Family Club. We call the coordinators of our groups "Fellows." A Fellow serves as a messenger whose job it is to inform members of the group about events happening in the Hippo world at large.

The Hippo Family Club also runs a number of Transnational Exchange Programs. As the name suggests, these programs provide an opportunity for club members to interact with people from all over the world. Besides arranging meetings with visitors to Japan from other countries, we organize homestays for them lasting anywhere from one night to long-term stays. Japanese members can also go overseas for homestays in twenty different countries. These exchanges help us to realize that the human family transcends national borders, and that we all speak the same human language.

Part 1

Chapter 1

Fourier Series

Our Fourier adventure is about to begin. Are you ready? In this chapter, we will try our hand at using mathematics to express the following concept: "A complicated wave is the sum of simple waves." But how do you represent a wave in mathematical terms? That's where the adventure starts!

This chapter on Fourier series is based on my own learning experience and the inspiring accomplishments of the "First Fourier Family." It's a true-life adventure story.

NONFICTION!

Hi! My name's Rie! It's time for us to set out on our

FOURIER SERIES GREAT ADVENTURE!

1. ¿Por que? Why Do We Need Math?!

We're trying to solve the riddle of human speech. When we try to decipher ancient Japanese texts, we look for hints in the Chinese characters in which they are written. In the same way, the key to deciphering speech is

MATHEMATICS!

Many of us feel like running away at the very mention of the word "mathematics." But Fourier analysis happens to be the perfect mathematical tool for unlocking the secrets of the human voice!

Relax, relax!

2. Math is the Universal Language!

Mathematical formulas can come in very handy.

Look at these long sentences...

○ 일 더하기 일은 이	(Korean)
○ Un et un font deux	(French)
○ Uno y uno igual dos	(Spanish)
○ One plus one equals two	(English)

$$1+1=2$$

There! That's a lot shorter!

3. The Shape of Sound

If we want to solve the riddle of the voice, we first have to ask

"何 is the voice?"
What

So let's see what the voice really is!

Experiment

Put your hand on your throat and say "Ahh!"

Results

Your throat vibrates.

Ahh!

Chirp!

Ahh!

VIBRATIONS OF THE AIR

When you say "Ahh," it isn't that a chunk of "Ahh" sound flies into the ear of the listener. What happens is that the "Ahh" makes your throat vibrate, which squeezes the air, which becomes denser, then thinner, over and over. These repeating vibrations of the air reach the ear and make the eardrum vibrate.

Ahh!

Wow! No kidding!

It'd be more fun if we could see it, though.

Guess what! You can!

HUH?!

TA-DAH!

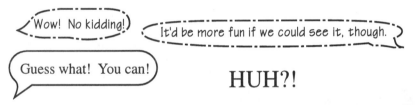

First or fast?

FFT: First Fourier Transform Analyzer

That's where FFT comes in!!
FFT is a fantastic machine that lets us see the vibration of the air — in other words, sound itself — with our own eyes.

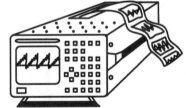

You already know about something similar!
In hospitals, they have machines that show the heartbeat as a wave, right?
...You don't want this:

BEEEEP

The voice is made of waves, too, remember?

4. Let's Look at Voice Waves!

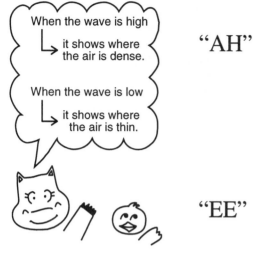

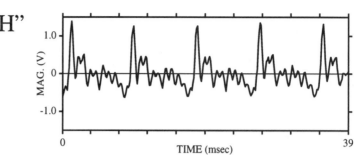

"AH"

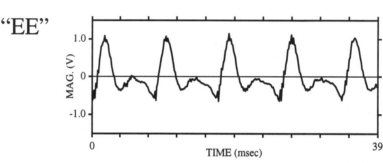

"EE"

These are waveforms of a male voice

What do you notice about these waves?

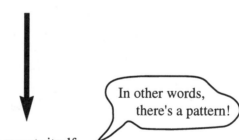

In other words, there's a pattern!

The same waveform repeats itself.

We call a repeating wave of this sort a *periodic* wave.

The time it takes for a single waveform pattern to repeat itself is called the *fundamental period*.

• A long fundamental period makes your voice sound low.

• A short fundamental period makes your voice sound high.

Women's voices have a shorter fundamental period than men's!

 Experiment

Let's get a lot of different people to say "AH"!

Ahh! Ahh! Ahh! Ahh! Ahh! Ahh!

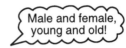 Male and female, young and old!

 Chirp!

Now let's change the volume of the voice!

"AH" in a loud voice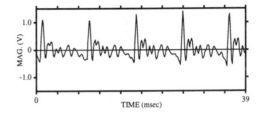

"AH" in a soft voice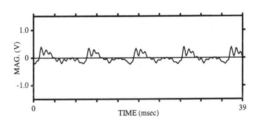

Now let's change the pitch of the voice!

"AH" in a high voice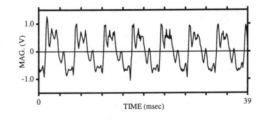

"AH" in a low voice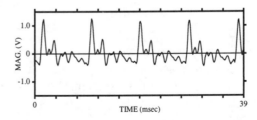

What have we learned from our experiment?

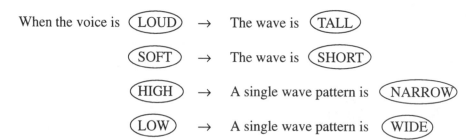

When the voice is (LOUD) → The wave is (TALL)

(SOFT) → The wave is (SHORT)

(HIGH) → A single wave pattern is (NARROW)

(LOW) → A single wave pattern is (WIDE)

 Results   Whether you're male or female, young or old, whether your voice is loud or soft, high or low, "AH" still sounds like "AH"!

We can recognize a vowel regardless of the fundamental period of the wave, or how steeply it rises and falls.

> But it's strange, you must admit -- "AH" sounds like "AH" even with completely different voices!

Strange??

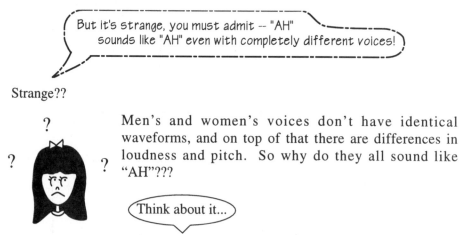

?   ?   ?

Men's and women's voices don't have identical waveforms, and on top of that there are differences in loudness and pitch. So why do they all sound like "AH"???

> Think about it...

There must be something unique about "AH" that makes it different from "EE" or "OO". And there must be something in common between the many different kinds of "AH" (loud, soft, high, low, etc.).

Take a more familiar example...

What are these?

> Dog on the left!

> Cat on the right!

> Who knows? - somewhere in this wide world there may be a place where people don't distinguish between cats and dogs. But let's not worry about "cognitive differences" here...!

But both of them have two eyes, two ears, one nose, one mouth, four legs, one tail... yet dogs are dogs, and cats are cats! If they were really the same, we wouldn't need separate names for them. We could call them all cogs or dats, or dots or cags... it wouldn't matter.

In other words, there's something about dogs that makes them different from cats. They might be Saint Bernards, Chihuahuas, chow chows, or bulldogs — yet they're all

DOGS!

But let's get back to the human voice...

Just what is it that's unique in a vowel sound, allowing humans to recognize it? Where is that uniqueness found in the sound wave?

Experiment — Take a close look at the five Japanese vowels and try to describe what makes each one unique!

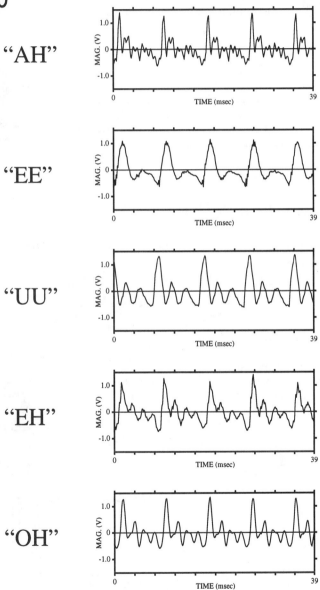

These are waveforms of a male voice

AH → A big mountain and skinny mountains

EE → Two big, rugged mountains

UU → Like "EE", but smoother

EH → Like "AH", but more rugged

OH → Like "AH", but smoother

Rocky! Like pencils! Bumpy mountains! Craggy! Pointy mountains!

 Hmm... not too clear, is it. Everybody has his or her own way of describing things. It's not completely apparent what the unique features of each wave are.

Gee whiz!
Sure would be nice if someone came up with a way to describe waves clearly!

Fourier analysis is a kind of mathematics that describes waves!

Looks like a job for **FOURIER!**

Instead of words like "smooth" and "rugged," Fourier analysis uses words that are clear to everyone.
Those words are called

FORMULAS.

Now here comes the real adventure!
We're going to learn how to use formulas to describe sound waves in language anyone can understand!

¡¡Vamos!!

DUM-DA-DUM-DUM...

5. Meet Mr. Fourier

Fourier, c'est moi!

Jean Baptiste Joseph, Baron de Fourier
(March 21, 1768 - May 16, 1830)

=He was a French mathematical physicist=

Huh? Fourier is somebody's name?!

Fourier was studying how heat flows through an object when it is heated up. This movement of heat also behaves like a wave.

Fourier studied this type of wave very closely. He discovered that, though very complicated, heat waves are periodic waves.

That means they consist of the same pattern or waveform repeated over and over.

FOURIER'S BIG DISCOVERY!

No matter how complicated it is,
a wave that is periodic - with a pattern that repeats itself -
consists of the sum of many simple waves.

A complicated wave is the sum of simple waves!

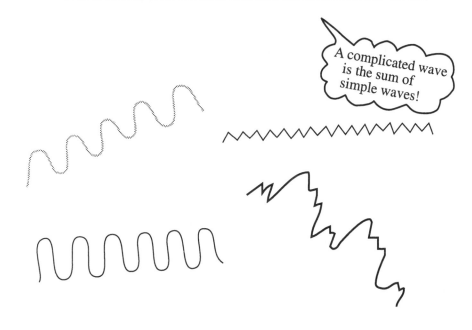

B-but - what's a "sum of waves"???

Well, suppose you have

a broad, rolling wave (A),
and
a narrow, choppy wave (B).

If you add them together,

you get wave (C),

which is both narrow and choppy, *and* broad and rolling at the same time (see the graph below).

Let's assume the horizontal axis on our graph shows time (*t*). To add the two waves, we find the sum of their heights *at a given time*. We do this for every time (*t*) on the graph.

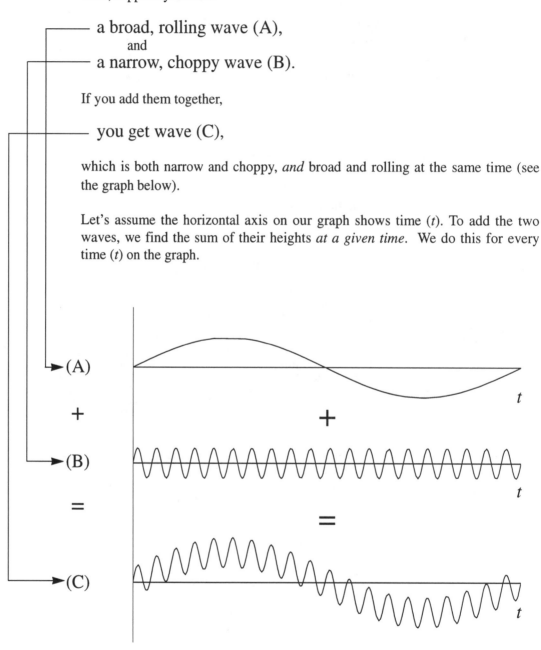

(A) + (B) = (C)

Experiment

Now let's try adding a couple of waves together ourselves!

Remember, we want to add their heights at each specific time. Moving along the vertical line, we'll add ①+②, and then ③+④, and so on...

See Appendix Item 1

It's at the back of the book!

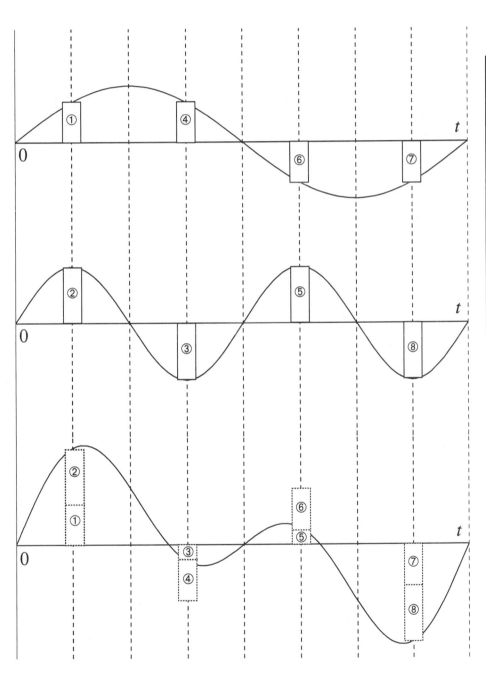

🔖 Method

1. Cut out the bars (showing wave heights) from the first page of the Appendix.

2. Paste the bars where they belong on the upper and middle graphs.

> * To keep them in place, it helps to use spray paste or some other kind of removable glue (see the Appendix).

3. Now, re-paste the bars at the proper points on the wave at the bottom of this page.

☆ Caution

Paste them in numerical order starting from line zero, in either the "plus" direction (up), or the "minus" direction (down) as appropriate!

Be especially careful when you're adding up a "plus" bar and a "minus" bar. Plot the difference as the wave height.

So how do we describe the features of a complicated wave in language that is clear to everyone - that is, in mathematical formulas? Simply by using a formula to describe each simple wave that forms part of the complicated wave, then adding these formulas together!

Let's express this idea as a formula...

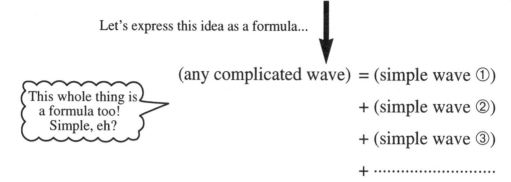

(any complicated wave) = (simple wave ①)

+ (simple wave ②)

+ (simple wave ③)

+ ....

This whole thing is a formula too! Simple, eh?

It's not easy to describe the features of a complicated wave by itself. But if you can split it up into simple waves, then it's easy - you just add 'em together!

"A single complicated wave is actually the sum of several simple waves"... does that still sound confusing?

Well, there are lots of examples of this you already know about!

Really?!

For example...

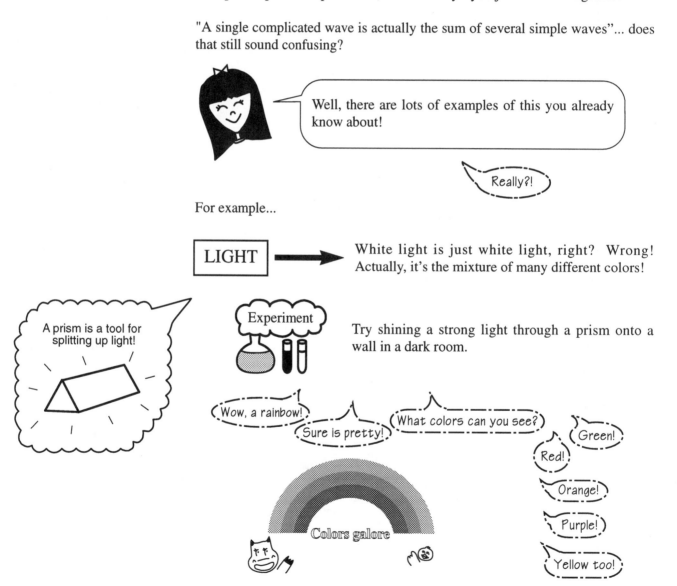

White light is just white light, right? Wrong! Actually, it's the mixture of many different colors!

A prism is a tool for splitting up light!

Experiment

Try shining a strong light through a prism onto a wall in a dark room.

Wow, a rainbow!

Sure is pretty!

What colors can you see?

Red!

Green!

Orange!

Purple!

Yellow too!

Colors galore

Here's something else we all know about!

| VEGETABLE JUICE | is the sum of many vegetables!

Right?

It's time for an...

INTERVIEW WITH
THE FOURIER GIRLS

We have three brands of vegetable juice here. We'd like you to sample them and describe the features of each one!

Miss A   Miss B   Miss C

You want us to tell you
how they taste, right?

| Interview results |

	Del Mondo	V4	Veggie-Veggie
Miss A	Fresh	Mellow	Rich
Miss B	Bright	Smooth	Heavy
Miss C	Crisp	Creamy	Very veggie!

Hmm... I guess this isn't such a great way
to figure out what makes these juices different, after all...

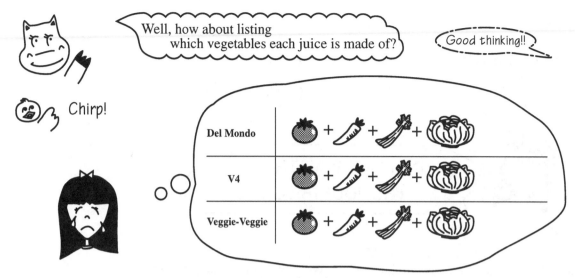

Well, how about listing which vegetables each juice is made of?

Good thinking!!

Chirp!

Del Mondo	🍅 + 🥕 + 🥬 + 🥗
V4	🍅 + 🥕 + 🥬 + 🥗
Veggie-Veggie	🍅 + 🥕 + 🥬 + 🥗

But, each juice contains the same vegetables in it !?

OKAY,

Then, let's measure the quantity of these vegetables!

Chirp!

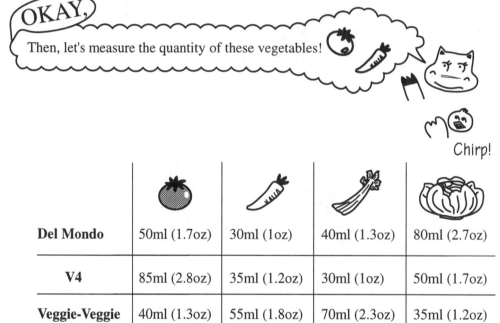

	🍅	🥕	🥬	🥗
Del Mondo	50ml (1.7oz)	30ml (1oz)	40ml (1.3oz)	80ml (2.7oz)
V4	85ml (2.8oz)	35ml (1.2oz)	30ml (1oz)	50ml (1.7oz)
Veggie-Veggie	40ml (1.3oz)	55ml (1.8oz)	70ml (2.3oz)	35ml (1.2oz)

Even when the vegetables are the same, you can say each juice is unique because it has different *quantities* of each vegetable!

You can't argue with the numbers!

Just as vegetable juice is a mixture of several vegetables, a complicated wave is a combination of several simple waves!

And just as we can describe a brand of vegetable juice as the sum of x-amount of tomato juice, y-amount of carrot juice, and so on, we can describe a complicated wave as the sum of the formulas that describe each simple wave.

So how do we go about expressing a complicated wave with a formula?

Well, first you have to know how to express a *simple* wave with a formula!

6. Trigonometric Functions

So how do we express a simple wave?

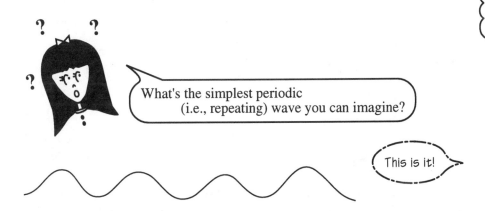

What's the simplest periodic
(i.e., repeating) wave you can imagine?

This is it!

But how do you describe this simple wave? "Single mountain"? "Gently rolling"? Never mind - there's a formula that precisely describes this wave better than words can!
This formula is called a TRIGONOMETRIC FUNCTION.

TRIGONOMETRIC??

That just means "measuring triangles" - in this case, right triangles.

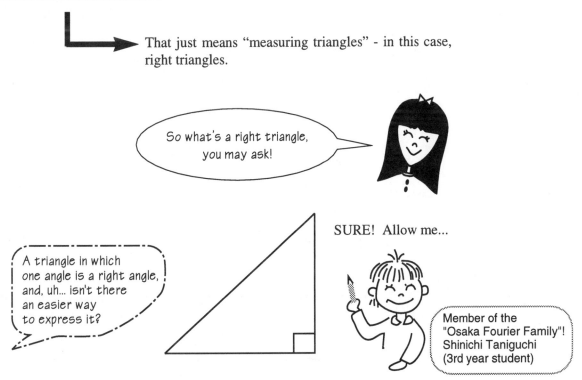

So what's a right triangle, you may ask!

SURE! Allow me...

A triangle in which
one angle is a right angle,
and, uh... isn't there
an easier way
to express it?

Member of the
"Osaka Fourier Family"!
Shinichi Taniguchi
(3rd year student)

Now *that's* a right triangle!

So now you understand the **TRIGONOMETRIC** part of trigonometric function.

Okay, what's a <u>**FUNCTION**</u>???

A relationship between two things where the value of one is determined by the value of the other.

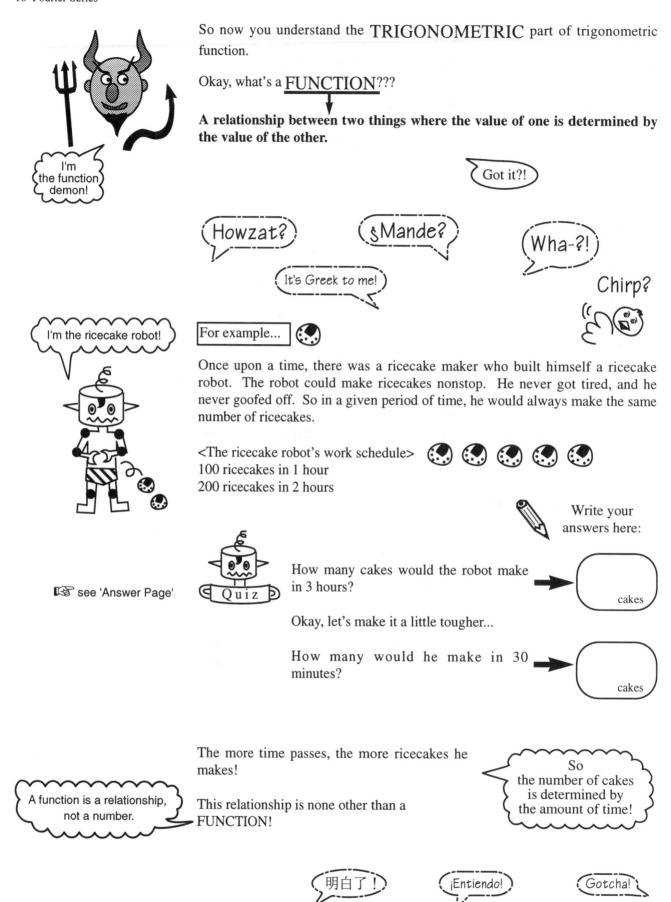

I'm the function demon!

Got it?!

Howzat?

¿Mande?

It's Greek to me!

Wha-?!

Chirp?

I'm the ricecake robot!

For example...

Once upon a time, there was a ricecake maker who built himself a ricecake robot. The robot could make ricecakes nonstop. He never got tired, and he never goofed off. So in a given period of time, he would always make the same number of ricecakes.

<The ricecake robot's work schedule>
100 ricecakes in 1 hour
200 ricecakes in 2 hours

Write your answers here:

☞ see 'Answer Page'

Quiz

How many cakes would the robot make in 3 hours?

→ cakes

Okay, let's make it a little tougher...

How many would he make in 30 minutes?

→ cakes

The more time passes, the more ricecakes he makes!

This relationship is none other than a FUNCTION!

A function is a relationship, not a number.

So the number of cakes is determined by the amount of time!

明白了！

¡Entiendo!

Gotcha!

Let's put this on a graph, which makes it easier to see.

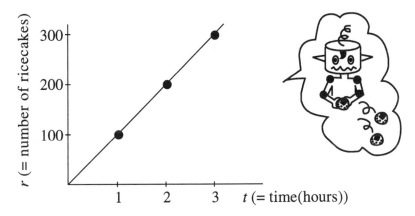

Now let's show this as a formula.

(number of ricecakes) = 100 × time t

You can write any time you want!!

- How many would he make in a certain period of time?

- How much time does he need to make a certain number?

It's easy to figure either of these things out!

Here's a shorter, more sophisticated way to write this formula:

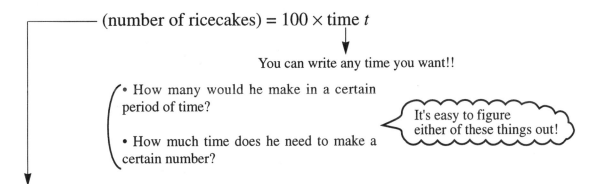

$$r(t) = 100 \cdot t$$

Multiply the time by the number of cakes made in 1 hour.

The equal sign defines the relationship.

This means the number of ricecakes is a function of time t.

The dot (·) between 100 and t means "multiply," just like "×"!

Normally, to show this is a function, you write it like this:

$$f(t) = 100t$$

Now that looks like a formula!!

Gee, all of a sudden it got complicated...

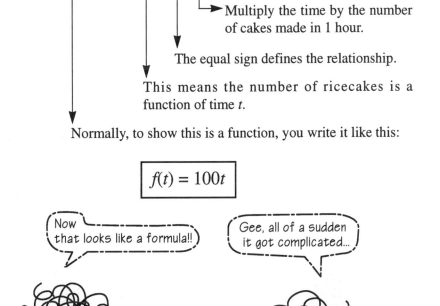

Relax! I said formulas were just a language, didn't I?

We'll figure it out!!

$$f(t) = 100t$$

The *f* is just the first letter of "function."

We use *f* for function the same way we use *r* for ricecake.

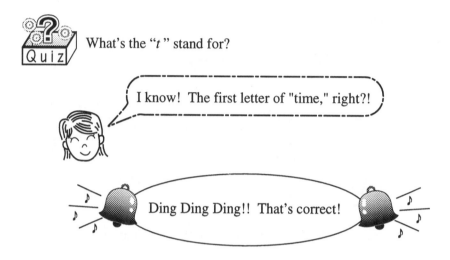

What's the *t* stand for?

I know! The first letter of "time," right?!

Ding Ding Ding!! That's correct!

But what happened to the multiplication sign - the dot or the "×"?

It's okay to leave it out!

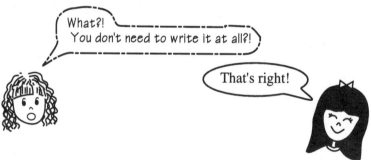

What?!
You don't need to write it at all?!

That's right!

Wow! Formulas really don't waste words!

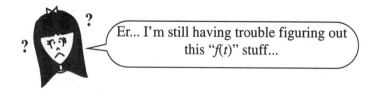

Er... I'm still having trouble figuring out this "*f(t)*" stuff...

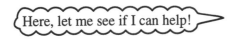

Here, let me see if I can help!

Mr. Aoto
A member of the
"Tokyo Fourier Family"

In the old days, we Japanese used to write the word "function" using the Chinese characters for "box" and "number."

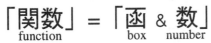

「関数」 = 「函 & 数」
function   box   number

"Box number," huh?
Why's that?

Because that's a perfect description of a function!

Think of $f(\ )$ as a box. You can put anything you want in box $f(\ )$. In the case of the ricecake robot, the number of cakes he makes depends on the amount of time he has. So the thing he puts in box $f(\ )$ is time t, and we write it as $f(t)$.

Likewise, a function of "a" would be written $f(a)$,
and a function of "x" would be written $f(x)$.

I see!

If a change in one thing is determined by a change in another, you put the thing that determines the change in box $f(\ )$. For example, how much your shoes wear out depends on how many miles you walk. You can write this as the function f(distance)!

So now you know what a function is, and that you can express a function as a graph or as a formula.

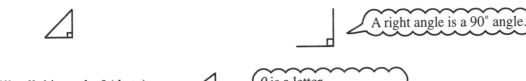

Let's get back to our talk about trigonometric functions!

So what's a **Trigonometric function**...?

In a right triangle, take one of the angles that is *not* a right angle.

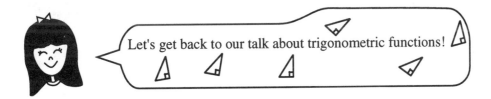

A right angle is a 90° angle.

We'll call this angle θ (theta)

θ is a letter in the Greek alphabet!

A trigonometric function is one that relates θ to the ratio of two sides of the triangle.

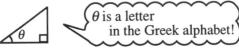

When θ changes, the ratio of the two sides changes too.

Suppose we draw a triangle with a right angle at the lower right corner, and angle θ at the lower left corner. Then:

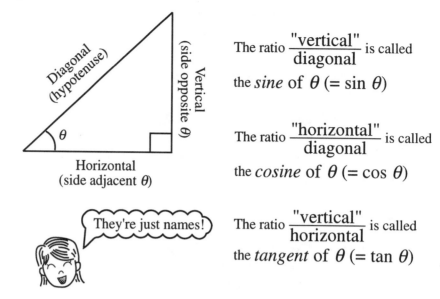

The ratio $\dfrac{\text{"vertical"}}{\text{diagonal}}$ is called the *sine* of θ ($= \sin\theta$)

The ratio $\dfrac{\text{"horizontal"}}{\text{diagonal}}$ is called the *cosine* of θ ($= \cos\theta$)

The ratio $\dfrac{\text{"vertical"}}{\text{horizontal}}$ is called the *tangent* of θ ($= \tan\theta$)

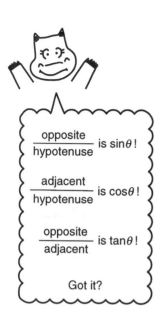

$\dfrac{\text{opposite}}{\text{hypotenuse}}$ is $\sin\theta$!

$\dfrac{\text{adjacent}}{\text{hypotenuse}}$ is $\cos\theta$!

$\dfrac{\text{opposite}}{\text{adjacent}}$ is $\tan\theta$!

Got it?

They're just names!

These values are the same no matter what size the triangle is. They are determined only by the size of θ.

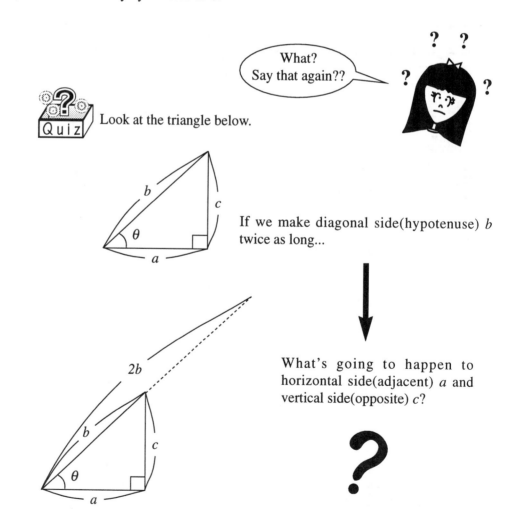

What?
Say that again??

Quiz Look at the triangle below.

If we make diagonal side(hypotenuse) b twice as long...

What's going to happen to horizontal side(adjacent) a and vertical side(opposite) c?

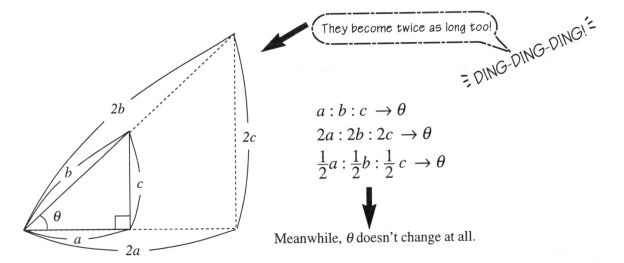

$$a : b : c \rightarrow \theta$$
$$2a : 2b : 2c \rightarrow \theta$$
$$\frac{1}{2}a : \frac{1}{2}b : \frac{1}{2}c \rightarrow \theta$$

Meanwhile, θ doesn't change at all.

In other words, when θ is set, the relationship between the sides is set too, no matter what length they are.

As long as θ doesn't change, these values don't change either, even if the size of the triangle does.

So these values can be determined from θ no matter how big or small the triangle is...

Look! Formulas!

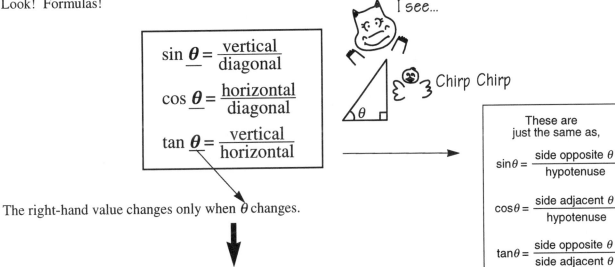

$$\sin \underline{\boldsymbol{\theta}} = \frac{\text{vertical}}{\text{diagonal}}$$

$$\cos \underline{\boldsymbol{\theta}} = \frac{\text{horizontal}}{\text{diagonal}}$$

$$\tan \underline{\boldsymbol{\theta}} = \frac{\text{vertical}}{\text{horizontal}}$$

I see...

Chirp Chirp

These are just the same as,

$$\sin\theta = \frac{\text{side opposite } \theta}{\text{hypotenuse}}$$

$$\cos\theta = \frac{\text{side adjacent } \theta}{\text{hypotenuse}}$$

$$\tan\theta = \frac{\text{side opposite } \theta}{\text{side adjacent } \theta}$$

The right-hand value changes only when θ changes.

And that, folks, is a TRIGONOMETRIC FUNCTION!!

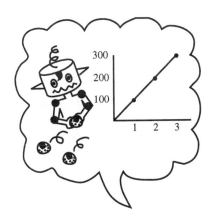

해보자!
(Let's try)

Now let's make some graphs of these functions, just as we did for the ricecake robot!

7. Sine Waves

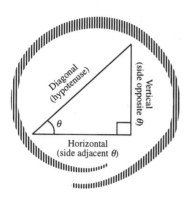

First, let's make a graph of changes in the value of

$$\sin \theta \ (= \frac{\text{vertical}}{\text{diagonal}})$$

when θ changes.
To keep it simple, let's give the diagonal a constant length "a".

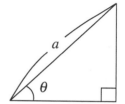

Then, as angle θ increases, it describes a circle of <u>radius a</u>.

↳ the diagonal side

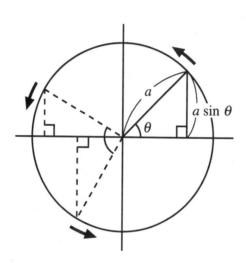

With diagonal a, you can always express the increase in θ from 0° to 360° as a circle of radius a! Circles are handy for describing things, aren't they?

$$\sin \theta = \frac{\text{vertical}}{a}$$

$$\underline{a \sin \theta = \text{vertical}}$$

To make it even simpler, let's use the number "1" for a!

$$\sin \theta = \frac{\text{vertical}}{1}$$

$$1 \sin \theta = \text{vertical}$$

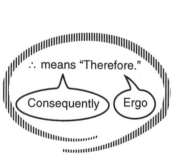

∴ means "Therefore."

Consequently   Ergo

And, since multiplying something by 1 doesn't change it ($1 \times 2 = 2$, $1 \times 3 = 3$, etc.)...

$$\therefore \ \underline{\sin \theta = \text{vertical}}$$

In other words, as θ changes, the value of $\sin\theta$ is the change of the length of the vertical side. We can make a graph showing how the vertical length changes as θ increases.

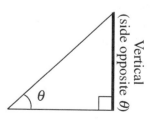

B-but wait!!
The right triangle loses its right angle if θ is 0°,
and it doesn't exist at all if θ is more than 90°...

Well, guess what!
Mathematics lets you get away with some crazy things!

Even if θ is greater than 90° - that is, even if our right triangle no longer exists -
$\sin\theta$ = (vertical/diagonal) still makes sense!

But why are we expanding the sine concept this way?
Let's construct a graph that'll help make the whole thing clear!

Here goes our construction project.

Get yourself a and a   See the next page.

and follow steps ① → ② → ③ below to make your own graph!

☆ Caution

When you connect the dots,
draw the line freehand!
Don't use your ruler!!

🐎 Method

① Paste in the triangles you'll find in the Appendix.

② Draw a line with your ruler.

③ Make a dot indicating the height of the vertical side at each time. Then draw a line connecting the dots.

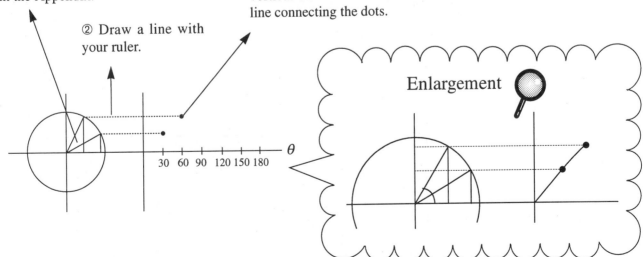

Enlargement

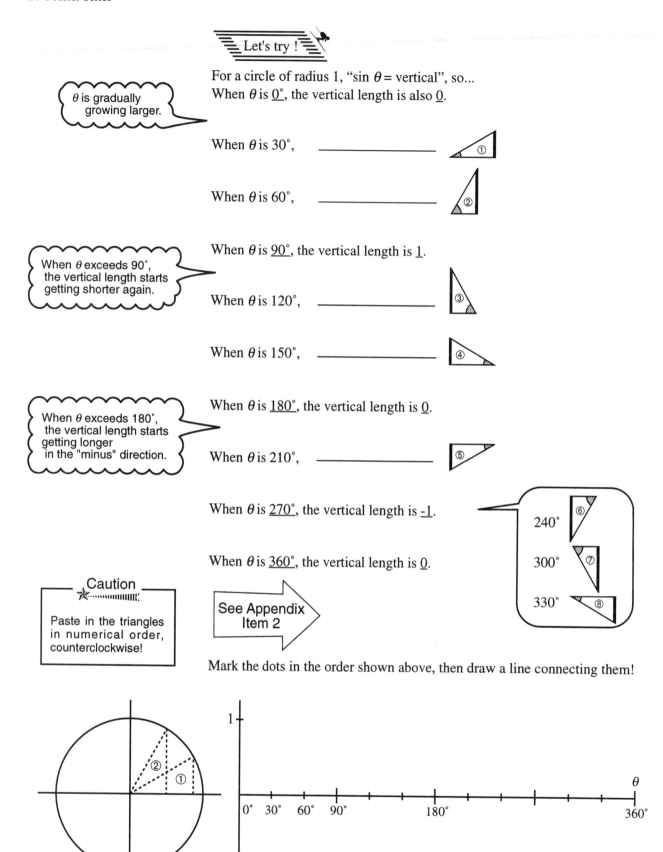

Let's try !

For a circle of radius 1, "sin θ = vertical", so...
When θ is $\underline{0°}$, the vertical length is also $\underline{0}$.

θ is gradually growing larger.

When θ is 30°, _____ ①

When θ is 60°, _____ ②

When θ exceeds 90°, the vertical length starts getting shorter again.

When θ is $\underline{90°}$, the vertical length is $\underline{1}$.

When θ is 120°, _____ ③

When θ is 150°, _____ ④

When θ exceeds 180°, the vertical length starts getting longer in the "minus" direction.

When θ is $\underline{180°}$, the vertical length is $\underline{0}$.

When θ is 210°, _____ ⑤

When θ is $\underline{270°}$, the vertical length is $\underline{-1}$.

240° ⑥
300° ⑦
330° ⑧

When θ is $\underline{360°}$, the vertical length is $\underline{0}$.

Caution

Paste in the triangles in numerical order, counterclockwise!

See Appendix Item 2

Mark the dots in the order shown above, then draw a line connecting them!

0° 30° 60° 90°   180°   360°

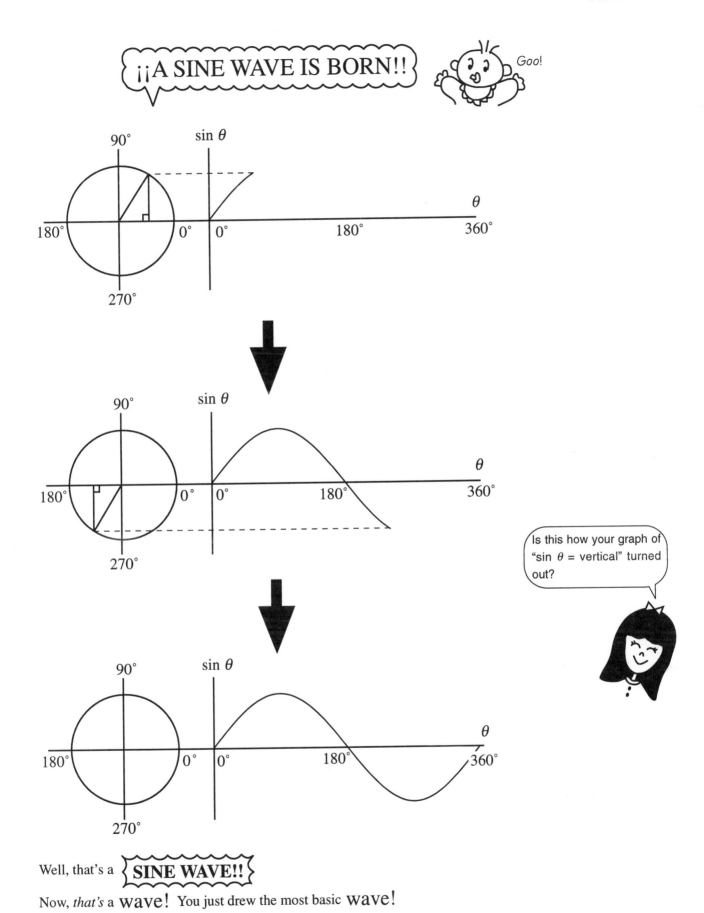

Well, that's a ⟮ **SINE WAVE!!** ⟯

Now, *that's* a wave! You just drew the most basic wave!

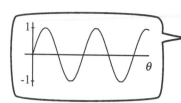

Now, even if you keep making θ larger (to 420°, 620°, or whatever), the wave on the graph will simply repeat itself over and over, rising and falling between +1 and -1.

In other words, to express the wave as a formula, all you need is sin θ.

This function is a function of θ, so you can place θ in the $f(\ )$ box...

$$f(\theta) = \sin \theta$$

You were wondering why math lets us get away with making θ greater than 90° when we talk about sinθ? So we can expand the sine concept to describe waves, that's why!

¡VIVA! This is great - we've succeeded in expressing a wave with a formula!

But...

¿**Problem?**

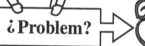 This formula only represents waves that oscillate (i.e., rise and fall) between 1 and -1!

And even if you add together several waves of this one type, they won't give you a complicated wave!

So how do you come up with a formula for a wave that oscillates between 2 and -2??

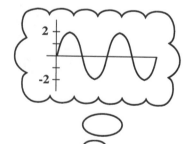

A wave between 2 and -2, hmm?

Let's see. When the diagonal side (i.e., the radius) was 1, it gave us a wave that oscillated between 1 and -1.

So let's try making a graph of changes in the vertical side when the radius is 2...

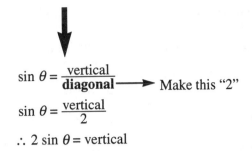

$\sin \theta = \dfrac{\text{vertical}}{\mathbf{diagonal}}$ ———→ Make this "2"

$\sin \theta = \dfrac{\text{vertical}}{2}$

$\therefore\ 2 \sin \theta = \text{vertical}$

Graph of $2 \sin \theta$

θ ——	$0°$ ——	The vertical is 0.
θ ——	$90°$ ——	The vertical is 2.
θ ——	$180°$ ——	The vertical is 0.
θ ——	$270°$ ——	The vertical is -2.
θ ——	$360°$ ——	The vertical is 0.

Look! We get a wave that oscillates between 2 and -2!

$$\boxed{f(\theta) = 2 \sin \theta}$$

And that means...

When the radius is 0.5,

→ the wave oscillates between 0.5 and -0.5 and can be written
$f(\theta) = 0.5 \sin \theta$

When the radius is 3

→ the wave oscillates between 3 and -3 and can be written
$f(\theta) = 3 \sin \theta$

In other words, we can use the following formula to represent any wave that oscillates between two values:

$$\boxed{f(\theta) = a \sin \theta}$$

Plug in any number you want for "a", and you'll get a wave that oscillates between a and -a!

This value *a*, which is the value of the highest point on the wave, is called the AMPLITUDE of the waveform.

With a voice wave, the louder your voice is, the bigger the amplitude!

You can tell your loud-mouthed friends, "Hey, easy on the amplitude!"

WAVES OF VARIOUS AMPLITUDES

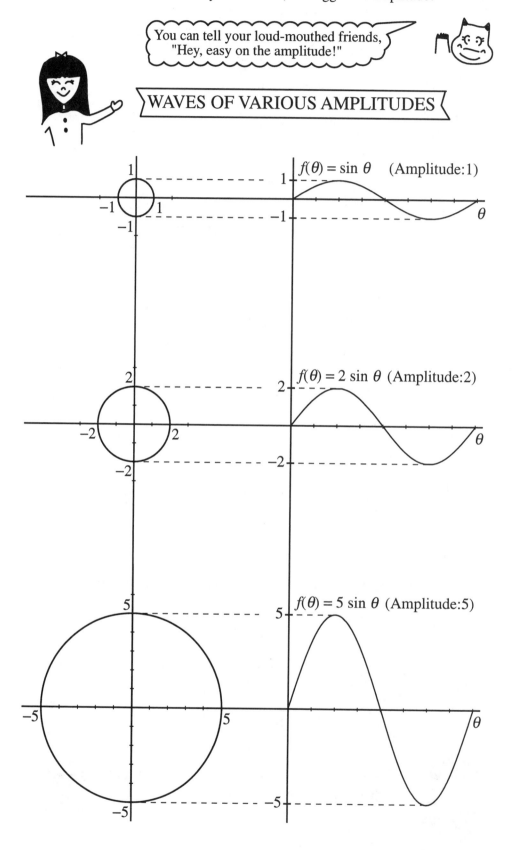

$f(\theta) = \sin\theta$ (Amplitude:1)

$f(\theta) = 2\sin\theta$ (Amplitude:2)

$f(\theta) = 5\sin\theta$ (Amplitude:5)

Great! This means we can write a formula for a simple wave of any amplitude starting from 0!

¿Problem? ➡ But...
This only lets us add up waves vertically (for example, $2 \sin \theta + 3 \sin \theta = 5 \sin \theta$). We still can't make complicated waves!

How can we find a formula to express waves that differ in the horizontal direction, not just the vertical??

8. Period, Frequency, and Angular Velocity

Our voice waveforms had time (t) as their horizontal axis.

Now, let's try adding a **change in time** to our graph of $\sin \theta$!

So θ is gonna change with time!

Let's assume the diagonal side (the radius) is rotating at a constant speed, just as a clock's hand does.

Let's also forget for a moment about the θ that was on our horizontal axis up till now. Instead, we're making a graph of how $a \sin \theta$ (that is, the vertical side) changes with <u>time</u>.

Change the horizontal axis from θ

to time t !

Think of it as a clock!

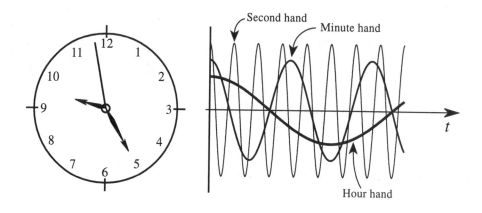

We wanted to make a graph of a real clock's movement, but then the second hand would go around 720 times for each rotation of the hour hand. So we cheated a bit to fit everything into this graph.

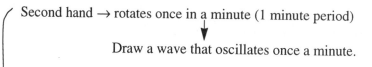

Second hand → rotates once in a minute (1 minute period)

Draw a wave that oscillates once a minute.

Minute hand → rotates once in an hour (1 hour period)

Draw a wave that oscillates once an hour.

Hour hand → rotates once in 12 hours (12 hour period)

Draw a wave that oscillates once in 12 hours.

If you draw all these waves on one graph, you'll find you have several waves with different patterns of oscillation - in other words, with <u>a range of widths</u> as well as heights!

Here are some terms we use to describe a wave that oscillates with time...

The <u>time</u> it takes for the wave to oscillate once is its

⌐→ PERIOD → Write this as T.

How many seconds does it take to complete one oscillation?

The unit is **sec** (for "seconds"!)

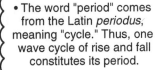

• The word "period" comes from the Latin *periodus*, meaning "cycle." Thus, one wave cycle of rise and fall constitutes its period.

• The word "frequency" owes its origin to the Latin *frequens*, meaning "numerous". Thus frequency refers to the <u>number</u> of waves in a given period.

The <u>number of times</u> the wave oscillates in 1 second is its

↓

FREQUENCY → Write this as f.

How many times does it oscillate in 1 sec?

The unit is **Hz** (Hertz)

When a wave oscillates many times per second, we say it has a "high frequency."
The higher your voice is, the higher its frequency!

So you can tell your squeaky-voiced friends, "What a high frequency your voice has!"

Chirp!

A 20 Hz wave oscillates 20 times per second, and a 20,000 Hz wave oscillates 20,000 times per second.

By the way, the human ear can hear sounds with frequencies from 20 Hz to 20,000 Hz!

Period T and frequency f ... I dunno, this is still kinda confusing!

They almost seem like the same thing!

How do they relate to each other, anyway?

All right, let's look at the relationship between period and frequency!

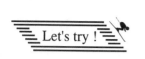

Read the problems and write the answers in this table!

☞ see 'Answer Page'

t	⑤ $\frac{1}{3}$	⑧	① 1	③ 2	⑩
f	⑥	⑦ 2	②	④	⑨ $\frac{1}{3}$

• What is the frequency f ② of a wave that has a period T of 1 ① - i.e., that takes 1 sec to oscillate once?

• What is the frequency f ④ of a wave that has a period T of 2 ③ - i.e., that takes 2 sec to oscillate once?

• What is the frequency f ⑥ of a wave that has a period T of 1/3 ⑤ - i.e., that takes 1/3 sec to oscillate once?

• What is the period T ⑧ of a wave that has a frequency of 2 Hz ⑦ - i.e., that oscillates twice in 1 sec?

• What is the period T ⑩ of a wave that has a frequency of 1/3 Hz ⑨ - i.e., that oscillates 1/3 times in 1 sec?

Notice that we're just looking at the same thing from two different points of view.

They're the inverse of each other, see?

The relationship between period T and frequency f is...

$$T = \frac{1}{f}$$

$$f = \frac{1}{T}$$

Awww!

Remember, we got rid of the θ function when we made time t the horizontal axis!
Sorry! That means we've **DUMPED** the wave formula

$$f(\theta) = a \sin \theta$$

you struggled so hard to find!

$$f(\theta) = \underline{a} \sin \theta$$

If we plug in the length of the clock hand here, we can change the amplitude.

But! We can't express the **speed at which angle θ changes** - that is, the speed of rotation of the clock hand!

So this time, let's think about the speed at which the hand rotates - in other words, its **VELOCITY!**

Remember the ricecake robot, who can make 100 cakes in an hour? That means his ricecake-making **velocity** is 100 cakes per hour.

Ricecake robot

So how do you calculate this velocity??

Use a stopwatch!

That's no good! A stopwatch can only tell how much time has elapsed!

How do we find the velocity from the time?

<No. 1>
You run a 100 meter race in 12.5 seconds.
What's your velocity per second?

m/sec

<No. 2>
The Bullet Train travels at 250 km(155miles) per hour.
In 2 hours, how far can it go?

km

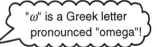 ☞ see 'Answer Page'

To solve these problems...

TA-DAH!! $$\text{velocity} = \frac{\text{distance}}{\text{time}}$$ Use this!

Right now, we're concerned with how many degrees an angle can move through in 1 second

We call this the **ANGULAR VELOCITY!** Write it like this: ω

"ω" is a Greek letter pronounced "omega"!

To find the angular velocity, use the formula you just learned.

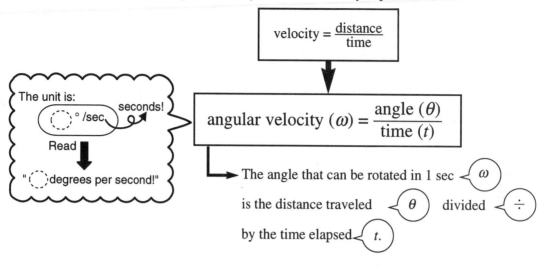

$$\text{velocity} = \frac{\text{distance}}{\text{time}}$$

$$\text{angular velocity } (\omega) = \frac{\text{angle }(\theta)}{\text{time }(t)}$$

The unit is:
°/sec ⟳ seconds!

Read

" ⃝ degrees per second!"

The angle that can be rotated in 1 sec ⟨ ω

is the distance traveled ⟨ θ divided ⟨ $\div$

by the time elapsed ⟨ t.

Angular velocity quiz

The ω

\<No. 1\>

So it took you 40 seconds to run around a circular 100 meter track, did it? What was your angular velocity per second?
Careful now - angular velocity has nothing to do with the size of the circle!

(💡 Hint) Don't worry about the size of the track. Think about the number of degrees in a circle...

°/sec

\<No. 2\>

It took the sun 12 hours to rise and set. What was its angular velocity?

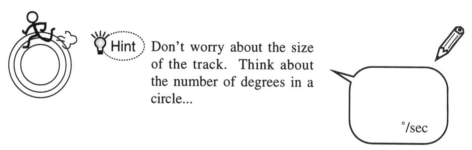

My dear husband made this quiz just for me! - Mrs. Unuma

(Member of the "Tokyo Fourier Family")

(💡 Hint) Here's the sun's path!
How many degrees is that?

°/hour

☞ see 'Answer Page'

Hurrah!

We can use this ω to write formulas for waves that rotate (i.e., rise and fall) at different speeds!

Great!

Okay, let's review the relationship of ω, θ, and t before things get too confusing!

Chirp!

$\theta \rightarrow$ the total angle rotated in a given time t (in degrees) $\longrightarrow$ Distance

$\omega \rightarrow$ the angle that can be rotated in 1 second (in degrees/sec) $\longrightarrow$ Velocity per second

$t \rightarrow$ the time (in seconds)

You can use ω and t to express θ.

If ω is 90°/sec, then after 1 second, $\theta = 90°$;
If ω is 90°/sec, then after 2 seconds, $\theta = 180°$.

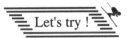 Let's try !

If ω is 180°/sec, what's θ after 2 seconds?

If ω is 360°/sec, what's θ after 5 seconds?

Let's use a table to figure this out!

☞ see 'Answer Page'

ω \ t	θ	1 sec	2 sec	3 sec	4 sec	5 sec
90°/sec	θ	90°	180°			
180°/sec	θ	180°				
360°/sec	θ	360°				

Values of θ after t sec when it rotates 90° in 1 sec

Values of θ after t sec when it rotates 180° in 1 sec

Values of θ after t sec when it rotates 360° in 1 sec

How did you come up with the answers you wrote in the table?

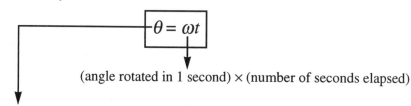

Easy! Since ω is the angle you can rotate in 1 second, I just multiplied that by the number of seconds to get the total angle rotated in the elapsed time!

Very good!
The formula $\omega = \dfrac{\theta}{t}$ we saw earlier does the same thing...

$$\theta = \omega t$$

(angle rotated in 1 second) × (number of seconds elapsed)

Tells you how many degrees you rotated in t seconds!

Now then, let's insert this into that other formula we **DUMPED** earlier!

our dumped formula

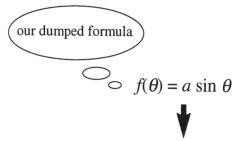

$$f(\theta) = a \sin \theta$$

Change the function of θ to a function of time:

$$f(t) = a \sin \underline{\theta}$$

You've got to change this too!

Replace θ with ωt

$$f(t) = a \sin \omega t$$

Chirp   Chirp   Chirp!!

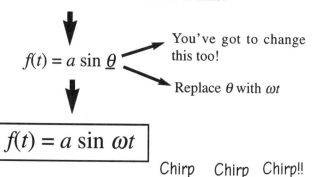

Hurrah, hurrah! Now we have a formula for expressing waves of any amplitude, any angular velocity, and any frequency!!

Let's review the definitions of period (t), frequency (f), and angular velocity (ω), and see how they relate to each other!

T — **Period** → the time it takes for a wave to oscillate once (in seconds) — sec

f — **Frequency** → the number of times a wave oscillates in 1 second (in Hertz) — Hz

ω — **Angular velocity** → the angle rotated in 1 second (in degrees per second) — °/sec

Let's try !

t (sec)	$\frac{1}{4}$	⑤ $\frac{1}{3}$	$\frac{1}{2}$	① 1	③ 2	3
f (Hz)	4	3	⑦ 2	1	$\frac{1}{2}$	⑨ $\frac{1}{3}$
ω (°/sec)	1440	⑥	⑧	② 360	④	⑩

Read the problems and write the answers in this table!

☞ see 'Answer Page'

• If a wave takes 1 second ($T = 1$ sec) ① to oscillate once, its angular velocity ω ② is 360°/sec.

• If a wave takes 2 seconds ($T = 2$ sec) ③ to oscillate once, what is its angular velocity ω ④?

• If a wave takes 1/3 second ($T = 1/3$ sec) ⑤ to oscillate once, what is its angular velocity ω ⑥?

• If a wave oscillates twice in 1 second ($f = 2$ Hz) ⑦, what is its angular velocity ω ⑧?

• If a wave oscillates 1/3 time in 1 second ($f = 1/3$ Hz) ⑨, what is its angular velocity ω ⑩?

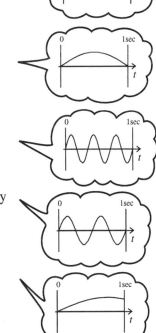

Big hint: A full rotation of a circle is 360°.
In other words,
when a wave oscillates once, it has travelled 360°!!!

So, did you fill out the whole table?
How did you calculate ω?

No problem! I just multiplied 360°
by the number of times the wave rose and fell in 1 second!

Very clever! So we can use this formula to get ω:

$$\omega = 360 \cdot f$$

and since $f = \frac{1}{T}$

$$\omega = 360 \cdot \frac{1}{T}$$

Ahem!

Now that you're so good at figuring out angular velocity ω...

Let's use the formula we came up with a little while ago:

$$f(t) = a \sin \omega t$$

...and write formulas for a bunch of different waves!
And then... let's add them together to produce a formula for a *really* complicated wave!!

GO FOR IT !

LET'S MAKE A FORMULA
FOR ALL THESE WAVES!

How do you take a complicated wave E and break it down into A, B, C, and D? That's one thing we haven't done yet!

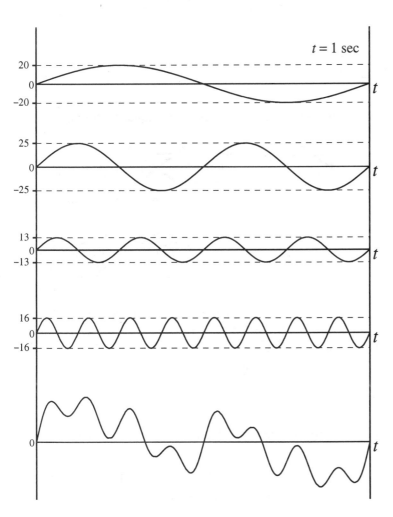

$t = 1$ sec

A   FREQUENCY 1 Hz   AMPLITUDE 20

B   FREQUENCY 2 Hz   AMPLITUDE 25

C   FREQUENCY 4 Hz   AMPLITUDE 13

D   FREQUENCY 8 Hz   AMPLITUDE 16

E $A + B + C + D = \boldsymbol{E}$

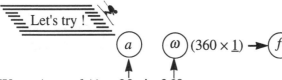

Let's try !

a ω $(360 \times \underline{1})$ → f

☞ see 'Answer Page'

Wave $A \rightarrow f_A(t) = \underline{20} \sin \underline{360}t$

Wave $B \rightarrow f_B(t) =$

Wave $C \rightarrow f_C(t) =$

Wave $D \rightarrow f_D(t) =$

Look at the equation for wave A and try making similar equations for waves B, C, and D!

Remember, I said a complicated wave is the sum of simple waves!

A through *D* are supposed to be *simple* waves! Did you get the formulas okay?

Now, as for complicated wave *E*, which is the sum of waves *A* through *D*...

$$f_E(t) = 20 \sin 360\,t + 25 \sin 720\,t$$
$$+ 13 \sin 1440\,t + 16 \sin 2880\,t$$

You can express it with this equation!

{CAREFUL!}

You can't just add up the numbers in the equation for *A*, *B*, *C*, and *D*!!

$$20 + 25 + 13 + 16 \qquad 360 + 720 + 1440 + 2880$$

Those numbers describe the features of each individual wave!

Look at the waves and you'll see!

To describe complicated wave *E*,
Don't use words like "rugged, uneven mountains" - say, "a wave that's the sum of wave 20 sin 360*t*, wave 25 sin 720*t*, wave 13 sin 1440*t*, and wave 16 sin 2880*t*"!! That's a lot more **PRECISE**!

Now let's make this into a <u>formula</u> into which any number may be inserted...

$$f(t) = a_1 \sin \omega_1 t + a_2 \sin \omega_2 t$$
$$+ a_3 \sin \omega_3 t + \cdots\cdots\cdots$$
$$+ a_n \sin \omega_n t$$

Chirp chirp!!

Here a_1 is the amplitude of the first wave, and ω_1 is the angular velocity of the first wave!

All the way to a_n for the amplitude of the nth wave, and ω_n for the angular velocity of the nth wave...

Hooray!

Now we can use formulas to express simple waves, *and* to express a complicated wave as the sum of these simple waves!

 We did it! Aw right!!

9. The Order of Wave Addition

Let's look more closely at a wave that looks complicated, but periodic, and at the simple waves that make it up!

Have you noticed the elegant structure of these waves?

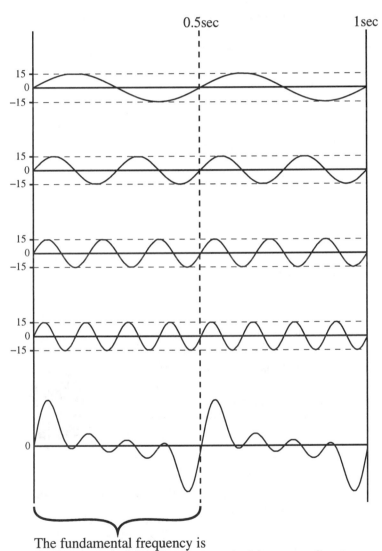

A FREQUENCY 2 Hz AMPLITUDE 15

B FREQUENCY 4 Hz AMPLITUDE 15

C FREQUENCY 6 Hz AMPLITUDE 15

D FREQUENCY 8 Hz AMPLITUDE 15

E FUNDAMENTAL FREQUENCY 2 Hz
$$A + B + C + D = E$$

The fundamental frequency is
the frequency of the biggest wave in this group of waves.

Wave *E* repeats the same shape every 0.5 second, so its

$$\begin{cases} \text{fundamental period} = 0.5 \text{ sec} \\ \text{fundamental frequency} = 2 \text{ Hz} \end{cases}$$

The four waves we've added together – *A, B, C,* and *D* – **all** repeat <u>the same shape every 0.5 second</u>!

Check it out!

If the fundamental frequency is 2 Hz, and there is even one wave that does not repeat every 0.5 second... then when you add them together, the resulting complicated wave will not repeat its shape every 0.5 second.

Well, then... what sort of waves are contained in a wave that repeats every 0.5 sec –
i.e., one with

$$\begin{cases} \text{a fundamental period of 0.5 sec} \\ \text{and a fundamental frequency of 2 Hz?} \end{cases}$$

Since it repeats the same shape every 0.5 second, it must contain waves that oscillate at a variety of different periods within that 0.5 second!

In other words, as long as you add waves that oscillate once, twice, three times and so on within 0.5 second, then no matter how many waves you add to form your complicated wave, that complicated wave will always repeat the same shape every 0.5 second!

IN FACT — A wave that repeats the same shape every 0.5 second... must be a wave with a frequency that is an **integral multiple** of the fundamental frequency of 2 Hz!

2, 4, 6, 8...

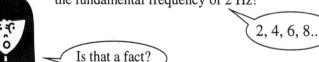

Is that a fact?

Experiment Let's see what happens when a wave has a frequency that *isn't* an integral multiple of 2 Hz!

 Cut out the 3 Hz wave and 5 Hz wave and place them above the waves on page 43!

 See Appendix Item 3

 Results Neither of these waves repeats the same shape every 0.5 seconds!

If we added these to the other waves, complicated wave E would take on a different shape after 0.5 seconds.
So wave E obviously doesn't contain waves of 3 Hz or 5 Hz.

Next, let's figure out the angular velocity (ω) of these waves!

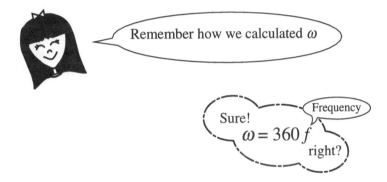

Remember how we calculated ω

Sure!
$$\omega = 360 f$$
Frequency
right?

- For a wave that oscillates once in 0.5 sec
  (i.e., 2 times per sec):

$$\omega = 360 \times 2 = 720° / \text{sec}$$

- For a wave that oscillates twice in 0.5 sec
  (i.e., 4 times per sec):

Doubled [× 2]

$$\omega = 360 \times 4 = 1440° / \text{sec}$$

Tripled [× 3]

- For a wave that oscillates three times in 0.5 sec
  (i.e., 6 times per sec):

$$\omega = 360 \times 6 = 2160° / \text{sec}$$

When the frequency is an integral multiple of the frequency of the fundamental wave (2 Hz × 2, × 3, etc.)...

Then ω is the integral multiple of the fundamental wave's ω, too!

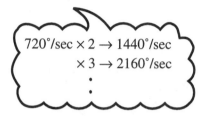

$720°/\text{sec} \times 2 \rightarrow 1440°/\text{sec}$
$\times 3 \rightarrow 2160°/\text{sec}$

No matter how complicated a periodic wave is, it is always the sum of waves with frequencies that are **integral multiples (× 1, × 2, × 3, etc.) of the fundamental frequency!**

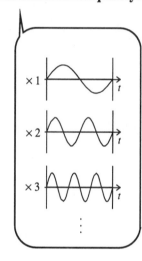

Meaning that each wave oscillates at a speed that's an integral multiple of the speed of the fundamental wave!

Hee hee!

1ω, that is

So if the angular velocity of the fundamental wave is ω, the angular velocities of the waves that were added together are **integral multiples – 2ω, 3ω, and so on!!**

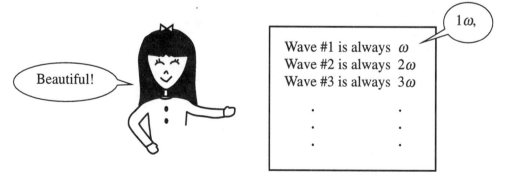

Beautiful!

1ω,

Wave #1 is always ω
Wave #2 is always 2ω
Wave #3 is always 3ω

If a complicated wave is periodic, it's going to be made up of waves like these!

Now let's try placing this perfectly symmetrical order in our <u>earlier formula</u> for expressing complicated waves!

$$f(t) = a_1 \sin \omega_1 t + a_2 \sin \omega_2 t$$
$$+ a_3 \sin \omega_3 t \cdots \cdots \cdots$$
$$+ a_n \sin \omega_n t$$

Substitute the beautiful order..

$$f(t) = a_1 \sin \omega t + a_2 \sin 2\omega t$$
$$+ a_3 \sin 3\omega t \cdots \cdots \cdots$$
$$+ a_n \sin n\omega t$$

Hip hip hooray!

Now we know we can use this order to add up as many simple sine waves as we want and get a formula for a complicated wave!

Chirp chirp!

We did it! We did it!

¡Que estupendo!

Are you sure about this?

10. Cosine Waves

Okay, let's look at a voice wave again and see if we can really use this formula for any wave!

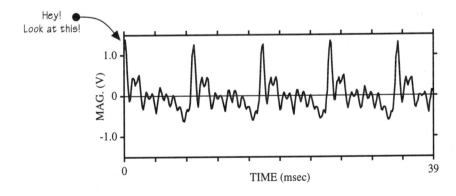

Hey! Look at this!

This is the waveform of a male "AH" sound

Look back– this wave doesn't start at 0!

That's because $\sin \omega t = 0$ when $t = 0$ ...

So far, our waves may have differed in amplitude, frequency, or angular velocity, but **they all started at 0, because they were sine waves.**

But there are plenty of waves that start from some point other than 0 – as you can see from the waveform on the preceding page.

Well, then, how do you represent a wave that doesn't start at 0??

This looks like a job for

COSINE ("cos" for short)!!

Er, what was "cos" again?

C'MON! Remember those trigonometric functions?

In other words,

$$\sin\theta = \frac{\text{side opposite } \theta}{\text{hypotenuse}}$$

$$\cos\theta = \frac{\text{side adjacent } \theta}{\text{hypotenuse}}$$

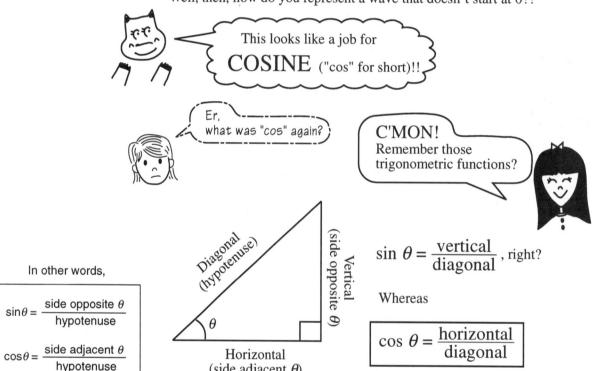

$$\sin \theta = \frac{\text{vertical}}{\text{diagonal}} \text{, right?}$$

Whereas

$$\cos \theta = \frac{\text{horizontal}}{\text{diagonal}}$$

Now, let's make a graph of changes in the value of

$$\cos \theta = \frac{\text{horizontal}}{\text{diagonal}}$$

when θ changes.

We'll do this exactly the same way we did for $\sin\theta$!

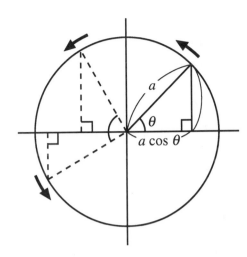

Again, let's give the diagonal a constant length "a". As angle θ increases, it describes a circle of <u>radius a</u>.

 (the diagonal side)

$$\cos \theta = \frac{\text{horizontal}}{a}$$

$$a \cdot \cos \theta = \text{horizontal}$$

With $a \sin \theta$, the vertical side changed – but with $a \cos \theta$, it's the horizontal side that changes!

We can use a graph to show what happens to the horizontal side as θ increases.

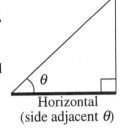

Horizontal
(side adjacent θ)

Remember our trick with $\sin\theta$! Even if θ is greater than 90˚,

$$\cos \theta = \frac{\text{horizontal}}{\text{diagonal}}$$

still makes sense in mathematical terms!

 Method

Time to make a graph!

Once again, get a and a

and follow steps ① → ② → ③ below to make your own graph!

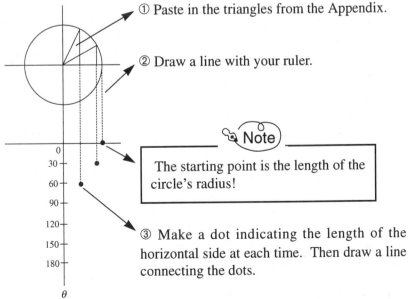

① Paste in the triangles from the Appendix.

② Draw a line with your ruler.

 Note

The starting point is the length of the circle's radius!

③ Make a dot indicating the length of the horizontal side at each time. Then draw a line connecting the dots.

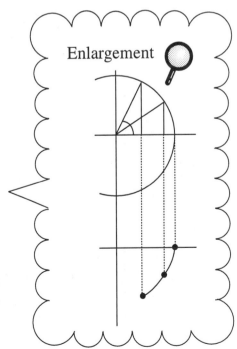

Enlargement

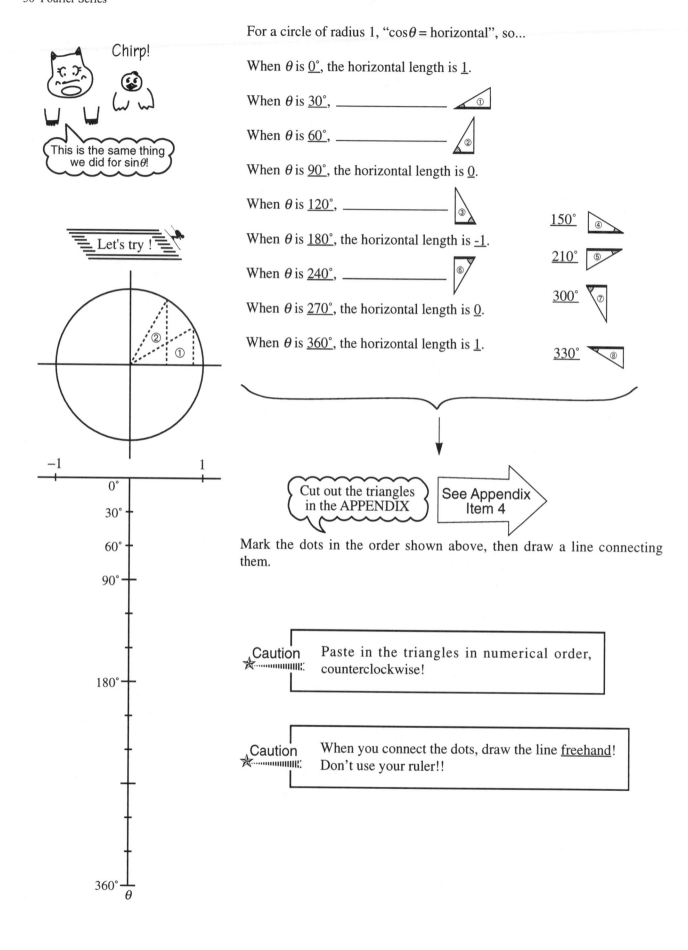

Chirp!

This is the same thing we did for sin θ!

Let's try !

For a circle of radius 1, "cos θ = horizontal", so...

When θ is 0°, the horizontal length is 1.

When θ is 30°, _____ ①

When θ is 60°, _____ ②

When θ is 90°, the horizontal length is 0.

When θ is 120°, _____ ③

150° ④

When θ is 180°, the horizontal length is -1.

210° ⑤

When θ is 240°, _____ ⑥

300° ⑦

When θ is 270°, the horizontal length is 0.

When θ is 360°, the horizontal length is 1.

330° ⑧

Cut out the triangles in the APPENDIX

See Appendix Item 4

Mark the dots in the order shown above, then draw a line connecting them.

Caution
☆········IIIIIIIIII: Paste in the triangles in numerical order, counterclockwise!

Caution
☆········IIIIIIIIII: When you connect the dots, draw the line freehand! Don't use your ruler!!

¡A COSINE WAVE IS BORN!

Ga ga goo !

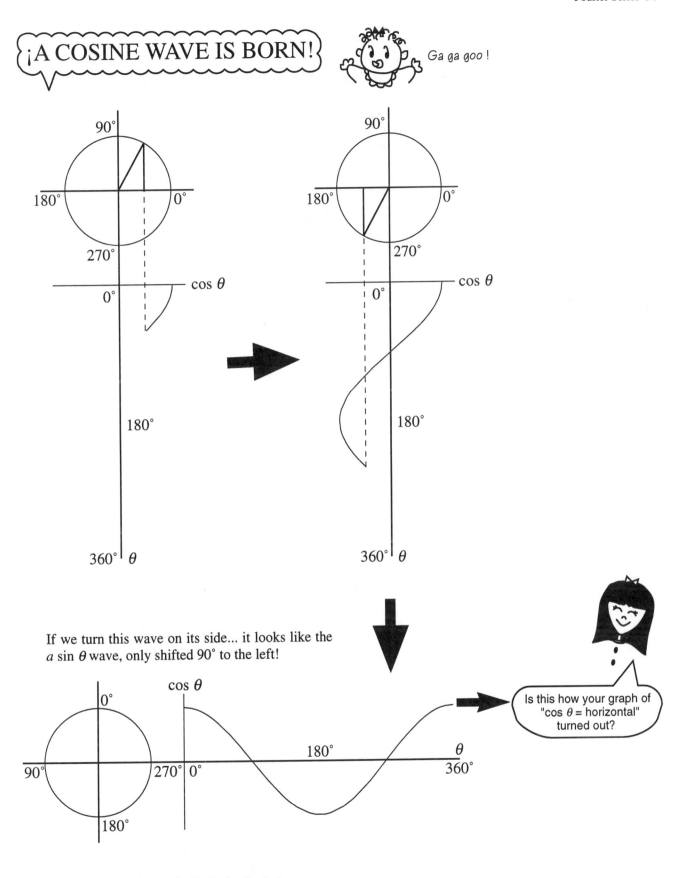

If we turn this wave on its side... it looks like the $a \sin \theta$ wave, only shifted 90° to the left!

Is this how your graph of "cos θ = horizontal" turned out?

Well, that's a COSINE WAVE!!

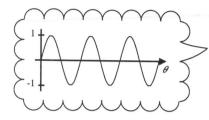

And even if you keep increasing θ (to 500°, 930°, or whatever), the wave keeps repeating itself, starting at +1 and oscillating between +1 and -1!

To express the wave as a formula...

$$f(\theta) = a \cos \theta$$

Then, to express cosine waves of various horizontal lengths... change the "time" component, just as we did for the sine wave!

Uhhh...ummm...

If you forgot this already, go back and review!

In other words, we're going to add the speed at which the wave oscillates (i.e., the speed at which the angle increases).

angular velocity ω

Our work with sines taught us this formula:

$$\theta = \omega t$$

Now we'll put it in

$$f(\underline{\theta}) = a \cos \underline{\theta}!$$

$\longrightarrow$ Change this to a function of time!

$$f(t) = a \cos \omega t$$

Now we can use any values we want for "a" and "ω" to get cosine waves of different amplitudes and frequencies!!

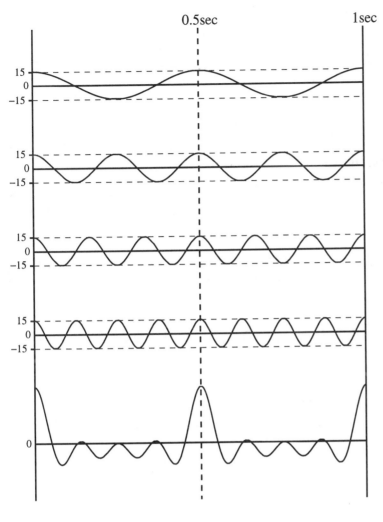

A	FREQUENCY 2 Hz AMPLITUDE 15
B	FREQUENCY 4 Hz AMPLITUDE 15
C	FREQUENCY 6 Hz AMPLITUDE 15
D	FREQUENCY 8 Hz AMPLITUDE 15
E	FUNDAMENTAL FREQUENCY 2 Hz $A + B + C + D = E$

And furthermore...

ω has exactly the same beautiful order we saw with the sine waves!

Just like with the sine waves!
Complicated wave *E* has a fundamental frequency of 2 Hz, repeating the same pattern every 0.5 seconds – the only difference is it doesn't start at 0!

So once again, this wave is just the sum of simple waves with frequencies that are **integral multiples of the fundamental frequency**!

"it doesn't start at 0!" means "the value is not zero at $t = 0$".

Now let's use this perfectly symmetrical order, with ω as the fundamental angular velocity, to write a formula for a complicated wave consisting of a lot of cosine waves!

$$f(t) = a_1 \cos \omega t + a_2 \cos 2\omega t$$
$$+ a_3 \cos 3\omega t \cdots\cdots$$
$$+ a_n \cos n\omega t$$

NOW THEN, suppose we add...

"Which begin with 0" means "which take the value zero at $t = 0$".
"Which begin with some other value" means "which take non zero values at $t = 0$".

A complicated wave made up of sine waves, which begin with 0

+

A complicated wave made up of cosine waves, which begin with some other value

↓

A VERY VERY COMPLICATED WAVE !

To avoid confusion between the amplitudes of sin and cos, we changed amplitudes a_1 and a_2 of sin to b_1 and b_2!

If we turn this into a formula...

$$f(t) = a_1 \cos \omega t + b_1 \sin \omega t$$
$$+ a_2 \cos 2\omega t + b_2 \sin 2\omega t$$
$$+ \cdots\cdots\cdots\cdots$$
$$+ a_n \cos n\omega t + b_n \sin n\omega t$$

Waves a_1 and b_1 have the same frequency (ditto for waves a_n and b_n, etc.)!

But what sort of wave are we going to get by adding sine waves and cosine waves?!

ULP! I-I dunno...

But it'll be complex, for sure...

That's a tough question!

TA-DAH!

But I'll be glad to answer it...

Meet our group leader, Odai!

If we add a sine wave to a cosine wave...

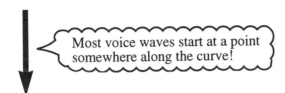

We get a wave that starts **part way up or down the curve!**

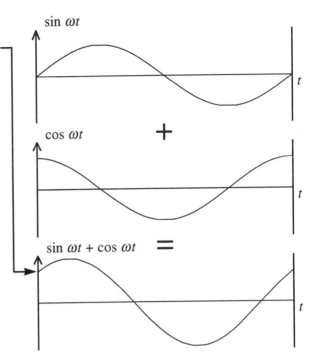

Most voice waves start at a point somewhere along the curve!

So:
If the wave consists only of sine waves, add only sine waves.
If the wave consists only of cosine waves, add only cosine waves.

And if the wave starts at a point along the curve, add sine waves **and** cosine waves!

That long formula covers all these possibilities!

11. a_0 ("A-zero")

This calls for another Hurrah!

Now we have a formula that can represent any wave, no matter how complicated!!

Chirp chirp!

...Well, almost. There's just one little problem.

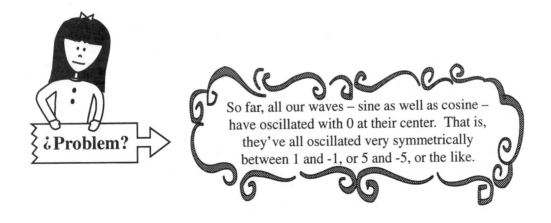

¿Problem?

So far, all our waves – sine as well as cosine – have oscillated with 0 at their center. That is, they've all oscillated very symmetrically between 1 and -1, or 5 and -5, or the like.

But we don't know how to represent a displaced wave that oscillates between, say, 5 and -2, or 10 and 3!

No matter how many waves you add together, if they all have 0 as their center, they'll only produce another wave with 0 as its center.

And you can bet there are complicated waves that are shifted away from 0!!

What are we gonna do?!

We'll figure something out!

Suppose we have the two waves below.

• One wave oscillates between 2 and -2.

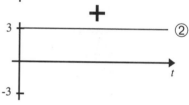

①

• The other wave not only doesn't oscillate around 0 – it doesn't oscillate at all! It just stays at 3!

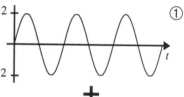

②

If we add these together, what sort of wave will we get?

Let's give it a try!!
At the beginning, it's

$$
\begin{array}{lll}
0 + 3 & \text{which gives us} & 3 \\
\downarrow & & \\
2 + 3 & = & 5 \\
\downarrow & & \\
0 + 3 & = & 3 \\
\downarrow & & \\
-2 + 3 & = & 1 \\
\downarrow & & \\
0 + 3 & = & 3 \\
\end{array}
$$

¡Si!
¡vamos!

Mark these numbers with dots on the graph on the next page, then draw a line connecting them!

Add the heights of the two waves at a given time(*t*) by tracing along the vertical lines.

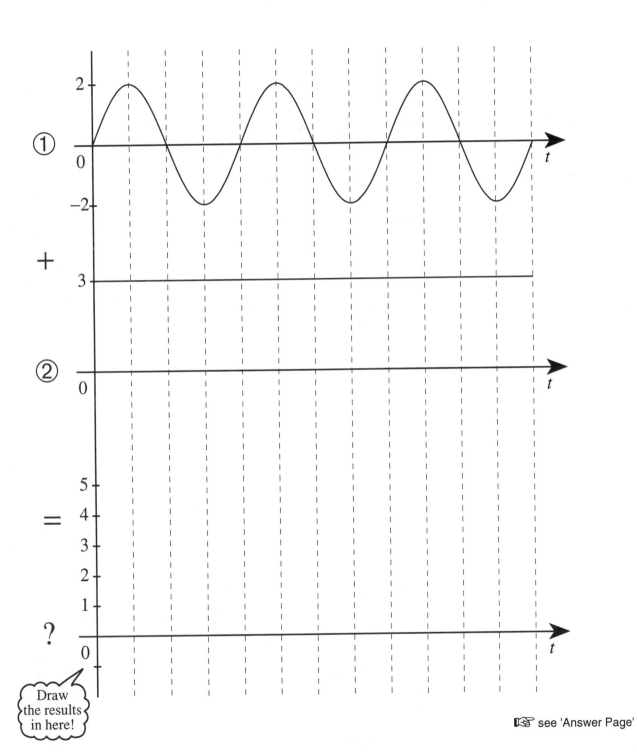

☞ see 'Answer Page'

You got a wave that oscillates between 5 and 1, with 3 as its center, didn't you?

Which means the whole wave was raised up by a height of 3!

If we write this as a formula...
we get

$$f(t) = \underline{3} + 2 \sin \omega t$$

So all we have to do is add the amount by which the entire wave is shifted!

where "a" is a number ≥ 0

• If the entire wave $b_1 \sin \omega t$ is raised by the amount a:

$$f(t) = a + b_1 \sin \omega t$$

• If the entire wave $b_1 \sin \omega t$ is lowered by the amount a:

$$f(t) = -a + b_1 \sin \omega t$$

• If the wave is neither raised nor lowered, a is 0, so:

$$f(t) = 0 + b_1 \sin \omega t$$

$$\therefore f(t) = b_1 \sin \omega t$$

Now let's add this information to the formula we had earlier!

Howdy!

$f(t) = a_1 \cos \omega t + b_1 \sin \omega t$
$\quad + a_2 \cos 2\omega t + b_2 \sin 2\omega t$
$\quad + \cdots \cdots \cdots \cdots \cdots \cdots$
$\quad + a_n \cos n\omega t + b_n \sin n\omega t$

Note If we just write "*a*", it'll get confused with the amplitude of cos, so we'll use a_0!

• which means the amplitude of cos $0\omega t$!

PRESTO!

We've got it!

$$f(t) = a_0 + a_1\cos \omega t + b_1\sin \omega t$$
$$+ a_2\cos 2\omega t + b_2\sin 2\omega t$$
$$+ \cdots\cdots\cdots\cdots\cdots$$
$$+ a_n\cos n\omega t + b_n\sin n\omega t$$

This is the ultimate wave formula!

Now this really, really deserves a Hip hip hooray!

 Chirrrp!

Por fin, we can really do it: break any complicated wave down into simple waves, express them as formulas – and add these simple waves to express the complicated wave as a formula!

This is called a **FOURIER SERIES FORMULA.**

We no longer have to rely on words like "rugged" or "gentle" to describe a complicated wave – we can use a formula to say **HERE IT IS!**

12. Σ (Summation)

We've reached our goal, and we could end our discussion of the Fourier series right here...

But now that you're on such friendly terms with mathematics, I wanted to show you just one more

MATH TRICK!!

Math has a lot of handy labor-saving devices.

A long formula like our Fourier series is tiring to write, and takes up a lot of space. But there's a shorter, faster way to write it!

Introducing the   SUMMATION (Σ) TRICK

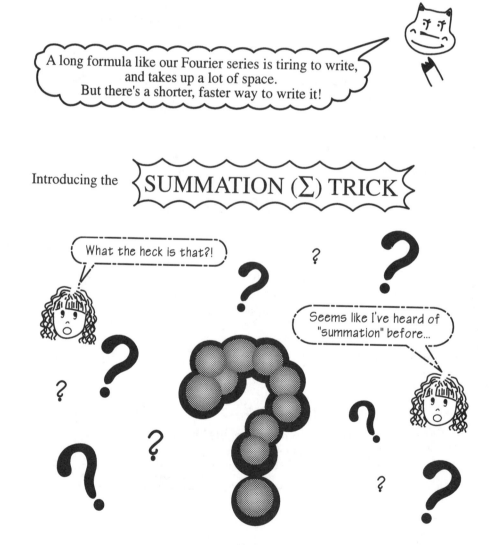

What the heck is that?!

Seems like I've heard of "summation" before...

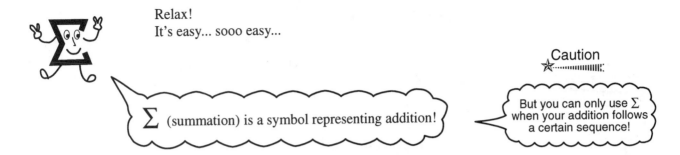

Relax!
It's easy... sooo easy...

Σ (summation) is a symbol representing addition!

Caution

But you can only use Σ when your addition follows a certain sequence!

For example...

♦ $A = 1 + 2 + 3 + 4 + 5 + 6 + 7$

Here is how you would use Σ to write this equation :

$$A = \sum_{n=1}^{7} n$$

This means you substitute the numbers 1 through 7 for "n", one after another, and add them together!
How to read the formula is
"A equals summation n from n equals 1 to 7."

Tip

Notice which parts change and which parts don't!

♦ $B = (x + 1) + (x + 2) + (x + 3)$

$$B = \sum_{n=1}^{3} (x + n)$$

Here the $(x +)$ part doesn't change – only "n" changes!

And another amazing thing about Σ!!

It doesn't just shorten long formulas
– it lets you write infinite formulas that go on adding forever!

For example...

♦ $C = Y_1 + Y_2 + Y_3 + Y_4 + \cdots\cdots$

This ribbon-like thing is the symbol for infinity!

Note

∞ : Infinity

an infinitely large number

$$C = \sum_{n=1}^{\infty} Y_n$$

Okay, here goes!

Asaka Naito
(5th year student)
She's with the
"Nagoya Fourier Family"

I know all about Σ!
I wrote this problem
all by myself!

$$A = (1 \div 2) + (2 \div 2) + (3 \div 2)$$
$$\rightarrow A = \sum_{n=1}^{3} (n \div 2)$$

I'm the Σ expert!!

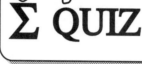

① $A = (W - 1) + (W - 2) + (W - 3)$
$\downarrow$
$A =$

② $B = (Z + 1) + (2Z + 2) + (3Z + 3)$
$\downarrow$
$B =$

③ $C = (1 \times 5) + (2 \times 5) + (3 \times 5)$
$\downarrow$
$C =$

☞ see 'Answer Page'

Now, let's give the Fourier series formula a try!!

$$f(t) = a_0 + a_1 \cos \omega t + b_1 \sin \omega t$$
$$+ a_2 \cos 2\omega t + b_2 \sin 2\omega t$$
$$+ a_3 \cos 3\omega t + b_3 \sin 3\omega t$$
$$+ \cdots \cdots \cdots \cdots \cdots$$
$\downarrow$

$f(t) =$

The answer's
on page 67!
Take a look!

Didja get it?

13. The Radian (Angular Measure)

Well, now you know about the Fourier series, and about the Σ method too! So we could stop here...

But! There's actually <u>one more way</u> to write a Fourier series formula!

The two methods have exactly the same meaning, but there are some things we'll be trying later that won't work unless we use this other method...

So we might as well learn it now!

We're talking about...

a different way of writing ω

We already know this about ω:

$$\blacklozenge \quad \omega = 360 \cdot f$$
$$\blacklozenge \quad \omega = 360 \cdot \frac{1}{T}$$

because $f = \frac{1}{T}$

The "360" here means 360°, i.e., the angle of a complete circle.
We're going to use a **different method of expressing 360°**.

What do we usually use to measure angles?

A protractor!

Not exactly
a household item!

That's right!
But you probably don't always have a protractor handy...

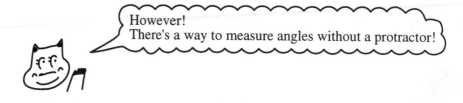

You'll need...

Scissors

&

This'll come in handy too!

And a good length of string!

Method

Stretch the string out along radius *r* of a circle,
and cut it off so it's the length of the radius.

Place the length *r* of string along the circumference of the circle.
Then draw a line from each end of the string to the center of the circle.

The angle you created is called 1 <u>RADIAN</u>!

A unit of measure, just
like the degree

By the way,
1 radian = 57.2958... degrees!

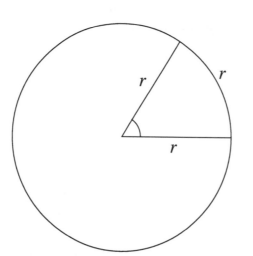

Okay, so how many radians are there in a complete circle??

Well, let's see how many radians fit in the circle below!

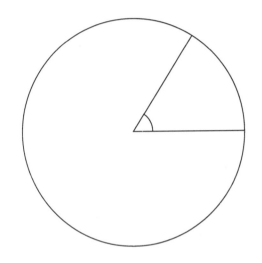

Cut the "radians" out of the Appendix and paste them into the circle!!

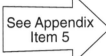

See Appendix Item 5

Six, plus a little bit extra

$\therefore (6 + \text{"a little extra"})$ radians $= 360°$

So exactly how much is this "a little extra"??
How do we figure that out??

$(6 + \text{"a little extra"})$ radians is an angle, but it also means we have $(6 + \text{"a little extra"})$ arcs of length r!

Which means we can find the circumference of the circle, then calculate how many times the arc length r goes into it.

So by **dividing the circumference by r**, we'll learn exactly how many radians are in a complete circle – none of this 6 + "a little extra" radian stuff!

What's the formula for finding the circumference?

Here!
circumference = diameter × 3.14

Actually, this is 3.1415... (and so on to infinity)

So we just call it π (pi)!

Chirp! Chirp!

Much easier, don't you think?

Which gives us...

$$2r \times \pi = 2\pi r$$

Diameter

So the circumference is $2\pi r$.

And since the number of radians in 1 circle is

circumference ÷ r

Circumference

$$\frac{2\pi r}{r} = 2\pi$$

A full 360° is 2π **RADIANS!**

$360° = 2\pi$ radians

You were wondering how much the "little extra" is in 6 + "a little extra" radians?

approx.

2π radians = 6.28 radians

3.14

approx.

approx.

6.28 − 6 = 0.28

So there you are! The "little extra" is about 0.28 radian.

Now that we have a different way to write 360°, let's stick it in our formula!

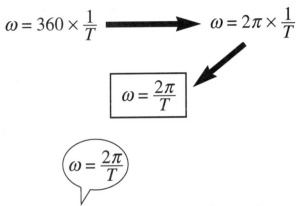

$$\omega = 360 \times \frac{1}{T} \longrightarrow \omega = 2\pi \times \frac{1}{T}$$

$$\omega = \frac{2\pi}{T}$$

$$\omega = \frac{2\pi}{T}$$

Remember?
$1/T = f$, so the equation can also be written
$\omega = 2\pi f$.

This is the angular velocity, expressed in radians, of a wave that has a fundamental frequency!

Now let's try using radians in our Fourier series formula!

$$f(t) = a_0 + \sum_{n=1}^{\infty} (a_n \cos n\omega t + b_n \sin n\omega t)$$

$$f(t) = a_0 + \sum_{n=1}^{\infty} (a_n \cos \frac{2\pi n}{T}t + b_n \sin \frac{2\pi n}{T}t)$$

These two formulas say exactly the same thing.
Only their way of expressing themselves is a little different!

Well, our long adventure with the Fourier series is finally over, and look at the treasure we've brought back!

Remember when we described vegetable juices like this:

"This juice contains !" "This juice contains !"

We were able to describe each brand of juice as a mixture of certain vegetables.

Now we can describe the seemingly complicated waves of the human voice in the same way...

By breaking a wave down into simple sine waves and cosine waves having frequencies that are integral multiples of a fundamental frequency, we can say "this wave is just the sum of all these simple waves!"

And we can express it with a FORMULA!!

Do you feel like you could do some real math now? You should, because you've already started to speak

BABY MATH!

Our Fourier series adventure may be over, but our adventures with the human voice have barely begun! As we embark on our quest for the unknown, let's not forget to bring along our new valuable tool, the Fourier series!

Never give up !

Fourier Coefficients

We now know that if you add simple waves together, you get a complicated wave. But how do you break a complicated wave down into simple waves?

In this chapter, we'll learn how to use the concept of "area" for this purpose.

Introduction

In our adventures so far, we have acquired a powerful weapon, the Fourier series. This weapon allows us to treat any wave, no matter how complicated, as the sum of simple waves – as long as the complicated wave is periodic. Furthermore, it allows us to instantly convert the wave into something very convenient – a mathematical formula. And if we can convert complicated waves into formulas ... that's right! We wanted to see the human voice, didn't we? Well, when the five Japanese vowel sounds form waves in the air, those waves are periodic. So we should be able to convert these vowels into formulas too!

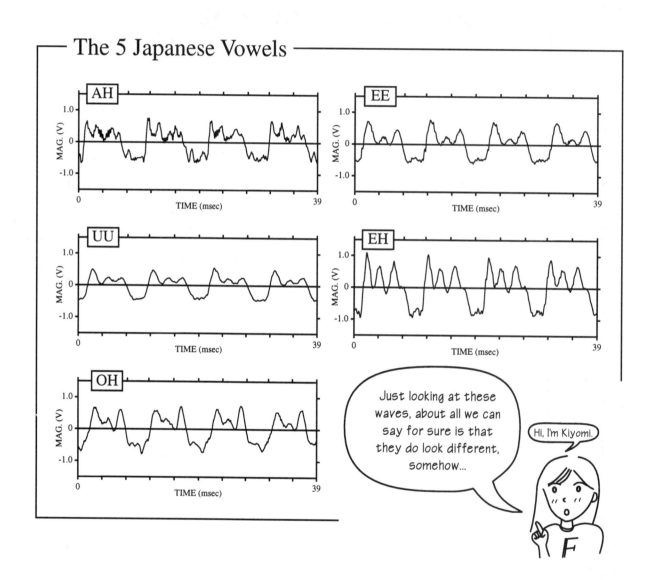

The 5 Japanese Vowels

If we can express these waves as formulas, maybe we'll be able to tell what it is that's different about AH and EE, for example. And maybe that will help us see how the human ear distinguishes between these two sounds. Once we understand that, we'll be a step closer to solving the riddle of human speech.

But how far will we get with our new weapons and techniques against a really complicated wave? Can we really work out formulas for the likes of AH, EE, UU, EH, and OH? Will we pick up some meaningful clues about the human voice? We'll never know unless we try, so let's get ready for our next adventure – converting vowel sounds to formulas!

1. Expressing AH and EE as Formulas

Before we set out, let's inspect our weapons. What sort of formula do we write for a periodic wave? Our old foe, the complicated wave, is the sum of simple waves, remember? So when we turn it into a formula, complicated wave $f(t)$ is:

$$f(t) = a_0 + a_1 \cos \omega t + b_1 \sin \omega t + a_2 \cos 2\omega t + b_2 \sin 2\omega t$$
$$+ a_3 \cos 3\omega t + b_3 \sin 3\omega t + a_4 \cos 4\omega t + b_4 \sin 4\omega t + \cdots$$

$$(\omega \text{ can also be } \tfrac{2\pi}{T})$$

And if we use Σ, we get:

Remember?

$$f(t) = a_0 + \sum_{n=1}^{\infty} (a_n \cos n\omega t + b_n \sin n\omega t)$$

Looks good! Now we're ready to venture forth on our quest for the complicated wave!

But first we're going to stop for a visit with the FFT analyzer. This is an amazing machine that produces a graph of air vibrations by displaying them as changes in air pressure. The analyzer will also find the Fourier coefficients process that we're going to try in a short while. Right now, we're going to ask it to produce graphs of the AH wave and EE wave for us. Talk about complicated waves!

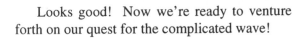

Bzzz...fzzt...bzzz...

FFT ANALYZER

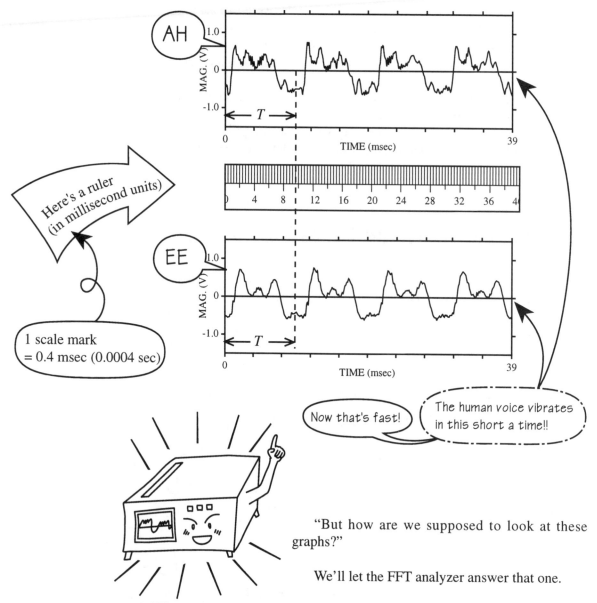

Here's a ruler (in millisecond units)

1 scale mark = 0.4 msec (0.0004 sec)

Now that's fast!

The human voice vibrates in this short a time!!

"But how are we supposed to look at these graphs?"

We'll let the FFT analyzer answer that one.

"The vertical axis is amplitude, meaning the loudness of the voice. The horizontal axis is time. The waveform I print out in a single graph is 39 msec (0.039 sec) long. So there's about 0.04 sec of time from one end of the graph to the other. Therefore I've made each scale mark along the edge of the graph represent 0.004 sec. And if you further divide each scale interval by 10, you get 0.0004 sec."

"Hey, then it should be easy to figure out the fundamental period T and the fundamental frequency f of the wave!"

Okay, let's start measuring our waves. We've already made a ruler that has scale marks for every 0.0004 second (see above). Using this ruler, we can see that a single pattern of the AH wave is 24 scale marks long.

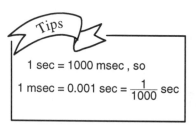

Tips

1 sec = 1000 msec , so

1 msec = 0.001 sec = $\frac{1}{1000}$ sec

You can make your own ruler, modeled after the one shown above!

$$24 \times 0.0004 = 0.0096 (\text{sec})$$

So the wave pattern takes 0.0096 sec to complete itself. In other words, the fundamental period T of the AH wave is 0.0096 sec. Then what is its fundamental frequency f?

$$f = \frac{1}{T}$$

– and all we have to do is plug in T:

$$f = \frac{1}{0.0096} = 104$$

The fundamental frequency is approximately 104 Hz.

"So the fundamental period of AH is 0.0096 sec, and the fundamental frequency is 104 Hz! Great!"

Next, how about the EE wave? Try measuring a single period of EE this time...

"Hey! It's the same 24 scale marks! Then we don't even have to calculate it – we know EE will also have a fundamental period of 0.0096 sec and a fundamental frequency of 104 Hz, right?"

We were able to figure out this much from looking at the waves themselves on paper. But now we've got to convert these AH and EE waves into formulas. Time for our secret weapon!

The concept behind the Fourier series is that "any periodic wave, no matter how complicated, can be treated as the sum of simple waves." Think back to what you learned about the Fourier series, and try to imagine how the AH or EE wave would look as the sum of simple waves. Did you come up with something like the graphs on the next page?

Tips

T = the time it takes for the wave to complete one pattern (i.e., the period)

f = the number of patterns repeated in 1 second (i.e., the frequency)

If we think of one pattern as a complete circle, it comes to 360°.

If you say "AH" or "EE" or "UU" or "EH" or "OH" at the same pitch, they'll all have the same fundamental frequency.

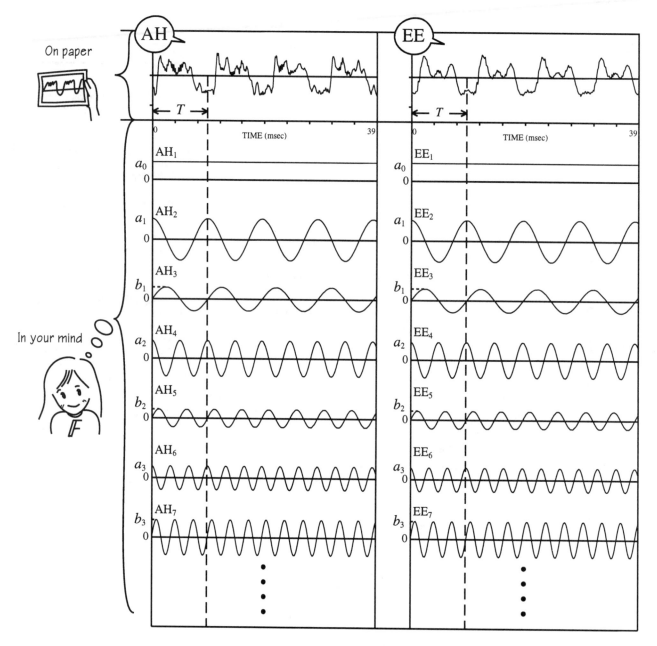

AH wave = AH$_1$ + AH$_2$ + AH$_3$ + AH$_4$ + ...   EE wave = EE$_1$ + EE$_2$ + EE$_3$ + EE$_4$ + ...

We can write a formula like this!

1. 1 Formula for the AH wave

Let's start with the AH wave. We want to develop formulas for the waves AH_1, AH_2, AH_3, AH_4, and so on, then add them together.

First we'll try AH_1. This one's simple, because it always has amplitude a_0 regardless of time t. So for the wave we'll call "AH(t)" (since the AH wave changes with time), we get

$$AH(t) = a_0 + \cdots \cdots \qquad \text{(formula 1)}$$

Next, what about wave AH_2? This is a cosine wave that completes a single pattern during each period of the AH wave.

"Okay, now we have to find the ω of $a_1 \cos \omega t$, right? Let's see... ω is the angular velocity, i.e., the amount the wave angle rotates per second. Since this cosine wave has the same fundamental frequency as AH, which is 104 Hz, that means it rotates 104 times per second. One rotation is 360°, so all we have to do is multiply 360° by 104 to get ω!"

$$360 \times 104 = 37440(°/\text{sec})$$

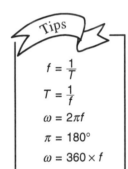

Tips

$f = \dfrac{1}{T}$

$T = \dfrac{1}{f}$

$\omega = 2\pi f$

$\pi = 180°$

$\omega = 360 \times f$

So now we have ω for wave AH_2. Let's write the formula with the actual value for ω plugged into it:

$$AH_2 = a_1 \cos 37440t$$

We can add this to formula 1.

$$AH(t) = a_0 + a_1 \cos 37440t + \cdots \cdots \qquad \text{(formula 2)}$$

That's two waves we have down so far. Next, wave AH_3! Like AH_2, this one completes a single pattern during each period of the AH wave, so it, too, rotates 104 times per second – but it's a sine wave.

"Hmmm... in that case, uh... I got it! It's a sine wave with the same angular velocity, 104×360, as wave AH_2! So $\omega = 37440°$/sec, right?"

Very good! Let's make a formula out of this for wave AH_3. We're using b_1 to represent the amplitude, since it's a sine wave.

$$AH_3 = b_1 \sin 37440t$$

Add this to formula 2:

$$AH(t) = a_0 + a_1 \cos 37440t + b_1 \sin 37440t + \cdots \cdots \quad \text{(formula 3)}$$

Now for our fourth wave, AH_4. This is a cosine wave that completes two patterns during each period (1 sec divided by 104, or 0.0096 sec) of the AH wave. In other words, its angle rotates through a circle twice in 0.0096 sec. That's twice the speed of AH_2 or AH_3, so:

$$2 \times \omega = 37440(^\circ\!/\mathrm{sec}) \times 2 = 74880(^\circ\!/\mathrm{sec})$$

"Meaning the angular velocity of AH_4 is 74880°/sec!"

That's right! Now we can write a formula for AH_4. All we have to do is substitute 74880 for the 2ω in $a_2 \cos 2\omega t$:

$$AH_4 = a_2 \cos 74880t$$

So we have:

$$AH(t) = a_0 + a_1 \cos 37440t + b_1 \sin 37440t$$
$$+ a_2 \cos 74880t + \cdots \qquad \text{(formula 4)}$$

On to wave AH_5. This one should be a breeze. We'll have our formula in no time! This is a sine wave that completes two patterns during every 0.0096 sec, exactly like wave AH_4. So its angular velocity is the same 74880°/sec, giving us the formula

$$AH_5 = b_2 \sin 74880t$$

Which brings us to:

$$AH(t) = a_0 + a_1 \cos 37440t + b_1 \sin 37440t$$
$$+ a_2 \cos 74880t + b_2 \sin 74880t + \cdots \qquad \text{(formula 5)}$$

The formulas are starting to pile up, aren't they. This is a good time to recall an important lesson we learned earlier:

These simple waves we're adding together all have frequencies that are integral multiples ($\times 1$, $\times 2$, $\times 3$, ...) of the fundamental frequency of the original complicated wave!

That means waves AH_6 and AH_7 will complete <u>three</u> patterns every 0.0096 sec, so they rotate at a speed (angular velocity) <u>three</u> times that of the fundamental wave:

$$37440(^\circ\!/\mathrm{sec}) \times 3 = 112320(^\circ\!/\mathrm{sec})$$

That gives us:

$$AH_6 = a_3 \cos 112320t$$
$$AH_7 = b_3 \sin 112320t$$

Add 'em on!

$$AH(t) = a_0 + a_1 \cos 37440t + b_1 \sin 37440t$$
$$+ a_2 \cos 74880t + b_2 \sin 74880t \qquad \text{(formula 6)}$$
$$+ a_3 \cos 112320t + b_3 \sin 112320t + \cdots$$

If we use Σ in formula 6:

$$AH(t) = a_0 +$$
$$\sum_{n=1}^{\infty} (a_n \cos 37440nt$$
$$+ b_n \sin 37440nt)$$

There's no end to it

In short, we can obtain wave AH by continuously adding on waves whose angular velocities are integral multiples of the second wave's angular velocity (37440°/sec). Although we could add them on to infinity, we won't try that here. The object of our quest still lies far ahead. But for now, at least we know that if we keep adding on cosine waves and sine waves with angular velocities that are integral multiples, we'll eventually get the formula for our complicated wave.

1. 2 Formula for the EE wave

If we refer back to our work on the AH wave, this shouldn't be too hard. We'll start with the first wave, and call our EE wave "EE(t)":

$$EE(t) = a_0 + \cdots \qquad \text{(formula 7)}$$

Try writing the formulas yourself, based on what you learned about the AH wave!

They're easy to calculate, so don't be shy!

How about waves EE_2 and EE_3? These are a sine wave and cosine wave, both of which complete a single pattern every 0.0096 sec.

$$EE_2 = a_1 \cos 37440t$$
$$EE_3 = b_1 \sin 37440t$$

"What? You mean these waves have the same angular velocity as AH_2 and AH_3 did for the AH wave?"

That's right. Both AH and EE complete a single pattern in the same amount of time, so they have the same fundamental frequency. That means EE_2 and AH_2 have the same angular velocity, as do EE_3 and AH_3. And since we will be adding up waves with angular velocities that are integral multiples of this same angular velocity, our formula for the EE wave will be:

$$EE(t) = a_0 + a_1 \cos 37440t + b_1 \sin 37440t$$
$$+ a_2 \cos 74880t + b_2 \sin 74880t \qquad \text{(formula 8)}$$
$$+ a_3 \cos 112320t + b_3 \sin 112320t + \cdots$$

If we use Σ in formula 8:

$$EH(t) = a_0 +$$
$$\sum_{n=1}^{\infty} (a_n \cos 37440nt$$
$$+ b_n \sin 37440nt)$$

"B-but – that's identical to the formula for the AH wave!!"

Yes! But are the two waves the same? No! They look completely different!

"Well, then, did we make a mistake in our calculations?"

No, we didn't. So how do we explain these identical formulas?

Let's review what we know so far.

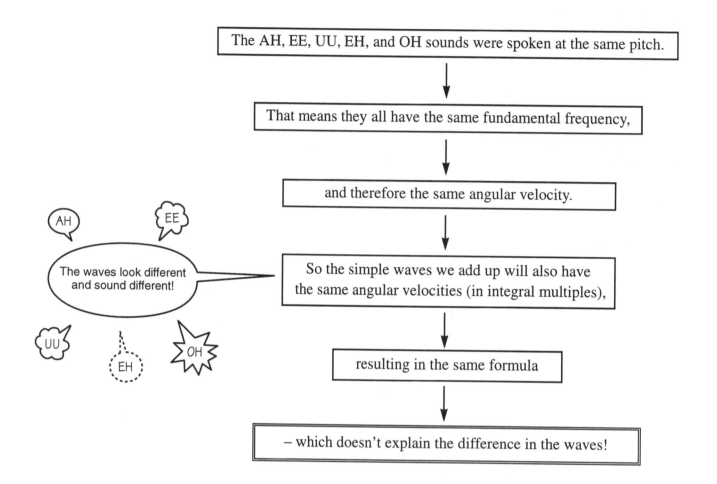

And here we thought we were one step closer to solving the riddle of the human voice! This is a sorry state of affairs!

"Maybe this Fourier series isn't so handy after all...?"

Well, let's look at the two formulas (6 and 8) again. Hmm...

"Those letters with subscripts – a_0, a_1, b_1 and so on – what was it they represented? Oh yeah, it was **amplitude**. Seems as if that might have something to do with... no, I still don't get it..."

Perhaps it's time we called on the great Dr. Fourier! Can you help us, Doctor?

"Harrumph! You've done quite well to get this far on your own, you know! Permit me to present you with a little quiz. This should give you the clues you need to resolve your present dilemma. Pay attention, now. I call this the Vegetable Juice Quiz!"

2. The Mystery of Vegetable Juice Flavors

Dr. Fourier began his quiz:

"I have here three types of vegetable juice, each in the amount of 200 ml. The brands are Del Mondo, V4, and Veggie-Veggie. First I would like you to drink each brand of juice and compare how they taste."

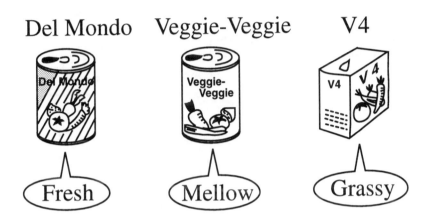

Del Mondo — Fresh

Veggie-Veggie — Mellow

V4 — Grassy

"Now how would you describe them?"

"They're all quite tasty, but each one tastes a little different!"

"Très bien! You're absolutely right. But why do they taste different? That's the first question in our quiz. Do you know the answer?"

"Hmm... Well, because they contain different kinds of vegetables, I suppose."

Dr. Fourier shook his head. "Non, non! Look at the labels! They list which vegetables are in each type of juice."

"By golly, all three of them contain the same vegetables – tomato, carrot, celery, and cabbage! Then I guess it's not the kinds of vegetables, but the relative amounts of each vegetable that make each juice different, right?"

"That is quite correct. But there is more to my quiz. Next question: How would you explain to someone precisely how the flavor of each juice differs? Words like 'fresh' or 'mellow' may mean different things to different people. How would you be more accurate?"

"By using the power of numbers. How about if you measure the quantity of each vegetable – for example, Veggie-Veggie Juice has X ml of tomato, Y ml of carrot, and so on – then arrange the figures in a table? Wouldn't that do the trick?"

If you know the quantity of each vegetable in each juice, you can make a table like this.

	Del Mondo	V4	Veggie-Veggie
Tomato	50ml (1.7oz)	85ml (2.8oz)	40ml (1.3oz)
Carrot	30ml (1oz)	35ml (1.2oz)	55ml (1.8oz)
Celery	40ml (1.3oz)	30ml (1oz)	70ml (2.3oz)
Cabbage	80ml (2.7oz)	50ml (1.7oz)	35ml (1oz)
Total	200ml (6.7oz)	200ml (6.7oz)	200ml (6.7oz)

"Magnifique!" Dr. Fourier replied. "That's a lovely table. But you can make things even clearer with some graphs – voilà!"

Juice at a glance!

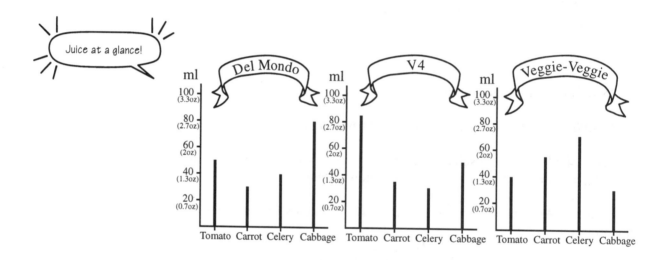

"Hey, no kidding! That's great! But what does this have to do with waves? You said this quiz would provide us with some clues, didn't you, Professor?"

"Oui, oui, and so it has! Just as vegetable juice is a mixture of various vegetables, a complicated wave is a combination of waves of various frequencies, remember? The difference in the flavors of these juices corresponds to the difference in the forms of various complicated waves. Taking this a step further, we can say that the different waveforms are produced by different "quantities" of each simple wave!"

"And just what is the 'quantity' of a wave? Why, its amplitude, of course! So the values a_0, a_1, b_1, a_2, and b_2 that we have in our formulas are like the quantities of tomato, carrot, celery, and cabbage in the vegetable juice!"

If we wrote formulas for the different juices, they would look something like this:

Del Mondo   200 ml = 50 ml tomato + 30 ml carrot + 40 ml celery
                                      + 80 ml cabbage

V4   200 ml = 85 ml tomato + 35 ml carrot + 30 ml celery
                                      + 50 ml cabbage

Veggie-Veggie   200 ml = 40 ml tomato + 55 ml carrot + 70 ml celery
                                      + 35 ml cabbage

"Even if you use the same vegetables to make your juice, different quantities of each vegetable will make the juices taste different. Likewise, even if you add together waves of the same frequency, different quantities – that is, amplitudes – of each wave will make the resulting complicated wave look different. Look at the graphs below."

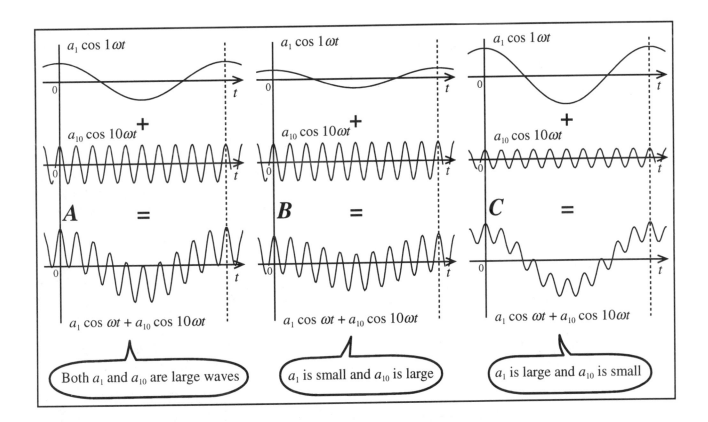

"If we don't find the values a_1 and a_{10} for these waves A, B, and C, they will appear to have identical formulas, n'est-ce pas? So if you wish to compare the waves for AH and EE, for example, you had better figure out the value of the amplitude of each wave – a_0, a_1, b_1, a_2, b_2, etc., etc.! Good luck, and au revoir!"

And with that, Dr. Fourier vanished into the ether.

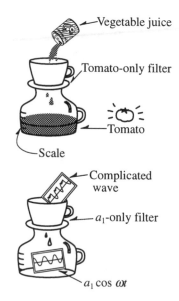

Values of amplitudes, eh? If we're talking about vegetable juice, that means the quantity of each type of vegetable – but how do you measure that, anyway? Once they're made into juice, the vegetables are all mixed together. What we really need is some kind of filter that only passes the part of the juice made from one vegetable – just the tomato juice, or just the carrot juice, or whatever. Then, if we run the juice through these different filters, we can measure the quantity of each vegetable ingredient.

But then how do we apply this to waves? What we need are <u>wave</u> filters – for a_0 only, or $a_1 \cos \omega t$ only, or $b_1 \sin \omega t$ only – that allow only the wave whose amplitude we want to know to pass through. Let's see what we can come up with...

Looks like our adventure won't be ending anytime soon.

3. Finding the Amplitude Through a Filter

3. 1 Finding a_0 ——— the a_0 filter puzzle

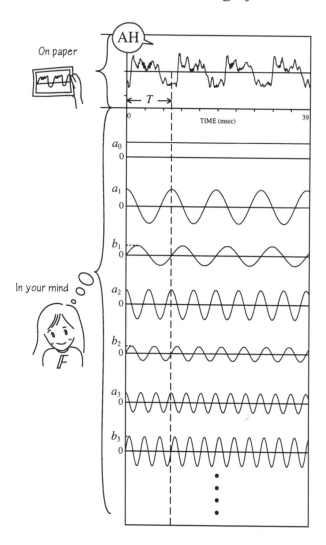

Let's start with a filter for a_0. First, of course, we have to figure out what a "filter" really is! At the moment, all we have in hand are two complicated waves – AH and EE. We want to pass these complicated waves through some sort of device that will let a_0 through, but leave everything else behind. A mathematical filter – but how do we construct one?

Let's see, a while back when we tried to imagine how the AH or EE wave would look as the sum of simple waves, we came up with some graphs of those waves. So what we want to do now is eliminate all the other waves and leave only a_0, right? But how to do that... gee, this is tough.

Wait a minute. . . We know the frequency of each of the simple waves that make up the complicated wave, right? Right. Maybe we're getting somewhere. But how – just a minute! When Dr. Fourier disappeared, he left something behind – an old scroll of some sort. Let's open it up and see what it says.

Aha! Two clues!

Plus and minus, eh? What is he talking about? Let's take a look at the simple waves on the previous chart again... Hmm...

Hey, look at this! The waves rise and fall, and when they're above the center line, they're positive, and when they're below the line, they're negative! That must be what he means by plus and minus! But what about this 'area'...?

Got it, got it! We can find the area of the space enclosed by the horizontal axis and one full period (i.e., time T) of each simple wave. For wave $a_1 \cos \omega t$, for example, the area of the plus part is the same as the area of the minus part, so the total area is 0! The same is true of wave $b_1 \sin \omega t$, so its area is 0 too. $a_2 \cos 2\omega t$, $b_2 \sin 2\omega t$, $a_3 \cos 3\omega t$ –all the other simple waves have areas of 0!

Then, if we add up the areas of all these simple waves, we should get the area of the complicated wave they form, right? And there's only one wave that doesn't have an area of 0 – the a_0 wave! So that's our a_0 filter!!

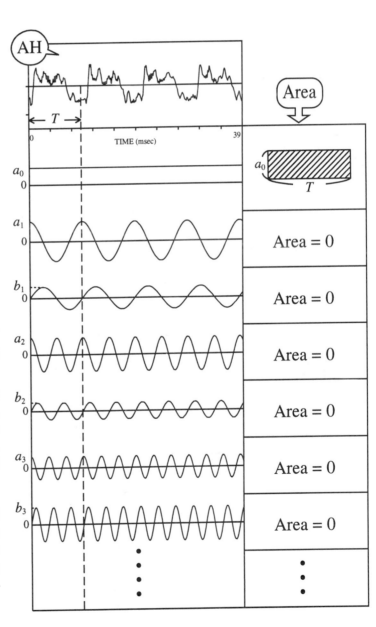

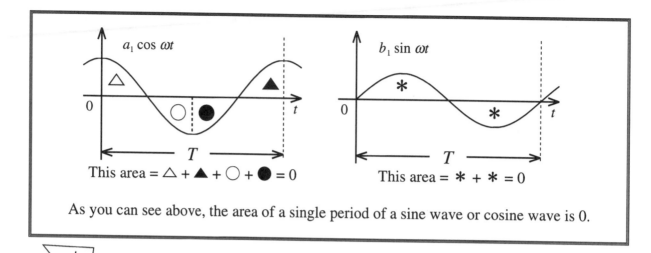

This area = $\triangle$ + $\blacktriangle$ + $\bigcirc$ + $\bullet$ = 0

This area = $*$ + $*$ = 0

As you can see above, the area of a single period of a sine wave or cosine wave is 0.

See Appendix Item 6

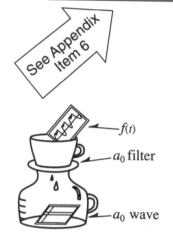

$f(t)$

a_0 filter

a_0 wave

All right, let's try to write that out as a formula. Since it's a pain to write the word "area" every time, we'll use "A" to represent the area of one period of a wave.

$$f(t) = a_0 + \underbrace{a_1 \cos \omega t}_{A = 0} + \underbrace{b_1 \sin \omega t}_{A = 0} + \underbrace{a_2 \cos 2\omega t}_{A = 0}$$

$$+ \underbrace{b_2 \sin 2\omega t}_{A = 0} + \underbrace{a_3 \cos 3\omega t}_{A = 0} + \underbrace{b_3 \sin 3\omega t}_{A = 0}$$

$$+ \cdots$$

So if we find the area of one period of a complicated wave, that should give us the area of just the a_0 wave, since all the other simple waves have areas of 0....

Well, what _is_ the area of a_0, then? Anyway, I don't want to know the area of a_0, I want to know its value!

Let's take a look at our chart again. Since the horizontal axis is time, the area of a_0 should be a rectangle with a length of time T (for one period), and a height of a_0. And since the area of a rectangle is

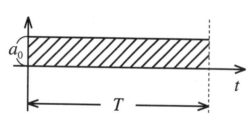

Area of a_0

a_0

T

(height) × (length)

that means the area of our rectangle here is:

$$a_0 \times T$$

Now, all we have to do to find the value of a_0 is divide this area by T!

And there we have our filter for a_0.

Let's review how we determined the value of a_0:

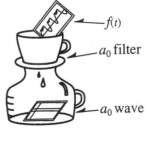

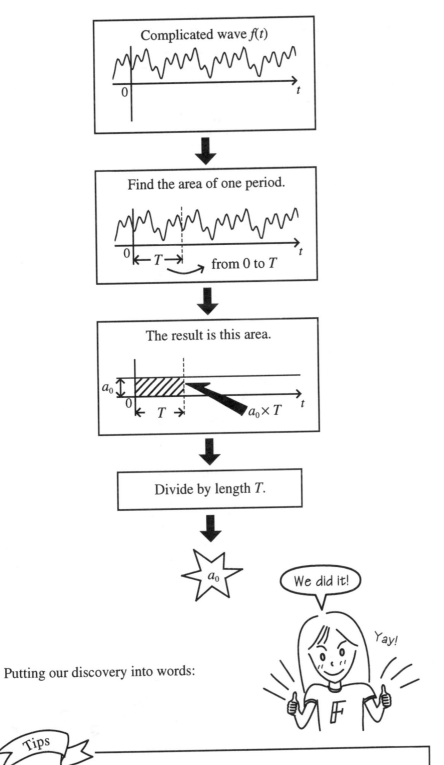

Putting our discovery into words:

Tips

To find a_0, find the area from 0 to T (one period) for complicated wave $f(t)$, then divide by T.

3. 2 Finding a_n —— the a_n filter puzzle

Here we go with our next puzzle. This time we have to come up with a filter for a_n. First things first, so we'll start by trying to find a_1.

Based on our experience with a_0, it seems as if "area" might again prove useful in filtering out all but one wave. But if we just find the area, we'll get stuck with wave a_0 again! This time we want a filter for a_1, one that will let only wave $a_1 \cos \omega t$ through and eliminate all the other waves. Let's take another look at that chart we used when we were finding a_0.

Okay, so we need to figure out a way to keep wave $a_1 \cos \omega t$ from disappearing, right?

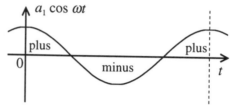

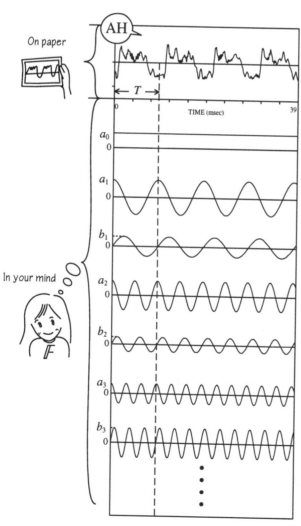

Yeah. Now if we just find the area above, the plus and minus parts will cancel each other out and give us 0, and our wave will disappear. If we can make the minus part "plus" instead, it won't disappear, but how...?

Whoa! It's Dr. Fourier, back from the ether, and he's got another scroll of clues with him! Let's see what this one says...

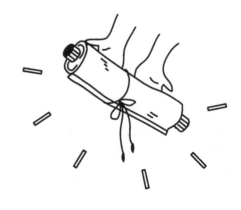

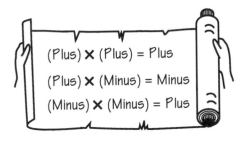

"Comprenez-vous, mon amie?"

"Uh, I think so. You mean like this?"

$$3 \times 5 = 15$$
$$3 \times (-5) = -15$$
$$(-3) \times (-5) = 15$$

"Exactement! When you multiply two numbers, you have to watch how their plus and minus signs change."

"But what does this have to do with the a_n filter?"

"Patience, patience! To solve your a_n filter puzzle, you must first be able to multiply two waves together. If you apply this multiplication process to waves on a graph, you will see some interesting things. Multiply the values of the two waves at various times t, and plot the resulting values (that is, draw dots) for the same times t. A real wave would be an infinite series of these dots. However, all we need here is to multiply the values at a few points on these waves, and draw a smooth curve connecting the results. Be careful of the plus and minus signs!"

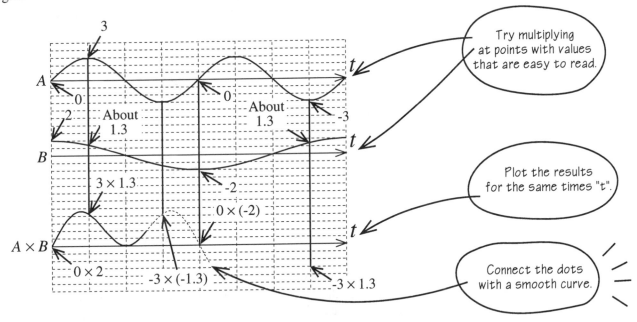

"Now try it yourself!

Multiplying two waves

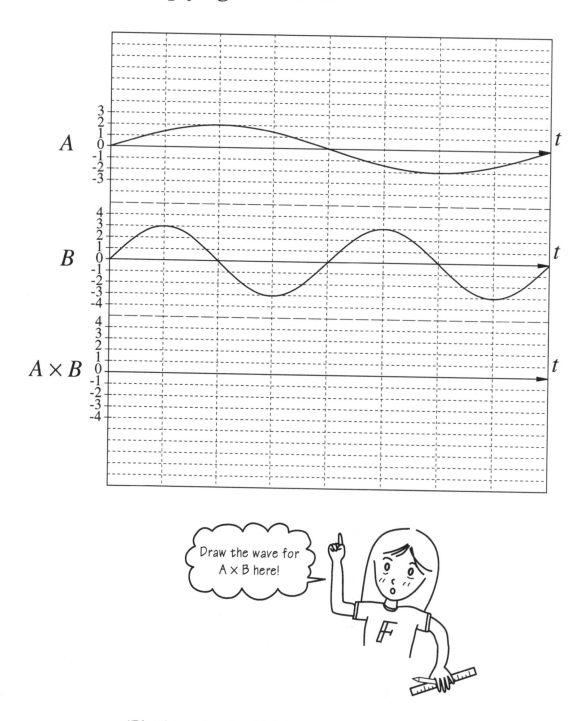

Draw the wave for A × B here!

"Plot the results of multiplying the value of *A* by the value of *B* for the same times "*t*". Assume that each scale mark has a value of 1, and watch your plus and minus signs! Pick several points where it's easy for you to read the values. And remember, use a smooth curve to connect the dots!"

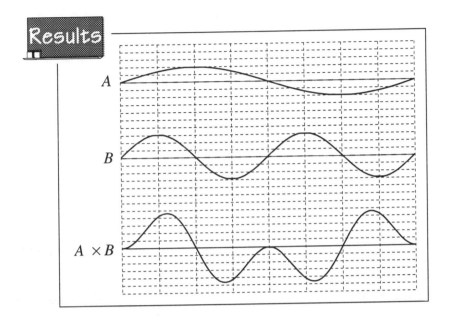

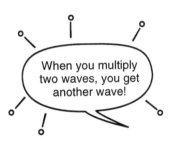

When you multiply two waves, you get another wave!

"All done, Professor!"

"Bon! Bon! But we must press onward! First, we must identify the wave you wish to extract from the complicated wave. You said you wanted to find $a_1 \cos \omega t$. If you change this wave's minus part to "plus", you will have solved your filter puzzle."

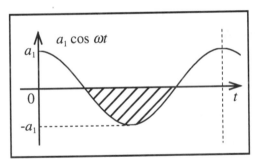

"You remember, of course, my little clue about how to change a negative value into a positive one?"

"Um, let's see, if you multiply a negative value by another negative value, it gives you a positive value, right?"

"Correct! However, if we multiply this entire wave by a negative number, the negative part will indeed become positive, but the positive part will become negative! What we want is to leave the positive part positive, and make the negative part positive as well. Can you see how to do that?"

"Leave the positive positive, and make the negative positive too, huh? Gee, I dunno..."

"To get a positive result in multiplication, you have to multiply a positive number by a positive number, or a negative number by a negative number."

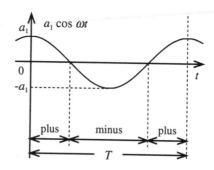

"So when the $a_1 \cos \omega t$ wave is positive, you have to multiply it by a positive value. When it's negative, you have to multiply it by a negative value..."

"Aha! I bet you can get an all-positive wave if you multiply it by a positive wave when the first wave is positive, and by a negative wave when the first wave is negative! In our case, we want a wave that's positive when $a_1 \cos \omega t$ is positive, and negative when $a_1 \cos \omega t$ is negative... Hey! All we need is to multiply $a_1 \cos \omega t$ by a wave that oscillates at the same angular velocity as $a_1 \cos \omega t$!"

Dr. Fourier grinned happily. "Oui! Oui! In other words, multiply it by a wave of the same frequency!"

"A wave of the same frequency, huh? Sounds good! Let's give it a try!"

"Just one thing – you must always use a wave with an amplitude of 1 for your multiplication. So, if you wish to get the wave $a_1 \cos \omega t$ as your result, you must multiply it by $\cos \omega t$."

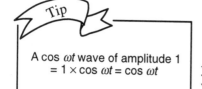

A $\cos \omega t$ wave of amplitude 1
$= 1 \times \cos \omega t = \cos \omega t$

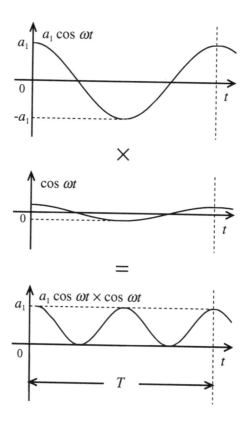

"Got it! This will guarantee that we don't get 0 when we try to find the area of $a_1 \cos \omega t$!"

But what's going to happen when we multiply the entire complicated wave $f(t)$ by $\cos \omega t$?

$$
\begin{aligned}
f(t) \times \underline{\cos \omega t} = (a_0 &+ a_1 \cos \omega t + b_1 \sin \omega t + a_2 \cos 2\omega t \\
&+ b_2 \sin 2\omega t + a_3 \cos 3\omega t \\
&+ b_3 \sin 3\omega t + \cdots) \times \underline{\cos \omega t}
\end{aligned}
$$

$$
\begin{aligned}
= a_0 &\times \underline{\cos \omega t} + a_1 \cos \omega t \underline{\times \cos \omega t} \\
&+ b_1 \sin \omega t \underline{\times \cos \omega t} \\
&+ a_2 \cos 2\omega t \underline{\times \cos \omega t} \\
&+ b_2 \sin 2\omega t \underline{\times \cos \omega t} \\
&+ a_3 \cos 3\omega t \underline{\times \cos \omega t} \\
&+ b_3 \sin 3\omega t \underline{\times \cos \omega t} + \cdots
\end{aligned}
$$

Well, there's our formula. If we multiply the entire complicated wave by $\cos \omega t$, it just seems to make it more complicated. It's easier to understand if we multiply each simple wave by $\cos \omega t$, one at a time. Then we can use graphs to illustrate each multiplication operation. Let's start with $a_0 \times \cos \omega t$.

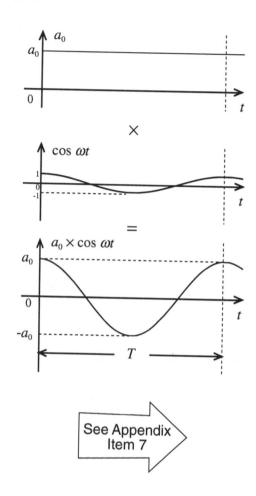

Look! The area for this one becomes 0!
We'll put this in our formula, using "A" for "area":

$$f(t) \times \cos \omega t \;=\; \underbrace{a_0 \times \cos \omega t}_{A\,=\,0} \;+\; a_1 \cos \omega t \times \cos \omega t$$

$$+\; b_1 \sin \omega t \times \cos \omega t \;+\; a_2 \cos 2\omega t \times \cos \omega t$$

$$+\; b_2 \sin 2\omega t \times \cos \omega t \;+\; a_3 \cos 3\omega t \times \cos \omega t$$

$$+\; b_3 \sin 3\omega t \times \cos \omega t \;+\; \cdots$$

So the wave $a_0 \times \cos \omega t$ has vanished.

Next, let's check out $b_1 \sin \omega t \times \cos \omega t$.

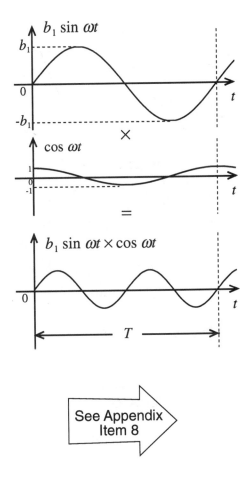

See Appendix
Item 8

Wow! The plus and minus areas are the same now, so this area's 0 too!
Add it to the formula:

$$f(t) \times \cos \omega t \;=\; \underbrace{a_0 \times \cos \omega t}_{A=0} \;+\; a_1 \cos \omega t \times \cos \omega t$$

$$+\; \underbrace{b_1 \sin \omega t \times \cos \omega t}_{A=0} \;+\; a_2 \cos 2\omega t \times \cos \omega t$$

$$+\; b_2 \sin 2\omega t \times \cos \omega t \;+\; a_3 \cos 3\omega t \times \cos \omega t$$

$$+\; b_3 \sin 3\omega t \times \cos \omega t \;+\; \cdots$$

So $b_1 \sin \omega t \times \cos \omega t$ is out of the picture too.

We're on a roll now – on to the next wave!

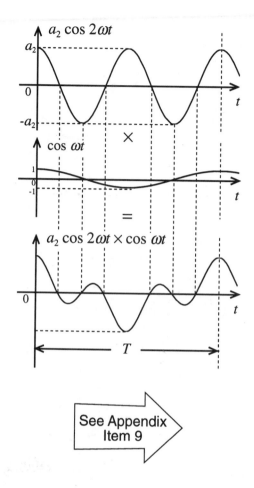

See Appendix
Item 9

Even with this one, the plus and minus parts cancel each other out!
So we get:

$$f(t) \underline{\times \cos \omega t} \;=\; \boxed{a_0 \underline{\times \cos \omega t}}_{\;A\,=\,0} \;+\; a_1 \cos \omega t \underline{\times \cos \omega t}$$

$$+\; \boxed{b_1 \sin \omega t \underline{\times \cos \omega t}}_{\;A\,=\,0} \;+\; \boxed{a_2 \cos 2\omega t \underline{\times \cos \omega t}}_{\;A\,=\,0}$$

$$+\; b_2 \sin 2\omega t \underline{\times \cos \omega t} \;+\; a_3 \cos 3\omega t \underline{\times \cos \omega t}$$

$$+\; b_3 \sin 3\omega t \underline{\times \cos \omega t} \;+\; \cdots$$

$a_2 \cos 2\omega t \times \cos \omega t$ – it's gone!

How about $b_2 \sin 2\omega t \times \cos \omega t$?

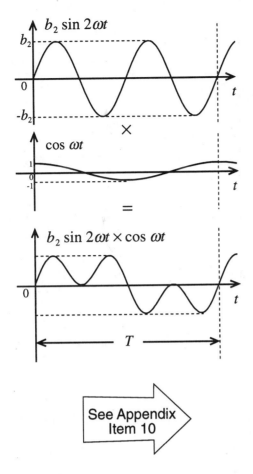

Once again, the area becomes 0, and our formula becomes:

$$
\begin{aligned}
f(t) \underline{\times \cos \omega t} \;=\; & \underbrace{a_0 \underline{\times \cos \omega t}}_{A\,=\,0} \;+\; a_1 \cos \omega t \underline{\times \cos \omega t} \\[2mm]
& +\; \underbrace{b_1 \sin \omega t \underline{\times \cos \omega t}}_{A\,=\,0} \;+\; \underbrace{a_2 \cos 2\omega t \underline{\times \cos \omega t}}_{A\,=\,0} \\[2mm]
& +\; \underbrace{b_2 \sin 2\omega t \underline{\times \cos \omega t}}_{A\,=\,0} \;+\; a_3 \cos 3\omega t \underline{\times \cos \omega t} \\[2mm]
& +\; b_3 \sin 3\omega t \underline{\times \cos \omega t} \;+\; \cdots
\end{aligned}
$$

$b_2 \sin 2\omega t \times \cos \omega t$ – poof!

Pressing ever onward...

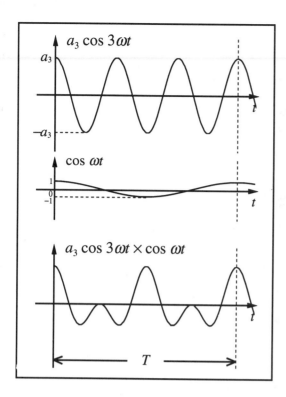

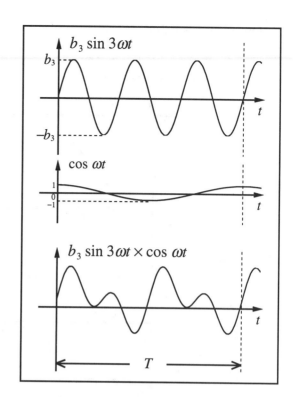

The plus and minus sides of this wave form may look quite different, but their areas are the same, so they add up to 0.

If you look closely, you can tell the areas are about the same – right?

In a nutshell, every one of these waves disappears when you find their area – except for $a_1 \cos \omega t \times \cos \omega t$!

See, their areas all became 0!

In other words, a wave's area always becomes 0 except when you multiply it by a wave of the same frequency.

$$f(t) \times \underline{\cos \omega t} = \underset{A=0}{\underline{a_0 \times \cos \omega t}} + a_1 \cos \omega t \times \underline{\cos \omega t}$$

$$+ \underset{A=0}{\underline{b_1 \sin \omega t \times \cos \omega t}} + \underset{A=0}{\underline{a_2 \cos 2\omega t \times \cos \omega t}}$$

$$+ \underset{A=0}{\underline{b_2 \sin 2\omega t \times \cos \omega t}} + \underset{A=0}{\underline{a_3 \cos 3\omega t \times \cos \omega t}}$$

$$+ \underset{A=0}{\underline{b_3 \sin 3\omega t \times \cos \omega t}} + \cdots$$

Finally, we have our a_1 filter. But we don't need to know the <u>area</u> of a_1, we want to find its actual value!

When we multiply complicated wave $f(t)$ by cos ωt, the value we get for the area is the shaded section shown below:

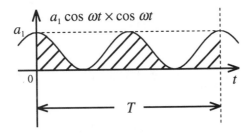

But how are we going to get the value of a_1 from this squiggly waveform?

Gee, the squigglier the waveform, the harder it looks to measure. But we know how to measure the area of a rectangle, don't we! Suppose we give these squiggles a vigorous shake and straighten them out into a rectangle.

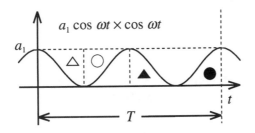

Yeah, that's it! All we have to do is move the ▲ section to the △ section, and the ● section to the ○ section. They're the same shape, so they fit perfectly, and they form a rectangle! So the area of this squiggly waveform is exactly the same as the area of the rectangle!

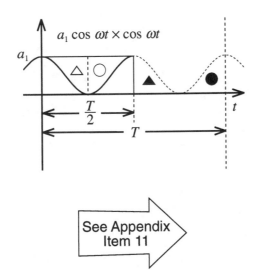

See Appendix
Item 11

Not only that, but the length of this rectangle is different from the length of a_0, because it's half of T, or $T/2$. So when we multiply the complicated wave by $\cos \omega t$, we'll get the following value for the area:

$$\text{Area} = a_1 \times \frac{T}{2}$$

Then all we have to do is divide this area by the length $T/2$ to get the value of a_1!!

At long last, we've solved the puzzle of the a_1 filter. Again, let's put what we've learned into words:

To find a_1, multiply complicated wave $f(t)$ by $\cos \omega t$, find the area from 0 to T (one period), then divide by $T/2$.

But what about the amplitudes of the other cosine waves – a_2, a_3, a_4, etc.? Can we find those values the same way?

Let's see, if we do the same thing for each of these other waves – that is, multiply them by a wave that has the same frequency and an amplitude of 1 – we'll always get the area of a rectangle whose height is amplitude a_n and whose length is $T/2$.

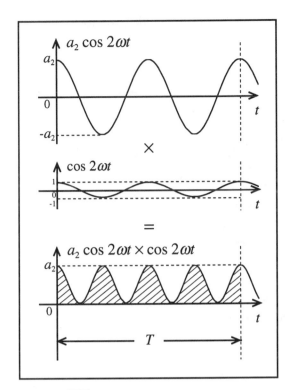

See Appendix Item 12

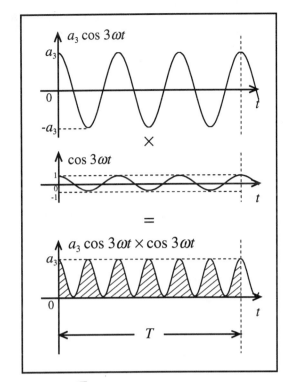

See Appendix Item 13

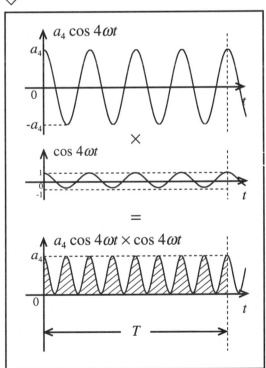

See Appendix Item 14

Use the numbered items in the appendix to make your own rectangles out of the shaded sections! They all have a length of $\frac{T}{2}$ It's fun – like putting together jigsaw puzzles!

So, to recap how we find the value of the amplitude a_n of any cosine wave:

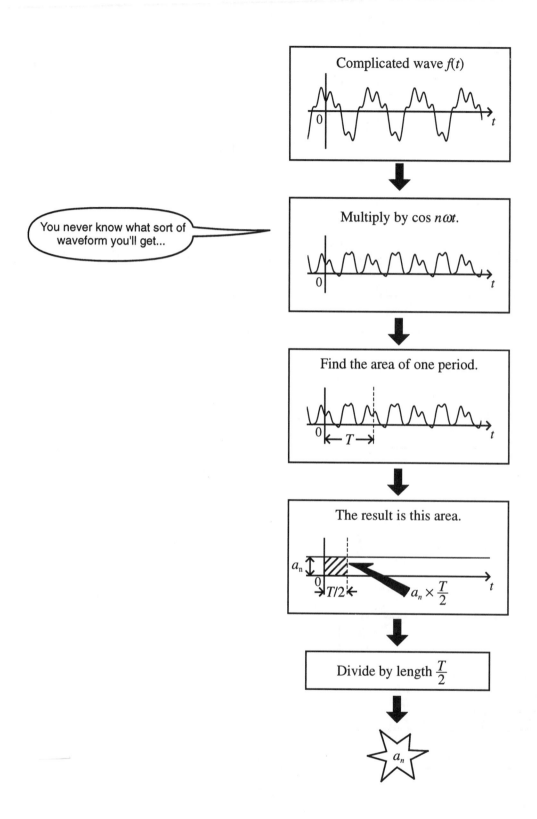

Now let's put it into words:

Tips

To find a_n, multiply complicated wave $f(t)$ by cos $n\omega t$, find the area from 0 to T (one period), then divide by $T/2$.

How to find a_n

See! You substitute the same number for the "n" in a_n and cos $n\omega t$ – 1, 2, 3, 4, or whatever – to get the amplitude of the wave with that frequency! So for a_1, you use cos $1\omega t$ (i.e., cos ωt). For a_2, you use cos $2\omega t$; for a_3, you use cos $3\omega t$, and so on...

So much for the a_n filter. Onward to b_n!

3. 3 Finding b_n —— the b_n filter puzzle

We now know how to find a_n – a_0, a_1, a_2, a_3 and the like. Next we'll try our luck with the b_n filter, which we need to help us find the amplitude of sine waves. This time, why don't we go straight to the amplitude of the b_2 sin $2\omega t$ wave.

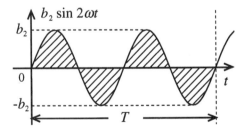

Once again, if we multiply the plus part of the wave by another plus, and the minus part by a minus, both the positive and negative parts will become positive. It seems as if we should be able to use the same method we used to find a_n.

On paper

In your mind

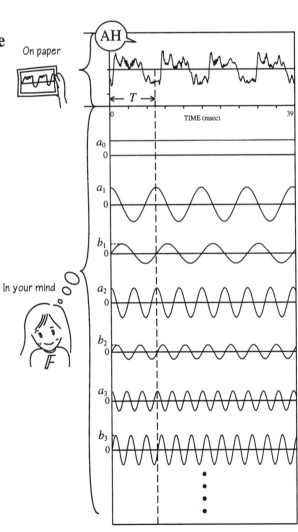

Since we're only going to try to extract $b_2 \sin 2\omega t$, we can just multiply $f(t)$ by a sine wave of the same frequency and an amplitude of 1 – which is $\sin 2\omega t$!

Okay, let's give it a try. What kind of formula do we get?. . .

$$
\begin{aligned}
f(t) \times \underline{\sin 2\omega t} = (a_0 &+ a_1 \cos \omega t + b_1 \sin \omega t + a_2 \cos 2\omega t \\
&+ b_2 \sin 2\omega t + a_3 \cos 3\omega t \\
&+ b_3 \sin 3\omega t + \cdots\cdot) \times \underline{\sin 2\omega t} \\
= a_0 &\times \underline{\sin 2\omega t} + a_1 \cos \omega t \times \underline{\sin 2\omega t} \\
&+ b_1 \sin \omega t \times \underline{\sin 2\omega t} \\
&+ a_2 \cos 2\omega t \times \underline{\sin 2\omega t} \\
&+ b_2 \sin 2\omega t \times \underline{\sin 2\omega t} \\
&+ a_3 \cos 3\omega t \times \underline{\sin 2\omega t} \\
&+ b_3 \sin 3\omega t \times \underline{\sin 2\omega t} + \cdots\cdot
\end{aligned}
$$

Now let's get right to the wave that we're interested in $- b_2 \sin 2\omega t \times \sin 2\omega t$.

Will it have an area that's not 0?

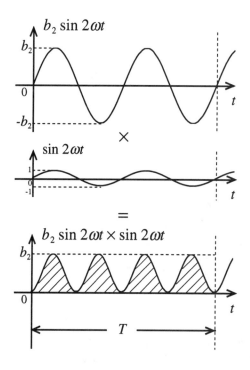

Yes! The area of $b_2 \sin 2\omega t \times \sin 2\omega t$ <u>isn't</u> 0! But what about the other waves? I have a hunch their areas will all become 0, but you never know...

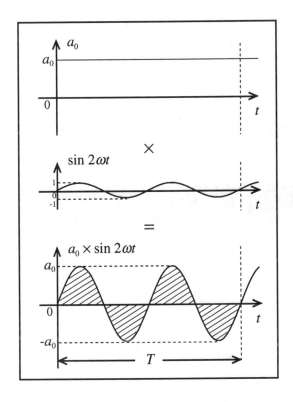

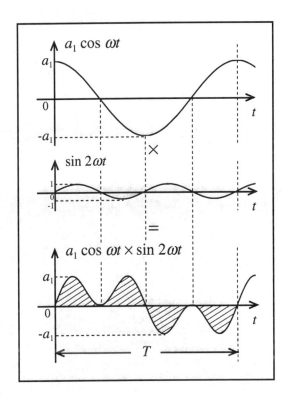

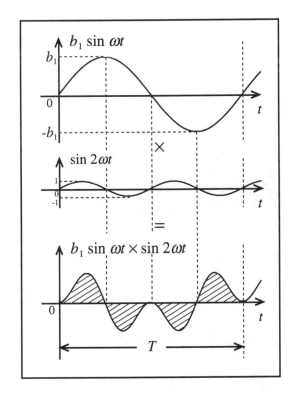

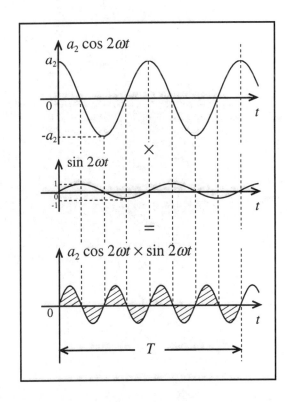

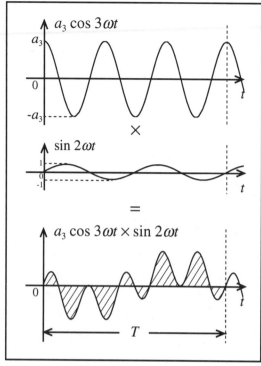

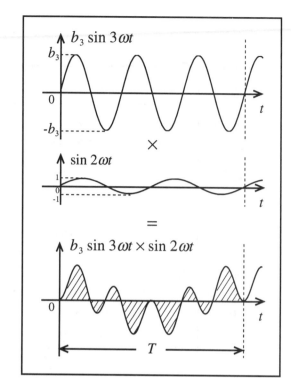

Hey, I was right! All the other waves except $b_2 \sin 2\omega t$ have areas of 0 now!!

$$f(t) \times \underline{\sin 2\omega t} = \underbrace{a_0 \times \sin 2\omega t}_{A=0} + \underbrace{a_1 \cos \omega t \times \sin 2\omega t}_{A=0}$$

$$+ \underbrace{b_1 \sin \omega t \times \sin 2\omega t}_{A=0} + \underbrace{a_2 \cos 2\omega t \times \sin 2\omega t}_{A=0}$$

$$+ b_2 \sin 2\omega t \times \underline{\sin 2\omega t} + \underbrace{a_3 \cos 3\omega t \times \sin 2\omega t}_{A=0}$$

$$+ \underbrace{b_3 \sin 3\omega t \times \underline{\sin 2\omega t}}_{A=0} + \cdots \cdots$$

So the resulting value of the area is:

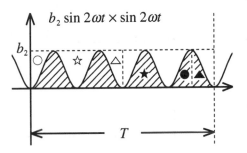

And if we straighten out the curves, the area looks like this:

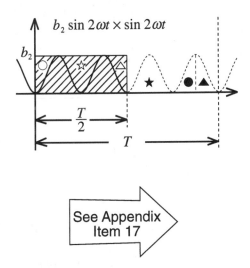

So the area of this shaded section is $b_2 \times T/2$. Then, if we divide the area value by $T/2$, we'll get the value of b_2!

Putting this in real English:

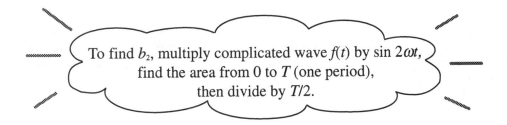

To find b_2, multiply complicated wave $f(t)$ by $\sin 2\omega t$,
find the area from 0 to T (one period),
then divide by $T/2$.

Okay, but what about b_1, b_3, b_4, b_5...? Will we get the same results we did with the cosine waves?

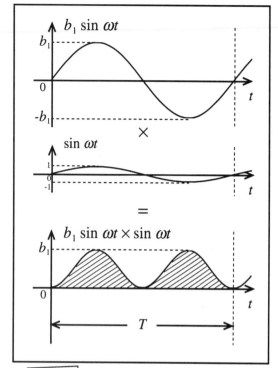

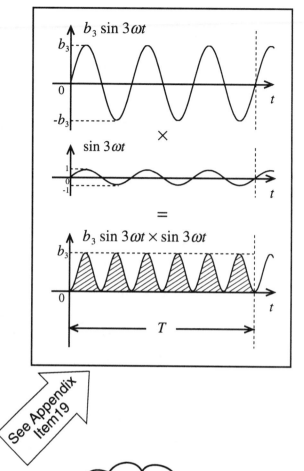

See Appendix Item 18

See Appendix Item 19

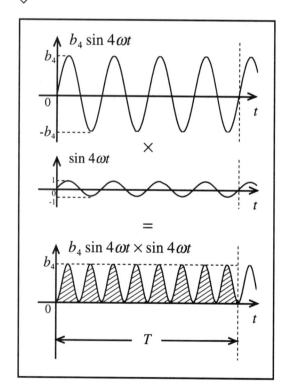

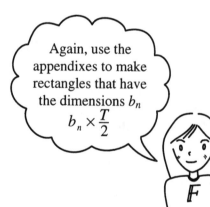

Again, use the appendixes to make rectangles that have the dimensions b_n

$$b_n \times \frac{T}{2}$$

So, we can deal with sine waves just as we did with the cosine waves: multiply them by a wave that has the same frequency and an amplitude of 1, and we'll get the area of a rectangle whose height is amplitude b_n and whose length is $T/2$.

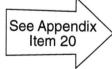

See Appendix Item 20

Summing up, this is how we find the value of the amplitude b_n of any sine wave:

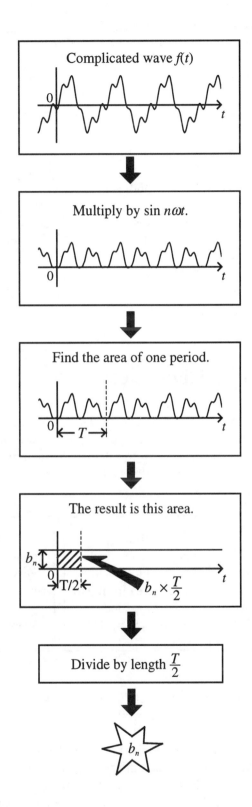

And putting this method into words:

Tips

How to find b_n

To find b_n, multiply complicated wave $f(t)$ by sin $n\omega t$,
find the area from 0 to T (one period),
then divide by $T/2$.

Just like the cosine waves – substitute
any number you want for the "n" in b_n and
sin $n\omega t$, and you'll get the amplitude of
the wave that has that frequency!
(For b_1, use sin $1\omega t$; for b_3, use sin $3\omega t$;
for b_{10}, use sin $10\omega t$...)

So now we have our b_n filter too!

4. The Fourier Coefficients Formulas

So far we have solved the riddles of three filters. And we have learned
how to use these filters to isolate a single simple wave from the many that
make up a complicated wave, and how to calculate the amplitude of that wave.
Let's put these three filters in writing and compare them side by side:

To find a_0,	**To find a_n,**	**To find b_n,**
find the area from 0 to T (one period) for complicated wave $f(t)$, then divide by T.	multiply complicated wave $f(t)$ by cos $n\omega t$, find the area from 0 to T (one period), then divide by $T/2$.	multiply complicated wave $f(t)$ by sin $n\omega t$, find the area from 0 to T (one period), then divide by $T/2$.

That seems clear enough! Just looking at those pretty descriptions makes
all the trials of our journey seem worthwhile!

However, there's a slight problem with these descriptions. They're not
very helpful if we want to convey this information to people who speak other
languages. Not only do you have to translate them into, say, French or Turkish
or Korean, but you'll never be absolutely sure they were translated accurately.

But the esteemed Dr. Fourier has yet another trick up his sleeve!

"Oui, mes amis, allow me to teach you a medium of communication understood around the world – the formula!"

Using the good doctor's formulas, we can break down one of our written descriptions as follows:

For a_0, take complicated wave $f(t)$, find the area from 0 to T
(1)   (2)   (3)

and divide by T.
(4)

---

(1) For a_0

$$a_0 =$$

(2) take complicated wave $f(t)$

$$a_0 = \quad f(t)$$

(3) find the area

"Wha-?! How do we write "find the area"?!"

"Like this!" $\quad a_0 = \displaystyle\int_0^T f(t)\, dt$

The symbol $\int$ is called an "integral". It is always followed by the symbol "dt", indicating that the area of the item appearing between these symbols is to be calculated. The range for which to find the area is written to the right of the $\int$ symbol at the top and bottom.

Caution

In the formula from (1) to (3), the equal sign does not represent an equality.
It is being used for the process of constructing the complete formula (4).

(4) and divide by T.

$$a_0 = \int_0^T f(t)\, dt \div T$$

"One more thing – instead of dividing by T, let's multiply instead. "Divide by T" means the same as "multiply by $1/T$". For example,

$$18 \div 3 = 6$$

can be written

$$18 \times \frac{1}{3} = 6$$

$15 \div 5 = 3$

$15 \times \dfrac{1}{5} = 3$

$16 \div 2 = 8$

$16 \times \dfrac{1}{2} = 8$

These mean the same thing!

"So we can write the formula for a_0 as:

$$a_0 = \int_0^T f(t)\, dt \times \frac{1}{T}$$

How to read the formula

"a_0 equals 1 divided by T multiplied by the integral from 0 to T of $f(t)\, d\, t$."
Of course, you can also say it in plain English:
"a_0 is the area from 0 to T for $f(t)$, divided by T."

"If we omit the "$\times$" symbol, which isn't necessary, and move the whole thing up to the front, we get:

$$a_0 = \frac{1}{T}\int_0^T f(t)\, dt$$

"Wow, Professor, this looks like a real, fancy, professional formula – and it's a lot shorter than writing it out in words!"

"C'est ça! Now try the same approach with a_n and b_n!"

First we'll give our description of a_n the treatment:

For a_n, take complicated wave $f(t)$ and multiply it by cos $n\omega t$;
(1) (2) (3)
find the area for the period 0 to T and divide by $T/2$.
(4) (5) (6)

(1) For a_n $\qquad\qquad a_n =$

Caution

In the formula from (1) to (5), the equal sign does not represent an equality.
It is being used for the process of constructing the complete formula (6).

(2) take complicated wave $f(t)$ $\qquad a_n = \; f(t)$

(3) and multiply it by cos $n\omega t$; $\qquad a_n = \; f(t) \times \cos n\omega t$

(4) find the area $\qquad\qquad a_n = \displaystyle\int f(t) \times \cos n\omega t\; dt$

(5) for the period 0 to T $\qquad\qquad a_n = \displaystyle\int_0^T f(t) \times \cos n\omega t\; dt$

(6) and divide by $T/2$. $\qquad\qquad a_n = \displaystyle\int_0^T f(t) \times \cos n\omega t\; dt \div \frac{T}{2}$

"Does that look okay, Doc?"

"Excellent! But again, let us multiply instead of dividing by *T/2*."

"Let's see... 'divide by *T/2*' means the same thing as 'multiply by 2/*T*', so...

$$a_n = \int_0^T f(t) \times \cos n\omega t\, dt \times \frac{2}{T}$$

"And if we eliminate the "×" symbol, we get:

$$a_n = \frac{2}{T} \int_0^T f(t) \cos n\omega t\, dt$$

"We did it again!!"

"We did it again!!" "Perfect! Now on to b_n!"

How to read the formula

"a_n equals 2 divided by *T*
multiplied by the integral
from 0 to *T* of *f(t)*
cosine *n* omega *t* d *t*."

Or you can just say
"a_n is the area from 0
to *T* for *f(t)* etc. etc..."

For b_n, take complicated wave $f(t)$ and multiply it by sin $n\omega t$;
(1)   (2)   (3)

find the area for the period 0 to *T* and divide by *T/2*.
(4)   (5)   (6)

---

(1) For b_n $\boldsymbol{b_n} =$

(2) take complicated wave $f(t)$ $b_n = \boldsymbol{f(t)}$

(3) multiply it by sin $\boldsymbol{n\omega t}$; $b_n = f(t) \times \boldsymbol{\sin n\omega t}$

(4) find the area $b_n = \int f(t) \times \sin n\omega t\, \boldsymbol{dt}$

(5) for the period 0 to *T* $b_n = \int_0^T f(t) \times \sin n\omega t\, dt$

(6) and divide by *T/2*. $b_n = \int_0^T f(t) \times \sin n\omega t\, dt \div \frac{\boldsymbol{T}}{\boldsymbol{2}}$

Caution

In the formula from (1)
to (5), the equal sign
does not represent an
equality.
It is being used for the
process of
constructing the
complete formula (6).

How to read the formula

"b_n equals 2 divided by T times the integral from 0 to T of $f(t)$ sine n omega t d t."

"Then omit the "×" symbol, and change the division to multiplication, right?"

$$b_n = \frac{2}{T} \int_0^T f(t) \sin n\omega t \, dt$$

"Et voilà! These formulas are referred to as the

"Fourier Coefficients"

"Be sure and hold on to these Fourier coefficients together with the Fourier series. Believe me, you will find them absolutely indispensable during your upcoming adventures!"

Fourier coefficients

$$a_0 = \frac{1}{T} \int_0^T f(t) \, dt$$

$$a_n = \frac{2}{T} \int_0^T f(t) \cos n\omega t \, dt$$

$$b_n = \frac{2}{T} \int_0^T f(t) \sin n\omega t \, dt$$

Wow, so now we have a universal language for expressing Fourier coefficients, too! Formulas are great – they're compact, and they're understood everywhere in the world!

Conclusion

This concludes our current adventure. We've learned how to convert a complicated wave into a formula and, with the help of Dr. Fourier, how to find the amplitude of each of the simple waves that determine the shape of the complicated wave. The method the good doctor taught us is called "Fourier coefficients."

From now on, whenever we encounter a complicated wave, we can first use the Fourier series to convert it into a sum of simple waves. Then we can bring our other weapon into play – Fourier coefficients – to find the amplitude of each of those simple waves. Once we know the values of all these amplitudes (a_0, a_1, b_1, a_2, b_2, and so on), we can make a precise numeric comparison of the difference between two waves – AH and EE, for example.

In this episode, we've learned a method for finding the amplitudes of a series of simple waves. We still haven't actually performed these calculations on a real complicated wave. But in the next chapter, that's exactly what we'll do!

Best of luck!

The Riddle of a_0

Does a_0 strike you as a bit of an oddball? Why do we call it a_0, anyway? And isn't there a b_0? The whole a_0 business seems rather strange, doesn't it. So we'll take this opportunity to shed some light on the subject.

As a type of "a", a_0 is obviously a member of the a_n family. We know that a_1 is the amplitude of $\cos 1\omega t$, so what does that make a_0? As you'd expect, it's the amplitude of $\cos 0\omega t$. But what is the value of $\cos 0\omega t$? The angle $0\omega t$ of $\cos 0\omega t$ is multiplied by 0, so regardless of the value of ω or t,

$$\cos 0\omega t = \cos 0.$$

And what is $\cos 0$? That's right, it's 1. At 0 degrees, the ratio "horizontal/diagonal" is 1. Therefore,

$$a_0 \cos 0\omega t = a_0 \times 1 = a_0.$$

So a_0 is actually an abbreviation for $a_0 \cos \omega t$ in the Fourier series formula

$$f(t) = a_0 + a_1 \cos 1\omega t + b_1 \sin 1\omega t...$$

But what about b_0? Why doesn't it appear in the formula? Just as a_0 belongs to the a_n family, b_0 belongs to the b_n family. That should make it the amplitude of $\sin 0\omega t$. What is the value of $b_0 \sin 0\omega t$, then? Since the angle $0\omega t$ is multiplied by 0, it will be 0 regardless of the value of ω or t. And $\sin 0$ is 0. Therefore, whatever b_0 may be,

$$b_0 \sin 0\omega t = b_0 \times 0 = 0.$$

That makes it impossible to determine the value of b_0.

Recapping what we've said so far, the formula for the Fourier series is actually

$$f(t) = a_0 \cos 0\omega t + a_1 \cos 1\omega t + b_1 \sin 1\omega t...$$

But since $\cos 0\omega t$ is always 1, we instead write it

$$f(t) = a_0 + a_1 \cos 1\omega t + b_1 \sin 1\omega t...$$

Now that we've solved the riddle of a_0 in the Fourier series, let's see how it behaves in the Fourier coefficients formulas. Here, too, the a_0 formula seems a bit out of place. If a_0 belongs to the a_n family, why does it have a formula like

$$a_0 = \frac{1}{T} \int_0^T f(t)\, dt \quad ?$$

Well, there is a reason. Suppose we put a_0 in a Fourier coefficients formula like the others, calculating it as

$$a_n = \frac{2}{T} \int_0^T f(t) \cos n\omega t\, dt$$

What we get is not a_0, but $2a_0$, or double the value of a_0! Notice that where the a_0 formula contains $1/T$, the a_n formula contains $2/T$. If we had originally decided to find a_0 in the formula

$$f(t) = \frac{a_0}{2} + a_1 \cos 1\omega t + \sin 1\omega t + \cdots\cdots$$

we could have used the a_n formula to find a_0. (You can try this calculation yourself if you're familiar with integration or the trigonometric identities.) But otherwise, we have to provide a_0 with its own special formula among the Fourier coefficients.

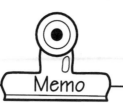

Memo

Chapter 3

Discrete Fourier Expansion

In the last chapter we learned how to break a complicated wave down into simple waves. Now it's time we tried this method out in some real calculations, to see what kinds of waves combine to form an actual complicated wave. The key phrase in this chapter is... "paper strip"!

1. What Have We Learned So Far?
A Quick Review

We learned that no matter how complicated a wave may be,

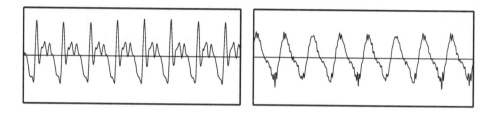

as long as it repeats itself – i.e., has a period – the wave can be described as a sum of simple waves.

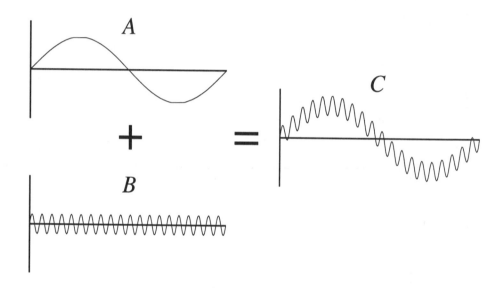

For example, wave *C* above is the sum of wave *A* and wave *B*.

For a more complicated wave, the equation looks like this:

complicated wave = simple wave 1 + simple wave 2 + simple wave 3 + ...

In our study of the Fourier series and Fourier coefficients, we also learned that we can break down the waves of the human voice this way!

Let's look for a moment at the waves you make when you say AH and EE, and think about the simple waves that will form them. Since AH and EE have the same fundamental period, they'll both consist of the sum of the types of waves shown on the following page.

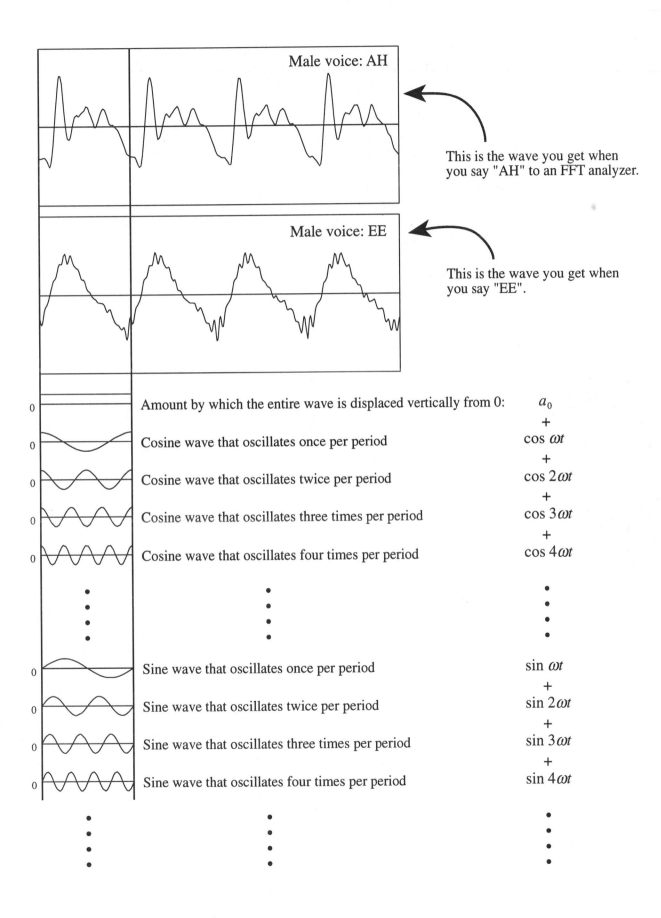

Male voice: AH

This is the wave you get when you say "AH" to an FFT analyzer.

Male voice: EE

This is the wave you get when you say "EE".

Amount by which the entire wave is displaced vertically from 0: a_0

$+$

Cosine wave that oscillates once per period $\cos \omega t$

$+$

Cosine wave that oscillates twice per period $\cos 2\omega t$

$+$

Cosine wave that oscillates three times per period $\cos 3\omega t$

$+$

Cosine wave that oscillates four times per period $\cos 4\omega t$

Sine wave that oscillates once per period $\sin \omega t$

$+$

Sine wave that oscillates twice per period $\sin 2\omega t$

$+$

Sine wave that oscillates three times per period $\sin 3\omega t$

$+$

Sine wave that oscillates four times per period $\sin 4\omega t$

To sum up, a lot of simple waves combine to form the jagged complicated waves AH and EE.

As a matter of fact, you have to add up around thirty sine and cosine waves each to get an AH wave or EE wave! Think about it – all those waves in the voice you use so casually every day! The mind boggles...

But why do the AH and EE waves look so different? They have the same period, which means they contain the exact same types of waves. And if they each have 30 sine waves and 30 cosine waves... well, why don't they look the same?

Because even if the simple waves that make them up are the same – cos ωt, sin ωt, cos $2\omega t$, sin $2\omega t$, cos $3\omega t$, sin $3\omega t$, and so on – the quantities of those waves are different!!

You recall our example of the vegetable juices...

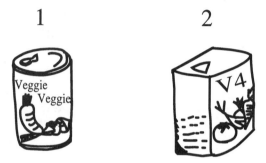

They all contained the same vegetables – tomato, carrot, celery, cabbage – and yet they tasted different. Why?

Because they had different quantities of each vegetable!

For example, Juice 1 might have equal amounts of each vegetable, while Juice 2 might consist mostly of tomato, with only a little of the other vegetables. Likewise, two complicated waves might have the same types of simple waves, but in different "quantities." The result is different waveforms, as we saw in the case of AH and EE.

For example, the AH wave has a lot of the cos $3\omega t$ wave, whereas the EE wave has only a little. On the other hand, the EE wave has more of the cos ωt and cos $8\omega t$ waves than the AH wave does.

But what do we mean by "quantity" when we're talking about a wave? Actually, we mean its **amplitude**! So if we can find the amplitude of each simple wave, we should be able to determine the form of the resulting complicated wave.

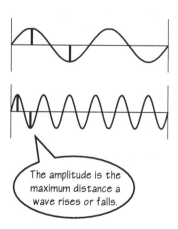

The amplitude is the maximum distance a wave rises or falls.

$$f(t) = a_0 + a_1 \cos \omega t + b_1 \sin \omega t$$
$$+ \, a_2 \cos 2\omega t + b_2 \sin 2\omega t$$
$$+ \, a_3 \cos 3\omega t + b_3 \sin 3\omega t$$

$$\vdots \qquad \vdots$$

This is the Fourier series formula, which shows that a complicated wave is the sum of simple waves. By finding the values of the amplitudes a_0, a_1, a_2, a_3,... and b_1, b_2, b_3,... we can tell what complicated wave $f(t)$ looks like.
So how do we find the amplitude?

With a filter, remember?!

All we need are the right filters, and it's a breeze...

$$a_0 = \frac{1}{T} \int_0^T f(t)\, dt$$

(Find the area of one period of complicated wave $f(t)$, and divide it by period T.)

$$a_n = \frac{2}{T} \int_0^T f(t) \cos n\omega t\, dt$$

(Multiply complicated wave $f(t)$ by $\cos n\omega t$, find the area of one period, divide it by period T and multiply by 2.)

$$b_n = \frac{2}{T} \int_0^T f(t) \sin n\omega t\, dt$$

(Multiply complicated wave $f(t)$ by $\sin n\omega t$, find the area of one period, divide it by period T and multiply by 2.)

If we run complicated wave $f(t)$

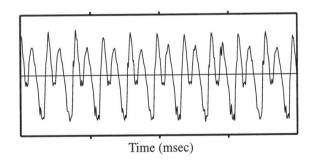

Time (msec)

through these filters, we'll be left with the amplitudes we were looking for!

But... can we really find the amplitudes of all those waves with just this method...?

"Today, let's find out whether this method really works."

"Oh! Hello, Prof!"

"Here, try your hand at calculating the amplitudes of the waves that make up a real-life complicated wave... this one!"

"I came up with this wave by inputting some values into a computer, so I know the correct answer already. If you find the same answer using the filters, that will prove the method works, right? Go ahead, give it a try!"

"Oh, all right... Geez, I feel like an amateur detective or something...Why don't all of you at home give it a try too!"

2. Finding the Amplitude of a Wave

Let's start with the period of the wave.

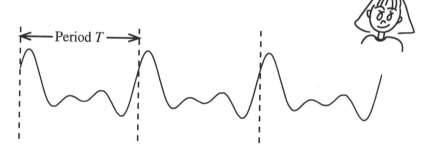

If we make an enlargement of one period, it looks like this:

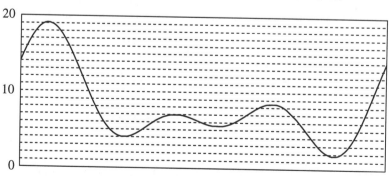

10 sec

This wave repeats itself every 10 seconds. That means its fundamental period is 10 seconds!

$$\boxed{\text{Fundamental period } T = 10 \text{ sec}}$$

Now then! Let's find the value of a_0, using the a_0 filter we learned about.

2. 1 Find a_0!

$$a_0 = \frac{1}{T}\int_0^T f(t)\, dt$$

(Find the area of one period of complicated wave $f(t)$, and divide it by period T.)

This filter should help us find a_0, which will tell us how much the entire wave is displaced above or below 0.

Well, let's go to it. Find the area of one period, eh? Hmm... Hey, how are we supposed to find the area of a weird shape like this?!

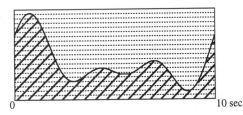

 Shapes like these, I can handle. But **this**...?!

"Hey, Prof! How do you expect us to do this, anyway?"

"Heh heh... Simple! Allow me to introduce the paper strip method!"

"The "**paper strip**" method? What the–"

"Paper strip – you know, a long, narrow, rectangular piece of paper!"

"Yeah, okay, but how–"

"Try dividing the wave up into 10 equal sections. Since period T is 10 seconds long, it's easy to divide the wave into 1-second parts. You can get the value of $f(t)$ for each second by reading the scale on the vertical axis. Think of each section as a strip of paper with a width of 1 and a height that is the value of $f(t)$ at that point in time."

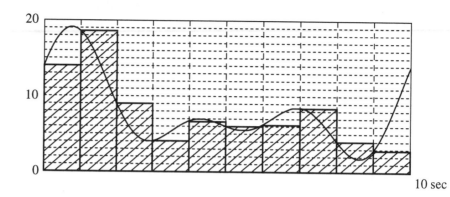

"Like this? I dunno, it looks kind of sloppy. A lot of the strips don't actually fit the wave..."

"That's true. Some of them aren't long enough, others stick out – but overall, wouldn't you say they appear to average out to 0, approximately?"

"Well, approximately, sure, but..."

"Approximations can be surprisingly precise, you'll find."

"But can't we make things less sloppy by using narrower strips?"

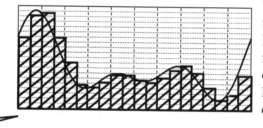

This approach is none other than the "integration" we'll be discussing later. By making the strips narrower and narrower, we can eventually find the "closest approximation of the area."

"Exactly! The narrower we make them, the more precise they'll be. But the more strips there are, the more work we have to do to calculate them all. So for now, let's stick with 10 strips and make do with 'approximate' precision!"

All right, here we go with 10 strips!

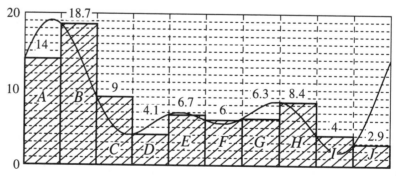

The first strip has a height of 14 and a width of 1, so its area is:

$$14 \times 1 = 14$$

Let's calculate the area of all the other strips in this fashion and write them in a table:

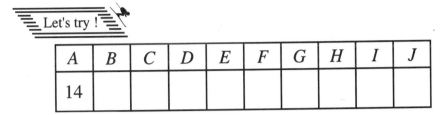

☞ Answer on page 131

A	B	C	D	E	F	G	H	I	J
14									

In other words, just write in the value of $f(t)$ for each of these 10 points.

Then add up these values to get the total area!

Total = _____

Finally, divide this total by T, that is, 10.

Total area ⬜ ÷ T ⬜ = a_0 ⬜

So the entire wave is displaced by a value of approximately 8 above 0. Now we know the value of a_0!!

2. 2 Find a_n!

Well, a_0 was pretty simple, wasn't it? Now let's give a_n a try! Our filter for finding a_n is:

$$a_n = \frac{2}{T} \int_0^T f(t) \cos n\omega t \, dt$$

> Multiply complicated wave $f(t)$ by cos $n\omega t$, find the area of one period, divide it by period T and multiply by 2.

Let's start with the value of a_1, the amplitude of the largest cosine wave contained in $f(t)$.

First, we have to multiply complicated wave $f(t)$ by cos $1\omega t$.

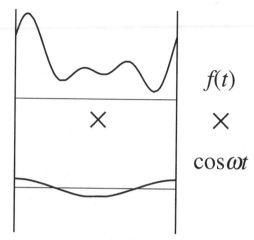

$f(t)$

$\times$ $\times$

$\cos \omega t$

Since we've already divided $f(t)$ into 10 equal sections, we should divide $\cos \omega t$ the same way. Then we can multiply the values of $f(t)$ and $\cos \omega t$ that occur at the same points in time t.

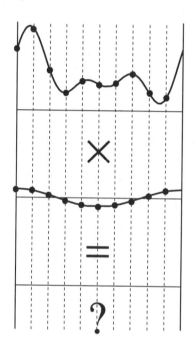

That will give us a new wave, and we can find this wave's area using the strip method, as we did before.

Okay, let's start multiplying the points shown in the chart above. We already know the values of the 10 points on wave $f(t)$, so all we need now is the values of those same 10 points on $\cos \omega t$.

This cosine wave passes through one period (i.e. 360°) in 10 seconds, so it passes through 36° in 1/10 of that period (1 second). That means we need to find the values of cos in 36-degree increments: cos 0°, cos 36°, cos 72° and so on up to cos 360°.

Let's see, since each of our 10 sections is 1 second long, the wave passes through 36° in 1 second... now, what was the angle through which a wave passes in 1 second? That's it! – angular velocity (ω)!

Angular velocity $\omega = 36°/\text{sec}$

Now we can do some multiplication! Since our first calculation is for $t = 0$ on both waves, we'll insert $\omega = 36$ and $t = 0$ in the formula $f(t) \times \cos\omega t$. That gives us:

$$f(0) \times \cos(36 \cdot 0)° = 14 \times \cos 0°$$
$$= 14 \times 1 = 14$$

Remember, a cosine wave starts at 1, so $\cos 0° = 1$!

Hey, that was simple! Onward, onward! Our next point is at $t=1$, so our multiplication should look like this:

$$f(1) \times \cos(36 \cdot 1)° = 18.7 \times \cos 36°$$

Whoa, wait a minute! What's $\cos 36°$?! We knew that $\cos 0°=1$, but how are we going to figure out $\cos 36°$? Our graph tells us it will be a smaller value than 1, but...

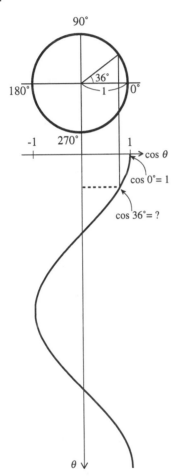

"How's it going?"
"Ah! Prof!"
"What's wrong?"
"What are we gonna do about $\cos 36°$?!"
"Ah yes! That would be very difficult for us to calculate on our own. Fortunately, it's already been done! Take a look at this handy table!"

Trigonometric Table

Angle	sin	cos	tan	Angle	sin	cos	tan
0°	0.0000	1.0000	0.0000	45°	0.7071	0.7071	1.0000
1°	0.0175	0.9998	0.0175	46°	0.7193	0.6947	1.0355
2°	0.0349	0.9994	0.0349	47°	0.7314	0.6820	1.0724
3°	0.0523	0.9986	0.0524	48°	0.7431	0.6691	1.1106
4°	0.0698	0.9976	0.0699	49°	0.7547	0.6561	1.1504
5°	0.0872	0.9962	0.0875	50°	0.7660	0.6428	1.1918
6°	0.1045	0.9945	0.1051	51°	0.7771	0.6293	1.2349
7°	0.1219	0.9925	0.1228	52°	0.7880	0.6157	1.2799
8°	0.1392	0.9903	0.1405	53°	0.7986	0.6018	1.3270
9°	0.1564	0.9877	0.1584	54°	0.8090	0.5878	1.3764
10°	0.1736	0.9848	0.1763	55°	0.8192	0.5736	1.4281
11°	0.1908	0.9816	0.1944	56°	0.8290	0.5592	1.4826
12°	0.2079	0.9781	0.2126	57°	0.8387	0.5446	1.5399
13°	0.2250	0.9744	0.2309	58°	0.8480	0.5299	1.6003
14°	0.2419	0.9703	0.2493	59°	0.8572	0.5150	1.6643
15°	0.2588	0.9659	0.2679	60°	0.8660	0.5000	1.7321
16°	0.2756	0.9613	0.2867	61°	0.8746	0.4848	1.8040
17°	0.2924	0.9563	0.3057	62°	0.8829	0.4695	1.8807
18°	0.3090	0.9511	0.3249	63°	0.8910	0.4540	1.9626
19°	0.3256	0.9455	0.3443	64°	0.8988	0.4384	2.0503
• 20°	0.3420	0.9397	0.3640	65°	0.9063	0.4226	2.1445
21°	0.3584	0.9336	0.3839	66°	0.9135	0.4067	2.2460
22°	0.3746	0.9272	0.4040	67°	0.9205	0.3907	2.3559
23°	0.3907	0.9205	0.4245	68°	0.9272	0.3746	2.4751
24°	0.4067	0.9135	0.4452	69°	0.9336	0.3584	2.6051
25°	0.4226	0.9063	0.4663	70°	0.9397	0.3420	2.7475
26°	0.4384	0.8988	0.4877	71°	0.9455	0.3256	2.9042
27°	0.4540	0.8910	0.5095	72°	0.9511	0.3090	3.0777
28°	0.4695	0.8829	0.5317	73°	0.9563	0.2924	3.2709
29°	0.4848	0.8746	0.5543	74°	0.9613	0.2756	3.4874
30°	0.5000	0.8660	0.5774	75°	0.9659	0.2588	3.7321
31°	0.5150	0.8572	0.6009	76°	0.9703	0.2419	4.0108
32°	0.5299	0.8480	0.6249	77°	0.9744	0.2250	4.3315
33°	0.5446	0.8387	0.6494	78°	0.9781	0.2079	4.7046
34°	0.5592	0.8290	0.6745	79°	0.9816	0.1908	5.1446
35°	0.5736	0.8192	0.7002	80°	0.9848	0.1736	5.6713
★ 36°	0.5878	[0.8090]	0.7265	81°	0.9877	0.1564	6.3138
37°	0.6018	0.7986	0.7536	82°	0.9903	0.1392	7.1154
38°	0.6157	0.7880	0.7813	83°	0.9925	0.1219	8.1443
39°	0.6293	0.7771	0.8098	84°	0.9945	0.1045	9.5144
40°	0.6428	0.7660	0.8391	85°	0.9962	0.0872	11.4301
41°	0.6561	0.7547	0.8693	86°	0.9976	0.0698	14.3007
42°	0.6691	0.7431	0.9004	87°	0.9986	0.0523	19.0811
43°	0.6820	0.7314	0.9325	88°	0.9994	0.0349	28.6363
44°	0.6947	0.7193	0.9657	89°	0.9998	0.0175	57.2900
45°	0.7071	0.7071	1.0000	90°	1.0000	0.0000	

"Wow! That's great! So cos 36° = 0.8090. That was easy!"

"Hold on! What about cos 91°, then?"

"Er, uh, I don't see it... Hey, where's the second page of the table, anyway?"

"There is no second page. This one page is all you need!"

"I don't get it."

"There's just one little trick you need to know."

"Trick?"

cos 91° is the same as
cos 89° with a minus
sign, so:

cos 91° = –0.0175

"Draw yourself a unit circle, and plot a graph showing changes in cos θ as it rotates through the circle."

"Done!"

"Very nice. Now, do you see any other points on the graph that have the same value for cos θ as cos 36°?"

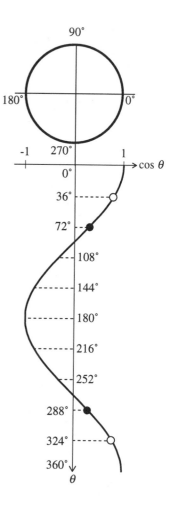

"Yes! There's cos 324°! And cos 288° is the same as cos 72°. Even for larger angles, the value of cos θ is always the same as one of its values between 0° and 90°!"

"All right, then, where would you find the value of cos 252°?"

"At cos 108°! Uh oh, but cos 108° isn't in the table either. Now what do we do?"

"Look at the graph again and think..."

"I get it! For cos 108°, you can just use the negative of cos 72°. Since cos 72° is 0.3090, cos 108° is -0.3090, right?"

"You've got it! So now you understand why the table only goes up to 90°. That's all you need. Just keep in mind how the wave is shaped, and you'll be able to find the value of any angle, no matter how large, in that table."

"Hey, now that I've got the hang of it, let me try some more... cos 45°, say. Since cos 45° is 0.7071, that's the value of cos 315° too. Then, on the minus side of the wave, cos 135° and cos 225° are both -0.7071!"

"Okay, what about cos 370°?"

"Hmmm... cos 370° is 10 degrees past one full rotation, so it would be the same as cos 10°, which is 0.9848!"

"Excellent! Now we can pick up where we left off."

Where were we? Oh yes, we were multiplying $f(t) \times \cos \omega t$. We didn't know the value of cos 36°, but now we do thanks to the trigonometric table: cos 36° is 0.8090, and cos 72° is 0.3090.

Now let's substitute the numbers 0 to 9 for time t, calculate the value of cos 36t for each point, and then calculate $f(t) \times \cos 36t$.

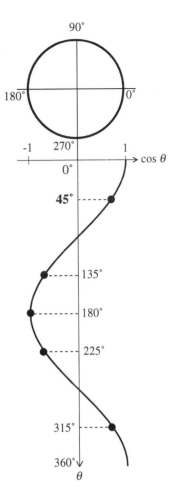

seconds

0 $\quad f(0) \times \cos (36 \cdot 0)° = 14 \times \cos 0° = 14 \times 1 = \mathbf{14}$

1 $\quad f(1) \times \cos (36 \cdot 1)° = 18.7 \times \cos 36° = 18.7 \times 0.8090 = \mathbf{15.1283}$

2 $\quad f(2) \times \cos (36 \cdot 2)° = 9 \times \cos 72° = 9 \times 0.3090 = 2.781$

3 $\quad f(3) \times \cos (36 \cdot 3)° = 4.1 \times \cos 108° = 4.1 \times (-0.3090) = \mathbf{-1.2669}$

4 $\quad f(4) \times \cos (36 \cdot 4)° = 6.7 \times \cos 144° = 6.7 \times (-0.8090) = \mathbf{-5.4203}$

5 $\quad f(5) \times \cos (36 \cdot 5)° = 6 \times \cos 180° = 6 \times (-1) = \mathbf{-6}$

6 $\quad f(6) \times \cos (36 \cdot 6)° = 6.3 \times \cos 216° = 6.3 \times (-0.8090) = \mathbf{-5.0967}$

7 $\quad f(7) \times \cos (36 \cdot 7)° = 8.4 \times \cos 252° = 8.4 \times (-0.3090) = \mathbf{-2.5956}$

8 $\quad f(8) \times \cos (36 \cdot 8)° = 4 \times \cos 288° = 4 \times 0.3090 = \mathbf{1.236}$

9 $\quad f(9) \times \cos (36 \cdot 9)° = 2.9 \times \cos 324° = 2.9 \times 0.8090 = \mathbf{2.3461}$

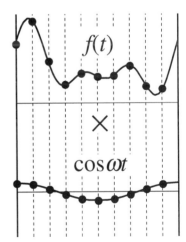

Plot these values and connect them with a smooth curve, and we'll have our new wave for $f(t) \times \cos \omega t$.

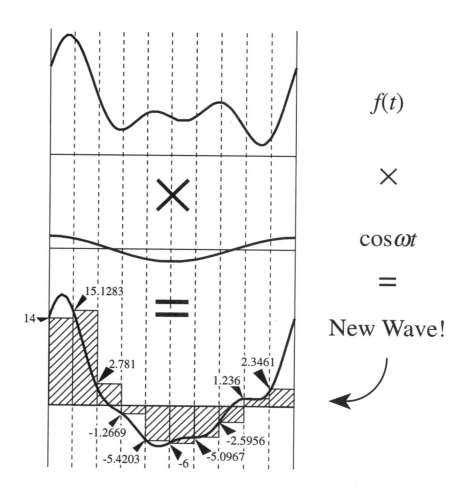

Now all we have to do is find the area of this wave, divide it by period T, and multiply that amount by 2 to get a_1! To find the area, we'll rely on our trusty strips, as shown above.

As in the case of a_0, the width of each strip is 1, so the area of the strip is simply the value of its height, which is the plotted value. Adding all of these up, we get 15.119. Multiply this by 2, and we get 30.2238. Divide that by period T, which is 10, and we get 3.0224.

So amplitude a_1 is 3.0224, or approximately <u>3.</u>

In other words, the cos ωt wave in $f(t)$ has an amplitude of about 3.

"Prof! We got a_1!"

"Well, how about coming up with the amplitudes of the other cosine waves? You can do that by filling in the table on the following page."

☞ Answer on page 132

Let's try !

t	$f(t)$	a_1 $f(t) \times \cos \omega t$	a_2 $f(t) \times \cos 2\omega t$	a_3 $f(t) \times \cos 3\omega t$	a_4 $f(t) \times \cos 4\omega t$	a_5 $f(t) \times \cos 5\omega t$
0	14	14				
1	18.7	15.1283				
2	9	2.781				
3	4.1	-1.2669				
4	6.7	-5.4203				
5	6	-6				
6	6.3	-5.0967				
7	8.4	-2.5956				
8	4	1.236				
9	2.9	2.3461				
Total area		15.1119				
a_n		3.0224				

Starting with a_2...

$$a_2 = \frac{2}{T} \int_0^T f(t) \cos 2\omega t \, dt$$

This time we multiply $f(t)$ by $\cos 2\omega t$, find the area, divide it by period T and multiply by 2. So the only difference from finding a_1 is that we multiply by $\cos 2\omega t$. Whereas wave $\cos \omega t$ moved at an angular velocity of 36° per second, or one period every 10 seconds, angle $\cos 2\omega t$ moves at twice that speed. That would be 72° per second, or 2 periods every 10 seconds.

So $f(t) \times \cos 2\omega t$ looks like this:

You'll find that a calculator is a big help. And if you have a scientific calculator, you won't even need to refer to the trigonometric table.

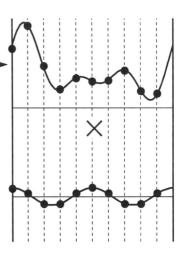

$$14 \times \cos (2 \cdot 36 \cdot 0)° = 14 \times \cos 0° = 14$$

.
.
.

The rest of your calculations are exactly the same as they were for a_1. Go ahead, fill in the table!

"Yahoo! I did it all by myself, Prof! The more I do, the easier it gets!"

"Congratulations! Now that you've mastered the a_n filter, the b_n filter should be a piece of cake. Our goal is in sight!"

2. 3 Find b_n!

$$b_n = \frac{2}{T} \int_0^T f(t) \sin n\omega t \, dt$$

(Multiply complicated wave $f(t)$ by $\sin n\omega t$, find the area of one period, divide it by period T and multiply by 2.)

This filter should give us the amplitude of any sine wave in a complicated wave. The key here is how $\sin \theta$ changes. If we plot it on a graph, we get:

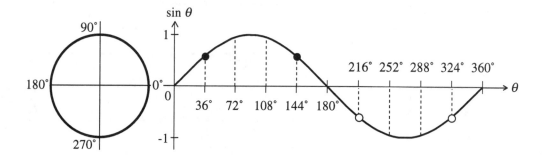

Keeping this graph in mind, we should be able to find the values of $\sin \theta$ in the trigonometric table without any trouble.

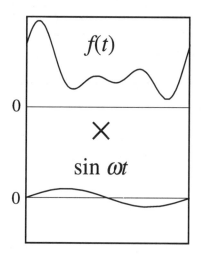

For example, $\sin 144°$ has the same value as $\sin 36°$ – both are 0.5878. On the minus side, both $\sin 216°$ and $\sin 324°$ are -0.5878.

Notice, however, that the negative part of a sine wave is different from the negative part of a cosine wave!

Just as we did with the cosine waves, let's start with the amplitude b_1 of the largest sine wave, $\sin \omega t$. find b_1, we multiply $f(t) \times \sin \omega t$. In all other respects, our method is the same as the one we used for a_n!

Let's draw another table.

Let's try !

t	$f(t)$	b_1 $f(t) \times \sin \omega t$	b_2 $f(t) \times \sin 2\omega t$	b_3 $f(t) \times \sin 3\omega t$	b_4 $f(t) \times \sin 4\omega t$	b_5 $f(t) \times \sin 5\omega t$
0						
1						
2						
3						
4						
5						
6						
7						
8						
9						
Total area						
b_n						

☞ Answer on page 132

That was fast!

Take a break while we review our answers for $f(t)$.

Results	A	B	C	D	E	F	G	H	I	J
	14	18.7	9	4.1	6.7	6	6.3	8.4	4	2.9

Total = <u>80.1</u>

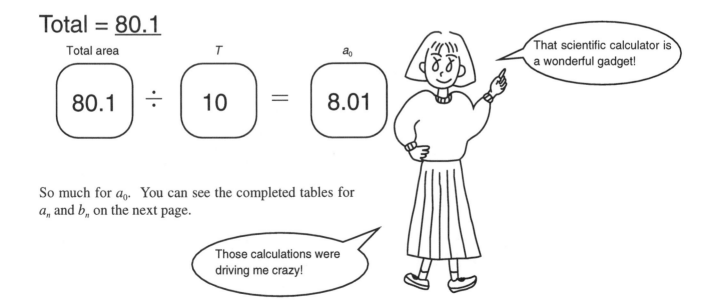

So much for a_0. You can see the completed tables for a_n and b_n on the next page.

Those calculations were driving me crazy!

<a_n table>

t	$f(t)$	a_1 $f(t) \times \cos \omega t$	a_2 $f(t) \times \cos 2\omega t$	a_3 $f(t) \times \cos 3\omega t$	a_4 $f(t) \times \cos 4\omega t$	a_5 $f(t) \times \cos 5\omega t$
0	14	14	14	14	14	14
1	18.7	15.1283	5.7783	-5.7783	-15.1283	-18.7
2	9	2.781	-7.281	-7.281	2.781	9
3	4.1	-1.2669	-3.3169	3.3169	1.2669	-4.1
4	6.7	-5.4203	2.0703	2.0703	-5.4203	6.7
5	6	-6	6	-6	6	-6
6	6.3	-5.0967	1.9467	1.9467	-5.0967	6.3
7	8.4	-2.5956	-6.7956	6.7956	2.5956	-8.4
8	4	1.236	-3.236	-3.236	1.236	4
9	2.9	2.3461	0.8961	-0.8961	-2.3461	-2.9
Total area		15.1119	10.0619	4.9381	-0.1119	-0.1
a_n		3.0224	2.0124	0.9876	-0.0224	-0.02

<b_n table>

t	$f(t)$	b_1 $f(t) \times \sin \omega t$	b_2 $f(t) \times \sin 2\omega t$	b_3 $f(t) \times \sin 3\omega t$	b_4 $f(t) \times \sin 4\omega t$	b_5 $f(t) \times \sin 5\omega t$
0	14	0	0	0	0	0
1	18.7	10.9919	17.7856	17.7856	10.9919	0
2	9	8.5599	5.2902	-5.2902	-8.5599	0
3	4.1	3.8995	-2.4100	-2.4100	3.8995	0
4	6.7	3.9383	-6.3724	6.3724	-3.9383	0
5	6	0	0	0	0	0
6	6.3	-3.7031	5.9919	-5.9919	3.7031	0
7	8.4	-7.9892	4.9375	4.9375	-7.9892	0
8	4	-3.8044	-2.3512	2.3512	3.8044	0
9	2.9	-1.7046	-2.7582	-2.7582	-1.7046	0
Total area		10.1883	20.1134	14.9964	0.2069	0
b_n		2.0377	4.0227	2.9993	0.0414	0

* We used the trigonometric table and rounded off the fifth decimal place for these calculations.

Since a_4, a_5, b_4, and b_5 are all 0, that means the waves $\cos 4\omega t$, $\cos 5\omega t$, $\sin 4\omega t$, and $\sin 5\omega t$ are not included in wave $f(t)$.

So now we know which waves make up $f(t)$. Let's try writing out an expression for $f(t)$ using the Fourier series formula:

$$f(t) = 8 + 3 \cos \omega t + 2 \cos 2\omega t + 1 \cos 3\omega t$$
$$+ 2 \, in \, \omega t + 4 \sin 2\omega t + 3 \sin 3\omega t$$

"Hey, those filters really work!"

"Of course! We don't call them Fourier coefficients for nothing! But we still haven't verified that the values we've calculated are accurate. Any ideas on how we should do that?"

"Well, since what we did was break a complicated wave down into simple waves, we could add them up and see if we get the original wave, couldn't we? If that works, it should prove our values are correct!"

3. Find the Original Wave $f(t)$

The values we've found for the various amplitudes are:

$$a_0 = 8$$
$$a_1 = 3 \quad a_2 = 2 \quad a_3 = 1 \quad a_4 = 0 \quad a_5 = 0$$
$$b_1 = 2 \quad b_2 = 4 \quad b_3 = 3 \quad b_4 = 0 \quad b_5 = 0$$

So what we can do is find the values at each second for the waves with these amplitudes, add all these values together, and plot the results.
For example, the value of the wave with amplitude a_1 after 3 seconds is:

amplitude $\times \cos\omega t$ (Remember, $\omega = 36°$/sec !)

$$3 \times \cos 36 \cdot 3°$$
$$= 3 \times \cos 108° \; (\cos 108° = -0.3090)$$
$$= -0.93$$

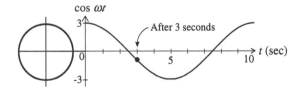

Easy, isn't it? Now start calculating values and plugging them into the table on the following page.

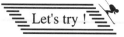 Let's try !

n	a_n $\diagdown$ t	0	1	2	3	4	5	6	7	8	9
0	8										
1	3				-0.93						
2	2										
3	1										
4	0										
5	0										
	b_n										
1	2										
2	4										
3	3										
4	0										
5	0										

$f(t)$										

Add up the values in each vertical column and write the sum in the $f(t)$ box at the bottom. Then plot the values of $f(t)$ on the graph below.

By comparing the result with the original $f(t)$ wave, you should be able to tell right away whether the process we've just gone through is correct or not.

Once you've plotted all the points on the graph, connect them with a smooth curve.

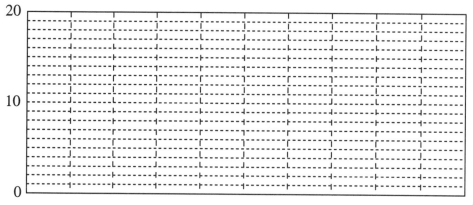

20

10

0

10 sec

☞ see 'Answer Page'

Perfect! So our method was correct after all!

It might be interesting – and easier to understand, too – if we draw the simple waves that make up $f(t)$, like so:

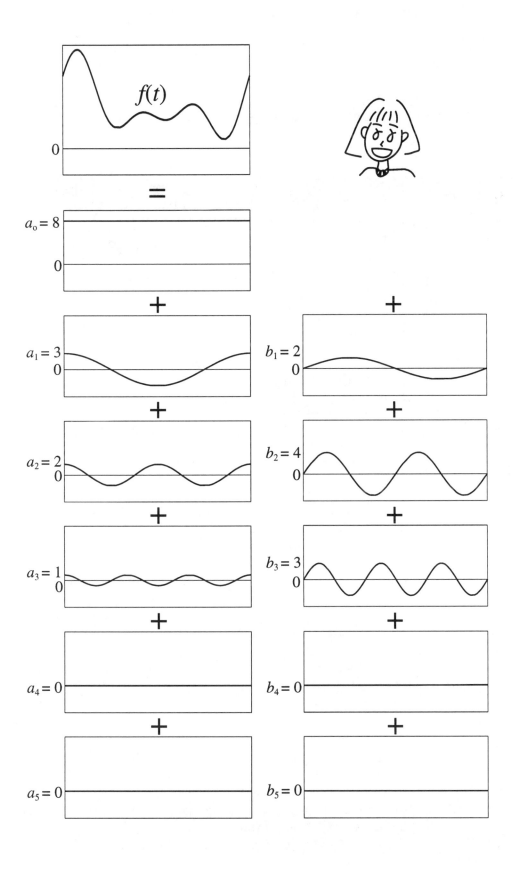

"Yes, that's very pretty, but what about these human voice waves that contain 30 or 40 simple waves? Do you expect us to draw them all?"

"Well, it just so happens we have a very handy device for illustrating waves like that: a graph known as a spectrum!"

"Spectrum?!"

"That's right! A spectrum is a graph like the one below, with frequency on the horizontal axis and amplitude on the vertical axis."

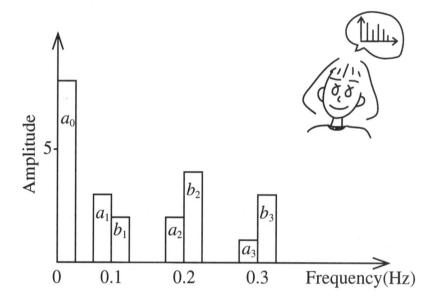

"This way, we can see right away what types of simple waves make up a complicated wave, and in what quantities. And we don't have to draw every single simple wave to find out. It's just like the graphs of vegetable juice ingredients we drew back in Chapter 2."

"In other words, a spectrum allows us to see the components of a complicated wave at a glance."

"That certainly does make things clearer."

"Today, when we found the actual values of a_0, a_n, and b_n, we were using a method called **discrete Fourier expansion**."

"Why 'discrete'?"

"A wave forms a continuous line, right? But today we analyzed $f(t)$ based on 10 points at 1-second intervals on this line. When we use the formulas of the Fourier coefficients to determine $f(t)$ in this manner – by dividing a continuous wave into fixed time intervals and calculating values for $f(t)$ at these **discrete** points – we call it discrete Fourier expansion."

"I see... and the smaller you make these intervals, the closer you get to the original continuous wave, right? But doing all those calculations can sure be a hassle! It's a lot easier if we can get more-or-less accurate values from just 10 points on the wave... Come to think of it, how did we manage that, anyway – finding the correct value of $f(t)$ from only 10 points?"

"Well, I'll let you in on a little secret. Tell me – what do you think are the minimum number of points needed to show a wave that rises and falls once?"

"Uh, two!"

"Why?"

"Because we can plot it like this."

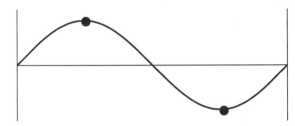

All you need is 2 points to plot a wave that oscillates once.

The wave $f(t)$ the Prof drew for us oscillates 3 times in a period, so it should require only 6 points to plot!

"So if you have 10 points, how many oscillations of a wave should you be able to plot?"

"Five!!"

"Correct! And that's why our 10 values for $f(t)$ allowed us to find the amplitudes of sine and cosine waves up to and including the waves (a_5 and b_5) that oscillated 5 times."

"I get it! That's really neat!"

"The $f(t)$ wave we've been looking at repeats itself every 10 seconds, so its fundamental frequency is 0.1 Hz. The AH and EE waves, on the other hand, vary with the individual speaker, but generally have a fundamental frequency of 100 to 250 Hz. A frequency of 100 Hz means the wave oscillates 100 times per second, which also means it passes through an angle of 36000° every second!"

"Wow – that's fast!"

"If you understand discrete Fourier expansion, you pretty much have all of Fourier analysis in your grasp. This is where it really starts to get interesting!"

"Hey, I'm ready – I'm seeing all kinds of things I never noticed before! Keep 'em coming! This is exciting!"

We've already seen a lot in our exploration of discrete Fourier expansion. What sights are in store for us next??

Coffee Break

Sampling theorem

In theory, it seems we should be able to plot a sine or cosine wave that oscillates half as many times as the number of points we have. But in practice, we always wind up with 0 for the amplitude of the sine wave with the most oscillations (b_5 if we have 10 points, b_9 if we have 18 points, and so on).

Why? Well, suppose we have 10 points and try to plot a sine wave that oscillates 5 times. We quickly find that the value for every one of those 10 points is 0, as shown in the graph below. So if we want to plot a sine wave that oscillates 5 times, we need more than 10 points. Likewise, even if we have 8 points, we still can't plot a sine wave that oscillates 4 times.

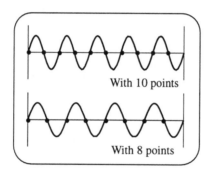

With 10 points

With 8 points

Therefore, when we perform a discrete Fourier expansion, we can only see as many waves as there are points plotted. (That's including a_0; if we have 10 points, for example, we can see waves: a_0 through a_5 and b_1 through b_4, or 10 in all.)

Chapter 4

The Spectrum of the Voice

If you understand Fourier series and Fourier coefficients, you have nearly all of Fourier analysis within your grasp. In this chapter we'll take a look at actual voice waves, based on what we now know about how to look at waves. By using the spectrum to study the characteristics of vowel sounds, we will see a hitherto hidden order in the phenomenon of the voice.

1. Of Waves and Language

1.1 Waves

Some time has passed since we began our Fourier adventure. Some of us may have had more fun than we expected, while others may have encountered steep mountains, sheer cliffs, and the occasional pitfall. But if you've made it this far, you have at least a general idea of what Fourier analysis is all about. Let's take a break from our journey right now and go on a little side trip.

At the very least, one thing you've learned so far is that Fourier analysis is a way to use formulas to describe waves. But what exactly are waves? Try naming as many examples of waves in your surroundings as you can think of...

Ocean waves, electric waves, wavy hair, mountain ranges, the heartbeat, brain waves...

And that's only a few! When we say someone is given to "mood swings," or that life has its "ups and downs," we're talking about waves – indeed, we attribute wave behavior to many things we feel but can't see. Light and sound both behave as waves, too. In short, we are surrounded by waves of all kinds. The words we speak are sounds, so they consist of waves too. There are many interesting things to see in these waves of language.

1.2 Language

All human beings speak a language. If you were born in Japan, you naturally ended up knowing how to speak Japanese; if you were born in Korea, you learned Korean the same way. Babies don't take language lessons; they simply grow up hearing the waves of language spoken by their parents and other people around them. Little by little, a baby starts uttering "baby talk," and by age three most children are able to speak in more or less the same way adults do. Mothers do not sit down and teach their babies a vocabulary list beginning with easy words, and in any case the baby is surrounded by a cacophony of words flying about at random. Yet the baby hears these words and gradually begins to speak them himself. This can only mean that somewhere in the seemingly random, complex mix of sounds there is a simple and elegant order that even a baby can grasp.

Those of us who listen to the language tapes of the Hippo Family Club have experienced something similar to the baby's experience. When we first listen to a tape, we can't understand a thing. After a while, however, we are able to tell what language is being spoken – Korean, French, or whatever. Little by little, we pick up phrases that we can repeat, and soon we find we can clearly distinguish the individual words in a long sentence. When we eventually get the opportunity to participate in a cultural exchange, we surprise ourselves with how well we are able to speak the language. We've internalized the language, yet we have no idea how we discovered an order in the language enabling us to speak it. Because everyone speaks a language, we tend to take it for granted and give no thought to how it's done. Once you start examining the process, however, you can't help being mystified by it. What is this order that lies hidden in the seemingly complex phenomenon of language? Wouldn't you like to see it? Normally, alas, we can't actually "see" language. But thanks to what we've learned on our Fourier adventure, we know how to see waves. Let's apply our newfound knowledge to solving the mystery of language.

1. 3 Language Waves and Vowels

Let's get right to the business of viewing "waves of language." Our friend the FFT analyzer will come in handy here. As you'll recall from our previous encounters with it, the FFT analyzer is a machine that lets us see in wave form the normally invisible world of sound.

Wave of a voice saying "SARU" ① → ② → ③

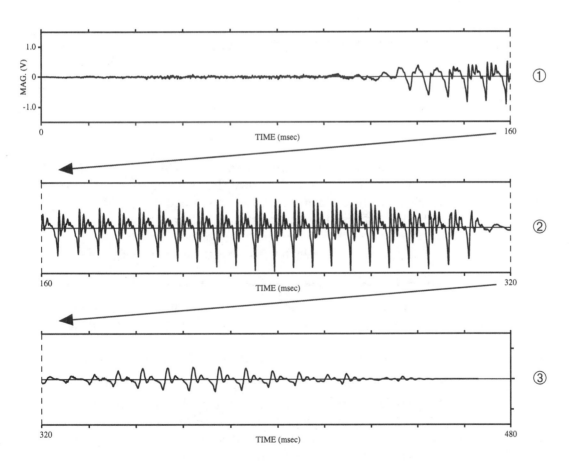

That was me saying the word "SARU" ("monkey" in Japanese!). This wave is a lot more complicated than the ones we've looked at so far. In fact, it's downright messy. We can't even tell where one part of the wave ends and the next begins. Next, let's look at three other waves – for the sounds "AH", "KA", and "SA".

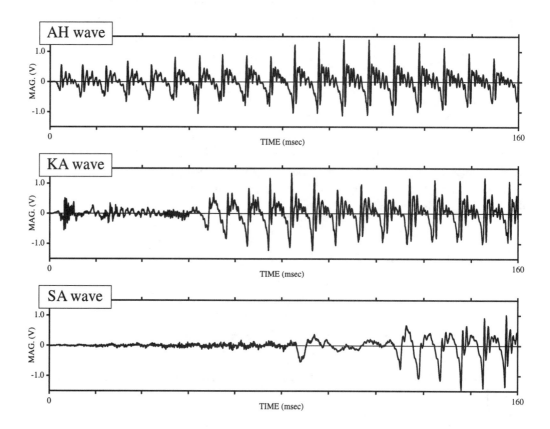

These three waves look simpler than the SARU wave. The AH wave repeats the same pattern over and over. The KA and SA waves both start off with jagged sections, which are the "K" of KA and the "S" of SA respectively. After that they take on the same form as the AH wave shown above.

Let us pause for a moment to review what we've learned so far:

Fourier series............ Expresses a wave that repeats itself, however complicated it may be, as the sum of simple waves.

Fourier coefficients... Finds the amplitude of each of these simple waves.

So we can use Fourier analysis to describe any wave, no matter how complicated it is – just as long as it repeats itself. This means that, of the waves we've illustrated above, we can at least describe the AH wave. Let's take a look at the waves of all five Japanese vowel sounds for comparison:

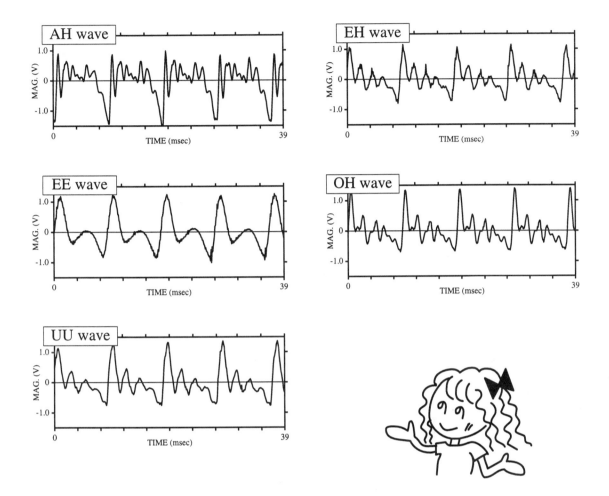

These charts make at least one thing clear: all of the vowel sound waves repeat themselves. That recommends them as excellent candidates for our Fourier explorations in this chapter.

1. 4 About Vowels

First of all, what is a vowel? The Japanese language has five vowel sounds: AH, EE, UU, EH, and OH. But if we were asked to come up with a sound midway between AH and OH, say, or between EE and UU but closer to EE, we could certainly respond with something that sounded appropriate. There really are infinite possibilities for vowels. Indeed, the human voice is capable of stringing together limitless combinations of sounds. Then why would any language limit itself to five vowel sounds? For some reason, the listener's mind distinguishes these five sounds from one another. And this is evidently not some random, arbitrary distinction, but one based on a natural order that is easily grasped by everyone. What, then, is that order?

2. Using the Spectrum to View Vowel Waves

2. 1 Fourier Analysis and Spectra

Our first step will be to use Fourier analysis to determine what kinds of waves these vowel waves are. But before that, let's review what we've done with our Fourier tools so far.

You recall the wave we used in our exploration of discrete Fourier expansion in Chapter 3. Remember how we found the Fourier coefficients for this wave? The graphic results looked like this:

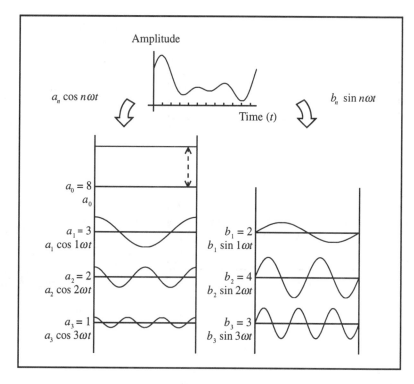

Using Fourier coefficients formulas is a way to find the size (i.e., amplitude) of the sine and cosine waves that make up a wave of this sort. Specifically, it gives us a numerical value for each of the various amplitudes a_0, a_1, a_2,... and b_1, b_2,...

But isn't there a simpler way to view the components of a complicated wave – some way to tell at a glance which sine and cosine waves make up the complicated wave, and in what quantities?

Well, that's precisely what a **SPECTRUM** does!

Without further ado, let's create a spectrum for this wave of ours. Remember that the wave repeats itself every 10 seconds.

• Spectrum of cos $n\omega t$

First we'll find the fundamental frequency of the wave. The other waves will have frequencies that are multiples (2×, 3×, 4×, etc.) of this one. Since the period T of the fundamental wave is 10 seconds, the fundamental frequency is:

$$f = \frac{1}{T} = \frac{1}{10} = 0.1 \text{(Hz)}$$

So the fundamental wave oscillates 0.1 times per second.

Now that we know the frequency of this wave, we also know the frequencies of the other waves, which are integral multiples of the fundamental. And since we know the amplitude of each of these waves, we can draw them on a graph with frequency on the horizontal axis and amplitude on the vertical axis, like this:

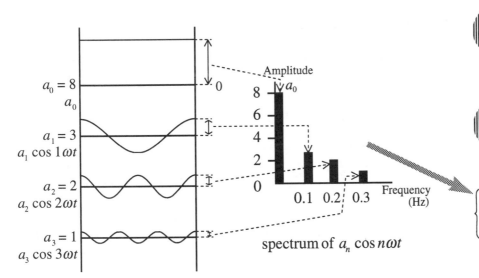

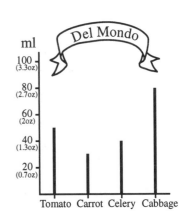

Angular velocity ω: how many degrees the wave moves through in 1 second

Frequency f: how many times the wave oscillates in 1 second

Period T: how much time one oscillation takes

Frequency of wave $\cos 1\omega t$: 0.1Hz
Frequency of wave $\cos 2\omega t$: 0.2Hz
Frequency of wave $\cos 3\omega t$: 0.3Hz

• Spectrum of $\sin n\omega t$

Once we have the $\cos n\omega t$ waves down, the $\sin n\omega t$ waves should be easy. Cosine and sine waves with the same value for n have the same frequency, so the frequencies on the horizontal axis of the sine wave spectrum will be exactly the same as those of the cosine wave spectrum. Now all we have to do is draw in the various amplitudes:

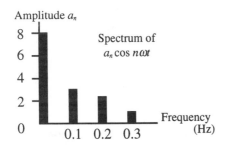

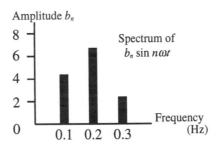

Let's place these two graphs side by side. Sure enough, they tell us at a glance the frequency and amplitude of each of the sine and cosine waves that make up the complicated wave. We no longer have to draw a bunch of waves as we did earlier. With only two spectra, we know all we need to know about the components of a complicated wave. The spectrum is certainly a handy tool for this purpose!

When we talked about vegetable juices, the graphs of juice ingredients (see Chapter 2) were the equivalent of spectra. Just as a glance at one of these graphs can tell you that a certain brand of juice contains a large quantity of tomato, a voice spectrum can tell you that a wave contains a large quantity of a component wave of a given frequency. Spectra should provide us with some clues about the special characteristics of vowel sounds, too.

2. 2 Looking at Vowel Spectra

Let's find the Fourier coefficients for the five Japanese vowel waves AH, EE, UU, EH, and OH, and create spectra for them. Think back again to the wave on which we performed discrete Fourier expansion. It turned out to be the sum of seven sine and cosine waves. It took us quite a while to find the Fourier coefficients for just those seven waves. Now, consider that a human voice wave consists of close to 100 sine and cosine waves! If we have to find the Fourier coefficients ourselves for every one of these waves, we'll never get around to solving the mystery of the vowels. Our objective here is not to spend our time searching for the Fourier coefficients, but to identify the waves that make up the five vowels. What we need is a quick, painless way to find the Fourier coefficients for vowel waves.

FFT stands for Fast Fourier Transform. See Chapters 12 and 13 for details.

And that's where the FFT analyzer comes in! Up until now we have thought of the analyzer primarily as a machine that makes the human voice visible to us, displaying it in the form of waves. But the analyzer has another remarkable talent – finding the Fourier coefficients of waves in a flash! (The name says it all: "FFT" is an abbreviation for "Fast Fourier Transform.") Even more amazingly, after finding the Fourier coefficients, the FFT analyzer provides us with the wave's spectrum! The whole process for a given wave takes only one second. Below is the spectrum of the AH wave generated by the analyzer.

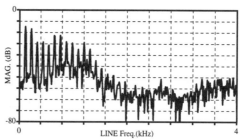

Notice that there are a number of differences between this spectrum and the ones we made for ourselves a moment ago:

(1)   We made two separate spectra for the sine waves and cosine waves, but the FFT analyzer generates only one spectrum for both.

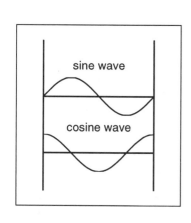

sine wave

cosine wave

As you can see from the graphs on the left, sin $n\omega t$ and cos $n\omega t$ have the same frequency when they have the same value for n; the only difference is that they begin at different points. We can use this relationship to find a single value to express the sine and cosine wave values together. "The Riddle of the Spectrum" – the "Coffee Break" column at the end of this chapter – explains how this is done.The resulting graph is viewed the same way as our graphs of the sine and cosine spectra.

(2)   Our previous graphs were bar graphs, but the FFT spectrum is a jagged line in which the "bars" are connected.

This is a result of the method of computation used by the analyzer, which connects the bars with a smooth curve. As with the earlier graphs, you only need to concern yourself with the spikes that represent the bars.

Now let's take a look at the spectra of the five vowels, leaving the search for Fourier coefficients to the FFT analyzer:

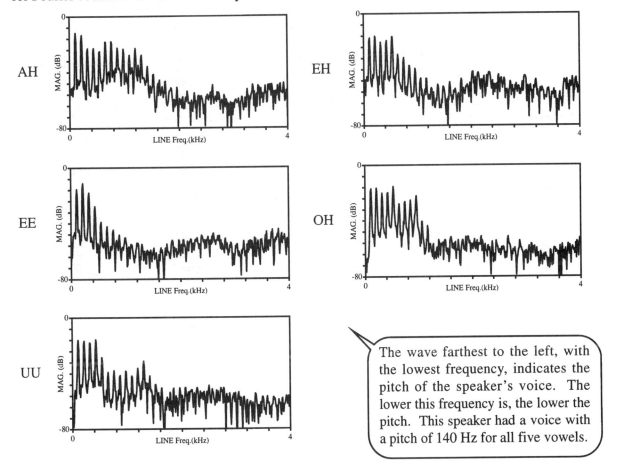

The wave farthest to the left, with the lowest frequency, indicates the pitch of the speaker's voice. The lower this frequency is, the lower the pitch. This speaker had a voice with a pitch of 140 Hz for all five vowels.

What can we say about these five spectra?

(1)   One thing common to the spectra of all five vowels is that their bars are all the same distance from one another. The position of each bar represents a frequency. The fact that the bars are located at equal distance simply means that their frequencies are in integral multiples. The wave farthest to the left has the lowest frequency (i.e., the largest period), which for the speaker in this case is 140 Hz. The next wave has a frequency twice that, or 280 Hz; the next, three times that, or 420 Hz. Thus all waves in this speaker's voice have frequencies that are integral multiples of 140 Hz.

(2)   Now let's look for differences. Although all five vowels are made up of waves with the same frequencies, the overall shape of the spectrum varies from vowel to vowel. What is different is the relative "quantity" of waves of each frequency. These differences make themselves apparent in the actual form of each wave. But we cannot tell if these differences are defining characteristics of each vowel simply by looking at the voice waves of one individual. For all we know, the shapes of these spectra may be unique to that person.

Therefore, let's examine the spectra of the five vowels as uttered by different people – five men and five women.

<Male voices>   Spectra of 5 vowels by 5 Japanese male voices

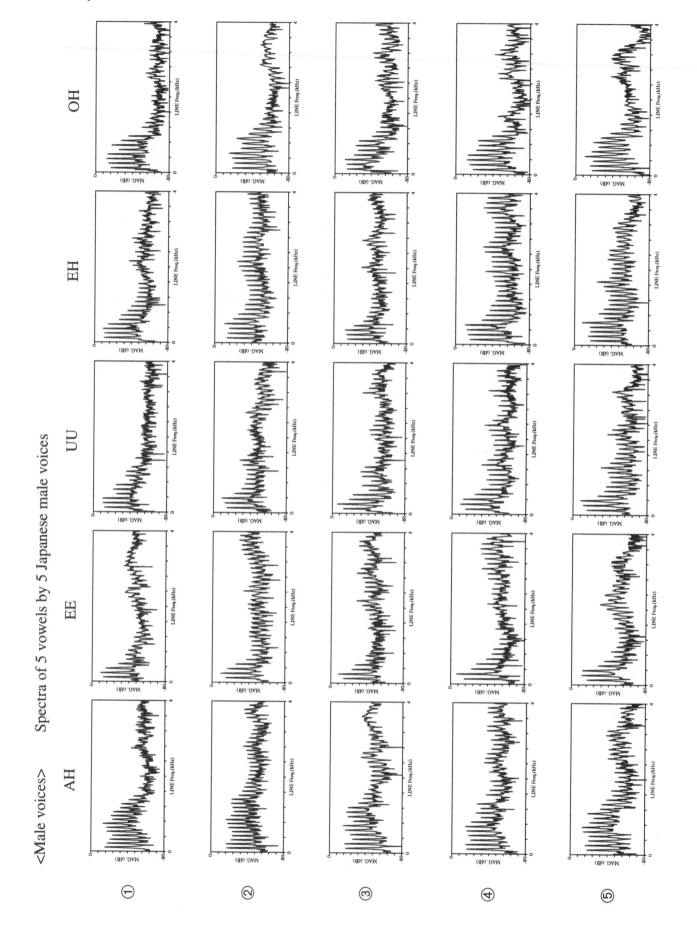

<Female voices>   Spectra of 5 vowels by 5 Japanese female voices

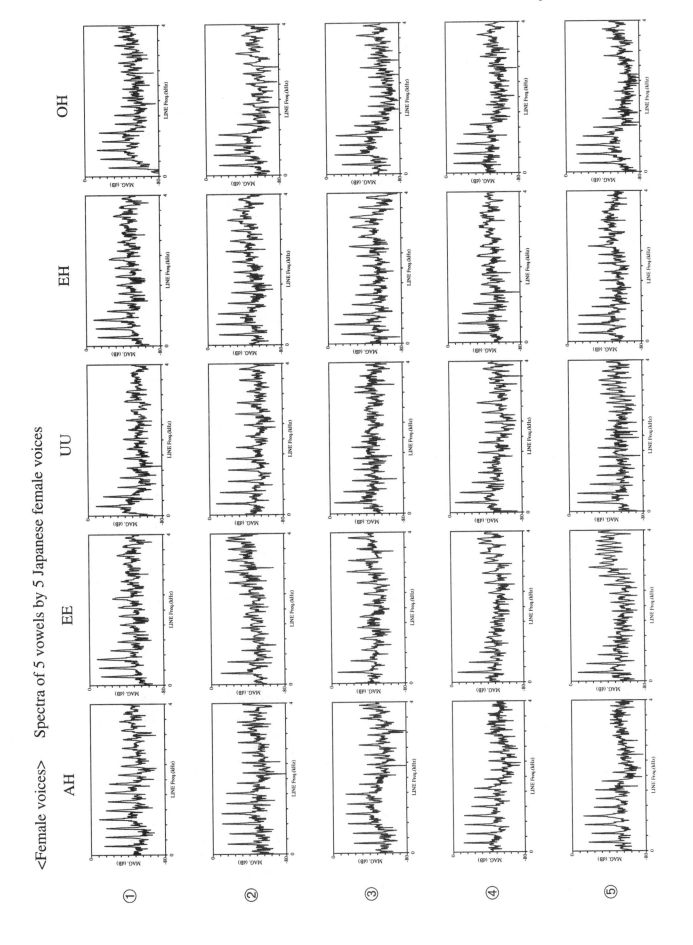

The spectra on the first page are from male voices and those on the second page are from female voices. When the spectra for the male voice is compared to the female voice, notice that the bars are spaced closer together for the male voice. This is because the men have deeper voices than the women. For example, compare male and female voices ①. The lowest frequency of male voice ① is 140 Hz, with subsequent frequencies at distance of 140 Hz: 280 Hz, 420 Hz, and so on. Female voice ①, on the other hand, has frequencies of 220 Hz, 440 Hz, 660 Hz, and so on – at distance of 220 Hz.

2. 3 Characteristics of the Five Vowels

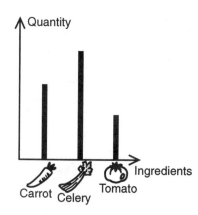

Male voice ——
Female voice ----

Every vowel has two
or three peaks.

Look carefully at the various graphs of the same vowel. Do they have anything in common? On closer examination, the spectra of AH, for example, do appear to have the same shape. The same goes for EE and the others. At first glance, the male and female voices may appear rather different. However, if you move the male spectrum to the right (in the direction of higher frequencies), you'll find it resembles the female spectrum. So spectra of the same vowel evidently share the same shape – that is, their peaks and valleys are in the same places. To be more precise, they share the same combination of relatively large or small quantities of waves at specific frequencies.

In vegetable juices, the ingredients that are present in the greatest quantities exert the greatest effect on the flavor of the juice. A juice with a lot of tomato in it will taste decidedly tomato-ey. It also makes sense to expect that waves present in large quantities have the greatest effect on the sound of the voice. The location at certain frequencies of peaks indicating waves in large quantities may well be an important characteristic, one that defines the nature of a vowel.

Isn't there some way we can verify the existence of these special characteristics for each vowel? Let's think about what we would do to determine the characteristics of vegetable juice.

Suppose we take a sip of a certain juice and say to ourselves, "This tastes a little bitter! I wonder why?" If we look at the ingredients chart on the left, we can see that the juice contains much more celery than carrot or tomato. So the celery must be the source of the bitter taste in the juice – but how do we prove that?

Of course – by removing the celery!

↑ Quantity

Ingredients

Carrot   Celery   Tomato

Experiment 1

Do you remember the special filters we used for the Fourier coefficients? We introduced the subject by talking about filters for vegetable juice – a filter that would pass only the carrot part of the juice, or the celery, or the tomato. Here we want a filter that removes the celery part of the juice. The remaining juice passing through the filter will contain no celery. We want to drink that juice and see what it tastes like.

Vegetable
juice

Celery
filter

Celery remains
behind

Vegetable juice minus celery

If the flavor is bitter → celery is not the source of the bitter taste.
If the flavor is not bitter → celery is the source of the bitter taste.

Let's try this same experiment with some vowels!

Experiment 2

Below is the spectrum of the vowel EH spoken by a male voice. We can identify three peaks in this spectrum, which we shall label Peak 1, Peak 2, and Peak 3, counting from the low-frequency end. We'll then use a sound filter to cut out these peaks one at a time, and find out what sort of sound we get as a result.

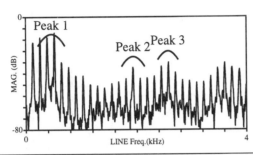

Spectrum of EH sound by a male voice ④

Peak 1 → When eliminated, the result is sort of a rough, jagged sound, which sounds like EE.

Peak 2 → When eliminated, the result sounds like EE.

Peak 3 → When eliminated, the result is a slightly murky sound whose speaker can no longer be identified – but it clearly sounds like EH.

These results tell us that Peaks 1 and 2 are defining characteristics of the EH sound. When we try cutting out the peaks of the other vowels, the same thing happens. For every vowel, cutting out either Peak 1 or Peak 2 makes the original sound unrecognizable – but cutting out Peak 3 has no such effect. In other words,

> ## "Peaks 1 and 2 are defining characteristics of every vowel."

Let's examine Peaks 1 and 2 for each vowel sound and see if we can find a relationship among the different vowels. For now, we'll only extract and compare Peak 2 from each vowel spectrum.

Since these peaks are such important characteristics, they would seem to deserve a name more substantial than "peak." And indeed they do have a name: **formant**. Peak 1 is called the first formant (F1), and Peak 2 is the second formant (F2).

Note

For the record, cutting out parts of the spectrum other than these peaks doesn't change the sound, so these other parts evidently are not important characteristics of the vowels.

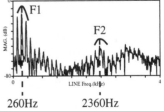

260Hz 2360Hz

Spectrum of EE sound by a male voice ①

2. 4 The Formant Order

To extract a formant, the first thing we do is read the value of its frequency. For example, if we look at the EE spectrum of a male voice ① shown on the previous page, we see that F1 (the first formant) is at 260 Hz and F2 (the second formant) is at 2360 Hz. However, the peaks of a given vowel do not occur in the same places for every speaker. There is a range of variation between individuals. We have therefore taken the average of the frequencies of the formants of the five vowels as spoken by 25 men and 25 women. The results are shown in the table on the right.

	Male		Female	
Vowel	F1	F2	F1	F2
AH	790Hz	1270Hz	980Hz	1640Hz
EE	280Hz	2310Hz	340Hz	2830Hz
UU	320Hz	1300Hz	390Hz	1550Hz
EH	520Hz	1950Hz	620Hz	2430Hz
OH	510Hz	860Hz	650Hz	1060Hz

Since it's hard to make sense of these figures when they're stacked in a table like this, let's try putting them on a graph like the one below.

Since the results for male and female voices are slightly skewed because of their difference in pitch, we'll keep things simple by looking only at the male voices from this point on.

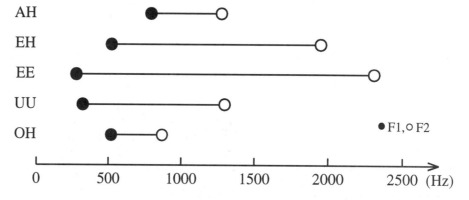

The graph above is not all that different from the spectra we've seen so far. All we've done is extract the formants from each spectrum (as in the spectrum below), then line them up in the sequence AH-EH-EE-UU-OH. By looking at this formant graph, can we see any sort of natural order to these vowel sounds?

Only this part was extracted:

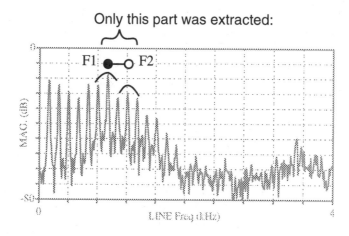

Spectrum of AH sound by male voice

2. 5 Logarithms

To be honest, it's hard to see anything suggesting an "order" in the graph on the previous page. To improve our vision, we'll introduce a new tool – the **LOGARITHM**.

Actually, the logarithm is not exactly new – in fact, it is a very familiar concept in our everyday lives. Here's an example:

Suppose you have only a dollar to your name, and you drop a dime of it down a grating. That lost dime means a lot to you! But suppose you have 100 dollars, and you lose the same dime – no big deal. How much of 100 dollars would you have to lose to suffer as much as you did when you lost 10 cents of your only dollar? That's right, you'd have to lose 10 dollars. Your feelings correspond to the **proportion** of your money you lost, not to the actual amount.

And that is how logarithms work. The logarithm is a means of expressing a very human trait – the perception of things in proportion. Our impressions of the severity of an earthquake, or the brightness of light, are logarithmic in nature. So are many other things – including our perception of sound.

The human ear senses the pitch of sounds logarithmically. Consider a musical scale, which repeats the same sounds over and over as it rises in pitch: do-re-mi-fa-so-la-ti, do-re-mi-fa-so-la-ti, and so on. More accurately, the human ear <u>senses</u> that the same distances are being repeated, and therefore hears the sounds as the same notes repeated higher and higher up the scale. Even when the notes are of different octaves, the distance between them sound the same. In other words, the distance from one DO to the next DO – or one LA to the next LA – seems to be constant, no matter how many octaves we climb. But when we look at the actual frequencies of these different DO's or LA's, we see that this is not really true.

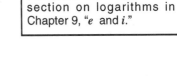

For more details, see the section on logarithms in Chapter 9, "*e* and *i*."

 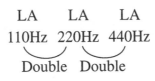 

As you can see, the frequency of the note LA at a certain pitch is 110 Hz, and the next LA an octave higher is 220 Hz. But the next LA above that is 440 Hz! So as far as frequency is concerned, the distance from one LA to the next is not constant. Then what is it that the human ear senses is the same about this distance? Let's compare the frequencies of three LA's. The lowest LA is 110 Hz. The next is 220 Hz, or double the frequency of the first one. And the next is 440 Hz – once again, double the frequency of the LA one octave below. Thus the distance between LA's is always doubled, yet the human ear senses this as the same distance.

The logarithmic graph below illustrates this human perception. Notice that the scale makes the distance between 100 and 200, 200 and 400, and 400 and 800 appear the same. Each of these distance represents a doubling of the previous distance. Let's do the same thing to our graph of the five vowels, changing it into a logarithmic graph.

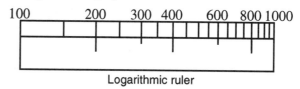

Logarithmic ruler

3. The Order of the Five Vowels

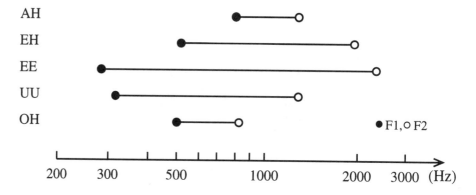

What do you think of that? Very orderly, wouldn't you say? See how symmetrical the five vowels suddenly look!

Now let's draw a line down the middle, as in the graph on the right. With this line as the axis of symmetry, we can now see that AH and OH are symmetrical relative to one another, as are EH and UU. EE is symmetrical to itself. So it turns out the five Japanese vowels are symmetrical around a certain central frequency!

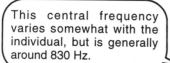

This central frequency varies somewhat with the individual, but is generally around 830 Hz.

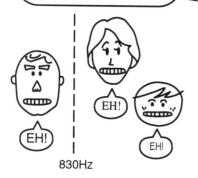

830Hz

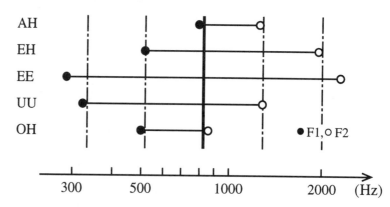

3. 1 The Formant Diamond

Next we're going to plot the first formant (F1) and second formant (F2) of the five Japanese vowels along a logarithmic axis again, but this time make separate graphs for the male voice and the female voice.

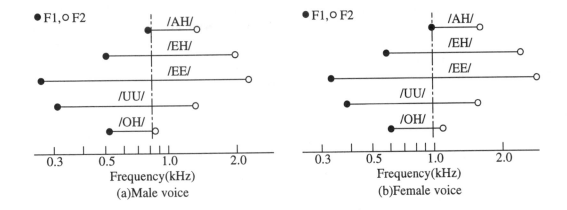

(a)Male voice

(b)Female voice

Let's take a closer look at the lovely symmetry we see in these graphs. The central axis of symmetry is at about 800 Hz for the male voice and 1 kHz for the female voice. In both cases, AH and EH lie primarily to the right of the axis (i.e., offset toward the high-frequency end), while UU and OH lie to the left (offset toward the low-frequency end). Also, we can see that the distance between F1 and F2 is shorter for AH and OH, and longer for EH and UU.

Thus we can say that AH, EH, UU and OH exhibit symmetry in two ways: in the length of their distance between F1 and F2, and in the offset of these distance to the left or right of the central axis:

AH is **short** and offset to the **right**.
EH is **long**　and offset to the **right**.
OH is **short** and offset to the **left**.
UU is **long**　and offset to the **left**.

EE doesn't seem to fit into this scheme. However, it is EE that sets the standard, providing the reference values against which we compare both the offset and distance of each of the other vowels.

First let's look at the offset. To define the offset of each distance, we need a center point as a reference value. We already mentioned that this center is at about 800 Hz for the male voice and 1 kHz for the female voice. But how did we come up with these frequencies?

When you change the shape of your mouth while uttering different vowel sounds, the values for F1 and F2 change too. If you try this while looking at the output from an FFT analyzer, you will notice that you can't move F1 down to a frequency below the F1 of EE. Likewise, you can't move F2 up to a

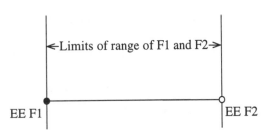

frequency above that of EE. In other words, EE defines the extreme lower and upper limits of F1 and F2 for the human voice.

When — and only when — we know the two endpoints of this range, we can determine the center. Thus 800 Hz and 1 kHz are the centers of the maximum range between F1 and F2 for the male and female voice respectively. Although these two frequencies are different, it still holds true for both men and women that the F1 and F2 of EE are the endpoints that define this center.

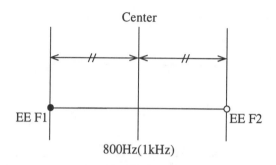

The same goes for distance: EE provides the standard against which to compare the length of the distance from F1 to F2 for each vowel. Since the F1 and F2 of EE represent the furthest limits possible for the human voice, the distance of EE is naturally the longest of all the vowels. Once we have this maximum distance as a point of reference, we can define the distance of the other vowels as relatively "long" or "short."

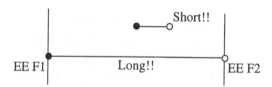

And that is how the F1 and F2 of EE provide the reference values that define the symmetry of the five Japanese vowels.

We saw that the F1 and F2 of EE are the lower and upper limits of the range within which the human mouth can move F1 and F2. Both F1 and F2 have their own respective upper and lower limits as well.

The lower limit for possible values of F1 is the value of F1 for EE, as we stated before. But what is its upper limit? If you try moving F1 around by changing the shape of your mouth while watching the results on the FFT analyzer, you'll see that the highest value you get is the F1 of AH.

Similarly, we already know that the upper limit for F2 is the F2 of EE. The lower limit, on the other hand, appears to be the F2 of OH. Both the F1 of AH and the F2 of OH lie more or less on the center line (the axis of symmetry). So roughly speaking, we can say:

The range of possible values of F1 is from the F1 of EE to the center.

The range of possible values of F2 is from the center to the F2 of EE.

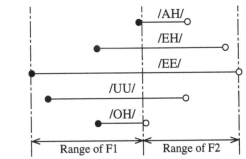

What we'd like to do now is come up with a graph that clearly illustrates the symmetry we've found in the five Japanese vowels. To do this, we'll plot "offset" values along the horizontal axis, and "distance" values along the vertical axis.

First of all, how do we represent values for the offset? Take AH, for example. What we really want to know is how far the distance for AH is offset from the center. We can indicate this by finding the center point between the F1 and F2 of AH, and then measuring how far this is from the center line for all five vowels. Writing this out as a formula, we get:

(Offset of AH) = (Center for AH) − (Center for all)

To express this mathematically, we can write:

$$X = \frac{F1 + F2}{2} - G$$

Here G is the value of the center for all five vowels — i.e., the center for EE.

$$G = \frac{F1(EE) + F2(EE)}{2}$$

Now, what about values for the distance? Since this distance is simply the distance from F1 to F2, all we have to do is find the difference between the value of F2 and the value of F1. Writing this out as a formula for AH, for example, we get:

(Distance of AH) = (F2 of AH) − (F1 of AH)

A more standard way of writing this is:

$$Y = \frac{F2 - F1}{2}$$

We divide the right side by 2 only to make this formula symmetric with the X formula; it doesn't change the meaning of the formula.

Here F1 and F2 are both logarithmic values of the formant frequency.

While we're at it, let's also display the range within which F1 and F2 can be moved.

The chart below on the left shows a vowel sound offset as far as it can go to the left. (The black dot is F1 and the white dot is F2.) If we plot this on the *x-y* coordinate plane we have just created, it appears as the point shown in the graph on the right.

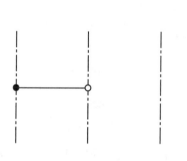 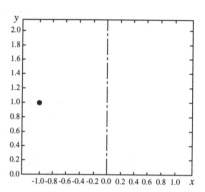

Now let's fix F1 where it is and move F2 to the right. If we move F2 until it can go no farther to the right, we have the distance for the vowel EE — i.e., the vowel with the longest distance.

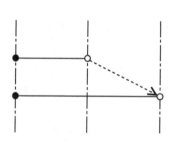 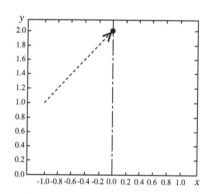

Next, suppose we fix F2 where it is now, and move F1 to the right. When F1 cannot be moved any farther, the result is a vowel sound offset as far as it can go to the right.

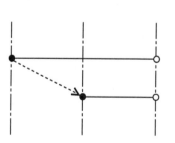 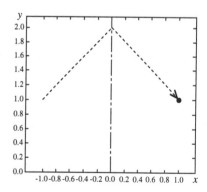

This time we'll fix F1 where it is and move F2 to the left. The result is a sound of distance 0.

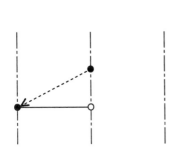
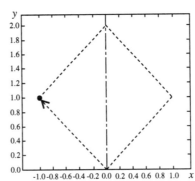

Finally, we'll fix F2 and move F1 to the left. This brings us back to where we started. The square we've just plotted represents the limits within which F1 and F2 can move.

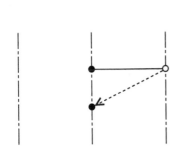
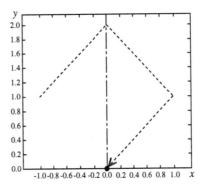

We are at last ready for the main act — plotting the five Japanese vowels, as spoken by male and female voices, on our x-y coordinate plane.

Let's start with a male AH. The F1 of the male AH is 790 Hz, and the F2 is 1270 Hz, so its x and y coordinates can be calculated as shown below. (The F1 and F2 of EE, which serve as reference values, are 280 Hz and 2310 Hz respectively.)

$$X = \frac{F1 + F2}{2} - G = \frac{\log_e(790) + \log_e(1270)}{2} - \frac{\log_e(280) + \log_e(2310)}{2} = 0.220$$

$$Y = \frac{F2 - F1}{2} = \frac{\log_e(1270) - \log_e(790)}{2} = 0.237$$

The tables below list the average values calculated in this manner for the x and y coordinates of each vowel, taken from a sample of male and female voices.

Average values for 25 Japanese male voices:

	AH	EH	EE	UU	OH
X	0.220	0.225	0.000	−0.221	−0.194
Y	0.237	0.661	1.055	0.701	0.261

Average values for 25 Japanese female voices:

	AH	EH	EE	UU	OH
X	0.257	0.224	0.000	−0.232	−0.167
Y	0.257	0.683	1.060	0.690	0.245

Now, at long last, we can plot average values for the five Japanese vowels along the x and y axes:

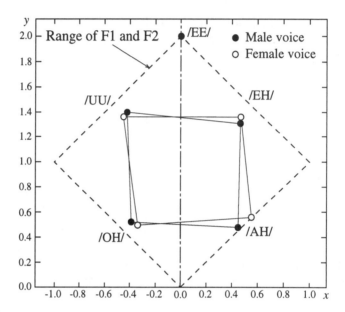

What do you know! The quadrangles formed by the values for AH, EH, UU and OH are nearly perfect squares! When we plot them according to the two criteria determined by EE ("offset" on the x-axis and "distance" on the y-axis), these four vowel sounds prove to be symmetrical indeed.

But what exactly does this mean? When we say two things are "symmetrical" in the sense of left vs. right or long vs. short, we are saying they are clearly recognizable as the opposite of one another. To say that four things are symmetrical, the only difference is that we need two sets of criteria against which to compare them instead of one. When we say that the five Japanese vowels are symmetrical, it simply means they are clearly distinct from one another.

This graph shows us one other interesting thing. The five vowels are spread as far apart as they can be within the permissible range for F1 and F2. Obviously, the farther apart they are from one another, the more distinct they are. In other words, the five vowels of the Japanese language sound as distinct from one another as they possibly can within the range of frequencies that can be uttered by the human mouth.

We call a coordinate plane like the one above, with offset and distance as its axes, a "**formant diamond.**" We decided to call it that because the range of movement of F1 and F2 plotted from these coordinates resembles a baseball diamond. In fact, you can refer to the location of EE as "second base," the angle on the far right as "first base," and so on.

Conclusion

F1 and F2 can be at pretty much any two frequencies independent of one another within their permissible range. This means that the human voice is capable of producing a virtually unlimited variety of vowel sounds.

And yet the Japanese language has only five vowels. This suggests that over the millennia, human beings have unconsciously isolated a few sounds that are the best suited for vocalizing language. The result is the symmetrical arrangement we have been looking at. Each vowel has been selected to maximize this symmetry of sounds.

Natural science can be described as the search for order in seemingly complex phenomena. At first glance, vowels do appear complex, but their formant frequencies vary with every individual, and the formants themselves are difficult to measure.

There are a number of voice researchers who have spent years studying vowels and who are familiar with every aspect of these sounds. To these phoneticians, facts such as the frequencies of the F1 and F2 formants of the five Japanese vowels are common knowledge. Yet until now, no one in the field had noticed the symmetrical order that we found among the five vowels when taking the average values of these formant frequencies.

Today, students at the Transnational College of LEX are searching for similar signs of order in consonants, in the melody and rhythm of language, and in the sounds of languages other than Japanese. If symmetry exists among the five Japanese vowels, surely it can be found in the vowels of other languages, as well as in their consonants, melody and rhythm. As a matter of fact, we are already beginning to detect hints of just such a symmetry among consonants! What could be more exciting than to join forces with friends and colleagues around the world in the quest for order in human language?

With just a little knowledge of Fourier analysis, we have made a remarkable discovery about the natural order of the five Japanese vowel sounds. Now we shall return from our slight detour and resume our adventures with Fourier.

The Riddle of the Spectrum

In Chapter 3, we showed separate spectra for a_n and b_n. Normally, however, these two values are displayed together as one. If you look at the output of the FFT analyzer, you'll notice that it displays only one spectrum value for a given frequency. In other words, a_n and b_n are somehow combined into one value. How does the FFT analyzer do this? As an example, let's look at the wave we used in our discussion of discrete Fourier coefficients. Right now we'd like to explain what is probably the biggest mystery of the sound wave spectrum: How does the FFT analyzer display a_n and b_n together as one wave? As an example, let's look at the wave we used in our discussion of discrete Fourier expansion.

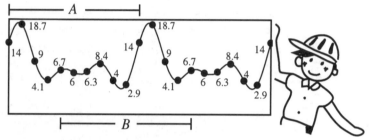

You've already used Fourier coefficients to determine which simple waves add up to make the wave shown above. Let's take a moment to review the Fourier coefficients process. The first thing you did was extract a single period of the wave. Fourier coefficients only works on waves that repeat, so we don't need to look at the entire wave; one period is enough. However, this "one period" is a very slippery concept. We agreed on what "one period" is back when we were studying Fourier series: a single repetition of the pattern of a wave. This definition says nothing about where the pattern starts or ends, so when we select one period, it doesn't necessarily have to start at the beginning of the wave. In this case, the period of our wave was 10 seconds, so we could extract any 10-second section we wanted – either section A or section B in the graph above would do, for example. As long as the section we select is 10 seconds long, we can call that a single period of the wave. When we did our discrete Fourier expansion exercise, we automatically chose to calculate the first 10 seconds of the illustrated wave – section A above. The results for A are shown below. But what would happen if we calculated section B instead? Would it be the same as A?

	A			B	
$a_0 = 8$			$a_0 = 8$		
$a_1 = 3$	$b_1 = 2$		$a_1 = -1.25$	$b_1 = -3.4$	
$a_2 = 2$	$b_2 = 4$		$a_2 = -3.2$	$b_2 = 3.13$	
$a_3 = 1$	$b_3 = 3$		$a_3 = 3.16$	$b_3 = 0$	

What's this?! We got completely different results for A and B!

Incidentally, if we move section A just a little bit to the right and pick that as our period, we can get Fourier coefficients values that are the exact reverse of the a_n and b_n values we found for A. That's because sine and cosine waves are identical except that they are 90° apart, which is 1/4 of 360°. Therefore if we move section A to the right by 1/4 of a period, the sine waves become cosine waves and vice-versa. In other words, we can extract different one-period sections from the same wave and find that the resulting component waves are completely different.

As you may have noticed, the results we got from Fourier coefficients were the simple waves required to perfectly reproduce the one period of the wave that we originally extracted. If we add together all the simple waves we get by breaking down section A, they will form a wave identical to A. If we add together the component waves of section B, they will give us a wave identical to B.

But this presents a real problem: our results differ depending on where we extract that one period! If we want to use a spectrum to show the characteristics of a complicated wave in a convenient format, it won't do us much good unless it can provide us with the same values for the wave regardless of which section we select as a period.

The FFT analyzer achieves this by taking the values of a_n and b_n (arrived at through Fourier coefficients) for the same frequency (i.e., a_1 and b_1, a_2 and b_2, etc.), and displaying them in such a way that they never vary, no matter which part of the wave was selected as its sample period. The key to this method is the formula $d_n = \sqrt{(a_n)^2 + (b_n)^2}$. The value d_n represents a_n and b_n together. The graph below shows how this is done.

As the graph indicates, a_n and b_n can be represented by a single point, d_n. For example, if $a_1 = 3$ and $b_1 = 2$, d_1 is the value of that point. The value shown in the spectrum is the distance from 0 to d_1. To find this distance, we use the Pythagorean theorem. Since $d_n = \sqrt{(a_n)^2 + (b_n)^2}$, that means $d_1 = \sqrt{3^2 + 2^2} = 3.61$.

For the wave we were using to study discrete Fourier expansion:

$A \quad a_0 = 8$

$$d_1 = \sqrt{3^2 + 2^2} \doteq 3.61$$

$$d_2 = \sqrt{2^2 + 4^2} \doteq 4.47$$

$$d_3 = \sqrt{1^2 + 3^2} \doteq 3.16$$

$B \quad b_0 = 8$

$$d_1 = \sqrt{(-1.25)^2 + (-3.4)^2} \doteq 3.62$$

$$d_2 = \sqrt{(-3.2)^2 + 3.13^2} \doteq 4.48$$

$$d_3 = \sqrt{(-3.2)^2 + 3.13^2} \doteq 3.16$$

So the values we get are more or less identical. If we draw a spectrum, we get:

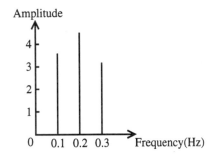

Thus the spectrum is a graphic representation of the value d_n, which is the same no matter where on the wave we select our sample period.

Memo

Part 2

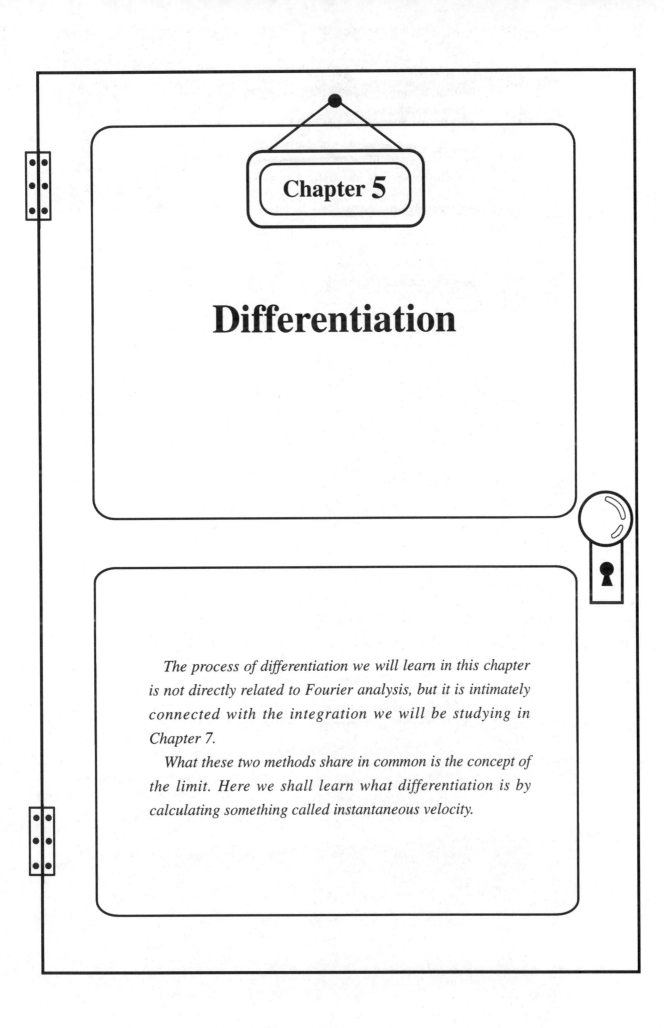

Chapter 5

Differentiation

The process of differentiation we will learn in this chapter is not directly related to Fourier analysis, but it is intimately connected with the integration we will be studying in Chapter 7.

What these two methods share in common is the concept of the limit. Here we shall learn what differentiation is by calculating something called instantaneous velocity.

The first part of our adventure has given us a view of the entire Fourier palace. We have learned how to express a complicated wave as the sum of simple waves. If we wanted, we could probably bring our adventure to a close right here. But after coming this far, you'll no doubt agree it would be nice to actually enter the palace, not just stare at it from the outside!

In Chapter 3, "Discrete Fourier Expansion," we calculated the area of a wave. We did this by dividing the wave into "strips." Unfortunately some of these strips were always too short, and others too long, so we were never able to find the precise area of the wave.

On the next part of our adventure, then, we will search for a more accurate way to find this area. It's time to enter the Palace of Fourier!

This palace contains many doors. Behind each door lies hidden a key to yet another door, which we must unlock if we are to learn how to find the "closest approximation of the area" of a wave. As we pick up each key and open these doors one after another, our adventure is bound to take us in unforeseen directions.

Now let us enter the palace and begin the second part of our adventure: the search for the "closest approximation of the area." The first door we come to opens into the "Differentiation Room."

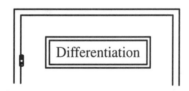

Our companions on this quest are:

Hana
(our guide to the
Differentiation Room)

Sir Isaac Newton
(the famous scientist)

Chommi
(Hana's lovely and
talented assistant)

Foo
(a young fellow who's a bit
slow on the uptake, but asks
plenty of questions)

And everyone else who took the course on Fourier together!

We'll start with a question.
This blackboard eraser is moving. Can anyone tell me why?

 Because you're pushing it with your hand.

 Try to be a little more specific!

 Because you're applying force?

That's better! The eraser moves because force is applied to it. You all know from personal experience that force is required to move an object.

Now, another question: If I let go off the eraser, it falls to the floor. We can say it's "moving downward." But I didn't push it "down" with my hand – so why did it move? If force is required to move objects, what sort of force is making this eraser fall?

 Gravity!

 And what kind of force is that?

 Uh...well, it's the force of the earth's pull.

That's right! When an object falls, it's because the earth is pulling it.

Now let's think some more about how things move.

You've all ridden a bicycle, haven't you? Think about what happens when you pedal a bike. If your bike is stationary and you want to move it, it takes some muscle, doesn't it. When you apply force by pedaling, the harder you pedal, the faster the bike goes. But then, when you reach a certain speed, suppose you stop pedaling, and even take your feet off the pedals. What happens then?

 You just keep coasting along.

 Exactly! Your bike keeps on moving, and hardly even loses any speed. When a bicycle reaches a certain speed, no more force is needed to keep it moving at that same speed. Then, if you start pedaling again, the bike speeds up even more, doesn't it!

Now let's think about what happens when you add some baggage to the bike. If your load is heavy, you'll have to exert quite a bit more force to get the bike moving than you did without the load. But even with this heavy load, once the bike reaches a certain speed, what happens if you quit pedaling? That's right, the bike keeps moving, just as it did without the extra load. The weight of the load doesn't matter – you can still make your bike coast at a constant speed.

So we've learned two things:

1. Force is required to move a stationary bicycle. But once the bicycle has reached a certain speed, force is not required to keep it moving at that speed.

2. The heavier the load on a stationary bicycle, the more force is required to get it moving. But once the bicycle has reached a certain speed, force is not required to keep it moving at that speed, no matter how heavy the load.

Hmmm. So that's the lowdown on the motion of objects, huh?

Yes! And actually, there's a way to say it all in one word!

What? One word in place of that long-winded description? I'd like to meet the genius who came up with that!

$$F = ma$$

This is my equation for motion, which describes in a word how objects move. The word is a mathematical formula, which people anywhere in the world can understand. It's pronounced "F equals m alpha."

What the heck does <u>that</u> mean? What's F? What's m? What's <u>alpha</u>, for heaven's sake?

F is force, m is the mass of an object, and a is acceleration.

Acceleration?

Acceleration is the rate at which a speed changes. For example, when you start to move your bicycle from rest, it gradually goes faster and faster, right? That change in the bike's speed over time is its acceleration, expressed as a in $F = ma$ (ma means "$m \times a$", of course!). What this equation tells us is that the force (F) required to move an object increases with the mass (m) of the object, but also with the acceleration (a) of the object. Remember, you didn't need force to keep the bike coasting along at a constant speed. When the speed doesn't change, the acceleration is zero. Looking at my equation, how much force do you think you'd need for zero acceleration?

Okay, if $F = ma$, and if acceleration a is 0, then $F = m \times 0$. That makes $F = 0$ too! So according to your formula, if the speed doesn't change, zero force is required, right?

For the purposes of this chapter, we are equating "weight" with "mass," but to physicists, the two words mean very different things.
You've probably heard that you would weigh less on the moon than you do on earth. "Weight" thus varies from place to place. "Mass," on the other hand, is the same wherever you go – anywhere in the universe, in fact. In other words, mass is the basic quantity of an object.

Quite right! By the same token, the greater acceleration a is, the greater the force F required – so the faster you want to speed up your bike from a full stop, the more force you have to exert.

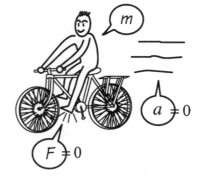

Now, you also pointed out earlier that the heavier your load is, the more force you need to move a stationary bike. The weight of the load is indicated by mass m, so let's use my equation to compare a heavy load (large mass m) with a light load (small mass m).

Okay! $F = ma$, and ma means "$m \times a$". If acceleration a stays the same, then the larger m is, the greater the value of $m \times a$ will be – that is, the value of force F. How's that?

Smashing! This equation lets us express everything we know about the motion of an object. We can use it to make precise calculations of anything from the movement of a bicycle to the way a blackboard eraser falls, or even the motion of the stars.

Wow! So now that I know this formula $F = ma$, I can calculate all those things, huh? Let's see, I can weigh something on a scale to get mass m. But how do I measure something like acceleration? I know it's zero when an object isn't moving, and that it gets bigger the faster the speed of the object changes. But I don't really know how to figure it out.

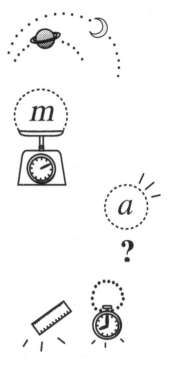

Well, that's what differentiation is for – to help us figure out things like acceleration. If you understand differentiation, you can calculate acceleration with nothing more than a ruler and a watch!

You can also use this same formula $F = ma$ to determine the gravitational pull of the earth. Let me ask you a question.

What happens to a tomato if you drop it from your hand? And what happens if it falls from the top of a building? I think you get the picture.

Something like this, right?

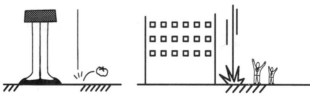

And do you know why that is?

It seems like it falls with more force from a high place, but I don't know exactly why.

That reminds me of the time I rode on a sled. At first it went nice and slow, and I was having a great time. But the farther downhill I slid, the faster it went, and soon I was scared stiff. Anyway I guess the farther an object falls, the faster it falls, right?

Jolly good story! You're absolutely right. Take a look at this chart I made of the movement of a ball as it falls. To make it easier to understand, I've shown how many meters the ball will fall at each second after you let go of it.

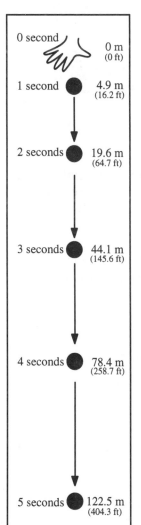

You can see it getting faster and faster.

We talked earlier about how the earth pulls on a blackboard eraser. The earth's pulling on this ball, too, huh!

When we were talking about bicycles, we saw that the speed of the bike didn't change unless we applied force to it. But as this ball falls, it goes faster and faster. Why is that?

A bike goes faster and faster if you keep pedaling it. Does that mean the ball falls faster and faster because the earth keeps pulling on it?!

Yes! The earth is continually pulling on the ball!

Hmm... so how much force is the earth pulling with?

That's where Mr. Newton's equation comes in!

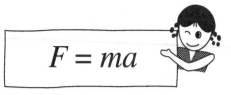

$$F = ma$$

Substitute the mass of the ball for *m*, and the acceleration of the ball as it falls for *a*, and you'll get the force with which the earth is pulling the ball.

Quick, show us how to figure out acceleration!

All in good time! But before we can find the acceleration, we have to find the speed.

So here's a question. Suppose you roll three balls, ①, ②, and ③, over a flat floor.

50 seconds	50 seconds	40 seconds
①	②	③
200m	400m	280m

Ball ① rolls past the 200-meter mark at 50 seconds.
Ball ② rolls past the 400-meter mark at 50 seconds.
Ball ③ rolls past the 280-meter mark at 40 seconds.

Can you tell which ball is fastest, and which is slowest?

After 50 seconds, ball ① has only rolled 200 meters, while ball ② has rolled 400 meters. So obviously ball ② is faster than ball ①. But I don't know where ball ③ fits in – it only traveled 280 meters, but it took only 40 seconds.

At times like this, the number "1" can come in very handy. Let's figure out how many meters each ball had traveled after 1 second. Then we have a way to compare them.

① $\dfrac{200 \text{ m}}{50 \text{ sec}} = 4 \text{ m/sec}$, so ball ① had rolled 4 meters after 1 second.

② $\dfrac{400 \text{ m}}{50 \text{ sec}} = 8 \text{ m/sec}$, so ball ② had rolled 8 meters after 1 second.

③ $\dfrac{280 \text{ m}}{40 \text{ sec}} = 7 \text{ m/sec}$, so ball ③ had rolled 7 meters after 1 second.

To calculate how far each ball traveled in 1 second, all we need is the formula:

$$\frac{\text{distance traveled(m)}}{\text{time elapsed(sec)}}$$

And that gives us the order of the balls, from fastest to slowest: ② → ③ → ①!

Here's a graphic representation:

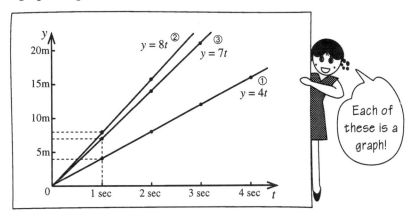

 Do you see how we drew these graphs? Ball ①, for example, reached 4 meters at 1 second, 8 meters at 2 seconds, and 12 meters at 3 seconds. We simply plotted these points and connected them to make a graph for ball ①. Then we did the same thing for balls ② and ③.

What does it mean where it says $y = 4t$ for ①, $y = 8t$ for ②, and $y = 7t$ for ③?

Those are the names of each graph. The value of y is the point on the vertical axis indicating the distance, and the value of t is the point on the horizontal axis indicating the time. Suppose the value of t is 1 second, or 2 seconds. What value do you get for y in each case?

If you substitute 1 for t in the equation $y = 4t$, you get 4 meters for y. If you substitute 2 for t, you get 8 meters, and 3 gives you 12 meters. So the equation gives you the position of the ball at the time you give for t. This is a formula for the motion of the ball, isn't it!

Yes indeed! You can describe the motion of objects in terms of distance and time – y and t. Did you notice anything else about these graphs?

Yes, the steeper the slope of the graph, the faster the speed it represents.

That's right – and you can calculate that slope without using a protractor! The slope of the graph is simply how far it advances vertically as it advances by a value of 1 horizontally. So you can use the ratio "vertical/horizontal".

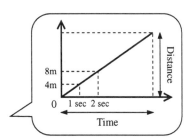

 Oh, I see. That means the same as "distance/time" on this graph.

In physics, speed and velocity are used separately. Both contain the rate of movement but velocity includes the direction in which the movement is made.

When we talk about how many meters something moves in 1 second, we're describing its speed – or, rather, its velocity.

Hey, so you don't need a speedometer to measure speed! You can calculate it yourself if you know how many meters the thing you're measuring has moved in 1 second.

Okay, here's a problem for you. A car traveling along at a constant speed reaches the 360-kilometer mark after 4 hours. What's the velocity of the car in kilometers per hour?

Well, if velocity is distance/time, that gives us 360 km/4 hours, or a velocity of 90 km/hour.

Good! Let's remember that formula:

$$\text{VELOCITY} = \frac{\text{DISTANCE}}{\text{TIME}}$$

But what about acceleration? How do we get that from velocity?

Hang on a sec! Now that you know how to calculate velocity, I have another problem for you. This one involves the falling ball we mentioned earlier. Do you think you can figure out the velocity at which the ball is falling?

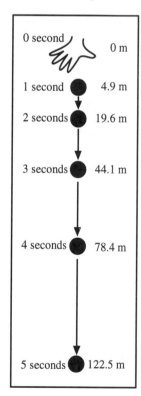

0 second   0 m

1 second   4.9 m

2 seconds   19.6 m

3 seconds   44.1 m

4 seconds   78.4 m

5 seconds   122.5 m

Well, it's fallen 122.5 meters after 5 seconds, so
$$\text{velocity} = \frac{122.5 \text{ m}}{5 \text{ sec}} = 24.5 \text{ m/sec}$$
can't we just say its velocity is 122.5 m/5 sec, or 24.5 m/sec? That's the answer, right?

If you say so! Now try the same calculation at 3 seconds, when it's fallen 44.1 meters.

No problem.
$$\text{velocity} = \frac{44.1 \text{ m}}{3 \text{ sec}} = 14.7 \text{ m/sec}$$
Huh? That's a different speed from the one I got for 5 seconds! What's going on here?

If you plot your results on a graph, you'll see what's happening.

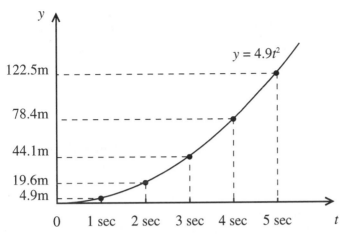

☞ see p.179 and p.192

This graph of a ball falling looks quite a bit different from the graph of the ball rolling on the floor, doesn't it.

 Yeah, this one's sort of curved.

 Do you know why?

 Maybe because the speed of the ball is increasing as it falls?

That's it! When the ball rolled across the floor, it was traveling at the same speed the whole time, so the graph was a straight line.

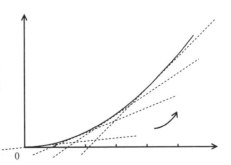

But this time the ball was dropped from above, and its speed kept changing as it fell.

Foo, you used this formula to figure out the ball's speed:

Distance fallen in 5 seconds, divided by 5 seconds = 122.5 m/5 sec

That's the speed of the ball if it had fallen at the same speed for the entire 5 seconds.

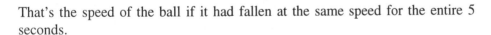

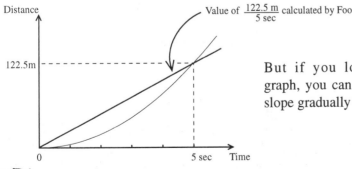

But if you look at this graph, you can see that the slope gradually gets steeper.

Yipes! How am I gonna figure out the velocity of the ball if it keeps changing like that? I'd have to come up with all these different speeds!

Hee hee! Relax, Foo! You can express the ever-changing velocity of this ball with just a single word!

First, let's try to find the velocity of the falling ball at exactly the 3-second mark. How do you think we should do that?

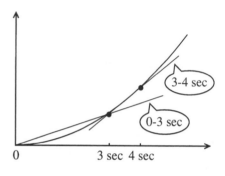

What if we figured out the slope of the graph between 3 seconds and 4 seconds? That would be a lot more accurate than the velocity from 0 to 3 seconds, at least!

3-4 sec

0-3 sec

That's true. Go ahead and give it a try!

Okay, the distance is from 44.1 to 78.4 meters, and the time is from 3 to 4 seconds. So:

$$\text{velocity} = \frac{\text{distance}}{\text{time}}$$

$$= \frac{78.4 \text{ m} - 44.1 \text{ m}}{4 \text{ sec} - 3 \text{ sec}}$$

$$= \frac{34.3 \text{ m}}{1 \text{ sec}}$$

$$= 34.3 \text{ m/sec}$$

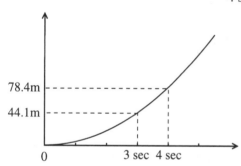

This is pretty much the speed at exactly 3 seconds, don't you think? The speed isn't going to change that much in just 1 second!

Don't be so sure! Let's take a closer look. Chommi, the magnifying glass, please!

One magnifying glass, coming up!

Right-o!

We'll place it right here...

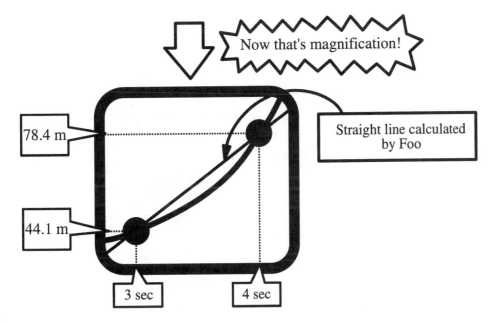

Now that's magnification!

78.4 m

44.1 m

Straight line calculated by Foo

3 sec   4 sec

Oh no! When you enlarge it like that, you can see the velocity changing even between 3 and 4 seconds!

Told you so! Try calculating the velocity between 3 and 3.1 seconds, and compare it to the velocity between 3.9 and 4 seconds. You'll find they're pretty different!

But how are you supposed to find the location of the ball at 3.1 seconds? The only velocities we know are at 1-second intervals!

Hey, the name of this graph is "$y = 4.9t^2$", right? We can use that formula to find the velocity, can't we?

Where'd that come from, anyway – "$y = 4.9t^2$"?

Er, um, actually, it's something Mr. Newton figured out a long time ago.

Never mind all that, let's just go ahead and use it! No doubt we'll learn more about it later. Meanwhile, let's plug "$t = 3.1$" into "$y = 4.9t^2$" and see what we get!

So the position of the ball at 3.1 seconds is

$$y = 4.9t^2$$
$$= 4.9 \times (3.1)^2$$
$$= 4.9 \times 9.61$$
$$= 47.089$$

47.089 meters! And if we figure out its position at 3.9 seconds the same way...

$$y = 4.9t^2$$
$$= 4.9 \times (3.9)^2$$
$$= 4.9 \times 15.21$$
$$= 74.529$$

...we get 74.529 meters. All right, now let's figure out the velocity!

• Velocity between 3 and 3.1 seconds:

$$\text{velocity} = \frac{\text{distance}(y)}{\text{time}(t)}$$
$$= \frac{47.089 - 44.1}{3.1 - 3}$$
$$= \frac{2.989}{0.1}$$
$$= 29.89 \text{(m/sec)}$$

• Velocity between 3.9 and 4 seconds:

$$\text{velocity} = \frac{\text{distance}(y)}{\text{time}(t)}$$
$$= \frac{78.4 - 74.529}{4 - 3.9}$$
$$= \frac{3.871}{0.1}$$
$$= 38.71 \text{(m/sec)}$$

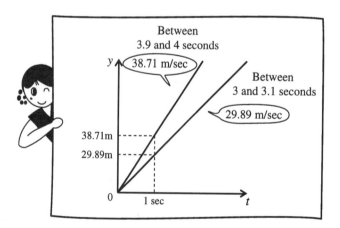

I can't believe how much the speed changed in only 1 second! But now we know the speed between 3 and 3.1 seconds! Sure, it might have changed a lot between 3 and 4 seconds, but it couldn't change in only 0.1 second, could it?

 We'll see!

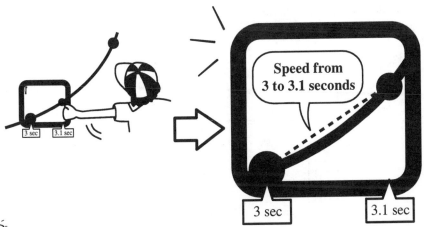

 Aagh! I can't stand it! Even in 0.1 second, the speed keeps changing! Forget it! We're never gonna find the speed at exactly 3 seconds! I mean, we're stuck with the formula

$$velocity = \frac{distance\ traveled}{time\ elapsed}$$

– so we can only find the velocity when the ball has traveled over a certain period of time, that is the average velocity over a given distance or time. But if the velocity changes so much in even 0.1 second, how are we supposed to find the true speed at exactly 3 seconds?!

 Heh heh! Don't worry, you can! And the person who discovered how to do it is none other than...

Pip pip! I'm back!

 Wow, it's Mr. Newton again! Gee, can you help us?

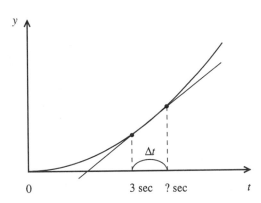

What you want, old chap, is to find the **instantaneous velocity** at exactly 3 seconds. Now this velocity must be distance/time, of course. So what you must do is divide a certain finite time into the distance traveled during that time.

The term Δt (pronounced "delta-t") means "time changed." Likewise, the distance changed during Δt is called "Δy".

To get that value as close as possible to the velocity at the instant of 3 seconds, you need to make the interval between 3 seconds and some other time ("? sec" in the graph) as short as possible. I call this time interval "Δt seconds." In other words, you want to make Δt as small as you can.

The smaller we make Δt,

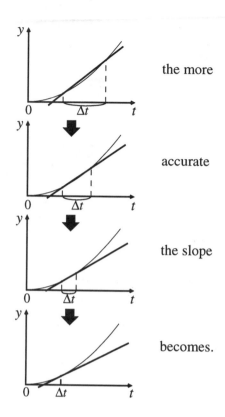

the more

accurate

the slope

becomes.

 In the graph at the bottom, it may look as if the two times are so close together they have become one. But in fact, they are still two separate points! Now here's the real trick: the smaller we make Δt, the closer we get to the actual speed. So that means...

We should make Δt be zero!

I say, old chap, we can't do that! If time $\Delta t = 0$, we can no longer divide distance by time, because it's impossible to divide by 0! So instead, we simply want Δt to become "infinitely close" to 0!

lim = limit !

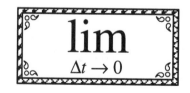

$$\lim_{\Delta t \to 0}$$

This is how we put that idea in writing. We can't let time Δt <u>be</u> 0, but we can let it get <u>infinitely close</u>. By that, we mean much, much closer to 0 than 0.1 second, or 0.000000001 second, or even 0.000...001 second with a million zeroes in a row!

No matter how small we make Δt, it's still a finite value, so we can still calculate distance/time. But at the same time, as Δt approaches 0, the change in speed during that interval becomes so small that we can ignore it.

 Uh, right. I'm not sure I follow you...

 Let's try using this method to calculate the speed at precisely 3 seconds. First, we'll find the speed for the interval between 3 seconds and $3 + \Delta t$ seconds. Do you think you can figure out the distance the ball has fallen during that interval?

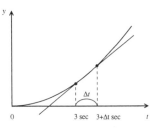

Can we use the formula $y = 4.9t^2$? If we can, the distance the ball fell in the time $3 + \Delta t$ seconds is:

$$y = 4.9(3 + \Delta t)^2$$

Then we can subtract the distance the ball fell in the first 3 seconds, which is:

$$y = 4.9 \times 3^2 = 44.1 \text{ (m)}$$

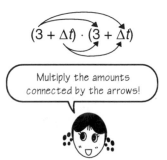

Multiply the amounts connected by the arrows!

 Right you are! Now try to calculate the velocity.

Let's see... first, we have:

$$\frac{\Delta y}{\Delta t} = \frac{4.9(3 + \Delta t)^2 - 44.1}{\Delta t}$$

And if we calculate that, we get:

$$\frac{\Delta y}{\Delta t} = \frac{4.9(3 + \Delta t) \cdot (3 + \Delta t) - 44.1}{\Delta t}$$

$$= \frac{4.9\{9 + 3\Delta t + 3\Delta t + (\Delta t)^2\} - 44.1}{\Delta t}$$

$$= \frac{4.9\{9 + 6\Delta t + (\Delta t)^2\} - 44.1}{\Delta t}$$

$$= \frac{44.1 + 29.4\Delta t + 4.9(\Delta t)^2 - 44.1}{\Delta t}$$

$$= \frac{29.4\Delta t + 4.9(\Delta t)^2}{\Delta t}$$

$$= 29.4 + 4.9\Delta t$$

So we now have the average velocity between 3 seconds and $3 + \Delta t$ seconds!

$\dfrac{29.4\Delta t + 4.9(\Delta t)^2}{\Delta t}$
is the same as
$\dfrac{29.4\Delta t}{\Delta t} + \dfrac{4.9(\Delta t)^2}{\Delta t}$
which cancel out like this:
$\dfrac{29.4\cancel{\Delta t}}{\cancel{\Delta t}} + \dfrac{4.9(\Delta t)^{\cancel{2}}}{\cancel{\Delta t}}$
giving us
$29.4 + 4.9\Delta t$.

The slope of a graph like the one on the right is called the "slope of the tangent."

This line is not a tangent!

Next, to find the velocity at precisely 3 seconds, we have to bring time Δt infinitely close to 0. Watch closely, now!

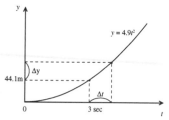

$$\lim_{\Delta t \to 0} (29.4 + 4.9\Delta t) = 29.4 + \cancel{4.9\Delta t}$$
$$= 29.4$$

Instantaneous velocity at 3 seconds: <u>29.4 m/sec</u>

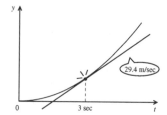

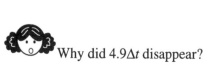 Why did $4.9\Delta t$ disappear?

Remember that Δt was infinitely close to 0. If you multiply 4.9 by a number infinitely close to 0, the number you get is also infinitely close to 0. In other words, the product of $4.9 \times \Delta t$ is practically the same as 0.

Wow, that's neat, Mr. Newton! I can't help thinking there's something sneaky about how you did it, but at least you helped us find the instantaneous velocity at 3 seconds!

Fine, so we found the speed of the ball at exactly 3 seconds – but the speed keeps changing as the ball falls! Hana, you said we could express this changing speed with a single word. So what is it, already?!

Hee hee hee! It's easy – all you have to do is take the same calculations we did for 3 seconds, and replace "3" with "t", representing any time t you want!

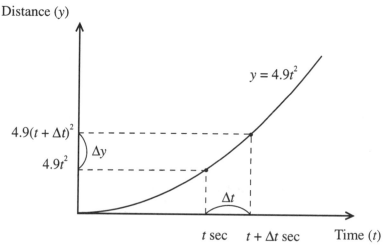

Distance (y)

$4.9(t + \Delta t)^2$

$4.9t^2$

Δy

$y = 4.9t^2$

Δt

t sec $t + \Delta t$ sec   Time (t)

Okay, I'm game. I need to calculate the instantaneous velocity at t seconds, is that it?

$$\frac{\Delta y}{\Delta t} = \frac{4.9(t + \Delta t)^2 - 4.9t^2}{\Delta t}$$

$$= \frac{4.9\{t^2 + 2t\Delta t + (\Delta t)^2\} - 4.9t^2}{\Delta t}$$

$$= \frac{4.9t^2 + 9.8t\Delta t + 4.9(\Delta t)^2 - 4.9t^2}{\Delta t}$$

$$= \frac{9.8t\Delta t + 4.9(\Delta t)^2}{\Delta t}$$

$$= 9.8t + 4.9\Delta t$$

$$\text{Velocity } v = \lim_{\Delta t \to 0} \left(9.8t + 4.9\Delta t\right)$$

$$= 9.8t$$

Instantaneous velocity at time t seconds: 9.8t (m/sec)

 So you get 9.8t, eh? What kind of number is that?!

 Suppose you replace t with 3. Then $9.8 \times 3 = 29.4$ – that is, 29.4 m/sec!

 That looks strangely familiar... Hey! That's the instantaneous velocity for 3 seconds we went to all that trouble to figure out! You mean you can insert any time t you want in "9.8t", and it'll give you the instantaneous velocity for that time?!

 Yes! This one word will express the velocity for any time you want it to! Let's draw ourselves a graph of $v = 9.8t$.

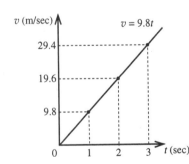

This is a graph of the velocity of a falling ball.

The graph we saw before, of $y = 4.9t^2$, was a graph of the location (i.e. distance) of the falling ball.

$\frac{dy}{dt}$ means $\lim_{\Delta t \to 0} \frac{\Delta y}{\Delta t}$. It's just an easier way to write it.

Just read "d-y-d-t."

Strictly speaking, dy/dt is a derivative. The process by which this derivative was determined is called differentiation.

By the way, when are we going to learn about differentiation?

Guess what! You've already done it! This is differentiation:

$$\boxed{\lim_{\Delta t \to 0} \frac{\Delta y}{\Delta t} \; \left(= \frac{dy}{dt} \right)}$$

Or, to be graphic:

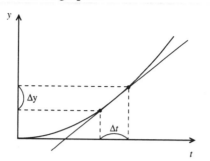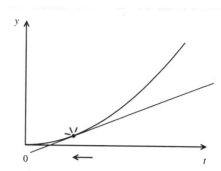

 We use differentiation to find the velocity "distance/time" at any given instant. If we perform differentiation on our graph of $y = 4.9t^2$, we get the graph of $v = 9.8t$. That is, if we perform differentiation to find the slope at every point in time on the curve shown on the left, and plot all these values on a new graph, we'll get the graph shown below. Does the result surprise you?

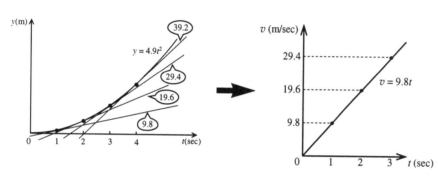

So by performing differentiation on a graph of distances – how many meters a ball has fallen at any given second – we can learn the speed at which the ball was falling in meters per second.

 What happens if we perform differentiation on the graph of $v = 9.8t$ this time?

Good question! Let's do it!

This graph is a straight line, so it should be easy to calculate the slope.

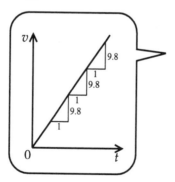

At any point on the graph of $v = 9.8t$, the speed increases by 9.8 for every 1 second of time, so the slope is always 9.8. If we plot this on a graph, it turns out like this:

This is actually a graph of the **acceleration** of the falling ball: $\alpha = 9.8$.

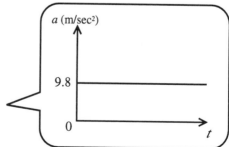

What, a graph of acceleration?!

Finally! But just what _is_ acceleration, then? Velocity is how much the distance changes in 1 second. So I suppose acceleration is how much the velocity changes in 1 second, right?

Right! The speed of the falling ball keeps changing, remember? The graph tells us the speed is increasing by 9.8 m/sec every second. That means the acceleration is 9.8 m/sec² (that is, 9.8 meters per second per second).

So when we want to find the acceleration of a moving object, all we need is a ruler and a watch, so to speak. We measure how many meters the object has traveled at any given second, plot this on a graph, and calculate a formula for the graph. The rest is easy – just perform differentiation twice, and we have our answer!

Now that we know the acceleration of the falling ball, let's go back to the equation $F = m\alpha$. We wanted to know the gravitational force of the earth on the ball, remember?

$$F \quad = \quad m \quad \cdot \quad a$$

$\begin{pmatrix} \text{force of earth} \\ \text{pulling on ball} \end{pmatrix}$ $\begin{pmatrix} \text{mass of ball} \end{pmatrix}$ $\begin{pmatrix} \text{acceleration of} \\ \text{falling ball} \end{pmatrix}$

We now know that the acceleration of the ball is $\alpha = 9.8$. Let's assume the ball mass 2 kilograms. Now we can figure out the gravitational pull of the earth on the ball!

$$F = m \times a = 2 \times 9.8 = 19.6$$

Force of earth pulling on 2 kg ball: 19.6 N ◄

"N" stands for "newton", which is a unit of force. It's named after Sir Isaac Newton, who invented it, of course!

But just how much force is 19.6 N? Can you give us an example we're familiar with?

Well, it's the force you feel when you hold a ball that weighs 2 kilograms!

By the way, our discussion of the falling ball really applies only to a ball falling through a vacuum, not through the air. If we had to take things like air resistance into account, that would require even more calculations. In a vacuum, you yourself would fall at the same rate as the ball – with an acceleration of 9.8 m/sec².

What? How could a human body fall at the same rate as a ball, when it's so much heavier?!

Well, it would! You, a ball, a feather, a raindrop – everything would fall at the same acceleration of 9.8 m/sec^2. Go ahead, try calculating the force at which the earth would pull *you*!

Okay, I weigh 35 kilograms, so:

$$F = 35 \times 9.8 = 343$$

Force of earth pulling on Foo: 343 N

Wow, that's a lot more than the force of the earth on the ball!

You're a lot heavier than the ball, Foo, so it takes a lot more force to pull you toward the earth at the same rate as the ball!

Huh. But only in a vacuum – that doesn't sound very real to me. Still, it's cool the way you can use a formula to measure a force you can't see, like gravity!

We may have figured out the gravitational force of the earth, but our quest is far from over. Before we leave the Differentiation Room, we have to pick up the key that opens the next door. You'll find the key on the next page – don't leave here without it!

To find the velocity of an object at a specific instant when its velocity is changing over time, calculate the velocity for the interval Δt seconds following the instant (t seconds) in question.

$$\frac{\Delta y}{\Delta t} = \frac{f(t + \Delta t) - f(t)}{\Delta t}$$

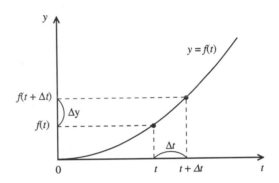

Then bring Δt as close as possible to 0.

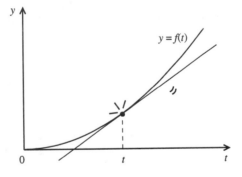

$$\frac{dy}{dt} = \lim_{\Delta t \to 0} \frac{\Delta y}{\Delta t}$$

$$= \lim_{\Delta t \to 0} \frac{f(t + \Delta t) - f(t)}{\Delta t}$$

Have you got the key firmly in hand? Despite all that time we spent wandering in the Differentiation Room, the key we picked up there was only one page long! But that doesn't mean the room doesn't contain many other fascinating treasures. If you have time, by all means come back and look around some more.

For example, Sir Isaac Newton's discoveries about force led to an entire field of study known as **mechanics**. Think of it as an opportunity for future adventures – we've barely scratched the surface here!

So, is that all differentiation is good for – finding velocity and acceleration?

Oh no! It has lots of other uses. Suppose you're climbing a hill. You can use differentiation to figure out which point on the hill is the steepest. Look at the graphs below. They show how differentiation can give you accurate numbers that indicate how steep each part of the hill is.

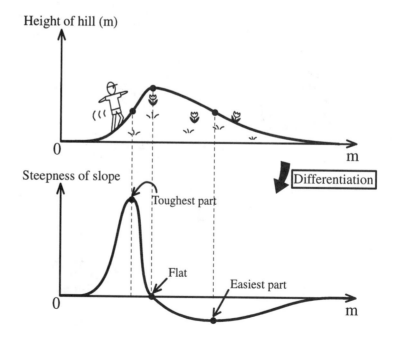

Differentiation can tell you how fat you'll get, the more candy you eat –

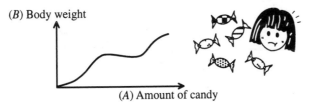

(*B*) Body weight

(*A*) Amount of candy

or how much you'll sweat, the farther you run –

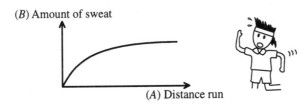

(*B*) Amount of sweat

(*A*) Distance run

or how loud a noise your stereo will make, the more you turn up the volume.

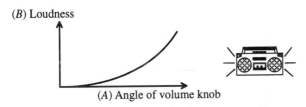

(*B*) Loudness

(*A*) Angle of volume knob

In a nutshell, differentiation helps us find out how a change in (*A*) affects (*B*).

When I look around now, I can see all kinds of things that make me say "Hey! That's differentiation too!!"

That's right! You'll be a professional differentiator before you know it! And next time, you can help out as a guide to the Differentiation Room!

Well, it's time for you to head out the door, key in hand, and unlock the next door! Good luck, everybody!

Why "$y = 4.9t^2$"?

What is that mysterious formula $y = 4.9t^2$, anyway? The "t(second)" is the time elapsed after an object is dropped, and the "y(meter)" is the distance the object has fallen. But where on earth does "4.9" come from? It's a rather strange number, don't you think? Your first impulse is probably to round it off to 5. But, like it or not, we are stuck with "4.9" as long as we live on the face of the earth. Any object – no matter where, or when, or how heavy – will always fall at the rate of $y = 4.9t^2$. Whether you weigh 40 or 50 kilograms, you yourself will fall at this rate. In Japan or Mexico, over the ocean or above the North Pole, any two objects dropped at the same time will hit the ground (or the water) at about the same time.

$y = 4.9t^2$ expresses the relationship between time and distance of objects falling to earth. Performing differentiation once yields the relationship $v = 9.8t$ between time and velocity. The number 9.8(m/sec^2) is the **gravitational acceleration** of the earth. Gravitational acceleration is proportional to the mass of the heavenly body in question. The moon is smaller than the earth and therefore has less gravitational acceleration to the same degree that it has less mass. Perhaps you saw the Apollo astronauts on T.V. when they first walked on the moon. Remember how they seemed to bounce gently over the surface? That was because things fall more slowly on the moon than they do on earth, due to the lower gravitational acceleration. Rather amazing, you must admit, that we can actually write a formula describing how objects behave on the earth's surface!

But in reality, the formula $y = 4.9t^2$ applies only to vacuum conditions, and does not take air resistance into account. In reality, if you dropped two ping pong balls from the roof of the World Trade Center at the same time – both having the same weight, but one much larger than the other – the smaller one would undoubtedly hit the street first. If it weren't for air resistance, parachutes would be useless – you would still fall at $v = 9.8t$ and meet with an untimely demise. To accurately describe the behavior of falling objects in the atmosphere, "$v = 9.8t$" is not enough; you must also figure air resistance into your calculations. For further details, you will need to find another book that can introduce you to the adventures of Messrs. Newton and Galileo!

Chapter 6

Differentiation of sin θ

Do you feel fairly comfortable with differentiation now? Good! In this chapter, we'll perform differentiation on the sine wave, a procedure that plays a prominent role in Fourier analysis. This differentiation process is by no means simple. But bear with us; we'll pick up several valuable keys along the way, starting with the "trigonometric identities."

In the previous chapter we had our first encounter with differentiation, and embarked on our quest in search of the closest approximation of the area of a wave. The key we picked up in the Differentiation Room looked like this:

$$\frac{df(t)}{dt} = \frac{dy}{dt} = \lim_{\Delta t \to 0} \frac{f(t + \Delta t) - f(t)}{\Delta t}$$

Perhaps you're thinking, "Now that we know how to differentiate, we should be able to find the closest approximation of the area right away!" Well, you'll have to be patient. First, we must use our differentiation key to perform differentiation on sin θ, with which we're already familiar. When we find the key to differentiating sin θ, we'll use that to unlock the Integration Room. And once inside the Integration Room, we'll find the key to calculating the closest approximation of the area.

Are you ready to venture forth on our quest for the key to the differentiation of sin θ? Off we go!

1. Differentiating a Sine Produces a Cosine?!

Do you remember sin θ and cos θ from Chapter 1?

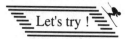

Try writing these out yourself. If you've forgotten, better go back and review them !

☞ see pages 24 and 48

sin θ = ——————

Vertical(side opposite θ) =

cos θ = ——————

Horizontal(side adjacent θ) =

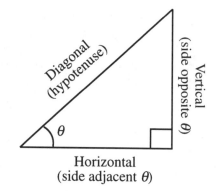

As angle θ gets larger and larger, sin θ and cos θ form graphs that look like this:

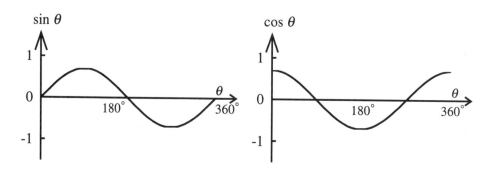

"Differentiating sin θ" means finding the slope of the tangent of the graph of sin θ, just as we did for a different sort of graph in Chapter 5. So without further ado, let's find the slope of the tangents of both sin θ and cos θ.

How do we find the slope of a tangent? You remember – by finding the ratio "vertical/horizontal". In the graph of sin θ, the value of the vertical is the value of sin θ, and the value of the horizontal is the angle itself. Here we shall measure the angle in radians. Using radians makes it extremely simple to find the answer when we differentiate sin θ. Do you remember how many radians there were in 360 degrees? That's right: 2π radians, which is approximately 6.28 radians. If we measure the horizontal axis in radians, our graph turns out like this:

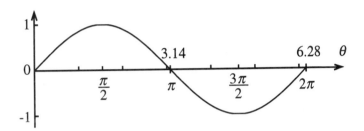

First let's find the result of differentiation(derivative) when the angle is 0. (When we measure angles in radians, we don't need to say "0 radians" or the like; just the number will do.) We'll try drawing the tangent at angle 0. What is the ratio "vertical/horizontal" for this tangent?

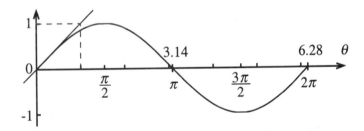

And the answer is... 1! Now, check out the tangent when angle θ is π/2:

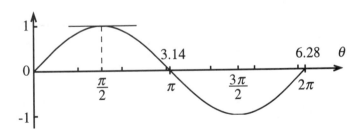

What is the slope of <u>this</u> tangent? When the angle is π/2, the graph of sin θ is right at the top of its curve, so the tangent is perfectly horizontal. That means its "vertical" value is 0, so the slope of the tangent (vertical/horizontal) is also 0.

How about when the angle is π?

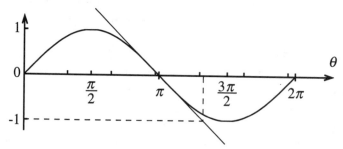

Look closely at the graph. Can you see why the slope of this tangent is -1? Now, on to angle $3\pi/2$. Once again, the slope of the tangent is 0, just as it was for $\pi/2$:

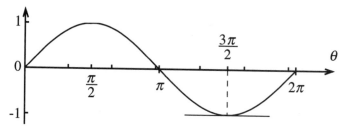

At angle 2π, we're back where we started; the slope is 1, as it was at angle 0.

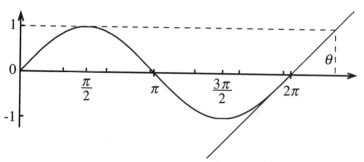

Now let's plot a graph of the values for the slope of the tangents that we've found so far. Then we'll connect the points with a smooth curve...

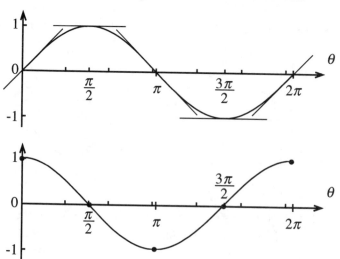

Whoa! Haven't we seen that curve somewhere before? Of course! That's the graph of cos θ!

Wait a minute! So when you differentiate sin θ, you get cos θ?! Well, then, what happens when you differentiate cos θ? Do you get sin θ? Let's try it and see.

Just as we did for the sine curve, we'll draw a tangent at each point and find the value of its slope – i.e., the ratio "vertical/horizontal".

Here's the result:

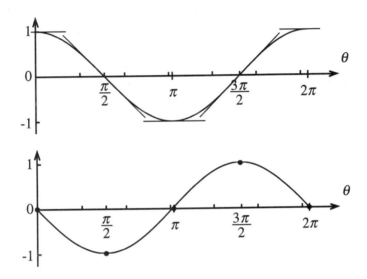

Hmm... This graph certainly looks a lot like the graph of sin θ, but with one significant difference: its highs and lows are reversed. When angle θ is π/2, the value of sin θ is 1. But on this graph, it's -1. When angle θ is 3π/2, the value of sin θ is -1, but here it's 1. In short, the signs of values on this graph are always the opposite of those on the sin θ graph. How should we describe a graph like this? Well, how does "-sin θ" sound?

And there you have it: **differentiate sin θ, and you get cos θ. Differentiate cos θ, and you get -sin θ.** Good enough! We've got our key to the differentiation of sin θ now! Onward, onward....

But hold on a minute. Maybe it would be a good idea to be a little more precise, don't you think? To find the slope of the tangent here, all we did was draw the tangent on a graph and read the slope off of that. But how can we be sure we drew these tangents accurately? Besides, we only found the slope of the tangents at 0, π/2, π, 3π/2, and 2π. For everything in between, we just drew a smooth curve and assumed it was accurate. So on the off-chance that you might want a more detailed look at how this really works, let's find out once and for all whether differentiating sin θ really gives us cos θ, and whether differentiating cos θ really gives us -sin θ.

2. sin $(\theta + \Delta\theta)$ Is Not the Same As sin θ + sin $\Delta\theta$!

Here is the key we picked up in the Differentiation Room:

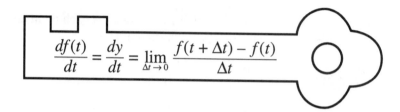

$$\frac{df(t)}{dt} = \frac{dy}{dt} = \lim_{\Delta t \to 0} \frac{f(t + \Delta t) - f(t)}{\Delta t}$$

This formula was for differentiating time t, or, in other words, for finding velocity. But as we learned in Chapter 5, differentiation doesn't have to be about time. We can use it to find the steepness of a hill, the loudness of a sound – any number of things. Right now, we're performing differentiation on angle θ. We want to see how much sin θ increases when we increase angle θ by just a little bit. So we want to replace t in the formula above with θ.

$$\frac{df(\theta)}{d\theta} = \frac{dy}{d\theta} = \lim_{\Delta\theta \to 0} \frac{f(\theta + \Delta\theta) - f(\theta)}{\Delta\theta}$$

Now, given $f(\theta) = \sin \theta$, let's do some calculations.

$$\frac{df(\theta)}{d\theta} = \lim_{\Delta\theta \to 0} \frac{\sin (\theta + \Delta\theta) - \sin \theta}{\Delta\theta}$$

But what comes next? The problem is with this part: <u>sin $(\theta + \Delta\theta)$</u>. If we do what we'd normally do, we get:

$$\sin (\theta + \Delta\theta) = \sin \theta + \sin \Delta\theta$$

But does that really work? Think about it for a moment. Suppose $\theta = 60°$ and $\Delta\theta = 30°$. Then $\theta + \Delta\theta = 90°$. If we place these values on a sine graph, they appear like this:

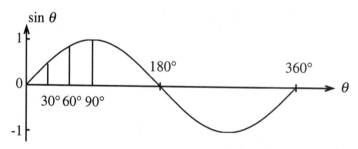

Let's pull these three sine values from the graph and line them up:

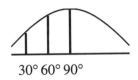

30° 60° 90°

Then we'll add the value of sin 30° to sin 60°:

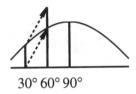

30° 60° 90°

What's this? The sum of sin 30° + sin 60° is greater than the value of sin 90°! That means

$$\sin 30° + \sin 60° \neq \sin (30° + 60°)$$

in other words,

$$\sin \theta + \sin \Delta\theta \neq \sin (\theta + \Delta\theta)$$

Well, that's a problem. Unless we can figure out another way to calculate sin ($\theta + \Delta\theta$), we're stuck. Let's put the differentiation of sin θ aside for a moment and concentrate on resolving this business with sin ($\theta + \Delta\theta$). For simplicity's sake, we'll replace sin ($\theta + \Delta\theta$) with sin ($\alpha + \beta$). (α is pronounced alpha, and β is pronounced beta.) Just bear in mind, we haven't finished differentiating sin θ yet!

3. Expressing sin ($\alpha + \beta$) with Trigonometric Functions of α and β

Think of a circle with a radius of 1. We call this type of circle a "unit circle." Now think of a triangle inside this circle, *COD*, which contains an angle α.

What would the value of sin α be here? The radius of the circle is 1, so:

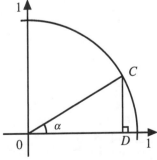

$$\frac{CD}{OC} = \sin \alpha = \frac{CD}{1}$$

In other words,

$$\sin \alpha = CD$$

Likewise, the value of cos α would be:

$$\frac{OD}{OC} = \cos \alpha = \frac{OD}{1}$$

That is,

$$\cos \alpha = OD$$

Now imagine another triangle inside this same circle, *AOE*, which contains an angle β. What is the value of sin β here? Got it? That's right, sin β is the length of segment *AE*. And of course, cos β is the length of segment *OE*.

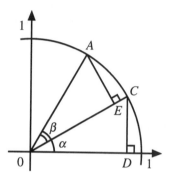

And now, let's consider yet another triangle – *AOB*. The angle *AOB* of this triangle has the value α + β. Taking the same approach we used with the first two triangles, we see that the value of sin (α + β) is the length of segment *AB*.

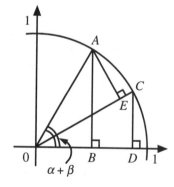

To summarize what we know so far:

$$\sin \alpha = CD$$
$$\cos \alpha = OD$$
$$\sin \beta = AE$$
$$\cos \beta = OE$$
$$\sin (\alpha + \beta) = AB$$

Now we're ready for our next step, which will be to express the value of sin (α + β) – that is, the length of segment *AB* – using the four values sin α, cos α, sin β, and cos β.

First we'll divide segment AB into two parts, *AF* and *FB*.

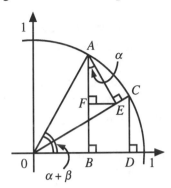

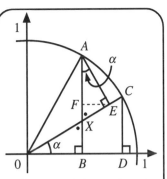

Notice that we've added a new triangle, *AFE*, in which angle *EAF* is α.
Therefore:

$$\frac{AF}{AE} = \cos\alpha$$

which gives us:

$$AF = AE\cos\alpha$$

Remember what the length of *AE* was? That's right, $\sin\beta$. So:

$$AF = \sin\beta\cos\alpha = \cos\alpha\sin\beta$$

> The sum of the angles of a triangle is 180˚.
>   Segments *AB* and *OC* intersect at point *X*, forming triangles *AXE* and *OXB*.
>   These triangles both contain right angles, and their angles *OXB* and *AXE* are opposing angles and therefore equal.
>   Since two of the three angles in both triangles are the same, their remaining angles *XOB* and *EAX* must also be the same – i.e., both are α.

Now let's look at segment *FB*. This should have the same length as segment *EG*.

> When you multiply, you can change the order without affecting the result.

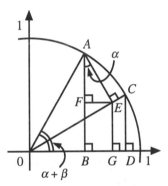

Instead of finding the length of *FB*, we're going to find *EG*, which will be the same thing. Angle *EOG* = α, so:

$$\frac{EG}{OE} = \sin\alpha$$
$$EG = OE\sin\alpha$$

Remember that the length of *OE* is $\cos\beta$. That gives us:

$$EG = \cos\beta\sin\alpha = \sin\alpha\cos\beta$$

And since *EG = FB*,

$$FB = \sin\alpha\cos\beta$$

So now we know what $\sin(\alpha + \beta)$ is.

We already know that sin $(\alpha + \beta) = AB$, and $AB = AF + FB$, so:

$$\sin(\alpha + \beta) = AB = AF + FB$$
$$= \cos\alpha\sin\beta + \sin\alpha\cos\beta$$

Now, what were we doing before we got into this? Ah yes, we were in the midst of trying to differentiate sin θ, weren't we! Well, then, let's pick up where we left off, this time using the formula we've just discovered.

$$\lim_{\Delta\theta \to 0} \frac{\sin(\theta + \Delta\theta) - \sin\theta}{\Delta\theta}$$

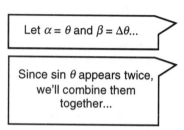

Let $\alpha = \theta$ and $\beta = \Delta\theta$...

Since sin θ appears twice, we'll combine them together...

$$= \lim_{\Delta\theta \to 0} \frac{\cos\theta\sin\Delta\theta + \sin\theta\cos\Delta\theta - \sin\theta}{\Delta\theta}$$

$$= \lim_{\Delta\theta \to 0} \frac{\cos\theta\sin\Delta\theta + \sin\theta(\cos\Delta\theta - 1)}{\Delta\theta}$$

$$= \lim_{\Delta\theta \to 0} \left\{ \frac{\cos\theta\sin\Delta\theta}{\Delta\theta} + \frac{\sin\theta(\cos\Delta\theta - 1)}{\Delta\theta} \right\}$$

First, take a look at this part:

If we bring the $\Delta\theta$ of cos $\Delta\theta$ infinitely close to 0,

$$\cos 0 = 1$$

Then:

$$\frac{\sin\theta(1 - 1)}{\Delta\theta} = \frac{\sin\theta \cdot 0}{\Delta\theta}$$

If we make the denominator $\Delta\theta$ become 0 as well, we get 0/0, which would seem to be the equivalent of 1. But it isn't! One of the rules of math is that you can't divide by 0. So unfortunately 0/0 is of no use, and we can't take our calculations any further in this example.

Now that we've come this far, let's try expressing cos $(\alpha + \beta)$ in the same manner – using the trigonometric functions of α and β.

4. Expressing cos $(\alpha + \beta)$
with Trigonometric Functions of α and β

Taking the same approach we used with sin $(\alpha + \beta)$:

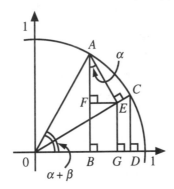

Here cos $(\alpha + \beta)$ is the length of segment OB. We can think of OB as the length of segment OG minus the length of segment BG, so:

$$\cos (\alpha + \beta) = OB = OG - BG$$

And since the length of BG is the same as the length of FE,

$$\cos (\alpha + \beta) = OG - FE$$

We can find OG and FE as follows:

$$OG = OE \cos \alpha = \cos \beta \cos \alpha = \cos \alpha \cos \beta$$
$$FE = AE \sin \alpha = \sin \beta \sin \alpha = \sin \alpha \sin \beta$$

And that means:

$$\cos (\alpha + \beta) = OB = OG - FE$$
$$= \cos \alpha \cos \beta - \sin \alpha \sin \beta$$

So we have now expressed both sin $(\alpha + \beta)$ and cos $(\alpha + \beta)$ using the trigonometric functions of α and β. Having come this far, why don't we try the same trick with sin $(\alpha - \beta)$ and cos $(\alpha - \beta)$.

5. Expressing sin $(\alpha - \beta)$ and cos $(\alpha - \beta)$
with Trigonometric Functions of α and β

For sin $(\alpha + \beta)$ and cos $(\alpha + \beta)$, we simply added angles α and β together. This time, however, we have to subtract β from α. What exactly _is_ sin $(\alpha - \beta)$, anyway?
For example, suppose we have $\alpha = 60°$ and $\beta = 20°$. Then:

$$\sin (60° - 20°) = \sin 40°$$

Simple, wasn't it? But what about $\alpha = 60°$ and $\beta = 120°$? This time we get:

$$\sin (60° - 120°) = \sin (-60°)$$

A positive angle is one measured in the counterclockwise direction, while a negative angle is one measured in the clockwise direction.

Take a moment to look at the diagram on the right. Note that sin 60° and sin (-60°) are the same size; only their signs are different. If you place a minus sign in front of the value of sin 60°, you get the same value as sin (-60°). So:

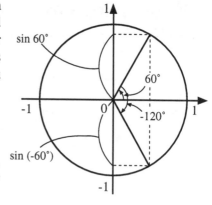

$$\sin(-60°) = -\sin 60°$$

And as for cos 60° and cos (-60°)... What's this? It turns out they're exactly the same:

$$\cos(-60°) = \cos 60°$$

In other words,

$$\sin(-\theta) = -\sin \theta$$
$$\cos(-\theta) = \cos \theta$$

So now we know that sin (α - β) is just sin (α + β) with the sign switched from plus to minus:

$$\sin(\alpha + \beta) = \sin \alpha \cos \beta + \cos \alpha \sin \beta$$
$$\sin(\alpha - \beta) = \sin \alpha \cos(-\beta) + \cos \alpha \sin(-\beta)$$
$$= \sin \alpha \cos \beta - \cos \alpha \sin \beta$$

And if we do the same thing for cos (α - β):

$$\cos(\alpha + \beta) = \cos \alpha \cos \beta - \sin \alpha \sin \beta$$
$$\cos(\alpha - \beta) = \cos \alpha \cos(-\beta) - \sin \alpha \sin(-\beta)$$
$$= \cos \alpha \cos \beta + \sin \alpha \sin \beta$$

Minus × minus = plus

That was easy! But where were we? Still in the middle of differentiating sin θ, right? Meanwhile, however, we've managed to come up with all these formulas. Let's list them:

[A]
$$\sin(\alpha + \beta) = \sin \alpha \cos \beta + \cos \alpha \sin \beta \cdots ①$$
$$\cos(\alpha + \beta) = \cos \alpha \cos \beta - \sin \alpha \sin \beta \cdots ②$$
$$\sin(\alpha - \beta) = \sin \alpha \cos \beta - \cos \alpha \sin \beta \cdots ③$$
$$\cos(\alpha - \beta) = \cos \alpha \cos \beta + \sin \alpha \sin \beta \cdots ④$$

Four new formulas in all... but to be honest, we can't use any of them in their present form to differentiate sin θ. Let's examine them more closely, though. Maybe we'll come up with some clues on to how to use them.

6. sin α cos β

A closer look at these four formulas reveals that sin α cos β appears twice – in formulas ① and ③. Maybe we can produce a formula for this part alone! Let's try adding formulas ① and ③ together:

$$\sin (\alpha + \beta) = \sin \alpha \cos \beta + \cos \alpha \sin \beta$$
$$\underline{+) \ \sin (\alpha - \beta) = \sin \alpha \cos \beta - \cos \alpha \sin \beta}$$
$$\sin (\alpha + \beta) + \sin (\alpha - \beta) = 2 \sin \alpha \cos \beta$$

$$2 \sin \alpha \cos \beta = \sin (\alpha + \beta) + \sin (\alpha - \beta)$$

$$\sin \alpha \cos \beta = \frac{1}{2}\Big\{ \sin (\alpha + \beta) + \sin (\alpha - \beta) \Big\}$$

That was pretty easy, and it seemed to do the trick all the same. Why don't you try the same method to find formulas for cos α sin β, cos α cos β, and sin α sin β? Go ahead!

- cos α sin β   (hint: ① – ③)

- cos α cos β   (hint: ② + ④)

- sin α sin β   (hint: ② – ④)

¡Ánimo, ánimo!

Here are the answers:

[B]

$$\sin \alpha \cos \beta = \ \frac{1}{2}\Big\{ \sin (\alpha + \beta) + \sin (\alpha - \beta) \Big\}$$

$$\cos \alpha \sin \beta = \ \frac{1}{2}\Big\{ \sin (\alpha + \beta) - \sin (\alpha - \beta) \Big\}$$

$$\cos \alpha \cos \beta = \ \frac{1}{2}\Big\{ \cos (\alpha + \beta) + \cos (\alpha - \beta) \Big\}$$

$$\sin \alpha \sin \beta = -\frac{1}{2}\Big\{ \cos (\alpha + \beta) - \cos (\alpha - \beta) \Big\}$$

It would be nice if we could apply these formulas directly to the differentiation of sin θ. Unfortunately, it's still too early for that.

But what's this? Take another look at our list of answers. One of them is **sin (α + β) - sin (α - β)**. The differentiation of sin θ included the subtraction of one sine from another, right?

7. $\sin A - \sin B$

Let's simplify $\sin(\alpha + \beta) - \sin(\alpha - \beta)$ to read $\sin A - \sin B$. That is,

$$\alpha + \beta = A, \text{ and } \alpha - \beta = B$$

Substitute these in the second formula of set above, and we get:

$$\cos \alpha \sin \beta = \frac{1}{2}\{\sin A - \sin B\}$$

Now let's use A and B to express α and β themselves:

$$\begin{array}{ll}
\alpha + \beta = A & \alpha + \beta = A \\
+)\ \alpha - \beta = B & -)\ \alpha - \beta = B \\
\hline
2\alpha\ \ = A + B & 2\beta = A - B \\
\alpha = \dfrac{A+B}{2} & \beta = \dfrac{A-B}{2}
\end{array}$$

If we insert $\alpha = (A + B)/2$ and $\beta = (A - B)/2$ into our formula, we get:

$$\cos \frac{A+B}{2} \sin \frac{A-B}{2} = \frac{1}{2}\{\sin A - \sin B\}$$

$$\boxed{\sin A - \sin B = 2 \cos \frac{A+B}{2} \sin \frac{A-B}{2}}$$

And there you have it – an effective way to subtract one sine value from another. Now try the same thing for $\sin A + \sin B$, $\cos A + \cos B$, and $\cos A - \cos B$, using the formulas in set :

- $\sin A + \sin B$
- $\cos A + \cos B$
- $\cos A - \cos B$

The answers are:

$$\sin A + \sin B = 2 \sin \frac{A+B}{2} \cos \frac{A-B}{2}$$

$$\sin A - \sin B = 2 \cos \frac{A+B}{2} \sin \frac{A-B}{2}$$

[C]

$$\cos A + \cos B = 2 \cos \frac{A+B}{2} \cos \frac{A-B}{2}$$

$$\cos A - \cos B = -2 \sin \frac{A+B}{2} \sin \frac{A-B}{2}$$

So far we have come up with three sets of four formulas each. All of the formulas in sets [A], [B], and [C] are called "trigonometric identities." These constitute our first key of the day:

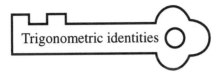

Trigonometric identities

Now that we finally have a key in hand, let us return immediately to the business of differentiating sin θ and see what secrets we can unlock.

8. Back to sin θ Differentiation

$$\frac{d}{d\theta}\sin\theta = \lim_{\Delta\theta\to 0}\frac{\sin(\theta+\Delta\theta)-\sin\theta}{\Delta\theta}$$

$$= \lim_{\Delta\theta\to 0}\frac{2\cos\frac{\theta+\Delta\theta+\theta}{2}\sin\frac{\theta+\Delta\theta-\theta}{2}}{\Delta\theta}$$

$$= \lim_{\Delta\theta\to 0}\left\{\frac{2}{\Delta\theta}\cos\frac{2\theta+\Delta\theta}{2}\sin\frac{\Delta\theta}{2}\right\}$$

$$= \lim_{\Delta\theta\to 0}\left\{\frac{2}{\Delta\theta}\cos(\theta+\frac{\Delta\theta}{2})\sin\frac{\Delta\theta}{2}\right\}$$

$$= \lim_{\Delta\theta\to 0}\left\{\cos(\theta+\frac{\Delta\theta}{2})\frac{\sin\frac{\Delta\theta}{2}}{\frac{\Delta\theta}{2}}\right\}$$

> Use the formula we just discovered!
> Let $\theta+\Delta\theta = A$ and $\theta = B$.
>
> $\sin A - \sin B =$
> $2\cos\frac{A+B}{2}\sin\frac{A-B}{2}$

> Why does it turn out like this? Because, for example,
>
> $$3\times\frac{2}{5}=\frac{6}{5}$$
>
> is the same as
>
> $$\frac{3}{\frac{5}{2}}=\frac{3}{\frac{5}{2}}\times\frac{2}{2}$$
>
> $$=\frac{6}{5}$$

Why did we come up with this strange format? Because it allows us to use a very convenient trick. Take a look at this part:

$$\frac{\sin\frac{\Delta\theta}{2}}{\frac{\Delta\theta}{2}}$$

If we take Δθ/2 to be θ, and bring θ infinitely close to 0, sinθ/θ becomes 1. However, this can only happen when θ is measured in radians. We learned a little about radians in Chapter 1, but this might be a good time to review the subject.

9. Radians

Think of a circle with radius r from which a piece has been cut out, like a slice of pizza.

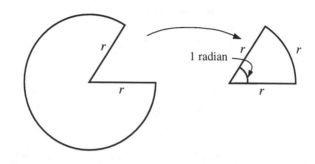

When the curved edge (i.e., the arc) of this pizza slice is the same length as the radius (r), the angle θ of the slice is defined as one radian. Now, how many radians are in the entire 360° of the circle?

The formula for finding the circumference of a circle is:

$$\text{circumference} = \text{diameter} \times 3.14 = 2\pi r$$

Actually, the number π goes on infinitely: 3.141592 . . . . . So we just call it "pi".

The length of the arc of 1 radian is r. So if we divide the circumference by r, we'll know how many radians there are in 360°:

$$2\pi r \div r = 2\pi \text{ (radians)}$$

And that's our second key for the day: 360° is 2π radians.

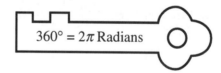

Let's pursue our study of radians using a unit circle of radius 1.

Since the radius of the circle is 1, when the arc of an angle is of length 1, the angle will be 1 radian.

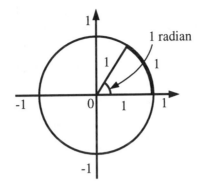

What if there's an arc of length 2?

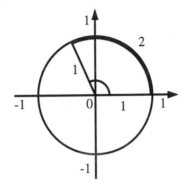

That's right, the angle is 2 radians!

And an arc of length 0.5?

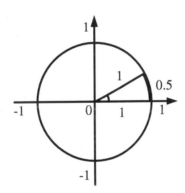

You guessed it: 0.5 radian.

Aha! When the radius is 1, the length of an arc and the value of its angle will always be the same – as long as the angle is measured in radians. How convenient!

Next, let's consider a pizza slice of radius 1 and an arc of length θ. That means the angle will be θ too. Now think about the sine of angle θ, or sin θ.

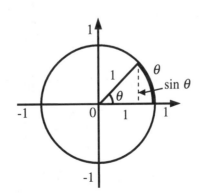

Since the radius is 1, the value of sin θ will be the length of the vertical dotted segment shown above.

Let's compare the length θ of the arc and the length of sin θ. What relationship can we find between these two values?

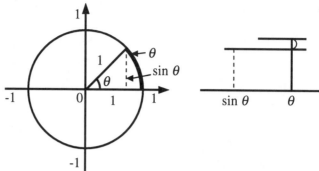

When θ is large, θ and sin θ are quite different in size, right? What happens when θ is smaller?

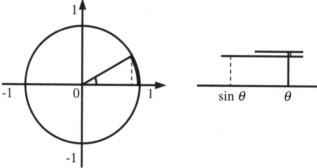

It appears that as θ gets smaller, the difference between θ and sin θ decreases too.

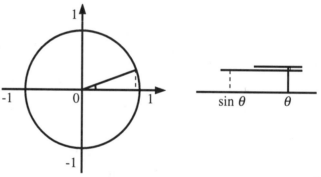

And if we bring the value of θ infinitely close to 0...

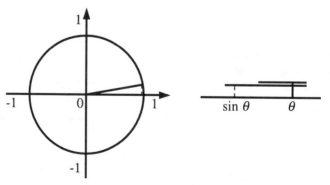

it looks as if the values of θ and sin θ may become identical! In other words,

$$\lim_{\theta \to 0} \sin \theta = \theta$$

And there we have our third key:

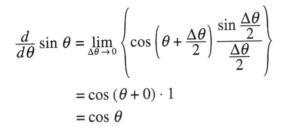

$$\lim_{\theta \to 0} \frac{\sin \theta}{\theta} = 1$$

Once again, let us return to our main business of the day, the differentiation of sin θ.

10. sin θ Differentiation. Take Three.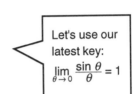

$$\frac{d}{d\theta} \sin \theta = \lim_{\Delta\theta \to 0} \left\{ \cos\left(\theta + \frac{\Delta\theta}{2}\right) \frac{\sin \frac{\Delta\theta}{2}}{\frac{\Delta\theta}{2}} \right\}$$

$$= \cos(\theta + 0) \cdot 1$$

$$= \cos \theta$$

> Let's use our latest key:
> $$\lim_{\theta \to 0} \frac{\sin \theta}{\theta} = 1$$

We've got it! At last, we've found the result of differentiating sin θ. It's cos θ! It's been a long road, but our efforts have paid off. We now have our most important key of the day:

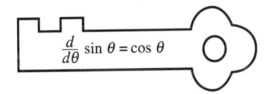

$$\frac{d}{d\theta} \sin \theta = \cos \theta$$

When we performed differentiation on sin θ, it gave us cos θ. What happens if we differentiate cos θ? When we first tried this with graphs at the beginning of this chapter, we got what appeared to be -sin θ. You should be able to perform the necessary calculations quickly now, using the keys we've picked up along the way. Come on, give it a try!

> Use this formula:
> $$\cos A - \cos B$$
> $$= -2 \sin \frac{A+B}{2} \sin \frac{A-B}{2}$$

We've now succeeded in differentiating sin θ. Unfortunately, Fourier analysis doesn't make much use of sin θ all by itself. But it does make a lot of use of the sine and cosine when θ changes over time, that is, when

$$\theta = n\omega t.$$

Let's see what happens when we differentiate the sine and cosine in such cases; that is, when:

$$f(t) = \sin n\omega t$$
$$f(t) = \cos n\omega t$$

Will the differentiation of sin nωt really give us cos nωt? We shall see.

11. Differentiation of sin $n\omega t$

$$\frac{d}{dt}\sin n\omega t = \lim_{\Delta t \to 0} \frac{\sin(n\omega t + n\omega\Delta t) - \sin n\omega t}{\Delta t}$$

Use that trigonometric identity!
$$\sin A - \sin B = 2\cos\frac{A+B}{2}\sin\frac{A-B}{2}$$

$$= \lim_{\Delta t \to 0} \frac{2\cos\dfrac{n\omega t + n\omega\Delta t + n\omega t}{2}\sin\dfrac{n\omega t + n\omega\Delta t - n\omega t}{2}}{\Delta t}$$

$$= \lim_{\Delta t \to 0}\left\{\frac{2}{\Delta t}\cos\frac{2n\omega t + n\omega\Delta t}{2}\sin\frac{n\omega\Delta t}{2}\right\}$$

$$= \lim_{\Delta t \to 0}\left\{\frac{2}{\Delta t}\cos\left(n\omega t + \frac{n\omega\Delta t}{2}\right)\sin\frac{n\omega\Delta t}{2}\right\}$$

$$= \lim_{\Delta t \to 0}\left\{\cos\left(n\omega t + \frac{n\omega\Delta t}{2}\right)\frac{\sin\dfrac{n\omega\Delta t}{2}}{\dfrac{\Delta t}{2}}\right\}$$

This is where we want to use our third key:

$$\lim_{\theta \to 0}\frac{\sin\theta}{\theta} = 1$$

But look closely at the section in the dotted box:

The denominator is $\Delta t/2$, but the numerator reads $(n\omega\Delta t)/2$! If $\theta = \Delta t/2$, the sine in the numerator is not $\sin\theta$. So what we'll do is try multiplying this by $(n\omega)/(n\omega)$. Since $(n\omega)/(n\omega) = 1$, it doesn't change anything in the equation.

Now back to where we were...

$$= \lim_{\Delta t \to 0}\left\{\cos\left(n\omega t + \frac{n\omega\Delta t}{2}\right)\frac{\sin\dfrac{n\omega\Delta t}{2}}{\dfrac{\Delta t}{2}}\cdot\frac{n\omega}{n\omega}\right\}$$

$$= \lim_{\Delta t \to 0}\left\{\cos\left(n\omega t + \frac{n\omega\Delta t}{2}\right)\frac{(\sin\dfrac{n\omega\Delta t}{2})n\omega}{\dfrac{\Delta t}{2}n\omega}\right\}$$

Move the coefficient up front!

$$= \lim_{\Delta t \to 0}\left\{n\omega\cdot\cos\left(n\omega t + \frac{n\omega\Delta t}{2}\right)\frac{\sin\dfrac{n\omega\Delta t}{2}}{\dfrac{n\omega\Delta t}{2}}\right\}$$

Here, we let
$$\theta = \frac{n\omega\Delta t}{2}$$
Then we can use
$$\lim_{\theta \to 0}\frac{\sin\theta}{\theta} = 1$$

$$= n\omega\cos(n\omega t + 0)\cdot 1$$

$$= n\omega\cos n\omega t$$

How's that? We expected to get cos $n\omega t$ for our result, but instead we got $n\omega$ cos $n\omega t$. Can that be right? Let's see what it looks like on a graph; maybe that will help make sense of it. Let's assume $n\omega = 2$.

$$\frac{d}{dt} \sin 2t = 2 \cos 2t$$

First, we'll draw the wave sin $2t$, find the slope of the tangents at certain points, and construct a graph of these values. Since we can't possibly do this for all points on the wave, we'll confine ourselves to a few points such as zero and the peaks and valleys of the wave.

Wave of sin2t:

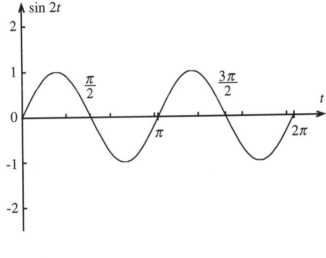

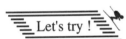 Let's try !

Now try making a graph of the values you found for the slope of the tangent at these points:

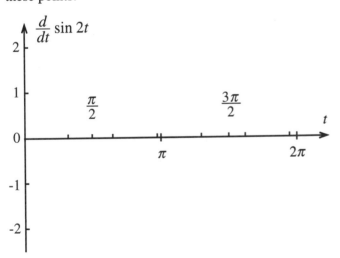

The answer is

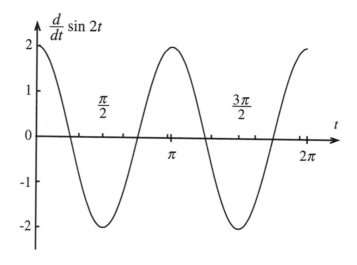

Well? Did you wind up with the wave 2 cos 2*t*? This will be the BIGGEST key we've picked up all day:

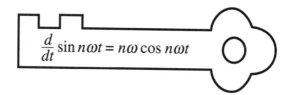

$$\frac{d}{dt} \sin n\omega t = n\omega \cos n\omega t$$

Hey, you've come a long way! Now that you've differentiated sin *n*ω*t*, you might find it interesting to differentiate cos *n*ω*t* too.

But that's enough for one day. Have you got all your keys in hand? Better check:

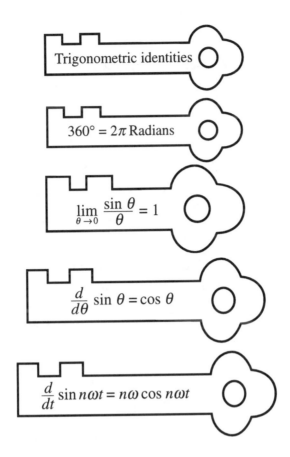

Trigonometric identities

$360° = 2\pi$ Radians

$\lim\limits_{\theta \to 0} \dfrac{\sin \theta}{\theta} = 1$

$\dfrac{d}{d\theta} \sin \theta = \cos \theta$

$\dfrac{d}{dt} \sin n\omega t = n\omega \cos n\omega t$

All we were planning to do was differentiate sin θ, and look at what we found! With these five keys, we shouldn't have too much to worry about. Now it's on to the Integration Room, where we will search for the key to finding the "closest approximation of the area." See you there!

A short cut to Differentiation

Here we'll take a look at a more convenient way to perform differentiation.

You may recall that in Chapter 5, we differentiated $f(t) = 4.9t^2$.

The result was $\frac{df(t)}{dt} = 9.8t$.

Now take a closer look at the values we have for $f(t)$ and $\frac{df(t)}{dt}$ here.

Notice that if you multiply 4.9 by the exponent of t, which is 2, you get 9.8. This is not a coincidence!

Let's try it with a different example. If we differentiate $f(t) = 3t^2$, we get $\frac{df(t)}{dt} = 2 \times 3t = 6t$.

Here is how we would arrive at this result using the differentiation method we learned in Chapter 5:

$$f(t + \Delta t) - f(t) = 3(t + \Delta t)^2 - 3t^2$$
$$= 3(t^2 + 2t\Delta t + \Delta t^2) - 3t^2$$
$$= 6t\Delta t + 3\Delta t^2$$

Next we divide by Δt and find the rate of change during Δt:

$$\frac{f(t + \Delta t) - f(t)}{\Delta t} = \frac{6t \cdot \Delta t + 3\Delta t^2}{\Delta t} = 6t + 3\Delta t$$

Finally, we let Δt approach 0:

$$\lim_{\Delta t \to 0} 6t + \underset{\downarrow}{3\Delta t} = 6t$$
$$0$$

And our result is indeed $6t$.

This suggests that when we differentiate $f(t) = at^n$, the result will be $\frac{df(t)}{dt} = ant^{n-1}$.

Let's see for ourselves whether the result of differentiating $f(t) = at^n$ is always $\frac{df(t)}{dt} = ant^{n-1}$.

We'll use the differentiation method with which we are already familiar:

$$f(t + \Delta t) - f(t) = a(t + \Delta t)^n - at^n$$

But now we're confronted with $(t + \Delta t)^n$. How do we deal with that???

Well, we know that

$$(a + b)^2 = a^2 + 2ab + b^2.$$

What about $(a + b)^3$? That would be

$$a^3 + 3a^2b + 3ab^2 + b^3.$$

We can also write it as

$$(a + b)(a + b)(a + b) = \ldots \ldots$$

In other words, $(a + b)$ multiplied three times yields the following:

one term of "a" multiplied three times (a^3);
one term of "b" multiplied three times (b^3);
three terms of "a" multiplied twice and "b" multiplied once ($3a^2b$);
and three terms of "a" multiplied once and "b" multiplied twice ($3ab^2$).

If we try the same thing with $a(t + \Delta t)^n$, we get:

$$a\left\{\underbrace{(t + \Delta t)(t + \Delta t)(t + \Delta t) \cdot \cdots \cdot (t + \Delta t)}_{n \text{ times}}\right\}$$

Here, $(t + \Delta t)$ is multiplied n times.

So that should yield one term consisting of t^n.
The next term consists of Δt multiplied once and t multiplied n-1 times ($t^{n-1}\Delta t$), and this term occurs n times (once for each time Δt can be selected) – in other words, $nt^{n-1}\Delta t$.
Continuing this process for each term, we get:

$$a\left\{t^n + nt^{n-1}\Delta t + \bigcirc t^{n-2}(\Delta t)^2 + \cdots + (\Delta t)^n\right\}$$

Now, going back to $f(t + \Delta t) - f(t)$ and substituting our new expression, we get:

$$f(t + \Delta t) - f(t)$$
$$= a(t + \Delta t)^n - at^n$$
$$= a\left\{t^n + nt^{n-1}\Delta t + \bigcirc t^{n-2}(\Delta t)^2 + \cdots + (\Delta t)^n\right\} - at^n$$
$$= ant^{n-1}\Delta t + a\bigcirc t^{n-2}(\Delta t)^2 \cdots + a(\Delta t)^n$$

Here the term t^n is cancelled out.
Next we divide by Δt:

$$\frac{f(t + \Delta t) - f(t)}{\Delta t}$$
$$= ant^{n-1} + \bigcirc t^{n-2}\Delta t + \cdots + a(\Delta t)^{n-1}$$

Now, as Δt approaches 0, all terms multiplied by Δt become 0, and all that we're left with is:

$$\lim_{\Delta t \to 0} \frac{f(t + \Delta t) - f(t)}{\Delta t} = a \cdot nt^{n-1}$$

In other words, if we differentiate $f(t) = at^n$, the result is indeed $\frac{df(t)}{dt} = a \cdot nt^{n-1}$.

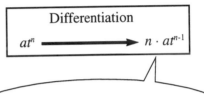

Multiply everything by the exponent "n", and subtract 1 from exponent n.

For example,

$$f(t) = t^3 \to \frac{df(t)}{dt} = 3 \cdot t^{3-1} = 3t^2$$

$$f(x) = \frac{1}{3}x^3 \to \frac{df(x)}{dx} = 3 \cdot \frac{1}{3}x^{3-1} = x^2$$

What a time-saver! Now that you understand this method, you can use it as much as you like!

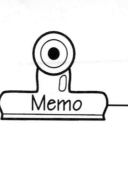

Memo

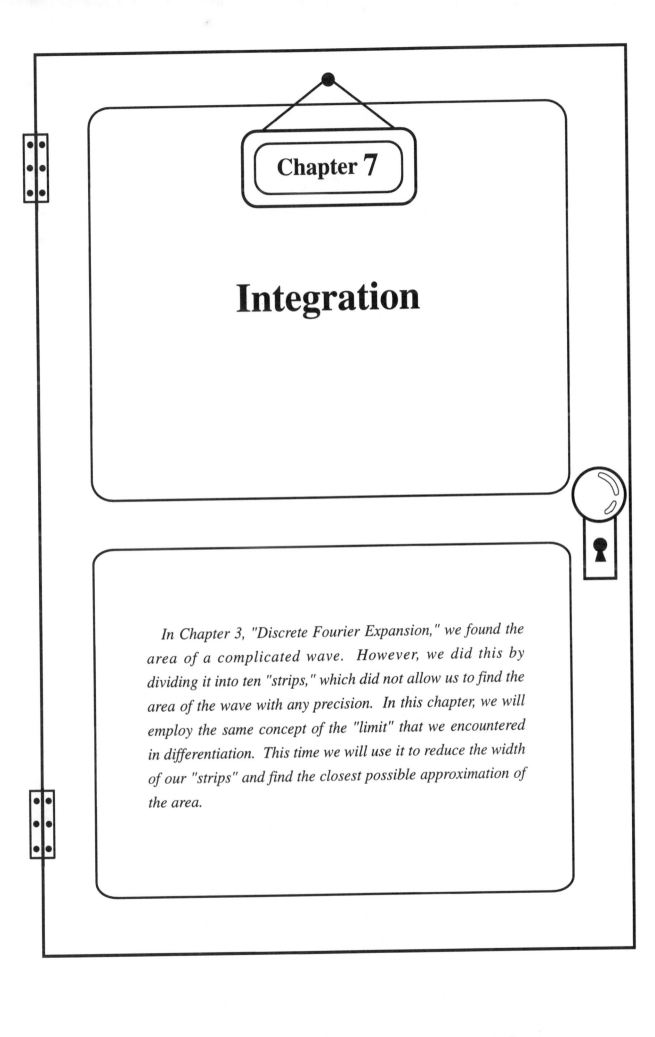

Chapter 7

Integration

In Chapter 3, "Discrete Fourier Expansion," we found the area of a complicated wave. However, we did this by dividing it into ten "strips," which did not allow us to find the area of the wave with any precision. In this chapter, we will employ the same concept of the "limit" that we encountered in differentiation. This time we will use it to reduce the width of our "strips" and find the closest possible approximation of the area.

Introduction

Since moving into the second part of this book, we've examined how a ball falls to the ground, figured out the slopes of sine and cosine waves... in short, our Fourier adventure has taken us in many different directions and some of you may be feeling a little confused. After all, our original goal was simply to solve the riddle of how human beings understand speech. That was our sole reason for getting involved with Fourier analysis to begin with. But don't fret – once you've read this chapter on integration, it will all fall into place. You'll realize that nothing we've done so far was a waste of time – indeed, that our experiences have been extremely valuable. Integration ties it all together; this is what we've been aiming toward all along.

1. What is Integration?

None other than this:

> Integration = finding the closest approximation of an area

Why, you may ask, do we want to find the area? Because we want to study the human voice, that's why. When the ear hears a voice, the sound quickly fades away, leaving nothing behind. But with a machine called the FFT analyzer, we can convert this sound into a waveform and view it. Fourier analysis is a method of analyzing these sound waves. Having already studied Fourier series and Fourier coefficients, you're probably feeling pretty good. You may even be telling yourself there can't be too many more surprises waiting down the road in our study of waves. But there is at least one – a very big one, in fact:

> We haven't yet mastered Fourier coefficients.

The Fourier series showed us that a complicated wave, if it repeats itself, consists of the sum of simple waves. Fourier coefficients showed us what types of waves make up that sum, and in what quantity. It was easy to determine the type of each wave. To find the speed (i.e., frequency) of the fundamental wave, all we had to do was measure the time of the longest repeating pattern in the complicated wave.

No matter how complicated a wave is, as long as it repeats, we know it consists entirely of sine and cosine waves that oscillate at speeds that are integral multiples (1 ×, 2 ×, 3 × ...) of the speed of the fundamental wave. So all we needed to do was measure the speed of the fundamental wave.

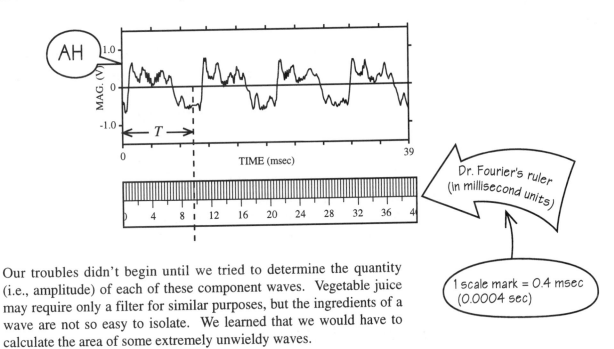

Our troubles didn't begin until we tried to determine the quantity (i.e., amplitude) of each of these component waves. Vegetable juice may require only a filter for similar purposes, but the ingredients of a wave are not so easy to isolate. We learned that we would have to calculate the area of some extremely unwieldy waves.

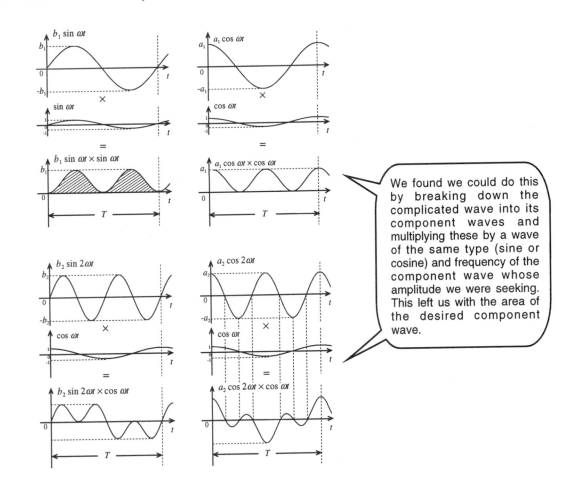

We found we could do this by breaking down the complicated wave into its component waves and multiplying these by a wave of the same type (sine or cosine) and frequency of the component wave whose amplitude we were seeking. This left us with the area of the desired component wave.

To determine the quantity (amplitude) of each sine and cosine wave in the complicated wave, we depended on scissors and glue, cutting out pieces of the wave and fitting them together to figure out the area. But if we're going to be serious about our study of the voice, we need a more precise method of finding the area than that.

$$\left(\begin{array}{c} \textbf{Finding the closest} \\ \textbf{approximation of the area} \end{array} \right) = \left(\begin{array}{c} \textbf{Finding the precise quantity} \\ \textbf{of each simple wave} \end{array} \right)$$

$$= \left(\begin{array}{c} \textbf{Getting a precise} \\ \textbf{look at the voice} \end{array} \right)$$

Scissors and glue are obviously not the answer. If you think you're skilled enough, you're welcome to keep using them. But it won't be easy cutting out the very squiggly waves we'll be encountering from now on, never mind trying to get a precise figure for their area that way. Surely there must be an easier way to determine the area of complicated waves.

2. How to Find Squiggly Areas

Is there really a way to calculate the area of an extremely squiggly wave?

Triangles...Circles...

What if we try fitting different shapes under the curve?
Sound familiar? Go back and look at Chapter 3, "Discrete Fourier Expansion."

That's right!

> We use strips to find the area.

The area of a strip is simple to find: height × width. That's all we need to know. Whatever shape the wave takes, as long as we use rectangular strips, we can get a reasonably accurate approximation of its area.

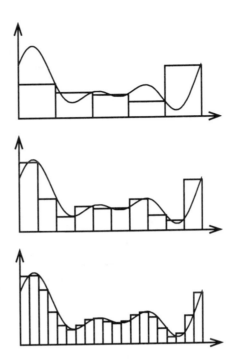

If the strips are too thick, of course, they can hardly be expected to provide us with anything resembling the "closest approximation of the area." But what happens when we make the strips narrower? The narrower the strips are, the smoother their pattern gets, until they actually begin to mimic the curve of the waveform. Then all we have to do is find the area of each of these strips and add them together to get the total area. A close approximation doesn't seem so far – fetched anymore for even the squiggliest of areas, does it? The use of strips is a powerful weapon indeed.

And that is precisely what integration is:

The use of strips to find the closest approximation of an area

---

3. Now for Some Real Integration

If all we have to do is use strips, this "closest approximation of area" doesn't sound so hard to calculate after all. Ready to give it a try? Well, how about finding the area of... this!!

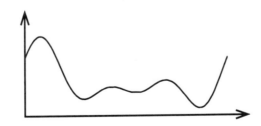

Whoa – that's one weird wave, and dividing its area into strips is going to be no picnic. Never mind, then, we'll start with something easier. How about the graph we drew for $v = 9.8t$ in Chapter 5 ?

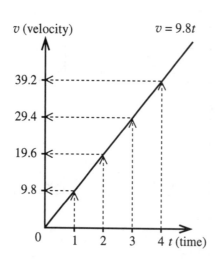

$v = 9.8t$

This formula expresses the relationship between time and the speed at which a ball falls. On the graph of this relationship, the vertical axis is speed or velocity (v), and the horizontal axis is time (t). As time passes, the ball falls faster and faster because the earth is steadily pulling on it. Finding the closest approximation of the area of this graph should be easy, so let's use it as our introduction to the wonderful world of integration.

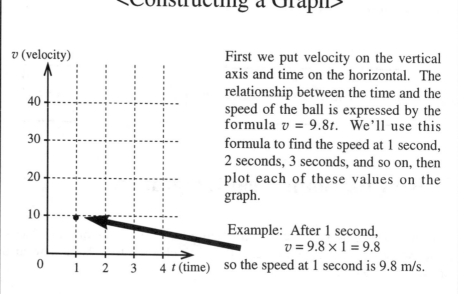

\<Constructing a Graph\>

First we put velocity on the vertical axis and time on the horizontal. The relationship between the time and the speed of the ball is expressed by the formula $v = 9.8t$. We'll use this formula to find the speed at 1 second, 2 seconds, 3 seconds, and so on, then plot each of these values on the graph.

Example: After 1 second,
$$v = 9.8 \times 1 = 9.8$$
so the speed at 1 second is 9.8 m/s.

Now let's find the closest approximation of the area under the graph from 0 to 4 seconds – i.e., the dotted space in the graph on the next page: ⬚
This ⬚ is a triangle, so:

$$\text{Area of triangle} = \frac{\text{base} \times \text{height}}{2}$$

We can use the formula above. For this particular triangle,

base = 4

height = velocity after 4 seconds

$= 9.8 \times 4$

$= 39.2$

Therefore,
the closest approximation of the area of

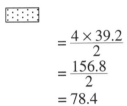

$$= \frac{4 \times 39.2}{2}$$

$$= \frac{156.8}{2}$$

$$= 78.4$$

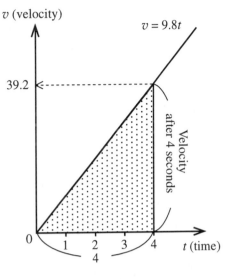

Closest approximation of area of ⬚ = 78.4

So the closest approximation of the area of ⬚ is 78.4. Does that mean 78.4 is the result of integrating ⬚?

NO – because we didn't follow the rules of integration!

Integration means using strips to find the closest approximation of an area. The strips are essential to the process, because they make it possible to find any area, no matter what its shape. Strips are what allow us to find the area of a complicated wave.

But can we really find the area of a triangle using rectangular strips?

4. Finding the Area By the Rules

This time we'll play by the rules and use strips to perform integration. We'll try slicing the area up into thin strips just as we did in Chapter 3 ("Discrete Fourier Expansion").

4. 1 Finding the Area with 4 Strips of Width 1

Area of strip = height × width

First, let's find the area of each of these strips. Then all we need to do is add up the areas of the four strips.

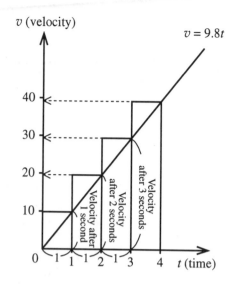

The width of every strip is the same – 1 – but their height varies with time. Since the vertical axis is velocity ($v = 9.8t$),

Height of strip 1
= velocity after 1 second
Height of strip 2
= velocity after 2 seconds

And so on. It's a tiresome process, but you'll have to calculate this value for each strip, one at a time.

	Height	Width	Area
Strip 1 →	9.8	1	9.8
Strip 2 →	19.6	1	19.6
Strip 3 →	29.4	1	29.4
Strip 4 →	39.2	1	39.2
Area of all four strips →	Total strip area		98.0

It helps to construct a table like this one.

For example, to find the area of strip 1,

width = 1
height = velocity after 1 second
= 9.8 × 1 = 9.8

So

the area of strip 1
= 9.8 × 1
= 9.8

Remember,

Closest approximation of area = 78.4

Compare this with the results we just got:

Width	Number of strips	Total strip area
1	4	98.0

What's this? Quite a difference, isn't there! One look at the graph tells us why: the strips are too wide. We'll have to make them narrower. Let's try making them exactly half as wide.

4. 2 Finding the Area with 8 Strips of Width 0.5

Our formula for finding the area is the same one we used for width 1, of course.
However, you'll have to pay close attention to the height of each strip.

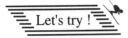 **Let's try !** Try filling in the
table yourself.

☞ see 'Answer Page'

Height	Width	Area
	0.5	
	0.5	
	0.5	
	0.5	
24.5	0.5	12.25
	0.5	
	0.5	
	0.5	
Total strip area		88.2

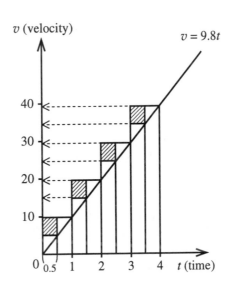

Did your total area come to precisely 88.2?

To find the area of strip 5,

width = 0.5
height = velocity after
2.5 seconds
= 9.8×2.5
= 24.5

So

the area of strip 5
= 24.5×0.5
= 12.25

Now compare your result to this:

Closest approximation of area = 78.4

Width	Number of strips	Total strip area
1	4	98.0
0.5	8	88.2

Look, we're
getting closer!

When we narrowed the strips down, we eliminated this part ▨ of the
surplus we had when the strips were wider. We're definitely getting closer to
the actual area. If we make the strips even narrower, we should get even closer.
Let's give it another try.

4. 3 Finding the Area with 16 Strips of Width 0.25

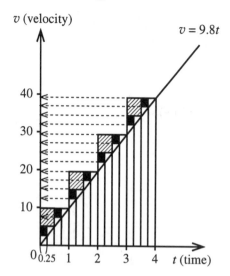

v (velocity)

$v = 9.8t$

40

30

20

10

0 0.25 1 2 3 4 t (time)

Let's try !

Height	Width	Area
	0.25	
Total strip area		

So now, in addition to this part ▨ , we've also eliminated this part ▮ of the surplus we had when the strips had a width of 0.5.

Unfortunately, the more strips there are, the more table there is for you to fill in.

☞ see 'Answer Page'

You'll find that a pocket calculator comes in handy. Thank goodness for modern technology!

All done? How much closer did you get?

Closest approximation of area = 78.4

Width	Number of strips	Total strip area
1	4	98.0
0.5	8	88.2
0.25	16	

Fill in the answer yourself (you'll find it at the bottom of the page).

The narrower, the better. As the strips get narrower, the jagged, stair – like triangle we began with gradually smooths out, and the more closely it resembles the figure we're actually looking for.

Answer: 83.3

So shall we continue to narrow them down? There seems to be no limit to how far we can go, but that's just the problem. How far <u>do</u> we go? It's clear that the further we reduce the width of the strips, the closer we get to the "closest approximation" of the area. Why don't we simply call this width "Δt" so we can change its value as much as we please?

$$\Delta t = \text{short time interval}$$

The "delta" (Δ) mark here indicates "small." In the graphs above, the horizontal axis represented time. So Δt, which is a short period of time on that axis, represents a short width of strip as well. In our effort to find the area, we can make this width as narrow as we like – 0.1, 0.01, you name it. However:

If we make the width **0.1**, we get **40** strips.
If we make the width **0.01**, we get **400** strips.

Obviously, finding the area of every one of these strips and adding them all together would be an absurdly time – consuming task. That's where Δt comes in handy. As a symbol representing "short width," Δt can be 0.1, or 0.01, or any width we want. At first, the use of an abstract symbol instead of a number may seem to make things even more complicated than they already are. But just think of Δt as another number, like 1 or 0.5. It really functions exactly like any other number.

Now then, given a certain width Δt, how many strips do we actually get? So far, we've seen the following relationship between the width and the number of strips:

When the width is **1**, the number of strips is **4**.
When the width is **0.5**, the number of strips is **8**.
When the width is **0.25**, the number of strips is **16**.

So the relationship is always "width $\times$ no. of strips = 4."

We can also say that:

$$\Delta t \times \frac{4}{\Delta t} = 4$$

Therefore, if the width is Δt, the number of strips is $\frac{4}{\Delta t}$.

4. 4 Finding the Area with 4/Δt Strips of Width Δt

First, we need to know how to find the height of a strip:

Height of strip 1 = velocity after Δt seconds = $9.8 \cdot \Delta t$
Height of strip 2 = velocity after $(\Delta t + \Delta t = 2\Delta t)$ seconds = $9.8 \cdot 2\Delta t$
Height of strip 3 = velocity after $(2\Delta t + \Delta t = 3\Delta t)$ seconds = $9.8 \cdot 3\Delta t$

That means the height of the last strip would be:

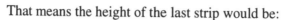

$$\text{Height of strip} \frac{4}{\Delta t} = \text{velocity after } \frac{4}{\Delta t} \cdot \Delta t \text{ seconds}$$
$$= 9.8 \cdot \frac{4}{\Delta t}\Delta t$$

We can use this formula to find the area of each strip.

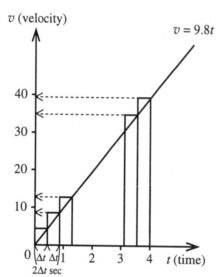

Height	Width	Area
$9.8 \cdot \Delta t$	Δt	$9.8 \cdot (\Delta t)^2$
$9.8 \cdot 2\Delta t$	Δt	$9.8 \cdot 2(\Delta t)^2$
$9.8 \cdot 3\Delta t$	Δt	$9.8 \cdot 3(\Delta t)^2$
$\sim\sim\sim$		$\sim\sim\sim$
$9.8 \cdot \frac{4}{\Delta t}\Delta t$	Δt	$9.8 \cdot \frac{4}{\Delta t}(\Delta t)^2$
Total strip area		

Now let's add up the areas of all the strips.

Given width Δt,

$$\boxed{\begin{array}{c}\text{Total area}\\\text{of strips}\end{array}} = \left\{9.8 \cdot (\Delta t)^2\right\} + \left\{9.8 \cdot 2(\Delta t)^2\right\} + \left\{9.8 \cdot 3(\Delta t)^2\right\} + \cdots + \left\{9.8 \cdot \frac{4}{\Delta t}(\Delta t)^2\right\}$$

That's one pretty formula! Look closely. The number in front of Δt^2 increases by an increment of 1 with each term: 1, 2, 3, ... **4/Δt**. Otherwise, the terms are identical, and they are added up in the order of increasing increments.

$(\Delta t)^2 = 1(\Delta t)^2$, of course.

☞ see p. 60

Could it be? Yes, it's our old friend Σ !

Remember how convenient it was to use Σ (summation) to represent the addition of terms that increase in a certain sequence?

 *Coffee Break*

Reviewing the Σ Trick

As you'll recall, Σ is a symbol representing addition.

If we write $\displaystyle\sum_{n=1}^{5} n$ it means "$1 + 2 + 3 + 4 + 5$".

(For details on Σ, see Chapter 1, "Fourier Series.")

By the way, did you know that $\displaystyle\sum_{n=1}^{3} 2n = 2\sum_{n=1}^{3} n$?

They mean the exact same thing.

$$\sum_{n=1}^{3} 2n = (2 \times 1) + (2 \times 2) + (2 \times 3) \quad \cdots \text{①}$$

$$2\sum_{n=1}^{3} n = 2 \times (1 + 2 + 3) \qquad\qquad \cdots \text{②}$$

If you add these two expressions up, you'll see that they both equal 12. On closer inspection, it's obvious why that is. . .

If you remove the parentheses from expression ② and multiply it out, you get:

$$2 \times (1 + 2 + 3) = (2 \times 1) + (2 \times 2) + (2 \times 3)$$

– which is identical to expression ①. So the two expressions mean exactly the same thing.

In other words, if you have a number (like 2 in this case) that is multiplied over and over again in every term of the expression, you can place it either before or after the Σ symbol – it doesn't matter which.

Now, remember that with Δt representing the width of the strips,

$$\boxed{\begin{array}{c}\text{Total area}\\\text{of strips}\end{array}} = \left\{9.8 \cdot (\Delta t)^2\right\} + \left\{9.8 \cdot 2(\Delta t)^2\right\} + \left\{9.8 \cdot 3(\Delta t)^2\right\} + \cdots + \left\{9.8 \cdot \frac{4}{\Delta t}(\Delta t)^2\right\}$$

Let's try rewriting this using Σ:

n Replace n	$\displaystyle\sum_{n=1}^{\frac{4}{\Delta t}} n$ with numbers from 1 to $4/\Delta t$ in sequence,	$\displaystyle\sum_{n=1}^{\frac{4}{\Delta t}} 9.8 \cdot n(\Delta t)$ multiply each number by 9.8 and Δt^2,	$\displaystyle\sum_{n=1}^{\frac{4}{\Delta t}} 9.8 \cdot n(\Delta t)^2$ and add these products together.

In other words,

$$\text{Total area of strips} = \sum_{n=1}^{\frac{4}{\Delta t}} 9.8 \cdot n(\Delta t)^2$$

Here's where we use our new trick. We can move everything that doesn't change to the front of the Σ – in this case, 9.8 and Δt^2, which remain the same even when n changes:

$$= 9.8(\Delta t)^2 \sum_{n=1}^{\frac{4}{\Delta t}} n$$

All right, let's calculate! But what are we going to do about this ungainly thing, $\displaystyle\sum_{n=1}^{\frac{4}{\Delta t}} n$? We won't get very far unless we can simplify it somehow. Let's write it out without using Σ.

This $\displaystyle\sum_{n=1}^{\frac{4}{\Delta t}} n$ actually means $1 + 2 + 3 + \cdots + \dfrac{4}{\Delta t}$.

When we add together a series of numbers that start with 1, we can find the answer by using the following formula:

$$\frac{(\text{first–number} + \text{last–number}) \times \text{last–number}}{2}$$

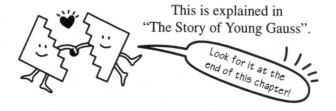

This is explained in "The Story of Young Gauss".

Look for it at the end of this chapter!

Here the first number is 1, and the last number is $4/\Delta t$.

$$\text{Total area of strips} = 9.8(\Delta t)^2 \sum_{n=1}^{\frac{4}{\Delta t}} n$$

$$= \overset{4.9}{\cancel{9.8}}(\Delta t)^2 \frac{\left(1 + \dfrac{4}{\Delta t}\right) \times \dfrac{4}{\Delta t}}{\cancel{2}_{1}} \qquad \text{Cancel out}$$

$$= 4.9(\Delta t)^2 \left(1 + \frac{4}{\Delta t}\right) \times \frac{4}{\Delta t} \qquad \text{Multiply each term}$$

$$= 4.9(\Delta t)^2 \left\{ \frac{4}{\Delta t} + \frac{16}{(\Delta t)^2} \right\} \qquad \text{Multiply each term}$$

$$= 19.6\Delta t + 78.4$$

Hang in there!
HI!
Don't give up!

In other words:

Given width Δt,
Total area of strips $= 19.6\Delta t + 78.4$

But what exactly does that mean? How large an area is "$19.6\Delta t + 78.4$"??

The joker in the deck is Δt. But it's not really all that tricky. Remember that Δt represents a "short width" of strip. Remember, too, that this width can be any value we want it to be – 0.1, or 0.01, or anything else. So to find the area $19.6\Delta t + 78.4$, all we have to do is replace Δt with the number of our choice.

Good grief!

What am I??

5. Finding the Area Using Actual Values for Δt

It almost sounds too easy. Just decide on a value for Δt – the width of a strip – and this simple formula will give you the total area of all strips! Let's double – check and see if this really works.

For width **1**, does this formula really give us the area **98.0** we calculated in section 4. 1?

$$19.6 \times 1 + 78.4 = 19.6 + 78.4$$
$$= 98.0 \qquad \text{Yes it does!}$$

For width **0.5**, does this formula really give us the area **88.2** we calculated in section 4. 2?

$$19.6 \times 0.5 + 78.4 = 9.8 + 78.4$$
$$= 88.2 \qquad \text{Yes again!}$$

Thanks to this formula, we don't have to calculate and add up the areas of each and every strip. This formula gives us the total in an instant! Instead of all that time – and space – consuming arithmetic, we have our answer in a single line, $19.6 \cdot \Delta t + 78.4$. In a single expression, this little formula sums up everything we've said so far about the strips. Formulas – what a nifty invention!

This formula also makes it easy to narrow the strips down even further. Just keep substituting smaller and smaller values for Δt in $19.6 \cdot \Delta t + 78.4$. What could be simpler?

Try substituting **0.1** for Δt:

$$19.6\,\Delta t + 78.4 = 19.6 \times 0.1 + 78.4$$
$$= 80.36$$

Now try substituting **0.01**:

$$19.6\,\Delta t + 78.4 = 19.6 \times 0.01 + 78.4$$
$$= 78.596$$

Remember,

Closest approximation of the area of ⬚⬚⬚⬚⬚ = 78.4

Width	Number of strips	Total strip area
1	4	98.0
0.5	8	88.2
0.25	16	83.3
0.1	40	80.36
0.01	400	78.596
0.0001	40000	78.40196

Now we're really getting close!

How would you like to make the strips even narrower? We seem to be on the verge of the "closest approximation," don't we?

To get there, though, we have to use our symbol for "infinitely close": the **limit** ("**lim**" for short).

$$\lim_{\Delta t \to 0} \text{let } \Delta t \text{ approach infinitely close to } 0$$

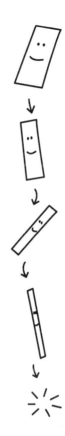

The purpose of the limit is to let a value get as close to 0 as it possibly can, <u>without actually becoming 0</u>. If the width of a strip becomes 0, we wind up with "height × width = height × 0 = 0", and the area of the strip vanishes.

But we <u>can</u> use a strip of infinitely narrow width...

$$\text{Total area of infinitely narrow strips} = \lim_{\Delta t \to 0} (19.6\Delta t + 78.4)$$

As Δt approaches 0, **19.6Δt** becomes:

$$19.6 \times 0.0000000 \cdots \cdots 0001 = \text{ a very, very small number}$$

...so small, in fact, that we might as well think of it as 0. In other words, it's so small that, just like 0, it has no effect whatsoever on the size of the area. Hey, math is nothing if not accommodating!

$$= 19.6 \times 0 + 78.4$$
$$= 78.4$$

$$\text{Total area of infinitely narrow strips} = 78.4$$

$$\text{Closest approximation of area of } \boxed{\vdots\vdots\vdots} = 78.4$$

It works! We've managed to find the area of a triangle using rectangular strips, simply by making them narrower and narrower!

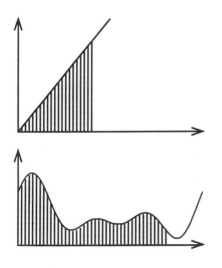

The narrower we make the strips, the closer they approach the true shape of the area we're trying to find. This is as true for the area of an irregular wave as it is for a triangle. Integration is both simple and convenient – all it does is use strips to find the closest approximation of an area!

6. Integrating a Triangle from 0 to *t*

So far we've only found the area up to 4 seconds. Now it's time to go a step further and find the area up to *t* seconds. When we do, we'll discover something very interesting.

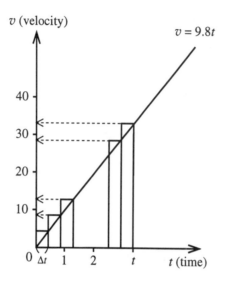

If we want the area from 0 up to 5 seconds, we simply substitute 5 for *t*; for the area up to 6 seconds, we substitute 6. Just like Δt, *t* represents any time we want it to. To find the area up to *t* seconds, we use strips of width Δt, which we bring as close to 0 as possible. Our method is exactly the same as the one we used to find the area up to 4 seconds. The only difference is the time is *t* seconds, not 4. So all we have to do is replace the "4" in our previous formula with "*t*".

Given width Δt,

$$\boxed{\begin{array}{c}\text{Total area}\\ \text{of strips}\end{array}} = \left\{9.8 \cdot (\Delta t)^2\right\} + 9.8 \cdot \left\{2(\Delta t)^2\right\} + \left\{9.8 \cdot 3(\Delta t)^2\right\} + \cdots + \left\{9.8 \cdot \frac{t}{\Delta t}(\Delta t)^2\right\}$$

The formula above is our formula for finding the area up to 4 seconds, with *t* replacing 4. The number of strips has changed from **4/Δt** to **t/Δt** – that's all.

As before, the terms we are adding up are identical except for the number in front of $(\Delta t)^2$, which increases incrementally – 1, 2, 3, ... **t/Δt**. Let's use Σ to write this formula. Once again, the only difference from our previous formula is that we have replaced 4 with *t*:

$$\text{Total area of strips} = \sum_{n=1}^{\frac{t}{\Delta t}} 9.8 \cdot n(\Delta t)^2$$

Now we'll apply our Σ trick, and move all the values that don't change to the front of Σ:

$$= 9.8(\Delta t)^2 \sum_{n=1}^{\frac{t}{\Delta t}} n$$

Before you go any further, please read "Supplement 3. The story of young Gauss" and the pages following it (pages 255 – 256) at the end of this chapter.

Now let's use the addition technique we learned from young Gauss. This will allow us to express $\sum_{n=1}^{\Delta t} n$ in a different fashion for the purpose of our calculations.

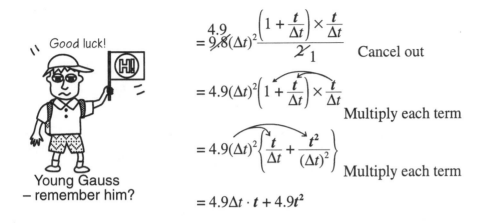

$$= 9.8(\Delta t)^2 \frac{\left(1 + \frac{t}{\Delta t}\right) \times \frac{t}{\Delta t}}{2_{\,1}} \quad \text{Cancel out}$$

$$= 4.9(\Delta t)^2 \left(1 + \frac{t}{\Delta t}\right) \times \frac{t}{\Delta t} \quad \text{Multiply each term}$$

$$= 4.9(\Delta t)^2 \left\{\frac{t}{\Delta t} + \frac{t^2}{(\Delta t)^2}\right\} \quad \text{Multiply each term}$$

$$= 4.9\Delta t \cdot t + 4.9t^2$$

Good luck!

Young Gauss – remember him?

To make the strip infinitely narrow, we need to use a limit:

$$\boxed{\begin{array}{c}\text{Closest approximation} \\ \text{of area}\end{array}} = \lim_{\Delta t \to 0} (4.9\Delta t \cdot t + 4.9t^2)$$

$$= 4.9t^2$$

$$\boxed{\text{Closest approximation of area up to } t \text{ (sec)} = \mathbf{4.9t^2}}$$

Now all you have to do is choose the range (i.e., "t") for which you want to find the area, and presto! You've got the closest approximation of that area from 0 to point t.

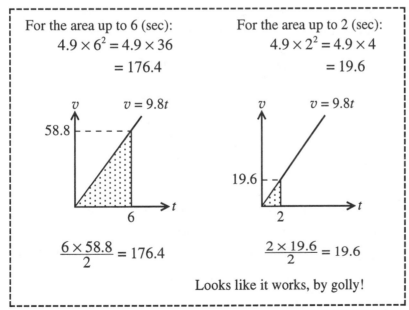

For the area up to 6 (sec):
$$4.9 \times 6^2 = 4.9 \times 36$$
$$= 176.4$$

For the area up to 2 (sec):
$$4.9 \times 2^2 = 4.9 \times 4$$
$$= 19.6$$

$$\frac{6 \times 58.8}{2} = 176.4$$

$$\frac{2 \times 19.6}{2} = 19.6$$

Looks like it works, by golly!

But what about this

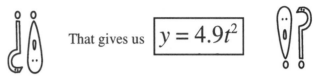

Closest approximation of area = **4.9t²**

Haven't we seen this formula before somewhere? Suppose we replace "closest approximation of area" with *y*:

That gives us $y = 4.9t^2$

This is the same formula we used for differentiation! When we performed differentiation on this formula, we got *v* = **9.8t**. This time, we performed integration on *v* = **9.8t**... which brought us right back to *y* = **4.9t²**!

7. The Relationship of Integration to Differentiation

What can this mean? What exactly happened? If you're confused, you're not alone. Let's review what we did to bring this about.

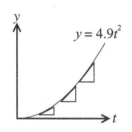

1)   In Chapter 5 ("Differentiation"), we differentiated *y* = **4.9t²**.
        We were trying to find the instantaneous speed of a falling ball.

2)   Our result was the formula *v* = **9.8t**,
        which tells us the speed of the ball at any given time.

3)   In this chapter, we performed integration on this same formula, *v* = **9.8t**.
        Even with the help of the strips, it was a long, painful process.

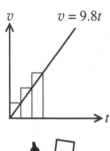

4)   And what did we get for our efforts, but the original formula *y* = **4.9t²**
        that we started out with in Chapter 5! What gives?!

Let's make a graphic representation of this phenomenon:

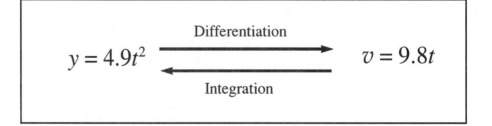

If we differentiate a formula, then integrate the result, we return to the original formula.

We can say that these two formulas, connected by the two opposing processes of differentiation and integration,

$$\text{are in an } \boxed{\text{inverse relationship}}$$

That means if we differentiate our integration result, $y = 4.9t^2$, we should get $v = 9.8t$ again.

If we had known about the relationship between these two formulas, we could have done our integration without resorting to those blasted strips! Integration is much, much easier if we take advantage of this

$\boxed{\text{inverse relationship}}$ between differentiation and integration

– which tells us "if you integrate something you differentiated, you get what you started out with."

It was a real ordeal to find the area by applying strips to the graph of $v = 9.8t$. Yet in the chapter on differentiation, we already learned that you can get $v = 9.8t$ by differentiating $y = 4.9t^2$, as illustrated below:

$$\boxed{y = 4.9t^2 \xrightarrow{\text{Differentiation}} v = 9.8t}$$

If we had known that an $\boxed{\text{inverse relationship}}$ existed between integration and differentiation, we simply could have drawn an arrow in the opposite direction:

$$\boxed{y = 4.9t^2 \; \substack{\xrightarrow{\text{Differentiation}} \\ \xleftarrow{\text{Integration}}} \; v = 9.8t}$$

and that would have said it all:

$$\text{"If you integrate } v = 9.8t, \text{ you get } y = 4.9t^2\text{."}$$

This inverse relationship is the crux of the trick. By viewing integration from a different perspective – that of differentiation – we discover we have a simple technique for integration. That's why we introduced you to differentiation first. Did it strike you as a bit odd that out of nowhere we had you find the velocity of a falling ball? Well, we had an ulterior motive: to demonstrate that you can use differentiation to integrate a formula.

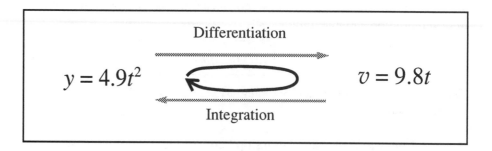

What goes around comes around. Differentiation and integration form a closed loop, cycling endlessly between two formulas.
And that is what makes our new trick possible.

From now on, we'll often take advantage of this │ inverse relationship │

between differentiation and integration to calculate the area of some very squiggly waveforms. How? By performing

 │ integration via differentiation! │

This is an extremely useful technique, so try not to forget it.

For example, if you want to integrate cos x, all you have to do is recall that differentiating sin x produced cos x:

see Chapter 6, "Differentiation of sin θ"

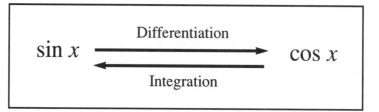

Which means that integrating cos x produces sin x.

It would be a terrible chore to cut the cos x wave into strips and find the area for each one. It's truly amazing that this new trick eliminates all that work so effortlessly <u>and</u> accurately!

But remember one thing – "integration via differentiation," however convenient, is just a trick. The essence of integration is still:

> Using strips to find the closest approximation of an area

This is the essence of integration even when we're integrating $v = 9.8t$. Integration is nothing more or less than the use of strips to find an area.

> Area of strip = height × width

The crucial point is this "use of strips." In the graph of $v = 9.8t$, where the vertical axis is velocity and the horizontal axis is time,

$$\text{height} \times \text{width} + \text{height} \times \text{width} + \text{height} \times \text{width} \ldots$$

represents the same thing as

$$\text{velocity} \times \text{time} + \text{velocity} \times \text{time} + \text{velocity} \times \text{time} \ldots$$

> velocity × time = distance

– right?

So when we were finding the area of each strip, one by one, we were calculating distances as well. When an object undergoes a steady change in velocity, the distance it advances from one instant to the next also changes. The slower it travels, the less it advances; the faster it travels, the more it advances. Therefore, to calculate the distance traveled by an object whose velocity keeps changing (like a falling ball), we must find the distance it has advanced from instant to instant. Then we have to add these distances together to find the total distance traveled. There is no other way to do it. Thus when we use strips to find a total area, we are actually finding a total distance:

> Closest approximation of area = distance

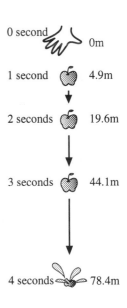

When we replaced "closest approximation of area" with the letter "y" at the end of section 6, it wasn't an arbitrary choice. We didn't use "y" just because the closest approximation of the area ⬚⬚⬚⬚⬚ happened to be $4.9t^2$. We chose "y" because it is the letter that symbolizes <u>distance</u>.

In other words, it is not the formula for <u>area</u> that is in an inverse relationship with the formula for the velocity of the ball. Rather, it is the formula for the <u>distance</u> the ball falls ($y = 4.9t^2$) that has this inverse relationship (via differentiation and integration) with the formula for the velocity of the ball ($v = 9.8t$). Makes sense if you think about it!

Moreover this inverse relationship arises precisely because the essence of integration is:

> Using strips to find the closest approximation of an area

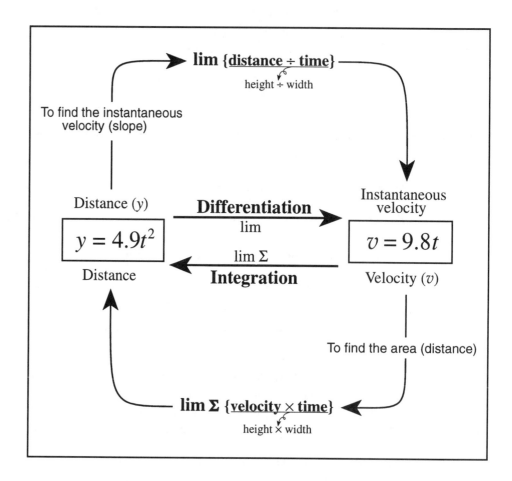

7. Adieu to Integration

Here ends our adventure with integration. You now know how to find the closest possible approximation of the area of any wave, no matter how convoluted. Congratulations – that's quite an accomplishment!

Remember: the basic method is the use of strips to find the area, but the trick is "integration via differentiation," utilizing the inverse relationship between the two.

In closing, we'd like to show you how calculations are actually performed in integration. Once that's out of the way, we can bring the curtain down on the subject (with one condition, however: that you promise to take a look at the last page of this chapter!).

Señor Strip

You've been a beautiful audience. . .
thank you! thank you!

Supplement 1. How to Integrate

Suppose we wish to find this area in the graph on the right: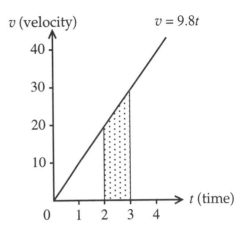
We describe the area of ⬚ as follows:

$$\int_2^3 (9.8t)dt$$

On the graph of $v = 9.8t$ $9.8t$	take the interval from 2 to 3, $\int_2^3 (9.8t)d$	and integrate. $\int_2^3 (9.8t)dt$

At first glance, this formula may look rather complicated, but it really isn't.
The term "*dt*" simply represents Δt brought to its lowest possible value.

In other words:

$$\lim_{\Delta t \to 0} \Delta t \to dt$$

See Chapter 5, "Differentiation"

The formula **9.8t** represents the height of the strip. Its height varies with time.
Since we can substitute any time we want for *t*, **9.8t** in effect represents all
possible heights.

That is,

$$\mathbf{9.8t} \times \mathbf{dt} = \text{height} \times \text{width}$$

What this formula means is simply "find the area in the form of strips."

The symbol $\int$ is just another form of the letter S, which stands for
"summation."

$$S \to \int \to \int$$

If you think about it, a skinny S is an appropriate symbol for integration, which
consists, after all, of adding up increasingly skinny strips...

In other words, the formula $\int_2^3 (9.8t)dt$

describes the entire process of integration – making strips infinitely narrow,
then adding them together. Not bad for a single formula!

When it comes to actually performing integration, we can drastically simplify the process by using the formula $y = 4.9t^2$, which represents the area of $v = 9.8t$.

We rewrite our formula like this:

$$\int_2^3 (9.8t)dt = \left[4.9t^2\right]_2^3$$

So as not to forget that we're integrating $v = 9.8t$, we put brackets [ ] around the formula representing its area, $y = 4.9t^2$. So as not to forget that our desired range is from 2 to 3, we write these numbers to one side of the brackets as well. To find the area of $v = 9.8t$ from 2 to 3, all we need to do is subtract the area up to 2 from the area up to 3.

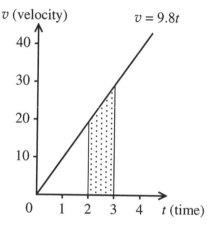

Area up to 3 $= 4.9 \times 3^2$
Area up to 2 $= 4.9 \times 2^2$

So we want to find:

$$(4.9 \times 3^2 - 4.9 \times 2^2)$$

All we did, in effect, was take the "range" numbers written next to the brackets in the formula, substitute them one at a time for t, and then subtract one from the other. The result:

$$= 24.5$$

Snip snip!

So by using a formula that is the result of integration, we can find the area in no time. If you harbor any doubts about the accuracy of this method, you can check for yourself by cutting and pasting in triangles!

Let's get a graphic look at our results:

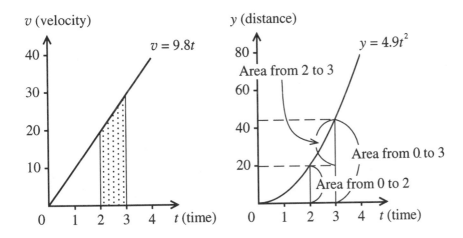

The value y in $y = 4.9t^2$ represents the area of $v = 9.8t$. The area from 0 of $v = 9.8t$ is represented by the vertical axis on the graph of $y = 4.9t^2$.

Next, let's find the area of cos x from 0 to $(1/2)\pi$. When we differentiate sin x, we get cos x, remember? Which means that integrating cos x produces sin x. Again, let's view this in graphic terms:

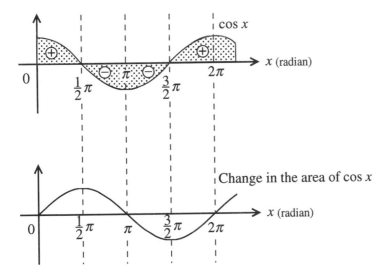

At first the area of cos x steadily increases. But when it passes $(1/2)\pi$, its negative area starts to increase instead. This causes the total area to decrease. At π, the positive and negative area values cancel each other out, so the total is 0. The total area continues to decrease until $(3/2)\pi$, at which point the area begins to increase on the positive side again. At 2π the positive and negative areas once again balance to 0, so the total area acquires a positive value again. It is clear that sin x really does express the change in the area of cos x.

The area of $\cos x$ from 0 to $(1/2)\pi$ can be written:

$$\int_0^{\frac{1}{2}\pi} \cos x \, dx$$

We use "dx" because the horizontal axis is x. In the square brackets [ ], we write the formula that, when differentiated, produces $\cos x$. (This is the formula produced by integrating $\cos x$.)

$$\int_0^{\frac{1}{2}\pi} \cos x \, dx = \left[\sin x \right]_0^{\frac{1}{2}\pi}$$

Now we can take the "range" numbers written next to the brackets, substitute them for x one at a time, and subtract one from the other:

$$= \left(\sin \frac{1}{2}\pi - \sin 0 \right)$$
$$= 1 - 0$$
$$= 1$$

Area of $\cos x$ from 0 to $(1/2)\pi = 1$

Simple, eh?

If we want to find the area of $\cos x$ from $(1/2)\pi$ to π, we get:

$$\int_{\frac{1}{2}\pi}^{\pi} \cos x \, dx = \left[\sin x \right]_{\frac{1}{2}\pi}^{\pi}$$
$$= \left(\sin \pi - \sin \frac{1}{2}\pi \right)$$
$$= 0 - 1$$
$$= -1$$

Area of $\cos x$ from $(1/2)\pi$ to $\pi = -1$

So the area of $\cos x$ from 0 to π is:

Area of $\cos x$ from 0 to $(1/2)\pi$ + Area of $\cos x$ from $(1/2)\pi$ to π
= Area of $\cos x$ from 0 to π
= **1 + (−1) = 0**

So the answer is 0, which is indeed correct.

We can now integrate in practically no time at all. You're a regular expert!

Supplement 2. Calculating Integration

– Finding the Fourier Coefficients of a Sawtooth Wave –

A sawtooth wave is...

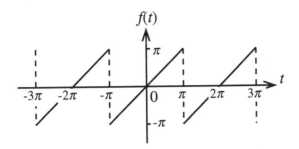

...a wave with a waveform that resembles the teeth of a saw. Here we shall perform the calculations required for the Fourier coefficients of a sawtooth wave. Can a wave that consists of straight lines really be expressed as the sum of sine and cosine waves, which consist of smooth curves? That's our riddle for the day. We shall see...

Before embarking on our calculations, let us review several crucial lessons from our studies so far. First, a reminder of what we learned at the very beginning about the Fourier series:

> **Any complicated wave, if it repeats itself,**
> **can be expressed as the sum of sine and cosine waves.**

Fourier series formula

$$f(t) = a_0 + \sum_{n=1}^{\infty} (a_n \cos n\omega t + b_n \sin n\omega t)$$

Next, a reminder about Fourier coefficients:

> **A complicated wave consists of the sum of several simple waves,**
> **and we can determine the quantity of each of these waves.**

Fourier coefficients formulas

$$a_0 = \frac{1}{T} \int_0^T f(t)dt$$

$$a_n = \frac{2}{T} \int_0^T f(t) \cos n\omega t\, dt$$

$$b_n = \frac{2}{T} \int_0^T f(t) \sin n\omega t\, dt$$

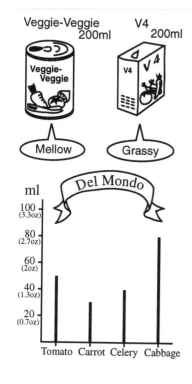

These "several simple waves" are sine and cosine waves. By finding the amplitude of each of these waves, we will learn what types of waves are added together to form the sawtooth wave. Remember our vegetable juice analogy? If this were vegetable juice, we'd be trying to determine the types and quantities of the vegetables contained in the juice. If that doesn't ring a bell, go back and reread Chapters 1 and 2, "Fourier Series" and "Fourier Coefficients."

Shall we begin?

First, let's examine a single period of the wave!

Why only a single period? Because the interval "0 to T" that we'll use in our Fourier coefficients formulas is precisely one period. What's more, this one period can start at any point on the wave we want. For example, it can be the period from 0 to 2π, or from -2π to 0 – it doesn't matter.

Here we'll use the period from $-\pi$ to π. The reason for this choice will become clear in a moment. On the graph, this section of the wave appears like this:

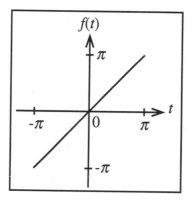

Is that all? A straight diagonal line?! This is supposed to be a <u>sawtooth</u> wave – it should look more like this:

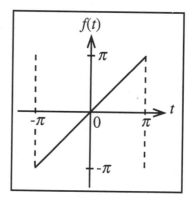

– shouldn't it?

Well, let's see what happens when t is π. Just <u>before</u> t becomes π, the sawtooth wave has a value close to π. But just <u>after</u> t becomes π, the wave has a value close to $-\pi$. On the graph, a dotted line is used to make these parts of the wave appear connected. But in reality, the sawtooth wave has no values along this interval. Rather, it changes quite abruptly from π to $-\pi$.

What sort of function can we use to express this graph as a formula? $f(t) = ??$

The graph shows that when t on the horizontal axis is π, $f(t)$ on the vertical axis is also π. In other words, $f(t)$ and t are the same: $f(t) = t$.

Now do you see why we chose the range from $-\pi$ to π as our period? It makes it easier to express and calculate $f(t)$, since $f(t) = t$. As long as we have a choice of periods, it makes sense to choose the simplest one, don't you think?

Period T is the time (in seconds) it takes the waveform to repeat itself, which in this case is from $-\pi$ to π, or 2π. Angular velocity ω is the number of radians the wave advances in one second (rad/sec). Since this wave advances 2π radians in 2π seconds, the value of ω is 1.

$$f(t) = t, \quad T = 2\pi, \quad \omega = 1$$

Now we can substitute these values for $f(t)$, T, and ω in our Fourier coefficients formulas. Let's start with a_0.

$< a_0 >$

a_0 indicates how far from the center the wave is displaced.

Let's insert $T = 2\pi$ and $f(t) = t$ into the Fourier coefficients formula for finding a_0:

$$a_0 = \frac{1}{T}\int_0^T f(t)dt$$
$$= \frac{1}{2\pi}\int_{-\pi}^{\pi} t\, dt$$

Next we have to integrate t. Since differentiation and integration have an inverse relationship, we should find the formula that produces t when differentiated, because that will be the result of integrating t.

Remember the relationship illustrated below?

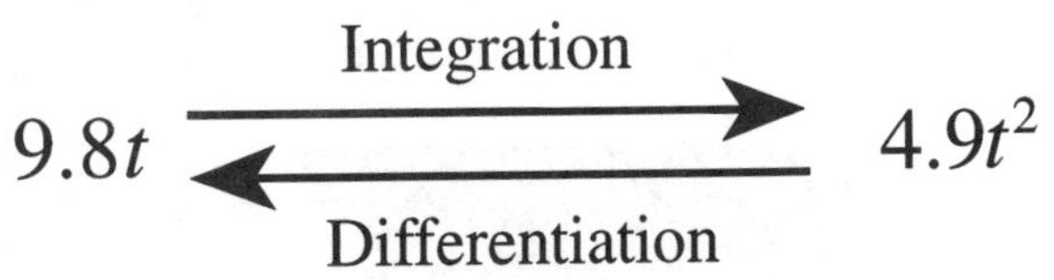

$$9.8t \quad \underset{\text{Differentiation}}{\overset{\text{Integration}}{\rightleftarrows}} \quad 4.9t^2$$

This indicates that when you integrate $9.8t$, you get $4.9t^2$. The value 9.8 is halved, yielding 4.9, while t becomes t^2. Is it possible that integrating t produces the result $1/2 \cdot t^2$?

Let's check it out by differentiating $1/2 \cdot t^2$. (If this is hard for you to follow, review Chapter 5, "Differentiation.")

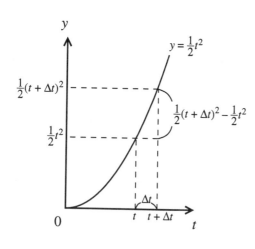

$$\frac{d}{dt}\left(\frac{1}{2}t^2\right) = \lim_{\Delta t \to 0} \frac{\Delta y}{\Delta t}$$

$$= \lim_{\Delta t \to 0} \frac{\frac{1}{2}(t + \Delta t)^2 - \frac{1}{2}t^2}{\Delta t}$$

$$= \lim_{\Delta t \to 0} \frac{\frac{1}{2}t^2 + t\Delta t + \frac{1}{2}(\Delta t)^2 - \frac{1}{2}t^2}{\Delta t}$$

$$= \lim_{\Delta t \to 0} \frac{t\Delta t + \frac{1}{2}(\Delta t)^2}{\Delta t}$$

$$= \lim_{\Delta t \to 0} \left(t + \frac{1}{2}\Delta t\right)$$

$$= t$$

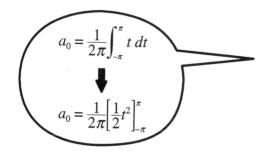

So now we know that the result of integrating t is $1/2 \cdot t^2$. All that's left is to insert the "range" numbers and perform the calculations we learned earlier:

$$a_0 = \frac{1}{2\pi}\left[\frac{1}{2}t^2\right]_{-\pi}^{\pi}$$

$$= \frac{1}{2\pi}\left\{\frac{1}{2}\pi^2 - \frac{1}{2}(-\pi)^2\right\}$$

$$= \frac{1}{2\pi}\left(\frac{1}{2}\pi^2 - \frac{1}{2}\pi^2\right)$$

$$= \frac{1}{2\pi} \cdot 0$$

$$= 0$$

$$\therefore a_0 = 0$$

So a_0 is not contained in this wave. If we look at the graph, that makes perfect sense: the sawtooth wave is not shifted from the center in either direction, so naturally $a_0 = 0$.

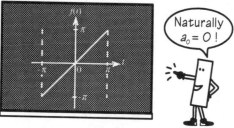

$< a_n >$

a_n represents the quantities in which cosine waves of different frequencies are contained in the wave.

Let's insert $T = 2\pi$, $f(t) = t$, and $\omega = 1$ into the Fourier coefficients formulas for finding a_n:

$$a_n = \frac{2}{T}\int_0^T \left\{ f(t) \cdot \cos n\omega t \right\} dt$$

$$= \frac{2}{2\pi}\int_{-\pi}^{\pi} (t \cdot \cos nt)\, dt$$

Since it's a bit difficult to integrate $t \cdot \cos nt$, we'll use a special trick for this purpose: We won't try to explain the trick here – it would take up too much space.

$$\int (t \cdot \cos nt)\, dt = \frac{\cos nt}{n^2} + \frac{t \cdot \sin nt}{n}$$

Anyway, don't look a gift formula in the mouth!

With your permission!

This trick is called "integration by parts." We picked this out of our grab-bag of formulas because the calculations would be too complicated otherwise.

$$= \frac{1}{\pi}\left[\frac{\cos nt}{n^2} + \frac{t \sin nt}{n} \right]_{-\pi}^{\pi}$$

$$= \frac{1}{\pi}\left[\left(\frac{\cos n\pi}{n^2} + \frac{\pi \sin n\pi}{n} \right) - \left\{ \frac{\cos n(-\pi)}{n^2} + \frac{(-\pi)\sin n(-\pi)}{n} \right\} \right]$$

$$\qquad\qquad\qquad\qquad 0 \qquad\qquad\qquad\qquad\qquad 0$$

$\sin n\pi = \sin n(-\pi) = 0$ at all times. Similarly, $\cos n\pi = \cos n(-\pi)$ at all times. The graphs below show why.

$$= \frac{1}{\pi}\left(\frac{\cos n\pi}{n^2} - \frac{\cos n\pi}{n^2} \right)$$

$$= \frac{1}{\pi} \cdot 0$$

$$\therefore\ a_n = 0$$

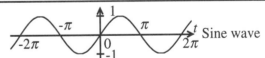

When t is an integral multiple of π (1π, 2π, 3π, etc.), the value of $\sin t$ is always 0.

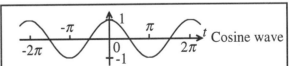

The values of $\cos t$ are always the same for any two values of t that differ only in sign (1π and -1π, 2π and -2π, etc.).

If there is no a_0 and no a_n, all that's left for this wave is b_n.

Before we try to find b_n ...

We used a special integration trick to find a_n. Now we need a similar trick to help us with b_n. Fortunately we have one, the formula shown below. Try using this to find b_n on your own, before looking at the answer!

To integrate $t \cdot \sin nt$:

$$\int (t \cdot \sin nt) \, dt = \frac{\sin nt}{n^2} - \frac{t \cos nt}{n}$$

$< b_n >$

b_n represents the quantities in which sine waves of different frequencies are contained in the wave.

Let's insert $T = 2\pi$, $f(t) = t$, and $\omega = 1$ into the Fourier coefficients formula for finding b_n:

$$b_n = \frac{2}{T} \int_0^T \left\{ f(t) \cdot \sin n\omega t \right\} dt$$

$$= \frac{2}{2\pi} \int_{-\pi}^{\pi} (t \cdot \sin nt) \, dt$$

Now we can use the formula for integrating $t \cdot \sin nt$ we introduced a moment ago:

$$= \frac{1}{\pi} \left[\frac{\sin nt}{n^2} - \frac{t \cos nt}{n} \right]_{-\pi}^{\pi}$$

$$= \frac{1}{\pi} \left[\left(\frac{\sin n\pi}{n^2} - \frac{\pi \cos n\pi}{n} \right) - \left\{ \frac{\sin n(-\pi)}{n^2} - \frac{(-\pi)\cos n(-\pi)}{n} \right\} \right]$$

$$\qquad \qquad \qquad 0 \qquad\qquad\qquad\qquad\qquad 0$$

As with a_n, the value of the sine terms is always 0. Also, we can replace $\cos n(-\pi)$ with $\cos n\pi$:

$$= \frac{1}{\pi} \left(-\frac{\pi \cos n\pi}{n} - \frac{\pi \cos n\pi}{n} \right)$$

$$= \frac{1}{\pi} \left(-2 \frac{\pi \cos n\pi}{n} \right)$$

$$= -\frac{2}{n} \cos n\pi$$

We're just about there. However, let's see if we can further simplify $\cos n\pi$.

The values for n are integers (1, 2, 3, ...). What happens when we plug these values in $\cos n\pi$?

We find that the resulting values of cos $n\pi$ alternate between -1 and 1 indefinitely: $-1, 1, -1, 1, -1, 1$, etc. That means cos $n\pi$ is the same as $(-1)^n$:

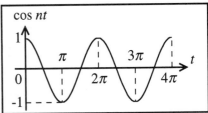

$$= -\frac{2}{n}(-1)^n$$

$$\therefore \ b_n = -\frac{2}{n}(-1)^n$$

We have now calculated a_0, a_n, and b_n. Let's add these values to the Fourier series formula.

Fourier series formula:

$$f(t) = a_0 + \sum_{n=1}^{\infty} (a_n \cos n\omega t + b_n \sin n\omega t)$$

Substituting $a_0 = 0$, $a_n = 0$, $b_n = -\frac{2}{n}(-1)^n$, $\omega = 1$ in the formula above, we get:

$$f(t) = \sum_{n=1}^{\infty} \left\{ -\frac{2}{n}(-1)^n \cdot \sin nt \right\}$$

But exactly what types of waves are being added together here? Let's substitute some actual values for n and see what they give us:

When $n = 1$,

$$-\frac{2}{1}(-1)^1 \cdot \sin 1t = 2 \sin 1t$$

When $n = 2$,

$$-\frac{2}{2}(-1)^2 \cdot \sin 2t = -1 \sin 2t$$

When $n = 3$,

$$-\frac{2}{3}(-1)^3 \cdot \sin 3t = \frac{2}{3} \sin 3t$$

When $n = 4$,

$$-\frac{2}{4}(-1)^4 \cdot \sin 4t = -\frac{1}{2} \sin 4t$$

When $n = 5$,

$$-\frac{2}{5}(-1)^5 \cdot \sin 5t = \frac{2}{5} \sin 5t$$

•

•

•

The wavy lines indicate the values of b_n. The sawtooth wave is the sum of the waves expressed by the right side of each of these equations. All we have to do is keep finding the waves for different values of n.

But how many of these waves do we have to add together to get the actual sawtooth waveform? Take a look at the graphs below.

This first wave is the result of adding only the first **three waves**. Doesn't look a bit like sawteeth, does it?

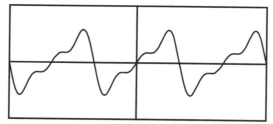

This is the result of adding the first **five waves**:

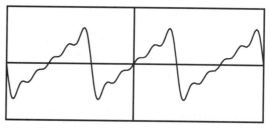

After the first **ten waves**, it begins to look like the real thing:

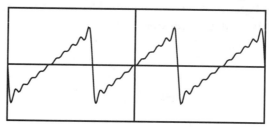

And after the first **20 waves**:

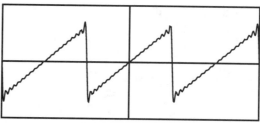

When we've added the first **50 waves**, the lines almost look straight from a distance. But we still have a way to go.

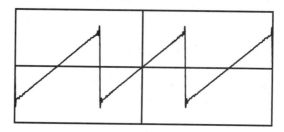

Not until we've added 100 waves, or 1000, or even an infinite number, will we get a bona fide sawtooth wave.

We now know that even a sawtooth wave consisting of nothing but straight lines can be the sum of smooth, curving sine waves – if we add an infinite number of such waves together. If you were wondering whether the Fourier series can really express any wave whatsoever, you should have your answer. If you still have any doubts, by all means try doing the calculations on your own again.

Supplement 3. The Story of Young Gauss

Now we're going to show you how young Gauss came up with his answer so quickly. Suppose we want to add together the numbers 1 through 5:

$$+\begin{array}{r} 1+2+3+4+5 \\ 5+4+3+2+1 \\ \hline 6+6+6+6+6 \end{array}$$

5 numbers

If we line up the numbers 1 through 5 above the numbers 5 through 1, and add them in pairs, we get 6 for each sum. If we add all five 6's together, we get $6 \times 5 = 30$. But we've added the same set of numbers twice, so we want to divide the total by 2. That should give us our answer.

If we make this into a formula, we get:

$$\frac{6 \times 5}{2} = \frac{30}{2} = 15$$

This agrees with the answer arrived at the conventional way:

$$1 + 2 + 3 + 4 + 5 = 15$$

Let's rewrite this formula so it can be used for sums up to any number we want:

$$\frac{(1 + 5) \times 5}{2} = \frac{(\text{first-number} + \text{last-number}) \times \underset{\sim}{\text{last-number}}}{2}$$

> This indicates how many numbers are added. If we add numbers in a sequence starting from 1, we can multiply by the last number of the series. But if we start from some other number, 2 or 3 for example, we must figure out how many numbers we are adding together and multiply by that number.

We can illustrate this method with the help of a couple of charts:

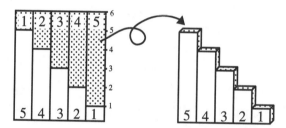

With the chart on the right, we have to add up every one of the quantities from 1 to 5 to get the total. However, if we combine two sets of these quantities together, as in the chart on the left, they form a square, making the total much easier to calculate. That's all there is to it.

Now then, what happens when we add all the numbers from 1 to 100? The first number is 1, and the last number is 100, so:

$$\frac{(1 + 100) \times 100}{2} = \frac{10100}{2} = 5050$$

You've got it!

This is the method young Gauss used to arrive at his answer so quickly. Here is how it looks in real mathematical jargon:

$$\sum_{n=1}^{k} n = \frac{(1 + k) \times k}{2}$$

This is an extremely useful formula, so be sure to take it with you!

 *Coffee Break*

Does Integrating a Differentiated Formula Produce the Original Formula?

In some cases, differentiating a formula, then integrating it, will not return you to the original formula. Take $y = 2x + 3$, for example. Let's try differentiating this.

$$y + \Delta y = 2(x + \Delta x) + 3$$

$$\Delta y = 2(x + \Delta x) + 3 - y$$

$$= \left\{2(x + \Delta x) + 3\right\} - (2x + 3)$$

$$= 2x + 2\Delta x + 3 - 2x - 3$$

$$= 2\Delta x$$

$$\frac{\Delta y}{\Delta x} = \frac{2\Delta x}{\Delta x} = 2$$

$$\lim_{\Delta x \to 0} \frac{\Delta y}{\Delta x} = \lim_{\Delta x \to 0} 2 = 2$$

$$\boxed{y = 2x + 3 \quad \xrightarrow{\text{Differentiation}} \quad y = 2}$$

If we integrate $y = 2$, which is the result of differentiating $y = 2x + 3$, we should get back to our original formula, $y = 2x + 3$, right? Well, let's give it a try.

To integrate $y = 2$, we want to find a formula that yields $y = 2$ when differentiated, remember? That formula is $y = 2x$.

Let's differentiate $y = 2x$ to make sure.

$$y + \Delta y = 2(x + \Delta x)$$

$$\Delta y = 2(x + \Delta x) - y$$

$$= 2(x + \Delta x) - 2x$$

$$= 2x + 2\Delta x + 3 - 2x - 3$$

$$= 2\Delta x$$

$$\frac{\Delta y}{\Delta x} = \frac{2\Delta x}{\Delta x} = 2$$

$$\lim_{\Delta x \to 0} \frac{\Delta y}{\Delta x} = \lim_{\Delta x \to 0} 2 = 2$$

Integrating $y = 2$ definitely produces $y = 2x$.

$$\boxed{y = 2x \quad \xleftarrow{} \quad y = 2 \atop \text{Integration}}$$

What's this? Differentiating either $y = 2x$ or $y = 2x + 3$ produces $y = 2$! So integrating $y = 2$ does not return us to the original formula, $y = 2x + 3$, after all.

$$y = 2x + 3 \xrightarrow[\text{Integration}]{\text{Differentiation}} y = 2 \;, \; y = 2x \xrightarrow[\text{Integration}]{\text{Differentiation}} y = 2$$

Here's the catch: if a constant, such as 3 in the example above, is attached to the formula, differentiation followed by integration will not return us to the original. Why?

Because differentiation only concerns itself with measuring the **slope** of a curve.

For $y = 2x$ or $y = 2x + 3$, or, for that matter, $y = 2x + 100$, the slope is the same.

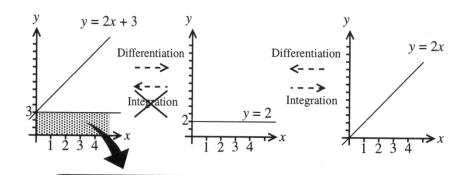

This part is ignored by the differentiation process.
But it is an important part of the area measured by integration.

When we integrate $y = 2$, we will always get $y = 2x$, nothing more, nothing less. That's because, when we differentiate $y = 2x + 3$, we only deal with the part $2x$, which changes with the variable x. Integration, on the other hand, is the process of finding an area. So when we integrate, we are confronted with the area of the part that was ignored by differentiation because it didn't change. A value like 3, which does not change when x does, is called a **constant**, or "**C**" for short. Whenever we integrate a formula, we always attach this "*C*" to it to remind us that something may have been ignored when the formula was differentiated.

Therefore, when we integrate $y = 2$,
we should write our result as follows: $y = 2x + C$.

Chapter 8

Projection
and
Orthogonality

In this chapter we're going to take off in a new direction, so to speak, and talk about vectors, which are quantities that have both magnitude and direction. (We therefore use arrows to represent them). This will be a bit of a departure from our discussion so far, so it may seem a little confusing at first. But our efforts will be rewarded: learning about vectors will help us view Fourier series and Fourier coefficients from an entirely different angle.

¡Hola!

I'm Tama.

¡Hola! Up to now we've been hanging out with Dr. Fourier, using a variety of approaches in order to answer the question, "What is a wave?" All along we've tended to take waves for granted, only to be surprised by one revelation after another about their true nature. What's in store for us now? "Projection and Orthogonality" is a pretty intimidating title. When I read it the first time, I cringed. Projection of what? And what on earth is orthogonality? What do either of these have to do with Fourier analysis? It made me tired just to think about it.

After a while, I was too drowsy to think...

Suddenly I came to – and found myself in a very odd place. Arrows were floating here and there in the air around me. As I stared at them in befuddlement, I heard a voice calling me.

Turning around, I beheld a European-looking gentleman dressed in extremely old-fashioned clothing. He was smiling.

"Bonjour! I am Jean Baptiste Joseph, Baron de Fourier! Comment-allez vous? I've come a long way just to escort you on this adventure, my friend!"

What?! It couldn't be – but it was! None other than the great Dr. Fourier himself!

"D-Dr. Fourier, I'm deeply honored! But... where the heck are we, anyway?!"

"Why, this is the world of vectors!"

"B-but aren't we supposed to be studying Fourier mathematics? What do vectors have to do with that?"

"Well, at first glance they may appear unrelated. But these two very different approaches describe the same phenomena.

"Take, for example, the word 'watermelon.' The Japanese call it *suika* and the Spanish say *sandia*. They all stand for the same thing, yet they all sound utterly different. Or, conversely, these seemingly unrelated sounds all express exactly the same concept: watermelon! Likewise, vectors express the same concepts as Fourier analysis, except that they do it with projection and orthogonality."

"Hmm. So Fourier analysis and vectors are just different ways of looking at the same thing, eh? Okay. But what is a vector, anyway, Doc?"

"With that question, let us begin our adventure!"

1. ¿¿Qué es un Vector??

Voici! This is a vector!
It may look like an arrow,
but believe me, this is no
mere arrow!

So all those arrows floating around me were vectors...

But I couldn't make sense of this notion that a Fourier wave ⌢⌣⌢⌣ and one
of these arrow-like vectors ➚ both represented the same thing. Whatever they
had in common was going to be a real eye-opener, because I for one could not
imagine what it might be!

Suddenly I noticed a guidepost right in front of me.

"A guidepost only points you in the direction of
something, so it serves as an arrow and nothing more.
What, then, is a vector? Well, you can find vectors in
the most unlikely places..."

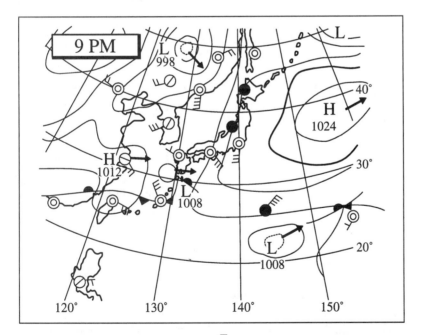

"This is a weather map. Notice all the ⊚ symbols on it! The ⊚ or ◑ part of
the ⊚ indicates the weather, while the ⌐ shows the direction of the wind.
What's important is that this wind symbol contains two pieces of information:
the direction and magnitude of the wind. And that's exactly what a vector
does."

"I see. An arrow by itself only shows direction. But a vector shows two things: direction **and** magnitude."

"Now, on these wind symbols, the strength of the wind is indicated by the number of lines sticking out from the tail: $\vdash, \digamma, \digamma$. Is this $\not\vdash, \not\digamma, \not\digamma$ how vectors show magnitude, too?"

"Non, non! The magnitude of a vector is indicated by the **length** of the arrow, which varies in multiples – doubling, tripling, and so on. But you must keep in mind that when the length of a vector changes, it only represents a change in magnitude, never direction. When only the size of a vector changes, we call it '**scalar multiplication**'."

I'd never heard the word 'scalar' before. I figured I'd just try to remember that it refers to a change in the magnitude of a vector, but not its direction.

"Time for a little trip to the seashore, mon ami!"

No sooner did Dr. Fourier utter these words than I found myself standing with him on a beach, wearing nothing but swimming trunks.

"Bon! Now I want you to swim in a straight line out to sea from where you are standing!"

I obediently started swimming, without any idea of what the good Doctor had in mind. After swimming for a while, I reached a sand bar and stood up in the water. But when I looked back, Dr. Fourier was gone. Nervously scanning the length of the beach, I finally caught sight of him standing far to the left. He was smiling at me as if nothing had happened; perhaps he had simply decided to go for a stroll.

I turned back and made a beeline for the beach. But when I reached the shore, I found that Dr. Fourier was even further to the left now, still grinning happily in my direction.

"Dr. Fourier, you went for a bit of a walk while I was swimming, didn't you?"

"Why no, I've been standing in the same place the whole time!" The Doctor grinned mischievously at me.

"How can that be? I was swimming straight out from the shore –yet when I looked back, you were way off to the left!"

"So you didn't notice that a current was carrying you, eh?"

A current?! So that's what happened – I thought I was swimming in a straight line, but the current was carrying me further and further to the left!"

"Précisément! Now, it just so happens that we can describe your experience very easily, through the addition of vectors."

Addition of vectors? Here was yet another unfamiliar concept. But at least now I had an idea why Dr. Fourier had insisted on visiting the ocean.

"When we speak of the addition of vectors..." As he spoke, Dr. Fourier began drawing in the sand with his finger.

"First, we shall use $\vec{B}$ to represent the direction and speed of your swim straight out from the beach, and $\vec{A}$ to represent the direction and strength of the current along the shore.

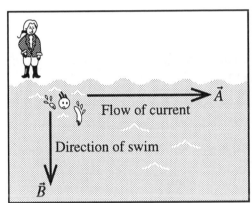

"If we add $\vec{A}$ and $\vec{B}$, we get $\vec{C}$, which represents the point you wound up at."

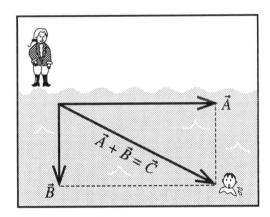

"But Dr. Fourier, how do we figure out where this $\vec{C}$ goes?"

"Well..."

Dr. Fourier picked up some pieces of driftwood that were lying nearby and placed them on top of the $\vec{A}$ and $\vec{B}$ arrows he had drawn in the sand.

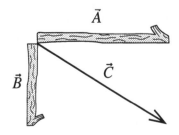

"Like this!"

The doctor suddenly moved twig ($\vec{B}$) to the right.

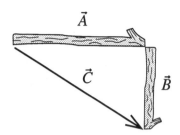

"Think of it as if you are first moving length $\vec{A}$, then moving length $\vec{B}$. That brings you precisely to the end point of $\vec{C}$, n'est-ce pas?"

"Why, so it does!"

"This is what it means to add vectors."

"But that's not the position I started swimming from, Doctor!"

"That's true. But in the world of vectors, we need not concern ourselves with **where** we are. For example, we could just as easily move branch $\vec{A}$ instead, like so:"

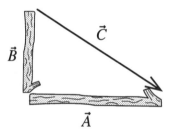

"Branch $\vec{A}$ represents the flow of the current. But we don't really know where the current started to flow from, do we!"

"I see! Vectors indicate magnitude and direction, but they have nothing to do with **position**! That's why vectors are perfect for representing things like currents or the wind! Right, Doctor?"

"Oui, oui! You are quite right. Vectors say nothing about position. If two vectors have the same direction and magnitude, they are the same vector even if they are located in different places. That allows us to move vectors around as we please when we wish to add them up!"

Dr. Fourier continued:

"After you swam out to the sand bar, you turned around and swam back to shore. We can express this by **subtracting** vectors."

As he said this, he moved twig $\vec{B}$ again.

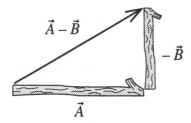

"Look! Vector $\vec{B}$ is now pointed in the opposite direction from your swim out to sea. We can express this by placing a minus sign (–) in front of $\vec{B}$, giving us " $-\vec{B}$ ". And voilà! Our previous addition becomes subtraction!"

$$\vec{A} + \left(-\vec{B}\right) = \vec{A} - \vec{B}$$

"Doctor, I can sort of see how that works – expressing the vector of my swim back to shore as " $-\vec{B}$ " makes it possible to perform vector subtraction. But why do you use a minus sign just because the direction of the vector is reversed?"

"Hmmm... to answer your question, I believe we must return to the world of vectors."

2. Orthogonal Coordinate Systems

Once again, I found myself with Dr. Fourier in the world of vectors. This time, however, the landscape was dominated by what looked like a huge piece of graph paper.

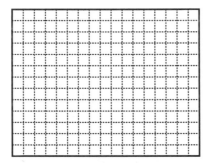

"What in the world is **this**, Doctor?"

"Mon cher ami, this is none other than the stage on which vectors perform!"

A stage? It looked like graph paper to me. And what did he mean by vectors performing...?

"Look at that vector there!" said the Doctor, pointing to an arrow floating in the air nearby.

"How do you think we should express the direction and magnitude of that vector?"

"Well, you said a few moments ago that vectors were represented by arrows..."

"Unfortunately, representing vectors by arrows has certain drawbacks. Allow me to show you..."

Suddenly the good Doctor and I were floating in midair. The vector he had pointed out was hovering right in front of us.

"Observe! The direction and size of this arrow now look different from before! That won't do. If you and I are in different positions, our individual perceptions of the direction and size of the vector will differ, too. That leaves us with no basis for an absolute measurement of the vector!"

"Well, can't we just look at it from the same position every time?"

"Yes indeed! That's why we use this grid, which as you say looks like graph paper. Let us promise ourselves that we will always draw our vectors on a grid of this sort. That way we can always be sure we are viewing a vector from the same position. In the past, what did you do when you drew graphs on graph paper?"

Note

When we create coordinates on straight lines that are perpendicular to one another, like those on graph paper, we say they form a "linear orthogonal coordinate system."

"Umm, let's see... first, I'd draw two axes, vertical and horizontal. Then I'd draw a graph up to a certain value on the x axis and a certain value on the y axis... Aha! I bet you're trying to tell me we can describe a vector the same way, in terms of a value in the x direction and another value in the y direction!"

"Excellent! If we abide by our commitment to draw vectors on a graph in this manner, then anyone looking at a vector can always be certain of its direction and magnitude."

Even as Dr. Fourier spoke, two perpendicular lines marked "x" and "y" appeared on the grid, together with a diagonal arrow marked " $\vec{A}$ ".

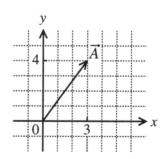

"For example, if we describe $\vec{A}$ as 'a vector of 3 in the x direction and 4 in the y direction,' we know exactly what kind of vector $\vec{A}$ is.

"What's more, we can use numbers to express this vector even more simply:

$$\vec{A} = (3, 4)$$

"Then, instead of talking about '3 in the x direction' and so on, we can say 'the x component is 3.' Much easier, don't you think?"

"Hmm. That **is** a different way of saying it. Okay, Doctor, I can see how this method clearly describes the direction of a vector – but what about its magnitude?"

"Well, the larger the x component or y component grows, the longer the arrow becomes – which indicates that the magnitude of the vector is increasing, you see?"

"Of course! Hey, wait a minute – the x and y axes form a right triangle with $\vec{A}$! And that means... Eureka! We can use the Pythagorean theorem, can't we!"

"Indeed we can! See if you can use it to find the magnitude of the vector."

"Okay, let's see. The horizontal value is 3, and the vertical value is 4, so that gives us:

$$3^2 + 4^2 = 25$$

and if we take the square root of this...

$$\sqrt{9 + 16} = 5$$

we get 5!"

"Correct! Now then, how would you find the magnitude of a vector $\vec{A}$ that has x component A_x and y component A_y?

"Well, that means the horizontal value is A_x and the vertical value is A_y, so:

$$\left(\text{magnitude of } \vec{A}\right)^2 = \left(A_x\right)^2 + \left(A_y\right)^2$$

"Say, isn't there an easier way to write 'magnitude of $\vec{A}$'?"

"But of course! Just write $\left|\vec{A}\right|$ – that means 'magnitude of $\vec{A}$'."

"So then we can write the formula above like this:

$$\left|\vec{A}\right|^2 = \left(A_x\right)^2 + \left(A_y\right)^2$$

"And if we take the square root, we get:

$$\left|\vec{A}\right| = \sqrt{\left(A_x\right)^2 + \left(A_y\right)^2}$$

"Does that look right?"

"Formidable, formidable! With this formula, you can describe the direction and magnitude of a vector to anyone – even an old Frenchman such as myself!"

Pythagorean theorem

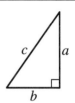

For the right triangle shown above,

$$c^2 = a^2 + b^2$$

Then, by using the square root:

$$c = \sqrt{a^2 + b^2}$$

we can find the value of c, that is, the length of the diagonal side.

3. What is 'Inner Product'??

"Dr. Fourier, what is this 'inner product' thing I've read about?"

"The inner product is one way to perform calculations involving two vectors. When we visited the seashore, we added and then subtracted two vectors, remember? But we didn't try multiplying or dividing vectors. Do you know why?"

"Uh . . . because it's too complicated?"

"Non, non! It's not merely complicated, it's **impossible** to multiply or divide vectors!"

"What? Impossible??"

"That's right. We've been using 'vector' to refer to a quantity that has both direction and magnitude. In the same way, we use 'scalar' to denote a quantity of magnitude only. In other words, all the quantities we dealt with before we encountered vectors were actually scalars. For example, 3, or 5000, or -1.5 – all these numbers are scalars. As you well know, we can multiply or divide numbers of this sort. That's because only their size, or magnitude, changes when we do so. But vectors indicate direction as well as size. How do you suppose this direction would change if we multiplied or divided two vectors together? It makes no sense! And that is why we cannot multiply or divide vectors."

The good Doctor's explanation only made me more confused.

"So what did you mean by 'scalar multiplication' when we were looking at the weather map?"

"Well, scalar multiplication looks like this:

$$2 \times \vec{A} = 2\vec{A}$$

In other words, it is the multiplication of a vector by a scalar. That **is** possible! Let us see how it looks on our graph paper.

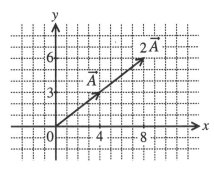

"Suppose we say that vector $\vec{A}$ = (4, 3). Now look carefully! The vector $2\vec{A}$ has a length twice that of the original $\vec{A}$. Not only that, its x and y components are both twice those of the original $\vec{A}$ as well. In other words, scalar multiplication increases both the x and y components of a vector by the same multiple."

"Then what happens if you multiply a vector by −1, say? Does it go in the opposite direction, the way it did when we performed subtraction?"

"That's right. Let's try it on the graph, using the same vector $\vec{A}$ = (4, 3) as before:

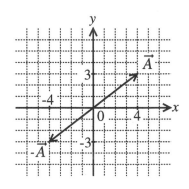

"And there you have it – in the opposite direction, just as you said!"

"So it is. Now I see how that subtraction worked earlier."

"In a nutshell, scalar multiplication only changes the **magnitude** of a vector. That's not really any more complicated than the multiplication of two scalars, is it?"

"Uh, I guess not..."

"Never mind, I'll try to make it even easier for you to understand."

Before Dr. Fourier had finished, the space around us was filled with words and numbers:

$$3 \quad + \quad 4 \quad = \quad 7$$
$$\text{(scalar)} + \text{(scalar)} \rightarrow \text{(scalar)}$$

$$6 \quad - \quad 2 \quad = \quad 4$$
$$\text{(scalar)} - \text{(scalar)} \rightarrow \text{(scalar)}$$

$$2 \quad \times \quad 3 \quad = \quad 6$$
$$\text{(scalar)} \times \text{(scalar)} \rightarrow \text{(scalar)}$$

$$9 \quad \div \quad 3 \quad = \quad 3$$
$$\text{(scalar)} \div \text{(scalar)} \rightarrow \text{(scalar)}$$

That much I could grasp. But the parade of equations continued:

$$(3, 4) + (2, 6) = (5, 10)$$
$$[\text{vector}] + [\text{vector}] \rightarrow [\text{vector}]$$

$$(6, 4) - (3, 1) = (3, 3)$$
$$[\text{vector}] - [\text{vector}] \rightarrow [\text{vector}]$$

$$(3, 2) \times 3 = (9, 6)$$
$$[\text{vector}] \times (\text{scalar}) \rightarrow [\text{vector}](\text{scalar multiple})$$

$$(8, 4) \div 2 = (8, 4) \times \frac{1}{2} = (4, 2)$$
$$[\text{vector}] \div (\text{scalar}) = [\text{vector}] \times \left(\frac{1}{\text{scalar}}\right) \rightarrow [\text{vector}](\text{scalar multiple})$$

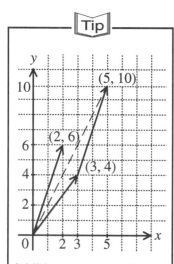

Tip

Addition or subtraction of vectors can be expressed as the addition or subtraction of their x and y components.

These are the only combinations in which vectors can be added, subtracted, multiplied, or divided.

"Does that help clear things up?"

"Oh yeah, that helps a lot! But I don't see anything about inner products in these formulas..."

"That's true. An inner product looks like this:

[vector] inner product [vector] → (scalar)

Once again, words appeared out of nowhere. They seemed to be saying that the inner product of two vectors is a scalar.

"The proper way to write out the calculation of an inner product is '$\vec{A} \cdot \vec{B}$'. But what this actually means is:

$$\vec{A} \cdot \vec{B} = A_x B_x + A_y B_y$$

"In other words, finding the inner product of two vectors means multiplying their x components and y components respectively, then adding up the results."

"But what exactly does this inner product represent?"

"By calculating the inner product and seeing if you get 0 for an answer, you can tell whether the two vectors are perpendicular to one another. Let's stick some numbers in our formula and see what happens."

Tip

The inner product symbol

An inner product is indicated by the symbol " • ". It's identical to the symbol for multiplication of scalars, but don't get them confused!

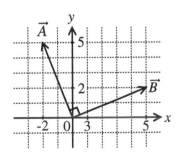

$$\vec{A} = (7, 2)$$
$$\vec{B} = (3, 6)$$
$$\vec{A} \cdot \vec{B} = 7 \times 3 + 2 \times 6$$
$$= 21 + 12$$
$$= 33$$

"Well, this inner product isn't 0. Are you saying it would be 0 if $\vec{A}$ and $\vec{B}$ were at right angles to each other?"

$$\vec{A} = (-2, 5)$$
$$\vec{B} = (5, 2)$$
$$\vec{A} \cdot \vec{B} = (-2) \times 5 + 5 \times 2$$
$$= -10 + 10$$
$$= 0$$

¡Muy bien! The inner product of these two perpendicular vectors is 0, all right!

"When two vectors intersect at right angles, their inner product is always 0."

"But why?"

"Would you like to find out?"

"Sure, but how?"

"Trust me, I'm a mathematician, remember? First, let's look at the angle θ between two vectors."

Suddenly, two of the arrows floating around us lined themselves up like this:

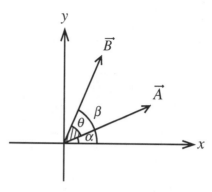

"Now suppose we have an angle θ between $\vec{A}$ and $\vec{B}$, an angle α between $\vec{A}$ and the x axis, and an angle β between $\vec{B}$ and the x axis. We can then use the trigonometric identities."

"Huh? You mean one of those formulas we used when we were differentiating $\sin \theta$ back in Chapter 6? Why do we want to use the trigonometric identities here?"

"Heh heh heh... chalk it up to a mathematician's intuition if you like, mon frère! You'd be surprised how often one's intuition proves correct in the solution of mathematical problems!"

"Say wha–?"

Dr. Fourier's talk about intuition caught me off guard. I'd always thought of math as a well-ordered collection of rigorously logical theories – not "intuitive."

"As you gain more experience solving various math problems on your own, you will come to appreciate what I'm saying!"

"Okay, I'll take your word for it, Doctor! But how do we use the trigonometric identities here?"

"Look at the graph. We can say that $\theta = \beta - \alpha$, can't we? In that case,

$$\cos \theta = \cos (\beta - \alpha)$$

n'est-ce pas? We can use one of the trigonometric identities to transform this as follows."

$$\cos \theta = \cos (\beta - \alpha)$$
$$= \cos \alpha \cos \beta + \sin \alpha \sin \beta$$

"Does this have anything to do with inner products?"

"All in good time, all in good time! Now, you know another way of expressing the $\sin \alpha$, $\cos \alpha$, $\sin \beta$ and $\cos \beta$ we have here, do you not?"

"I do? Another way...? Oh, you mean '$\sin \theta$ = vertical/diagonal' and '$\cos \theta$ = horizontal/diagonal'?"

"Exactement! Try using those formulas to rewrite the sine and cosine for α and β respectively!"

"Uh, let's see... cos α is horizontal/diagonal...

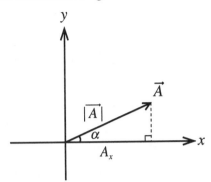

"Here the diagonal is $|\vec{A}|$ and the horizontal is A_x, so:

$$\cos\alpha = \frac{A_x}{|\vec{A}|}$$

"Right, Doctor?"

"Now do the same thing for the other cosine and the sines."

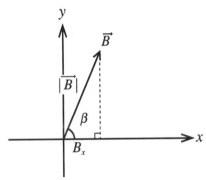

"The diagonal of cos β is $|\vec{B}|$ and the horizontal is B_x, so:

$$\cos\beta = \frac{B_x}{|\vec{B}|}$$

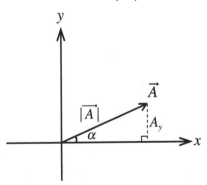

"As for sin α, which is vertical/diagonal, the diagonal is $|\vec{A}|$ and the vertical is A_y, so:

$$\sin\alpha = \frac{A_y}{|\vec{A}|}$$

In other words,

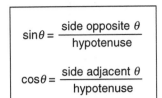

$$\sin\theta = \frac{\text{side opposite }\theta}{\text{hypotenuse}}$$

$$\cos\theta = \frac{\text{side adjacent }\theta}{\text{hypotenuse}}$$

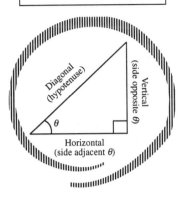

"And the diagonal of $\sin \beta$ is $|\vec{B}|$ and the vertical is B_y, so:

$$\sin \beta = \frac{B_y}{|\vec{B}|}$$

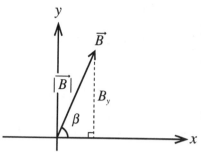

"Bon! Well done! Now try inserting these into the one of the trigonometric identities."

"Okay, it looked like this:

$$\cos \theta = \cos (\beta - \alpha)$$
$$= \cos \alpha \cos \beta + \sin \alpha \sin \beta$$

"So we can rewrite it as follows:

$$\cos \theta = \frac{A_x}{|\vec{A}|} \frac{B_x}{|\vec{B}|} + \frac{A_y}{|\vec{A}|} \frac{B_y}{|\vec{B}|}$$
$$= \frac{A_x B_x + A_y B_y}{|\vec{A}||\vec{B}|}$$

"Whoa! What's this? The numerator is the same as that formula you showed me for the inner product!"

"You're absolutely right. Now get rid of the denominator by multiplying both sides of the equation by $|\vec{A}||\vec{B}|$."

"Yes, sir! If we multiply both sides of $\cos \theta = \dfrac{A_x B_x + A_y B_y}{|\vec{A}||\vec{B}|}$ by $|\vec{A}||\vec{B}|$, we get:

$$A_x B_x + A_y B_y = |\vec{A}||\vec{B}| \cos \theta$$

"Is this another formula for the inner product, Doc?"

"Indeed it is. This formula means that the inner product $(A_x B_x + A_y B_y)$ can be found by multiplying the magnitude $|\vec{A}|$ of $\vec{A}$, the magnitude $|\vec{B}|$ of $\vec{B}$, and the cosine of the angle θ between them. This formula makes it easier to see the relationship between the angle made by two vectors and the value of their inner product."

"Wow! So what happens when the two vectors are at right angles?"

"Try it and see!"

"I was afraid you'd say that... Okay, that means I need to find the cosine for two vectors that form a right angle... Wait! I've got it! A right angle means θ is 90°, and since cos90° is 0, that gives us:

$$A_x B_x + A_y B_y = |\vec{A}||\vec{B}|\cos 90°$$
$$= |\vec{A}||\vec{B}| \times 0$$
$$= 0$$

"So the inner product is 0!"

So now you know that two vectors intersecting at right angles always yield an inner product of 0. And you know that, conversely, if the inner product is 0, you can be certain that the two vectors intersect at right angles. This information will prove very useful on our subsequent adventures, so make a note of it!

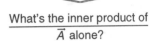

4. The World of the nth Dimension

Dr. Fourier handed me a sheet of blank paper.

"The x and y coordinates we have seen so far form a two-dimensional system. The world of two dimensions is just like this sheet of paper. It has only two axes, vertical and horizontal; the world is flat."

"Then in a two-dimensional world, I'd be flat as a pancake too, wouldn't I."

"Vraiment! But now, if we add one more axis to these two dimensions, we find we have length, width, and height – three dimensions! The world we live in, of course, is three-dimensional. But what do vectors look like in three dimensions? Let's take a look.

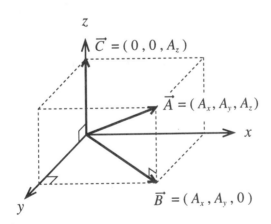

"Here we can express $\vec{A}$ like this:

$$\vec{A} = (A_x, A_y, A_z)$$

"Notice that we have a new component in the direction of the z axis!"

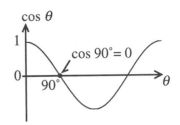

| Tip |

What's the inner product of $\vec{A}$ alone?

All you have to do is insert $\vec{A}$ twice in the inner product formula:

$$\vec{A} \cdot \vec{A} = |\vec{A}||\vec{A}|\cos 0°$$
$$= |\vec{A}||\vec{A}| \times 1$$
$$= |\vec{A}|^2$$

Since this is the inner product of $\vec{A}$ by itself, angle $\theta = 0°$, and

$$\cos 0° = 1$$

So the inner product of $\vec{A}$ is the magnitude of $\vec{A}$, or $|\vec{A}|$, squared.

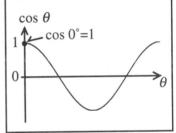

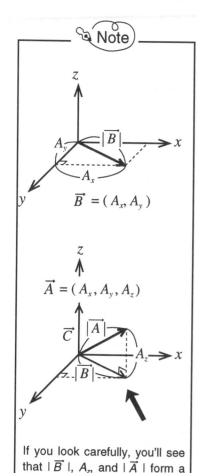

$\vec{B} = (A_x, A_y)$

$\vec{A} = (A_x, A_y, A_z)$

If you look carefully, you'll see that $|\vec{B}|$, A_z, and $|\vec{A}|$ form a new right triangle. That's why we can use the Pythagorean theorem again to find $|\vec{A}|$.

"But how do we calculate inner products, now that we have an extra dimension?"

"It's not all that different with three dimensions. Let's try finding the magnitude of $\vec{A}$, for example. The components of $\vec{B}$ consist of the x and y components of $\vec{A}$, so we can use them to figure out the length of $\vec{A}$.

"To begin with, we'll use the Pythagorean theorem to find the magnitude of $\vec{B}$:

$$|\vec{B}| = \sqrt{A_x^2 + A_y^2}$$

"Next, we want to find $|\vec{A}|$. To do this we'll use $|\vec{B}|$ and $|\vec{C}|$ (A_z), once again applying the Pythagorean theorem:

$$|\vec{A}|^2 = |\vec{B}|^2 + |\vec{C}|^2 = A_x^2 + A_y^2 + A_z^2$$
$$|\vec{A}| = \sqrt{A_x^2 + A_y^2 + A_z^2}$$

"So now we have the magnitude of $\vec{A}$. As you see, we can find the magnitude of a vector in three dimensions through the same calculations we used in two dimensions."

"What about four dimensions, then?"

"Can you imagine what a four-dimensional space would look like, mon ami?"

Four-dimensional space... whew...

"Yow!"

A cry escaped my lips. The ground under my feet had suddenly vanished, and I seemed to be floating in the middle of nowhere. There was no up or down, and the space around me seemed strangely distorted. Was this the fourth dimension??

The disembodied voice of Dr. Fourier emanated from the void.

"You are now in the world of four dimensions, at least as people like to imagine it!"

Dr. Fourier went on:

"The fourth dimension is often defined as time. Whenever people get in a time machine in science fiction movies, they always pass through the fourth dimension to reach some other period in history. The idea is that, since time is just another dimension, it's possible to travel through it as we would any other type of space. But that's only conjecture; we have no idea if it would really work."

"Why's that?"

"Because so far no one has been found who's actually visited the world of four dimensions! So no one knows what these four dimensions actually are. All we can do is try to picture them in our minds. Can you picture a graph with four mutually perpendicular axes?"

I tried to imagine four axes, but three was as far as I could get.

"And yet," said Dr. Fourier, "mathematics allows us to catch a glimpse of the true nature of four dimensions."

"First of all, we have to name them differently. Up to now we've been using x, y, and z, but there are no letters after z. So from now on, we'll use a_1, a_2, a_3, and a_4. That allows us to describe a four-dimensional vector $\vec{A}$ as follows."

$$\vec{A} = (a_1, a_2, a_3, a_4)$$

I was a little disappointed at how easy it sounded. Weren't four-dimensional vectors more complicated than that?

"Doctor, does this mean you can just write a_5, a_6, or a_{10}, or, for that matter, a_{100}? Is that all there is to it?"

"Essentially, yes. Mathematics allows you to describe 10,000 dimensions if you like! We can use the following formula to represent all the possibilities:

$$\vec{A} = (a_1, a_2, a_3, \cdots\cdots, a_n)$$

"That n at the end can be any number you want."

It all seemed too easy somehow, but who was I to complain? Besides, I was struck by the idea that math could conceive of an absurdly large number of dimensions, 10,000 or whatever, simply as an extension of our notion of three dimensions.

"Now then," said the Doctor, "when we found the magnitude of $\vec{A}$ before, all we did was square each of its components, add them together, then take the square root. So this time, we can do this:

$$\left|\vec{A}\right| = \sqrt{a_1^2 + a_2^2 + a_3^2 + \cdots\cdots + a_n^2}$$

"We can also use the same procedure as before to define the inner product.

$$\vec{A} = (a_1, a_2, a_3, \cdots\cdots, a_n)$$
$$\vec{B} = (b_1, b_2, b_3, \cdots\cdots, b_n)$$

"Then the inner product of the n-dimensional vectors $\vec{A}$ and $\vec{B}$ is:

$$\vec{A} \cdot \vec{B} = a_1 b_1 + a_2 b_2 + a_3 b_3 + \cdots\cdots + a_n b_n$$

"Not bad, eh?"

"But even with that many dimensions," I asked, "is it still true that, if their inner product is 0, the two vectors intersect at right angles?"

"Alas, we can't tell if they really intersect at 90°. It's impossible to know, because we can't even imagine, much less actually see, how they would intersect in four or more dimensions. Therefore, when we deal with that many dimensions, we don't say the vectors 'intersect at right angles' when their inner product $\vec{A} \cdot \vec{B} = 0$. We simply say they're **orthogonal**."

"Orthogonal, huh?"

This discussion was getting pretty deep, I thought to myself. Even though you couldn't picture it in your own head, mathematical formulas allowed you to talk about vectors in 10,000 dimensions. And if the inner products of all those vector were all 0, that meant all 10,000 axes were orthogonal! It's inconceivable. And yet, with the help of mathematics, we can sort of understand it as an extension of the world of three dimensions.

So the language of math allows us to describe the unimaginable. Another example of this is black holes, the existence of which was deduced from complex equations that made use of four-dimensional space. No doubt math will continue to reveal all sorts of amazing things. It certainly seems to qualify as the most useful language in the world!

5. Projection

"Projection" means the casting of a shadow or image on a surface. But what on earth could that have to do with vectors? My own notion of the "casting of shadows" looked like this:

So when I thought of projecting vectors, this is all I could come up with:

It must mean something else, I decided.

As I was pondering the mysteries of projection, a series of lines suddenly sprouted beneath my feet. Before I knew it, they had formed a graph of orthogonal vectors.

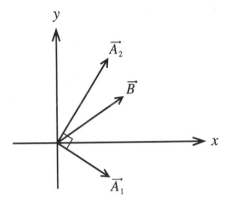

What caught my eye, however, was the presence of a third vector between the two orthogonal vectors $\vec{A_1}$ and $\vec{A_2}$.

"Say, Doc, what's this vector $\vec{B}$ doing here?"

"We're going to project it onto vectors $\vec{A_1}$ and $\vec{A_2}$. We do this by casting two lines, which are perpendicular to $\vec{A_1}$ and $\vec{A_2}$ respectively, from the tip of $\vec{B}$. The points where these lines intersect with $\vec{A_1}$ and $\vec{A_2}$ define two new projective vectors, $\vec{P_1}$ and $\vec{P_2}$."

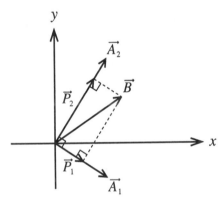

"If you say so! But just what do these projected vectors **do**?"

No sooner were the words out of my mouth than a large watermelon appeared where "$\vec{B}$" had been written.

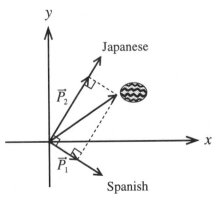

Moreover, the $\vec{A_1}$ vector was now labeled "Spanish" and the $\vec{A_2}$ vector "Japanese."

So now 🍉 was projected onto the Japanese vector and the Spanish vector – what did that mean??

"When we project 🍉 onto the Japanese vector, the word that represents 🍉 appears out of all the thousands of words in the Japanese language."

"Then, since the Japanese word for 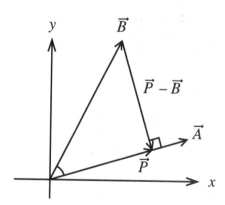 is *suika*, that means $\vec{P_2}$ must be *suika*, right?"

"Very good. And when we project 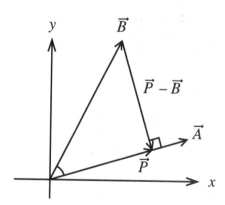 onto the Spanish vector?"

If we think of *suika* and *sandia* as elements of 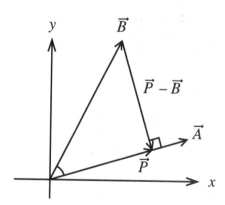, then adding them together allows us to describe 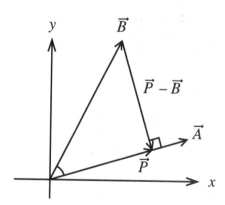 in more detail.

"We get *sandia*!"

"The *suika* and *sandia* we get by projecting 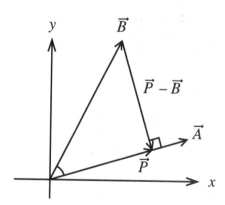 onto Japanese and Spanish are basically the same thing – 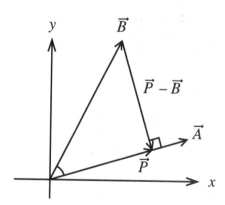. So we can think of *suika* and *sandia* as elements (components) of 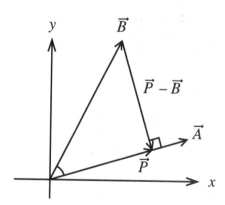, and express this relationship by addition:"

$$suika + sandia = \text{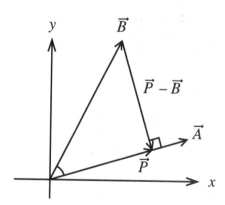}$$

"Likewise, we can express the relationship between $\vec{B}$ and the projected vectors $\vec{P_1}$ and $\vec{P_2}$ as follows."

$$\vec{P_1} + \vec{P_2} = \vec{B}$$

It began to dawn on me that projection was simply a way of looking at the same thing from different points of view.

"Now let us see how projection is expressed in the language of mathematics."

"How does vector $\vec{B}$ project onto vector $\vec{A}$? First we drop a line from the tip of $\vec{B}$ that intersects at right angles with $\vec{A}$. Then we can assign a name, $\vec{P}$, to the vector along $\vec{A}$ up to the point of intersection."

The perpendicular line we cast from $\vec{B}$ down to $\vec{A}$ can also be thought of as a vector expressed as ($\vec{P} - \vec{B}$).

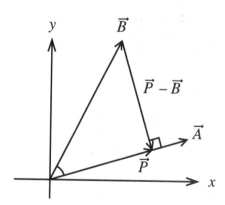

"What we're going to do now is find the value of the projected vector $\vec{P}$."

"Since ($\vec{P} - \vec{B}$) and $\vec{A}$ intersect at right angles, their inner product is 0, right?"

"Right you are. So we can write the formula for their inner product like this:"

$$\vec{A} \cdot (\vec{P} - \vec{B}) = 0$$

"Now, we can think of vector $\vec{P}$ as a scalar multiple of $\vec{A}$, so:

$$\vec{P} = x\vec{A}$$

"Through substitution and expansion, we get:

$$\begin{aligned}
\vec{A} \cdot \left(\vec{P} - \vec{B}\right) &= \vec{A} \cdot \left(x\vec{A} - \vec{B}\right) \\
&= x\vec{A} \cdot \vec{A} - \vec{A} \cdot \vec{B} \\
&= 0
\end{aligned}$$

"If we know how many multiples of $\vec{A}$ make $\vec{P}$, we can find the value of $\vec{P}$. So we want to find x:

$$x\vec{A} \cdot \vec{A} - \vec{A} \cdot \vec{B} = 0 \qquad \therefore x = \frac{\vec{A} \cdot \vec{B}}{\vec{A} \cdot \vec{A}}$$

"And now, we can finally find $\vec{P}$. Since $\vec{P} = x\vec{A}$, that gives us:

$$\vec{P} = \frac{\vec{A} \cdot \vec{B}}{\vec{A} \cdot \vec{A}} \vec{A}$$

Note

Why $\vec{P} = x\vec{A}$?

Vectors $\vec{P}$ and $\vec{A}$ face in the same direction, but their magnitudes are different. That means we can treat $\vec{P}$ as a scalar multiple of $\vec{A}$. Therefore $\vec{P} = x\vec{A}$

Note

What about calculating $\vec{A} \cdot (x\vec{A} - \vec{B})$?

$\vec{A} \cdot (x\vec{A} - \vec{B})$ can be calculated the following way:

$$\begin{aligned}
\vec{A} \cdot \left(x\vec{A} - \vec{B}\right) \\
= \vec{A} \cdot x\vec{A} - \vec{A} \cdot \vec{B}
\end{aligned}$$

"This is the value of the vector $\vec{P}$ that is projected from $\vec{B}$ onto $\vec{A}$. Take a close look at this formula, s'il vous plaît!"

"Hey! Both the numerator and denominator are inner products!"

"So they are. Now then, suppose vectors $\vec{A}$ and $\vec{B}$ are orthogonal. What happens when we project $\vec{B}$ onto $\vec{A}$ this time?"

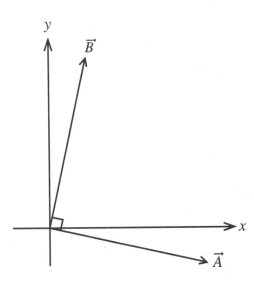

$\vec{A}$ and $\vec{B}$ are orthogonal, so their inner product is 0. Thus, $\vec{P}$ would equal 0. And since the inner product of $\vec{A}$ and $\vec{B}$ would be 0, the formula above would give us:

$$\vec{P} = \frac{0}{\vec{A} \cdot \vec{A}} \cdot \vec{A} = \vec{0}$$

"Right! When two vectors are orthogonal, their inner product is 0, so when $\vec{B}$ is projected onto $\vec{A}$, the result is $\vec{0}$."

Zero, eh? That seemed logical enough. But without having actual numbers in front of me, it was hard to see exactly how we arrived at that result.

"Why don't you try this with some actual numbers, then!"

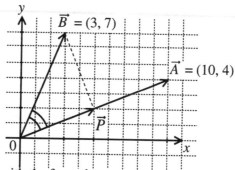

Okay, first we start with the formula:

$$\vec{P} = \frac{\vec{A} \cdot \vec{B}}{\vec{A} \cdot \vec{A}} \vec{A}$$

Here we can use the following values for $\vec{A} \cdot \vec{B}$ and $\vec{A} \cdot \vec{A}$:

$$\vec{A} \cdot \vec{B} = (10 \times 3) + (4 \times 7)$$
$$\vec{A} \cdot \vec{A} = (10^2 + 4^2)$$

Now, inserting these in our formula for $\vec{P}$, we get:

$$\vec{P} = \frac{10 \times 3 + 4 \times 7}{10^2 + 4^2} \vec{A}$$
$$= \frac{30 + 28}{100 + 16} \vec{A}$$
$$= \frac{58}{116} \vec{A} = \frac{1}{2} \vec{A}$$
$$= \frac{1}{2} (10, 4) = (5, 2)$$

Good, that seemed to work. Now then – Dr. Fourier just finished telling us that when two vectors are orthogonal, a projected vector has a value of 0. Time to check it out!

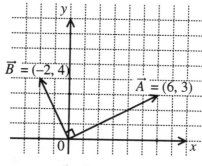

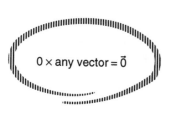

$0 \times$ any vector $= \vec{0}$

$$\vec{P} = \frac{\vec{A} \cdot \vec{B}}{\vec{A} \cdot \vec{A}} \vec{A}$$

$$= \frac{6 \times (-2) + 3 \times 4}{6^2 + 3^2} \vec{A}$$

$$= \frac{-12 + 12}{36 + 9} \vec{A}$$

$$= \frac{0}{45} \vec{A} = \vec{0}$$

He was right! I guess it should be pretty obvious, since the inner product $\vec{A} \cdot \vec{B}$ is always 0. But it's nice to see that it really works.

"Satisfied? Now I have something else for you to try. Remember how we learned that we could rewrite $\vec{A} \cdot \vec{B}$ as $|\vec{A}| |\vec{B}| \cos \theta$, and $\vec{A} \cdot \vec{A}$ as $|\vec{A}|^2$? Let's substitute these in our projection formula:

$$\vec{P} = \frac{\vec{A} \cdot \vec{B}}{\vec{A} \cdot \vec{A}} \vec{A}$$

$$= \frac{|\vec{A}| |\vec{B}| \cos \theta}{|\vec{A}| |\vec{A}|} \vec{A}$$

$|\vec{A}|$ is a scalar quantity, so we can cancel out $|\vec{A}| / |\vec{A}|$. Then we can group $\vec{A}$ and $|\vec{A}|$ together.

$$= |\vec{B}| \cos \theta \frac{\vec{A}}{|\vec{A}|}$$

This shows that $\vec{P}$ has a magnitude of $|\vec{B}| \cos \theta$ in the direction of $\vec{A}$.

"To make this easier to comprehend, let's draw it on a graph:

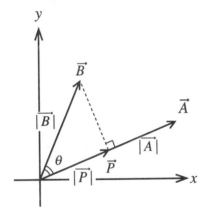

If the angle between $\vec{A}$ and $\vec{B}$ is θ, then:

$$\cos \theta = \frac{|\vec{P}|}{|\vec{B}|}$$

We can change this around to read:

$$|\vec{P}| = |\vec{B}| \cos \theta$$

So the magnitude of $\vec{P}$ is $|\vec{B}| \cos \theta$.

"And of course, the direction of $\vec{P}$ is the same as the direction of $\vec{A}$. That's why, in the formula we arrived at a moment ago...

$$\vec{P} = |\vec{B}| \cos \theta \frac{\vec{A}}{|\vec{A}|} \qquad \cdots\cdots\cdots \text{ formula } ①$$

"...$|\vec{B}| \cos \theta$ indicates the magnitude $|\vec{P}|$ of vector $\vec{P}$, and $\frac{\vec{A}}{|\vec{A}|}$ indicates the direction of $\vec{P}$."

"But Doctor, what's this $\frac{\vec{A}}{|\vec{A}|}$ thing??"

"That's a vector divided by its own magnitude; we call it a 'unit vector.' Simply put, the unit vector is a vector with a magnitude of 1 in the direction of $\vec{A}$."

"So in formula ① above, $\frac{\vec{A}}{|\vec{A}|}$ represents the direction of $\vec{P}$, which in this case is the direction of $\vec{A}$."

I found myself staring at the watermelon vector again.

"Before, we saw a 🍉 projected onto the Japanese and Spanish vector," said Dr. Fourier. "This time, we'll use proper mathematical symbols to identify those axes instead."

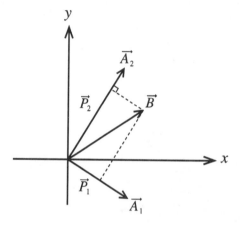

"Let's try our hand at finding values for $\vec{P_1}$ and $\vec{P_2}$ here:

$$\vec{P_1} = x_1\vec{A_1}, \quad x_1 = \frac{\vec{A_1} \cdot \vec{B}}{\vec{A_1} \cdot \vec{A_1}}$$

$$\therefore \vec{P_1} = \frac{\vec{A_1} \cdot \vec{B}}{\vec{A_1} \cdot \vec{A_1}} \vec{A_1}$$

$$\vec{P_2} = x_2\vec{A_2}, \quad x_2 = \frac{\vec{A_2} \cdot \vec{B}}{\vec{A_2} \cdot \vec{A_2}}$$

$$\therefore \vec{P_2} = \frac{\vec{A_2} \cdot \vec{B}}{\vec{A_2} \cdot \vec{A_2}} \vec{A_2}$$

"Now look at our graph. If we add $\vec{P_1}$ and $\vec{P_2}$ together, we should get, $\vec{B}$ remember?"

That's right – the Doctor had already told me that adding two projected vectors gives you the original vector – *suika* + *sandia* = 🍉, and all that...

"Doc, is this another rule that applies no matter how many dimensions you have?"

"Well, going back to our friend the 🍉, why don't you try adding another vector– for English, say? Then, when you project onto it..."

"You get watermelon!"

"That's right! And you can keep adding axes – for German, Korean, what have you. As you increase the number of axes, the elements (components) of 🍉 increase in number as well. The more of these you add together, the more detailed a description you get of 🍉.

"Now let's write this description out in mathematical terms.

$$\vec{A_1}, \vec{A_2}, \vec{A_3}, \vec{A_4}, \vec{A_5}, \cdots\cdots\cdots, \vec{A_n}$$

"We shall assume these vectors are all orthogonal in a coordinate system of n dimensions. Now, when we project n-dimensional vector $\vec{B}$ onto $\vec{A_i}$, $(i = 1, 2, 3, \cdots n)$ we can use this formula to find the projected vector $\vec{P}$:

$$\vec{P_i} = \frac{\vec{A_i} \cdot \vec{B}}{\vec{A_i} \cdot \vec{A_i}} \vec{A_i}$$

"And when we add up all these projected vectors, they return us to the original vector, $\vec{B}$:

$$\vec{P_1} + \vec{P_2} + \vec{P_3} + \vec{P_4} + \cdots\cdots + \vec{P_n} = \vec{B}$$

"In other words, if we project a 100-dimensional vector $\vec{B}$ onto 100 orthogonal axes, we get 100 different components of $\vec{B}$.

"To find these components, we perform projection. And when we add all 100 of these components together, they produce $\vec{B}$. So $\vec{B}$ is the sum of its components..."

Hadn't I heard something like this before? Now where did I hear that...?

6. Vectors and Fourier

I suddenly realized I was standing in complete darkness. Feeling a bit anxious, I tried to find Dr. Fourier, but he was nowhere to be found. Then I noticed a pale blue light off in the distance ahead of me. Framed in the light was a door. I walked toward the door until I could see a message of some sort written on it:

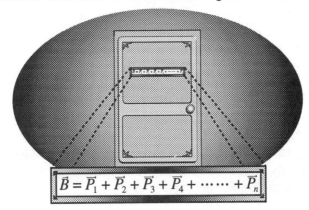

What was this? The addition formula for projected vectors I had just learned! Why was it on this door? It must have some kind of significance, but what?

The door opened easily. But when I walked through it, my jaw dropped. Floating all around me were Fourier waves. Some of these waves had lined themselves up in an orderly fashion:

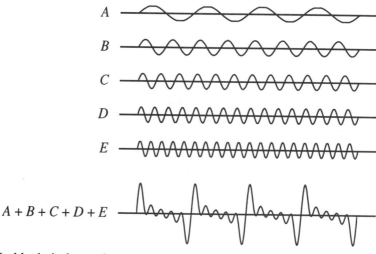

Suddenly it dawned on me.

"A complicated wave is the sum of its simple waves..."

"Vector $\vec{B}$ is the sum of its components..."

Eureka! No wonder the discussion about $\vec{B}$ had seemed strangely familiar. Adding up a Fourier series and adding up projected vectors were just two different ways of looking at the same thing!

Even as I pondered this new revelation, another door appeared in front of me. This one had a message too:

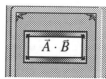

The inner product formula! Was there a connection between Fourier analysis and inner products too? When an inner product is 0, it means the two vectors are orthogonal, but...

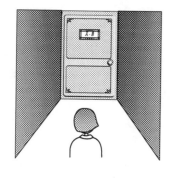

Now another message appeared on the door:

WHAT HAPPENS WHEN YOU MULTIPLY SINE AND COSINE AND THEN INTEGRATE THE RESULT?

The door wouldn't budge. I had a feeling it wouldn't open until I answered the question. Looking down, I saw the book **WHO IS FOURIER? A Mathematical Adventure** lying at my feet. Hurriedly I picked it up and opened it to the chapter on Fourier coefficients.

My eyes fell on a chart showing how to integrate the result of multiplying two sine waves together.

Suppose you multiply two sine waves that have the same period , for example sin $1\omega t$ and sin $1\omega t$, and integrate the result – it's never 0. But when you multiply and integrate two waves that have different periods, for example sin $2\omega t$ and sin $1\omega t$, the result is always 0. The same thing applies to cosine waves.

So what happens when you multiply a sine wave by a cosine wave, and integrate the result? It turns out that you always get 0.

Somehow that rang a bell. What was it with 0 all the time, anyway?

"It can't be! Could it? Does this mean sine and cosine waves are orthogonal...?"

As I stood there muttering to myself, the door suddenly creaked open. I rushed through it and nearly bumped into a wooden signpost with a lengthy message carved on it.

You're right! If we use vectors to represent sine and cosine waves, their inner product is always 0. But you'll find this easier to grasp if you learn it through formulas.

Beyond the signpost, a road stretched off into the distance. If I followed this road, would I reach the junction between the inner product concept and Fourier analysis? I had a hunch I might, so I set off down the road filled with great expectations.

I hadn't gone very far, however, before I came face to face with a high wall blocking my path. The road appeared to continue on the other side of the wall, but it was too high for me to climb over.

Had I gone the wrong way? I began to get nervous. I stared at the wall – and suddenly noticed some graffiti on it:

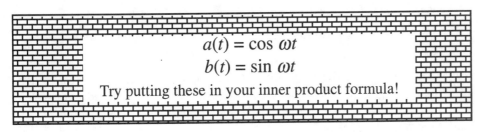

$a(t) = \cos \omega t$

$b(t) = \sin \omega t$

Try putting these in your inner product formula!

 Note

Expressing waves as vectors

When we performed discrete Fourier expansion, we drew a discontinuous wave by plotting values at fixed time intervals. By obtaining an infinite number of such values, we were able to draw a continuous wave.
Likewise, we can describe a vector of infinite dimensions in terms of an infinite number of components:

$$\vec{A} = (a_1, a_2, a_3, \cdots, a_n, \cdots)$$

Focusing on this point that they are both expressed by an infinite number of values (components), we can think of a wave as a vector of infinite dimensions.

The inner product formula was $\vec{A} \cdot \vec{B}$, so I figured the message meant substituting them like this:

$$\cos \omega t \cdot \sin \omega t$$

I took out my trusty spray can and spray-painted the new formula on the wall. Instantly a ladder appeared out of nowhere. I climbed up the ladder and hopped over the wall.

Before me towered another wall, much higher than the first. I couldn't even see the top of this one. A ladder wouldn't be much help. Yet I was strangely confident; I figured that if I could solve the problem on the wall, I'd get over it somehow.

This is what the wall said:

"Assume that the waves $\cos \omega t$ and $\sin \omega t$ are both made up of an infinite number of components. You must list these components in a table. But since you can't possibly write them all, you may instead write values for n components obtained at regular intervals of Δt seconds."

I strode up to the table that now appeared on the wall and began writing in the formulas for component waves, relying on what I remembered about the Fourier series.

t	0	Δt	$2\Delta t$	} }	$n\Delta t$
$\cos \omega t$	$\cos 0$	$\cos \omega \Delta t$	$\cos \omega 2\Delta t$	} }	$\cos \omega n\Delta t$
$\sin \omega t$	$\sin 0$	$\sin \omega \Delta t$	$\sin \omega 2\Delta t$	} }	$\sin \omega n\Delta t$

When I was done, another message materialized next to the table:

"Multiply each of these $\cos \omega t$ and $\sin \omega t$ pairs together, then add them all up."

$$(\cos 0 \cdot \sin 0) + (\cos \omega \Delta t \cdot \sin \omega \Delta t) + (\cos \omega 2\Delta t \cdot \sin \omega 2\Delta t) + \cdots\cdots$$
$$\cdots\cdots + (\cos \omega n\Delta t \cdot \sin \omega n\Delta t)$$

Now that I'd written the requested answer, I expected the wall to vanish, allowing me to get on with my journey. Unfortunately, the wall didn't appear to be in much of a hurry to go anywhere. Finding the inner product would require a little more work, it seemed.

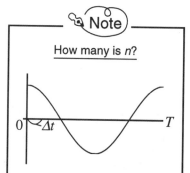

Note

How many is n?

If we take a value at every Δt seconds in one period ($0 \le t \le T$), the number of values obtained is:

$$n = T/\Delta t$$

(Example)
If we divide $T=10$ (seconds) into 1-second intervals:

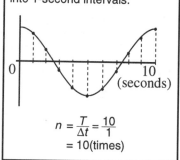

$$n = \frac{T}{\Delta t} = \frac{10}{1}$$
$$= 10 \text{(times)}$$

I'd already written out the components at Δt intervals. Now, if I multiplied them according to my formula and placed the results on a graph, they'd look like this:

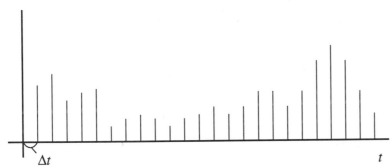

Since I only had values for the components at a few isolated intervals, multiplying them produced a very spiky version of the wave. To perform multiplication across the entire wave, I needed to multiply each value by Δt. That would fill in the space between the individual points.

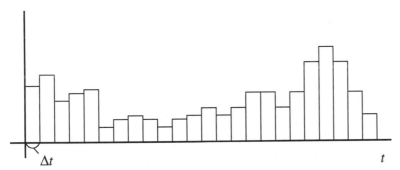

$$(\cos 0 \cdot \sin 0)\, \Delta t + (\cos \omega\Delta t \cdot \sin \omega\Delta t)\, \Delta t$$
$$+ (\cos \omega 2\Delta t \cdot \sin \omega 2\Delta t)\, \Delta t + \cdots\cdots$$
$$\cdots\cdots + (\cos \omega n\Delta t \cdot \sin \omega n\Delta t)\, \Delta t$$

As I set down my spray can, there was a loud rumble and the entire wall collapsed. Relieved, I resumed my journey down the road.

The next obstacle I encountered was a door with a large Greek letter engraved on it:

I assumed it was telling me to write a new formula using Σ. I remembered that Σ was a convenient shorthand for writing formulas in which you wanted to add many incremental terms together. It was perfect, in fact, for the formula I had just come up with. So I wrote:

$$\sum_{k=0}^{n} (\cos k\omega\Delta t \cdot \sin k\omega\Delta t)\, \Delta t$$

The door opened, only to reveal another door with another message:

This message presumably meant: To find values for every point on the wave, bring Δt infinitely close to 0.

$$\lim_{\Delta t \to 0} \sum_{k=0}^{n} \left(\cos k\omega\Delta t \cdot \sin k\omega\Delta t \right) \Delta t$$

As soon as I added the limit symbol, this door opened too. But now another door stood in my way. This one had the following written on it:

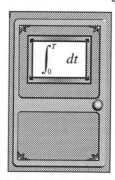

An integral sign!

Integration, eh? That would mean multiplying each component value by Δt at its lowest possible value (dt) then adding all the results together. So I wrote:

$$\int_{0}^{T} \cos \omega t \cdot \sin \omega t \, dt$$

Whoa! I was integrating a product (cos ωt, sin ωt), like in the chapter on Fourier coefficients!

The purpose of my quest was to learn how to use Fourier formulas to express the inner product of vectors. Now I had my answer. Integrating the product of two waves was the same thing as finding an inner product of vectors!

And since the result of integrating a sine and cosine wave is always 0, I could write the formula as follows:

$$\vec{A} \cdot \vec{B} = \int_{0}^{T} \cos \omega t \cdot \sin \omega t \, dt$$
$$= 0$$

So the inner product of a sine vector and cosine vector is 0!

> The inner product of a wave with any wave other than itself is always 0. That means all waves are orthogonal to one another!

The door swung open, revealing an open space flooded with bright light. There was Dr. Fourier, beaming proudly at me.

"Hey Doc, it was enough of a shock to learn that adding projected vectors is the same as adding a Fourier series. But this takes the cake – finding **an inner product is the same as integrating a product!**"

"Ho ho, you think that's a shock – hold on to your chapeau, mon vieux!"

Suddenly a familiar graph reappeared – the one I'd seen when Dr. Fourier was teaching me about projection. This time, however, the watermelon was gone and a Fourier series, $f(t) = a_1 \cos \omega t + b_1 \sin \omega t$, was in its place.

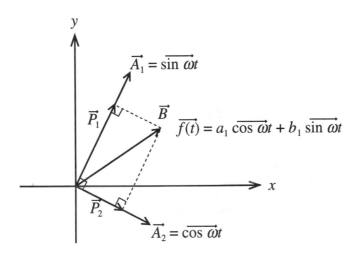

"What do you suppose will happen if we treat this complicated wave $f(t)$ as a vector and project it?" asked the Doctor.

Project it...? That would give us the components of $\overrightarrow{f(t)}$ on each vector, wouldn't it?

"I've got it!" I yelled. "The projection onto the $\overrightarrow{\sin \omega t}$ axis would be $b_1 \overrightarrow{\sin \omega t}$, and the projection onto the $\overrightarrow{\cos \omega t}$ axis would be $a_1 \overrightarrow{\cos \omega t}$!"

"Exactly so. When you project $\overrightarrow{f(t)}$, you produce its components. Doesn't that remind you of something you did with Fourier analysis?"

"F-Fourier coefficients!!" I blurted.

"Bon! Vector projection and Fourier coefficients express the same thing. To find the vector $\overrightarrow{P_1}$ projected onto $\overrightarrow{\sin \omega t}$ from vector $\overrightarrow{B}$ (that is, $\overrightarrow{f(t)}$) we use this formula:

$$\overrightarrow{P_1} = \frac{\overrightarrow{A_1} \cdot \overrightarrow{B}}{\overrightarrow{A_1} \cdot \overrightarrow{A_1}} \overrightarrow{A_1}$$

"Now, we know we can use the integral sign $\int$ to express the inner products in this formula, so:

$$\vec{P_1} = \frac{\displaystyle\int_0^T \sin \omega t \cdot f(t)dt}{\displaystyle\int_0^T \sin \omega t \cdot \sin \omega t \, dt} \vec{A_1}$$

"And since the result of integrating two sine waves (or two cosine waves) of the same period is $T/2$ over one period, we get:

$$\vec{P_1} = \frac{\displaystyle\int_0^T \sin \omega t \cdot f(t)dt}{\dfrac{T}{2}} \vec{A_1}$$

$$= \frac{2}{T}\int_0^T \sin \omega t \cdot f(t)dt \, \vec{A_1}$$

"Et voilà! The part $\dfrac{\vec{A_1} \cdot \vec{B}}{\vec{A_1} \cdot \vec{A_1}}$ that is, $\dfrac{2}{T}\displaystyle\int_0^T \sin \omega t \cdot f(t)dt$ is identical to b_n in

the formulas of the Fourier coefficients!"

I was very, very impressed.

The formula for finding the number of multiples ($\times$) of vector $\vec{A_1}$ that make up a vector $\vec{P_1}$ projected onto $\vec{A_1}$, and the formulas of the Fourier coefficients for finding an amplitude, were one and the same!

Vectors and Fourier... At first glance, arrows and waves seemed to have nothing in common, and I couldn't see any connection between the two. Now it turns out that they describe the same phenomenon; they simply approach it from different angles.

Integrating the product of two waves is the same as finding the inner product of vectors. The process of using Fourier coefficients to find the components of a wave is the same as the process of finding projected vectors. And when we add all the projected vectors up, we are employing the same concept as the Fourier series.

In short, vector language and Fourier language express the same thing!

I was overjoyed at this revelation. I looked around for Dr. Fourier so I could thank him, but he was nowhere to be found.

"Dr. Fourier! Dr. Fourier!" I shouted, but there was no reply. Gradually my surroundings grew dimmer, and I began to get drowsy...

I awoke with a start. I was sitting at my desk, with **WHO IS FOURIER? A Mathematical Adventure** lying open in front of me. I must have dozed off while I was reading, I thought. I felt groggy, but I clearly recalled my adventures with Dr. Fourier. I must have been dreaming, yet they seemed incredibly real.

I glanced at the Fourier book on my desk. It was open to the last page of the chapter "Projection and Orthogonality." I looked at the page and gasped. There was a note to me from Dr. Fourier!

I couldn't believe my eyes. Hurriedly I flipped through the preceding pages. There, in print, was the entire story of my adventure with Dr. Fourier!

Just then I thought I heard a faint but familiar voice off in the distance:

"Even now, a new adventure awaits you, mon ami!"

Coffee Break

Heisenberg and Schrödinger

On the Transnational College of LEX reading list is a book entitled **Physics and Beyond**. The author, Werner Heisenberg, created mathematical formulas for Quantum Mechanics, a branch of modern physics that describes phenomena such as light and electrons. His name is a familiar one to students at the College. But Heisenberg had a contemporary, Erwin Schrödinger, who also developed formulas for Quantum Mechanics. These two men described the same phenomena with completely different equations, yet both were absolutely correct. If this situation sounds familiar, it should; Heisenberg used vectors to describe Quantum Mechanics, while Schrödinger used functions.

Eventually it was proven that the two approaches were simply different views of the same thing. Both were accepted as equally valid descriptions of Quantum Mechanics. Heisenberg received a Nobel Prize in 1932, and Schrödinger was awarded one in 1933.

Part 3

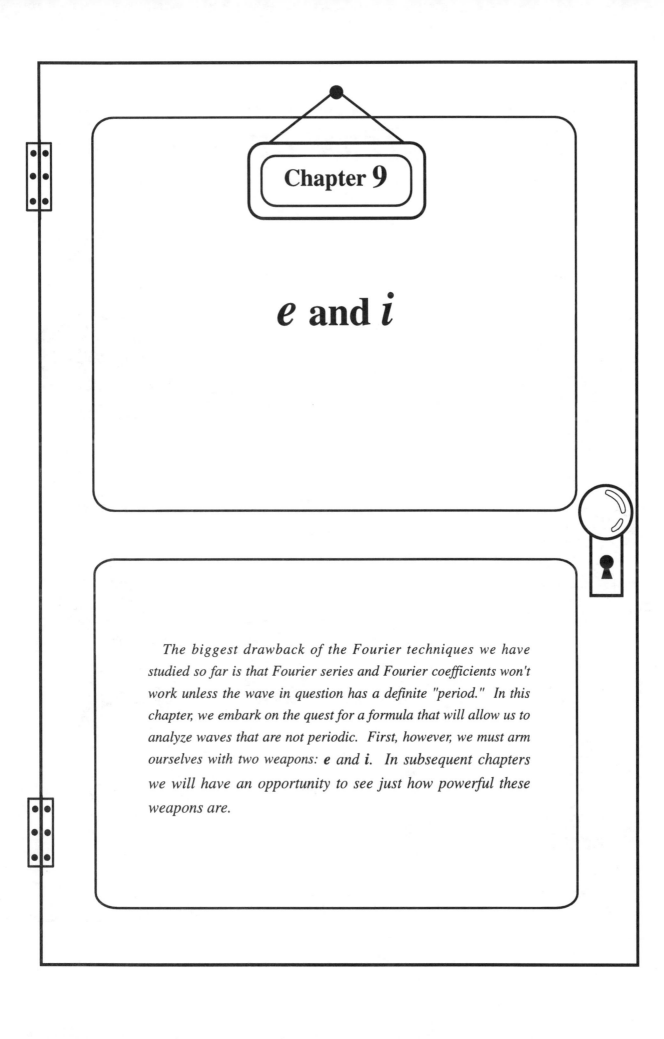

Chapter 9

e and *i*

*The biggest drawback of the Fourier techniques we have studied so far is that Fourier series and Fourier coefficients won't work unless the wave in question has a definite "period." In this chapter, we embark on the quest for a formula that will allow us to analyze waves that are not periodic. First, however, we must arm ourselves with two weapons: **e** and **i**. In subsequent chapters we will have an opportunity to see just how powerful these weapons are.*

Fourier Casebook:

The Mystery of *e* and *i*

Cast of characters:

"Still raining!" the Town Magistrate muttered in disgust as he stared out the window of his office. It had been raining steadily for days.

Suddenly Constable Kogoro dashed in. In a voice loud enough to drown out the rain, he shouted: "Your Honor! There's a new thief in town!"

The Magistrate glared at him irritably. "What, another Ninja cat burglar?"

"No sir, this one's much worse! You're not going to believe this, but this one calls himself the Non-Periodic Kid!"

"The what?!"

1. The Mystery of *e* and *i*

An hour later, the Magistrate was conferring with his assembled police officers.

"As all of you may know by now, a new thief, the Non-Periodic Kid, has been making mischief in town. Previously we were able to use the Fourier series and Fourier coefficients to catch 'Complicated Waver' Namizaemon, but this one's a whole new breed of cat."

"But Your Honor," said Constable Chugo, "up till now we've been able to catch every wave that came along, no matter how complicated! What's there to worry about this time?"

"In fact" said Sergeant Tatsuemon, shifting his massive frame, "Fourier series and Fourier coefficients are only effective on periodic waves. When I interrogated 'Complicated Waver' Namizaemon, he eventually confessed that he was really the Periodic Kid. We know that the Non-Periodic Kid is his older brother."

"This is terrible!" Constable Kogoro moaned. "We thought we'd caught all the complicated waves around these parts, but we obviously haven't!"

"There's no need to lose heart." Sergeant Tatsuemon sounded confident. "I've obtained intelligence that should help us catch the Non-Periodic Kid."

"Really? Where did you get your information?"

"From a physician here in town, a Dr. Fu Riei. He's picked up quite a reputation lately for his use of new-fangled treatments from abroad."

"Well, we can meet with this Fu Riei fellow later. Meanwhile, tell us what you learned!"

"He says we need to adopt a strategy known as Fourier transformation to apprehend the Non-Periodic Kid."

Fourier transform formula:
$$G(f) = \int_{-\infty}^{\infty} g(t)e^{-i2\pi ft}dt$$

Inverse Fourier transform formula:
$$g(t) = \int_{-\infty}^{\infty} G(f)e^{i2\pi ft}df$$

"These are two formulas used for Fourier transformation," Tatsuemon continued. "But the doctor says no one knows what they mean or how to use them."

"Perhaps we should bring this Dr. Fu Riei in right now!" said the Magistrate.

Dr. Fu Riei was promptly summoned. He proved to be a man of quiet but imposing demeanor.

"Doctor Fu, I've been told no one knows how to use these so-called Fourier transform and inverse Fourier transform formulas. Is there nothing you can do to help us ?" The Magistrate sounded discouraged.

"Actually, Your Honor, there are only two items in these formulas that we can't identify," replied the doctor. "Please look closely, everyone – do you see any unfamiliar terms there?"

"Got it!" yelled Constable Kogoro. "We don't have any files on *e* or *i*!"

"That's true," Constable Fuminojo muttered, half to himself. "If we thoroughly investigate these *e* and *i* characters, maybe we'll find out what these formulas have to tell us..."

"You're absolutely right!" Dr. Fu replied enthusiastically. "If you can identify *e* and *i*, you can decipher the formulas in their entirety, no doubt about it! And I shall be glad to offer what help I can towards catching this Non-Periodic rascal!"

2. On the Trail of the Exponential Function

Sergeant Tobei was the first one to pick up a clue about the identity of *e*.

"Your Honor, I found this scrap of paper at the scene of one of the Non-Periodic Kid's crimes!"

> "When you differentiate $y = e^x$,
> the values are the same."
> Try that on for size, coppers!
> It's all Greek to you, anyway...
>
> *The Non-Periodic Kid*

"That no good punk! Who does he think he is?" Hot-headed young Constable Chugo turned beet red with anger.

"Keep your hat on, my friend. He's provided us with a valuable clue. We should remain calm and do our best to analyze it." Dr. Fu radiated serenity even as he spoke.

Just then Constable Konoshin, known for his mathematical prowess, hurried into the room.

"Just the man we need!" boomed the Magistrate. "Can you help us with this, Constable?"

"Yes, Your Honor! The structure of the formula $y = e^x$ leads me to believe that, since 'x' is a variable, e must represent some special, fixed value -- in other words, a constant. Therefore, if we wish to analyze this formula, we should first substitute an ordinary constant 'a' for e. That gives us $y = a^x$, which we can then try to differentiate."

Wiping the sweat from his brow, Sergeant Tatsuemon harrumphed, "If that were $y = ax$ or $y = x^a$, we could differentiate it in no time flat! Any reason we have to use this other formula instead?"

"Well, let's try differentiating $y = ax$ and $y = x^a$, and see what happens to them. We'll substitute the value 2 for the constant 'a'."

Constable Konoshin began drawing a graph.

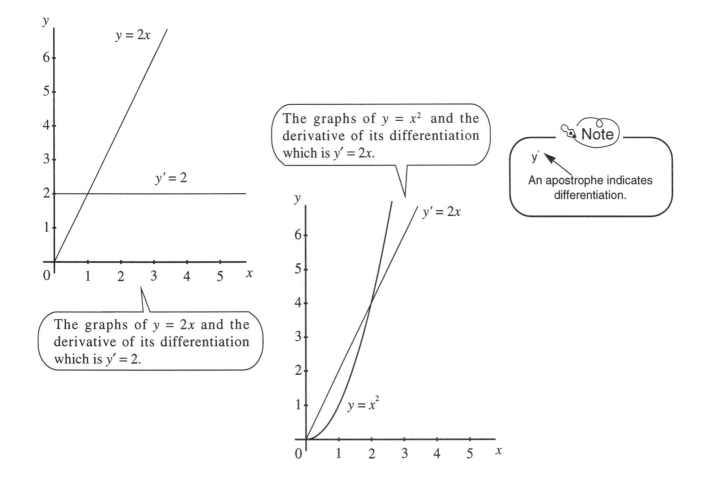

The graphs of $y = 2x$ and the derivative of its differentiation which is $y' = 2$.

The graphs of $y = x^2$ and the derivative of its differentiation which is $y' = 2x$.

Note

y'

An apostrophe indicates differentiation.

"Aha! So when you differentiate $y = ax$ or $y = x^a$, you get a graph that's not at all like the original one, eh?"

"Now then," said Constable Konoshin, "allow me to draw a graph of $y = a^x$, with the value 2 for a."

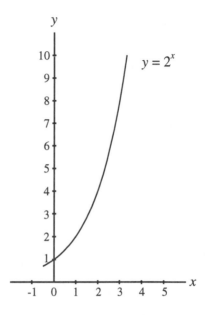

Constabe Fuminojo took one look at Konoshin's graph and exclaimed, "Say, that's an exponential function, isn't it!"

Dr. Fu frowned and muttered, "I'm afraid this formula can't be differentiated as easily as $y = ax$ or $y = x^a$."

Constable Kogoro spoke up. "Doctor, $y = ax$ always has the same slope, but with $y = a^x$, the slope keeps rising as the value of x increases!"

Constable Chugo slapped his knee. "Aha! And since 'differentiation' simply means finding the slope, when you differentiate an exponential function, you'll wind up with the curve of an exponential function again!"

The Magistrate, who had been silently following the discussion, now rose from his seat. "So differentiating an exponential function produces an exponential function, eh? I'll wager, then, that if you differentiate a function like $y = e^x$ with its special value e, you'll wind up with the exact same function $y = e^x$! That's what the Non-Periodic Kid meant when he said the values are the same! Our task is clear now -- we must determine the identity of this pesky constant e! Men, we cannot rest until we have tracked e down!"

The Magistrate's men shouted their agreement. But how would they go about solving the mystery of e?

3. What Is an Exponent?

That night the Magistrate invited Dr. Fu to his quarters for sushi and saké. The rain that had been falling for so many days had stopped, and the moon floated in the clear night sky.

"The moon seems to shine more brightly than usual tonight, Your Honor."

"Yes, the moonlight goes nicely with the saké, don't you think?"

"Ah, but no better than this delicious fish! Pray tell, where did you obtain such a fine, fresh catch?"

"Heh heh! I have a good friend who works at the local fish market. Once in a while he brings me some choice filets!"

"Well, I am honored to be the beneficiary of his kindness."

"The honor is all mine, Doctor. Without your help, we would never have made the progress we did today!"

"Don't thank me too soon. The worst is yet to come!"

"No doubt you mean the exponential function we encountered at the end of today's meeting. Tell me, Doctor – what exactly is an exponent?"

"Well, Your Honor, it's a small number written as a superscript to the right of another number -- the 4 in 2^4, for example. 2^4 means 2 multiplied by itself 4 times -- $2 \times 2 \times 2 \times 2$. We read it as '2 to the **fourth power'**."

"So if you want to multiply 5 by itself 10 times, instead of writing out $5 \times 5 \times 5 \times \cdots$ and so on, you can simply write 5^{10}, eh?"

"Precisely. If you'd like, I can list some of the rules that apply to the use of exponents."

Rules for Exponents (part 1)

1. $a^m = \underbrace{a \times a \times a \times \cdots \times a}_{m \text{ times}}$

2. $a^m \times a^n = a^{(m+n)}$

3. $a^m \div a^n = a^{(m-n)}$

"Hmmm. Rules 2 and 3 are a bit hard to figure out. Take rule 2, for instance. If we have $2^2 \times 2^3$, we know $2^2 = 4$ and $2^3 = 8$, so $2^2 \times 2^3 = 4 \times 8 = 32$. According to rule 2, that should be the same as 2^5, which is $2 \times 2 \times 2 \times 2 \times 2 = 4 \times 4 \times 2 = 32$. Oh ho! It works!"

"Actually, Your Honor, there is an easier way to demonstrate how this rule works. Allow me:

$$2^2 \times 2^3 = (2 \times 2) \times (2 \times 2 \times 2)$$
$$= \underbrace{2 \times 2 \times 2 \times 2 \times 2}_{5 \text{ times}}$$
$$= 2^5$$
$$= 2^{(2+3)}$$

"Now, if you understand these basic rules, you will have no trouble with the following rules as well."

Rules for Exponents (part 2)

4.	a^0	$=$	1
5.	a^{-n}	$=$	$\dfrac{1}{a^n}$
6.	$\left(a^m\right)^n$	$=$	a^{mn}
7.	$a^{\frac{1}{m}}$	$=$	$\sqrt[m]{a}$

> **Note**
>
> • The formula $\sqrt[m]{a}$ which we read as "the *m*-th root of *a*", means "the number that gives the result '*a*' when multiplied by itself *m* times." For $\sqrt[2]{a}$ (which is called the **square root** of "*a*"), we normally write $\sqrt{a}$ without the superscript 2.

"Eh?! What's this? Is a^0 always 1?"

"Yes, Your Honor. That is why, on graphs of $y = a^x$, the curve always passes through $y = 1$ when $x = 0$."

"I find that hard to believe, but let me see for myself. I'll try applying rule 3. If $m = n$ in $a^{(m-n)}$, that's the same as $a^{(m-m)}$, which is a^0. And $a^{(m-m)} = \dfrac{a^m}{a^m} = 1$ . . . so it's true, $a^0 = 1$!"

"Quite so. Next, let's look at a^{-n}. We'll use $a^{(m-n)}$ again. If $m = 0$, then $a^{(0-n)} = \dfrac{a^0}{a^n} = \dfrac{1}{a^n}$. So $a^{-n} = \dfrac{1}{a^n}$!"

"All right, I'll try proving rule 6 using $(2^2)^3$ as an example.

$$\left(2^2\right)^3 = \left(2^2\right) \times \left(2^2\right) \times \left(2^2\right)$$
$$= (2 \times 2) \times (2 \times 2) \times (2 \times 2)$$
$$= 2^6$$
$$= 2^{2 \cdot 3}$$

"By thunder, it works!"

"This last rule is a bit of a challenge, Your Honor. Allow me to demonstrate. First we'll use rule 6.

"Based on rule 6, $(a^{1/m})^m = a^{m/m} = a^1 = a$. That means, if we raise both sides of the equation $a^{1/m} = x$ to the power of exponent m, we get $x^m = a$. If we rewrite this as a formula expressing a root, we get $x = \sqrt[m]{a}$. And since $x = a^{1/m}$, that means $a^{1/m} = \sqrt[m]{a}$."

"Thank you, Doctor! I think I've got the hang of exponents now. I look forward to working with you tomorrow on the differentiation of that exponential function!"

4. Differentiating $y = a^x$

The next day, the Magistrate's office was filled with a mood of tense

$$y + \Delta y = a^{(x + \Delta x)}$$

"To perform differentiation, we first add infinitesimal (i.e., extremely small) values to y and x."

Constable Konoshin's pronouncement jogged the memories of the Magistrate's men, most of whom had forgotten how differentiation worked.

$$\Delta y = a^{(x + \Delta x)} - y$$

"Since $y = a^x$, we can change the y on the right side of the equation to a^x.

$$\Delta y = a^{(x + \Delta x)} - a^x$$

"Next, we want to find $\Delta y / \Delta x$.

$$\frac{\Delta y}{\Delta x} = \frac{a^{(x + \Delta x)} - a^x}{\Delta x} = \frac{a^x \times a^{\Delta x} - a^x}{\Delta x}$$

$$= a^x \frac{a^{\Delta x} - 1}{\Delta x}$$

"And finally, we want to find its limit."

$$\lim_{\Delta x \to 0} \frac{\Delta y}{\Delta x} = \lim_{\Delta x \to 0} a^x \left(\frac{a^{\Delta x} - 1}{\Delta x} \right)$$

$$= a^x \underline{\lim_{\Delta x \to 0} \left(\frac{a^{\Delta x} - 1}{\Delta x} \right)}_{*}$$

"That's it!"

At Dr. Fu's words, the whole room erupted in excitement. But the men's euphoria was quickly dashed by Sergeant Tobei's curt remark:

"This won't help us find the value of *e*!"

5. The Debut of the Logarithm

Sergeant Tobei went on. "In order to get

$$\lim_{\Delta x \to 0} \frac{\Delta y}{\Delta x} = a^x$$

for an answer, we've got to find a way to make all that stuff to the right of a^x equal 1." The sergeant drew a line under part of the equation and put an asterisk (*) under it for good measure.

"That way we'll be multiplying a^x by 1, which will give us a^x, of course. But in this formula, 'a' appears inside $\lim_{\Delta x \to 0}$ as well. So the content of $\lim_{\Delta x \to 0}$ is going to vary with the value of 'a'."

Dr. Fu seemed stumped too. Suddenly Constable Kogoro spoke up. "There's a saying that when the front gate is locked, a good soldier checks the back gate."

Everyone looked blank. Finally the Magistrate said, "And what exactly is that supposed to mean, Constable?"

"Just a suggestion, sir! If exponents are the front gate, I thought maybe there's a back gate we could try – a different approach of some kind."

Constable Fuminojo snapped his fingers and exclaimed, "Of course! We've forgotten all about logarithms!"

"How's that? What's a logarithm?"

"If exponents are the front gate, then logarithms are the back gate!"

Dr. Fu joined in. "You're right. A logarithm is simply a different way of expressing the formula $a^b = c$, using $b = \log_a c$ instead. Logarithms can be extremely useful!"

The Magistrate brightened upon hearing this and leaned forward eagerly.

Constable Konoshin quickly drew up a list.

Rules for Logarithms

1. $\log_a 1 = 0$ corresponds to $a^0 = 1$
2. $\log_a a = 1$ corresponds to $a^1 = a$
3. $\log_a(M \times N) = \log_a M + \log_a N$
4. $\log_a \dfrac{M}{N} = \log_a M - \log_a N$
5. $\log_a N^P = P \log_a N$

"As you can see, $\log_a 1 = 0$ corresponds to the exponent rule $a^0 = 1$, and $\log_a a = 1$ corresponds to $a^1 = a$. Likewise, rules 3 and 4 correspond to the exponent rules $a^m \times a^n = a^{(m+n)}$ and $a^m/a^n = a^{(m-n)}$, respectively. Logarithms are just exponents viewed from a different angle; basically they're the same thing."

"But what about rule 5?"

"Allow me to explain.

$$\log_a N^p = \log_a(N \times N \times N \times N \times \cdots \cdots \times N)$$
$$\underbrace{\qquad\qquad}_{P \ times}$$

"Then, by applying rule 3:

$$= \log_a N + \log_a N + \cdots \cdots \cdot \log_a N$$
$$\underbrace{\qquad\qquad}_{P \ times}$$

"Since $\log_a N$ is added to itself P times, we can write it like this:

$$= P \log_a N$$

"And therefore, $\log_a N^p = P\log_a N$."

"Well done, gentlemen!" declared the Magistrate. "I think it's time for a short break."

Human beings perceive things logarithmically

While the Magistrate's office takes its afternoon siesta, we may as well get some rest too. But what's this? The Magistrate and Dr. Fu are sitting in the tea house in the back of the garden. Let's listen in on their conversation.

"A cup of tea, Doctor?"

"Much obliged, Your Honor."

"It's rather warm for early May, wouldn't you say?"

"Yes indeed, it's tiring to have to think so hard on a day like this!"

"Ah, but I'm finding this discussion of logarithms extremely interesting. If you can't push a door open, try pulling, as it were... How about a refill, Doctor?"

"I'm fine, thank you. Actually, Your Honor, there's something about logarithms that interests me as a physician. I'd like to share it with you."

"Go ahead, Doctor, I'm all ears!"

"It turns out that logarithms are a very accurate reflection of how human beings perceive things."

"How so?"

"Well, the brightness of light and the musical scale are two examples that come to mind."

"Musical scale, as in ha-ni-ho-he-to-i-ro?"
(The traditional Japanese equivalent of "do-re-mi-fa-so-la-ti" is "ha-ni-ho-he-to-i-ro.")

"Yes. Incidentally, I'm told that in the West, they say 'do-re-mi-fa-so-la-ti' instead. Now, if you sing 'do-re-mi-fa-so-la-ti do-re-mi-fa-so-la-ti do,' it sounds as if the interval between each do is the same, does it not?"

"Well, isn't it?"

"It's quite natural to think so. But if we measure the frequency of each do, we find that the frequency of the second do is double that of the first, and the frequency of the third one is four times that of the first! Allow me to draw a little chart to illustrate this."

```
          DO—DO—DO————DO————————————DO
   2 times └──┘
   4 times └────┘
   8 times └──────────┘
  16 times └────────────────────────┘
```

"I find that hard to believe, Doctor!"
"But if we express these intervals as logarithms, we see the following pattern:

$$\log_2 2 \ = 1$$
$$\log_2 4 \ = 2$$
$$\log_2 8 \ = 3$$
$$\log_2 16 = 4$$

"While the frequency increases in multiples – 2 times, 4 times, 8 times, and so on – its logarithm increases at equal intervals – 1, 2, 3, 4 – just the way our ear hears it. So your perception of these do's as being the same interval apart is logarithmically correct, Your Honor!"

"Human beings perceive things logarithmically, eh? Can you give me some more examples?"

"Our perception of the brightness of light is one. And a colleague of mine recently told me of a new theory that a baby's ability to speak develops at a pace that can be perfectly expressed by a logarithm."

"Baby talk, eh? Now that takes the cake! I had no idea logarithms could be so fascinating. Doctor, I thank you for introducing me to this intriguing subject. Can I interest you in a final cup of tea?"

"Why, thank you very much."

The Magistrate's office was in a hubbub again.

"Attention, everyone! We're about to employ logarithms to differentiate $y = a^x$."

Armed with his fresh understanding of the subject, the Magistrate was in an upbeat mood.

6. Differentiating $x = \log_a y$

Constable Konoshin started things off. "If we change $y = a^x$ into a logarithm, what do we get?"

Constable Fuminojo, who had appeared to be dozing, sat up abruptly and blurted, "$x = \log_a y$!"

"Correct! Now, let's differentiate $x = \log_a y$ in the same way we did $y = a^x$ earlier today."

Before Constable Konoshin had finished speaking, Dr. Fu was already writing out the calculations:

$$x + \Delta x = \log_a\!\left(y + \Delta y\right)$$
$$\Delta x = \log_a\!\left(y + \Delta y\right) - x$$
$$= \log_a\!\left(y + \Delta y\right) - \log_a y$$
$$= \log_a\!\left(\frac{y + \Delta y}{y}\right)$$
$$= \log_a\!\left(1 + \frac{\Delta y}{y}\right)$$

"What's this? How did you get that fraction in there?" Constable Chugo asked Dr. Fu, a little indignantly.

The Doctor calmly replied, "Try using logarithm rule 4 and you'll see how it's done."

$$\frac{\Delta x}{\Delta y} = \frac{1}{\Delta y} \log_a\!\left(1 + \frac{\Delta y}{y}\right)$$

"Now let's clean the formula up a little."

$$\frac{\Delta x}{\Delta y} = \frac{y}{y} \times \frac{1}{\Delta y} \log_a\!\left(1 + \frac{\Delta y}{y}\right)$$

"Why are you multiplying it by y/y?" This time it was Constable Kogoro's turn to sound annoyed.

"We're using y/y to change the appearance of the formula," Constable Konoshin explained. "Since $y/y = 1$, multiplying the formula by it doesn't have any effect on the formula's actual value."

$$\frac{\Delta x}{\Delta y} = \frac{1}{y} \times \frac{y}{\Delta y} \log_a\left(1 + \frac{\Delta y}{y}\right)$$

$$= \frac{1}{y} \log_a\left(1 + \frac{\Delta y}{y}\right)^{\frac{y}{\Delta y}}$$

"Ah ha! You just used logarithm rule 5, didn't you, Doctor!"

"You're absolutely right, Your Honor! You seem to have an excellent grasp of what's going on. Now let's find the limit, $\lim\limits_{\Delta y \to 0}$."

To make it easier to view the formula, we can substitute "*A*" for the part of $\lim\limits_{\Delta y \to 0}$.

$$\lim_{\Delta y \to 0} \frac{\Delta x}{\Delta y} = \lim_{\Delta y \to 0} \frac{1}{y} \log_a\left(1 + \frac{\Delta y}{y}\right)^{\frac{y}{\Delta y}}$$

$$= \frac{1}{y} \log_a\left\{ \underbrace{\lim_{\Delta y \to 0} \left(1 + \frac{\Delta y}{y}\right)^{\frac{y}{\Delta y}}}_{A} \right\}$$

Dr. Fu looked up from his calculations. "We've completed the transformation of the formula."

$$\frac{dx}{dy} = \frac{1}{y} \log_a A$$

Sergeant Tatsuemon leaned his great bulk forward. "Is that really enough?"

Dr. Fu looked a little harried. "Actually, it's not. This is a formula for $\frac{dx}{dy}$. But what we really need to find is $\frac{dy}{dx}$."

Constable Konoshin, the math whiz, spoke up confidently. "That's no problem! All we have to do is change $\frac{dx}{dy}$ into $\frac{dy}{dx}$. Let's give it a try."

"What, is that possible? Quick, show us how!" Sergeant Tatsuemon sounded impatient. Doctor Fu obliged by fluidly writing out a formula.

"Here you are. It's really very simple."

Caution

⋆

This is a crude technique, and it does not work in every case.

$$\frac{dy}{dx} = \frac{1}{\frac{dx}{dy}}$$

"Can you really do that?" The men all looked a little skeptical.

"Well, let's test it with some actual numbers. We'll use 2/3, how's that?

$$\frac{1}{\frac{2}{3}} = 1 \div \frac{2}{3} = 1 \times \frac{3}{2} = \frac{3}{2}$$

"Satisfied? Now, let's put it to work for us:

$$\frac{dx}{dy} = \frac{1}{y}\log_a A$$

$$\frac{dy}{dx} = \frac{1}{\dfrac{dx}{dy}}$$

$$= \frac{1}{\dfrac{1}{y}\log_a A}$$

$$= \frac{y}{\log_a A}$$

$$= \frac{a^x}{\log_a A}$$

> We replaced *y* with a^x because $y = a^x$, remember?

"Now then our Honor, I have a question for you. What should we do to obtain the result $\frac{dy}{dx} = a^x$ – indicating, in other words, that even when we perform differentiation, we still get the same result a^x?"

"Hmm, you've got me there, Doctor... Wait a minute! We get that result if $\log_a A = 1$, don't we?

$$\frac{dy}{dx} = \frac{a^x}{\log_a A}$$

$$= \frac{a^x}{1}$$

$$= a^x$$

– how's that?"

"Right on the money, Your Honor!"

"Heh heh! Not bad if I do say so myself!"

Constable Konoshin elaborated.
"Since $\log_a A = 1$ means '*a*' is raised to the power of 1, that means $a = A$. In fact, this '*A*' is none other than *e* itself!"

The Magistrate's men had made remarkable progress. Now they were about to close in on their quarry – the actual value of *e*.

7. Finding $A = \lim\limits_{\Delta y \to 0}\left(1 + \dfrac{\Delta y}{y}\right)^{\frac{y}{\Delta y}}$

It's time for the grand finale. Let's get back to the Magistrate's office and see how Dr. Fu and the others are doing . . . . .

Constable Konoshin looked around the room and said solemnly, "It's time to find '*A*'. First, we must alter the formula to make it easier to calculate."

Constable Kogoro raised his hand tentatively. "How about replacing $\frac{\Delta y}{y}$ with '*t*'?"

$$A = \lim_{t \to 0}(1 + t)^{\frac{1}{t}}$$

Note

We can't substitute 0 for *t* in the formula for *A*. If we use 0, $1/t$ becomes $1/0$, which is meaningless and makes the value of the formula impossible to calculate.

"Excellent idea!" Constable Konoshin said admiringly. "That makes the formula much easier to work with. Let's put in some actual values for *t* and draw a graph of the results."

t	$(1 + t)^{1/t}$
-1	∞
0	- - -
1	2.000
2	1.732
3	1.587
4	1.495

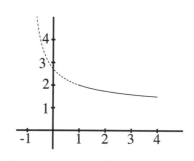

"That doesn't help a whole lot!" groused Constable Fuminojo. "We want to see what happens as *t* approaches 0, don't we? How about using a finer scale and trying some decimal values for *t*?"

t	$(1 + t)^{1/t}$
-0.5	4.00000
-0.1	2.86797
0	- - - - -
0.1	2.59347
0.5	2.25000

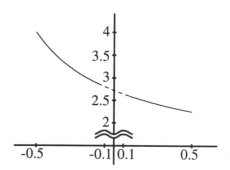

"I can't draw a graph that's going to be accurate for values beyond this point, so let's just look at the numbers themselves," said Constable Konoshin. He proceeded to draw up a table:

t	$(1 + t)^{1/t}$
-0.01	2.73200
-0.001	2.71964
-0.0001	2.71842
-0.00001	2.71830
0	- - - - -
0.00001	2.71827
0.0001	2.71815
0.001	2.71692
0.01	2.70481

Constable Chugo took one look at the table and shouted, "Look! As *t* gets closer to 0, the value of *A* converges on 2.718···!"

"You're right! This number 2.718... must be **e**!" Even Constable Konoshin couldn't contain his excitement.

The Magistrate rose to his feet. "We've done it! Thanks to all of you, we now have at least one clue as to how to catch the Non-Periodic Kid!"

"Hurrah!"

Now that they've found **e**, we'll leave the Magistrate's men to their celebration and return to the 20th century for a moment.

Today we can use computers to find the value of **e** to several thousand decimal places. This value is actually a number that goes on forever: 2.71828182....

Back at the Magistrate's, the evening had turned chilly. Everyone had gone home, leaving the office silent except for the drip-drip of water from a bamboo pipe in the garden.

The Magistrate and Dr. Fu sat on the veranda, quietly sipping saké.

"Well, Your Honor, at least we've solved the riddle of **e**."

"Yes, and I must say, my men did themselves proud. But our job's not over yet."

"Indeed. We still have **i** to deal with."

"To tell the truth, we covered so much ground today that I'm feeling a little overwhelmed. Would you be so kind as to go over the main points for me, Doctor?"

"I'd be glad to, Your Honor. Here's a quick outline."

$$e = \lim_{t \to 0} (1 + t)^{\frac{1}{t}} = 2.71828182\cdots$$

$$\left(e^x\right)' = e^x$$

Exponent: $\underbrace{a \times a \times a \times a \times \cdots \times a}_{m \text{ times}} = a^m$

Logarithm: If $a^b = c$, then $b = \log_a c$

"In any case, this calls for celebration. Drink up, Doctor!"

"Don't mind if I do. With all the work on **i** we have waiting for us tomorrow, tonight we must fortify ourselves!"

"My thoughts exactly!"

Note

Do you remember the differentiation for $y = a^x$?

On page 311,
when $y = a^x$,

$$\frac{dy}{dx} = \frac{a^x}{\log_a A}$$

$A = e$, so

$$\frac{dy}{dx} = \frac{a^x}{\log_a e}$$

And

$$\frac{a^x}{\log_a e} = \log_e a \times a^x$$

Because
$$\frac{1}{\log_a e} = b$$
$$1 = b \log_a e$$
$$1 = \log_a e^b$$
$$a^1 = e^b,$$
$$b = \log_e a$$
So, $\frac{1}{\log_a e} = \log_e a$

This is a general formula for differentiation of $y = a^x$.

$$\frac{dy}{dx} = \log_e a \times a^x$$

When $a = e$, $y = e^x$.

Then $\frac{dy}{dx} = \left(e^x\right)'$

$$= \log_e e \times e^x$$

$$= e^x.$$

(This is because $\log_e e = 1$)

So, $\left(e^x\right)' = e^x$

8. The Imaginary Number *i*

The next morning, the Magistrate had just finished his breakfast and was looking over some papers when Constable Kogoro burst in the door.

"Your Honor! Your Honor! The Non-Periodic Kid struck again last night!"

"There's no need to get excited. Where did this happen?"

"At the noodle shop on the corner, sir!"

"The noodle shop? That's right across the street from our office! Where were you?"

"S-sorry, sir, I didn't see anything out of the ordinary. And oddly enough, the thief didn't steal anything."

"Well, that figures. There's not much worth stealing from a noodle shop besides noodles."

"But he did leave this note behind."

"This message is a blot on our reputation! We must do everything in our power to find *i*! Gather the men immediately!"

So you found *e*, did you? Sorry, but you'll need more than that to catch me! "Bonne chance quand même!"

The Non-Periodic Kid

"Yes, sir!"

Moments later the Magistrate's sergeants, constables, and detectives had filled the chamber, and the meeting commenced.

"Did you all have a look at this scrap of paper? Our honor is at stake! We've got to crack this case, no matter what it takes! To begin with, can anyone here read this strange lettering in the middle of the note?"

"Must be some kind of foreign language. Maybe it gives a clue about how to find *i*, just like that note about *e* did!"

Sergeant Tobei's words created a stir of excitement.

"Once we decipher this part, we might have the whole case solved! This should be easy!" Constable Tatsuemon made it sound as if they had already found *i*.

Just then Dr. Fu strode into the room.

"Take a look at this, Doctor!"

Dr. Fu glanced at the note briefly and said, "This is French – one of the European languages."

Sergeant Tobei peered at Dr. Fu suspiciously. "And how does it happen that you know this barbarians' tongue, Doctor?"

"I used to live in the foreign quarter of Nagasaki," the doctor replied offhandedly.

Sergeant Tobei looked as if he wanted to pursue his questioning further, but Dr. Fu cut him short. "Anyway, this French simply means 'Good luck just the same'!"

"The punk's got a lot of nerve!" Constable Chugo muttered angrily.

"Attention, everyone!" barked Sergeant Tobei. "We have no leads to follow this time. I want you all to fan out across town and find whatever clues you can. Be ready to go in five minutes!"

In moments the entire force was out the door and on the streets.

9. The Discovery of Zero

Constable Kogoro and Detective Tamizo were assigned to the South Side.

"Tamizo, I have a hunch this *i* character is a number that hasn't existed before."

"Hasn't existed before? You don't say." Tamizo had no idea what Kogoro was talking about.

The two entered a dry-goods store and greeted the owner.

"Well, if it isn't Constable Kogoro and Detective Tamizo!"

"How's business these days?"

"Too good, actually! I'm having some problems dealing with it."

"How's that?"

"Some items have been selling so fast that I keep running out of stock. But I don't know how to keep a record of 'nothing' in my books. For example, if I have eight of an item and I sell five, I can record it as '8 - 5 = 3.' But what about '8 - 8'? How do I express that?"

"Ha ha ha!" laughed Kogoro. "That does make things rough! Luckily, there is a number that expresses 'nothing': zero! Apparently, it was invented in ancient India or something like that."

"Zero, eh? Thank you, Constable! That'll be a big help!"

When they had left the store, Tamizo turned to Kogoro.

"So there's a number for 'nothing,' is there?"

"Yep. Long ago, people invented numbers so they could count things – the same numbers we commonly use today. If we think of these on a number line, they look like this:

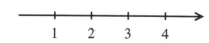

"These are called the 'natural numbers'."

"They are? But where's zero?"

"Not so fast! The invention of zero came later, expanding the world of numbers that already existed."

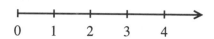

Natural numbers
1, 2, 3, ···

10. Integers

The two officers next paid a visit to the local shipping agent's office.

"Anybody in?"

A clerk emerged from the back of the office. "Sorry, the owner is out right now, but... oh, it's Constable Kogoro! How've you been?"

"Fine, thanks. How's business?"

"Well, if you want to know the truth..."

"What's the matter?"

"The shipping business has been in terrible shape lately. We're in hock up to our eyeballs. And on top of that, I have no way of recording our debts in my account book."

"What do you mean?"

"Well, suppose we have 100 pieces of silver in gross income and 90 in expenses. I can express that as 100 - 90 = 10, so I know we have 10 pieces of silver in net income. But if we need to spend 130 pieces of silver, and we have only 100 available, then we have to borrow 30 more. That's 100 - 130, which equals what? How do we express the 30 pieces of silver we borrowed? It's driving me up the wall!"

"Relax, there's a simple solution for that. All you have to do is add a minus sign to the amount of your debt. The minus sign indicates the amount by which you came up short."

"100 - 130 = -30, eh? That's great! Constable, you've made my day! Here, take some of this dried kelp for yourself and the boys. It just arrived today!"

"Hey, thanks!"

Once again, Tamizo had a question for Kogoro. "So did the minus sign help expand the world of numbers too?"

"Sure did. When you add zero and numbers with minus signs to the natural numbers, you have 'integers'."

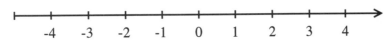

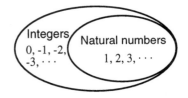

11. Fractions and Decimals

As Tamizo and Kogoro walked along the riverbank, they ran into the shipping agent's daughter, Ohana. Tamizo recognized her.

"Hello there, Ohana! How are you today?"

"Oh, hello, Mr. Tamizo! Actually, I'm feeling a little down right now."

"Really? That's not like you!"

"Well, the problem is, I wanted to get presents for my boyfriends, but then I somehow wound up getting ten presents!"

"Your boyfriends! You mean to say you have ten boyfriends, Ohana?"

"No, that's just the problem, I only have four! So even if I give each of them two presents, I still have two left over."

"That's what you're so depressed about?! It's a little hard to feel sorry for you!"

But Constable Kogoro was thinking. "So, Ohana, are you saying you can't divide 10 by 4?"

"Well, I can't, can I? I mean, 10 ÷ 5 or 8 ÷ 4 would work, but..."

"People ran into the same problem a long time ago, but they came up with a solution – a new kind of number."

"Really? Oh, please tell me about it, Constable!"

"The answer to 10 ÷ 4 can be written like this: 10/4. This is called a 'fraction'. Suppose you want to divide a piece of candy three ways. 1 ÷ 3 = 1/3, so each person gets 1/3 of a piece of candy."

"Oh, neat! So that means I can give each of my boyfriends 10/4 presents!"

"But Constable," interjected Tamizo, "I can see what 1/3 of something would be, but talking about 10/4 of something doesn't make any sense at all!"

"You've got a point," said Kogoro. "That's why we use a 'decimal' for numbers like that."

"A what?"

"Try calculating 10 ÷ 4. Without using a fraction, that is."

"Let me see, that would be 2 with a remainder of 2."

"Now divide that remainder 2 by 4."

"Okay, I know 2 is half of 4. But I can't write that without using a fraction!"

You see, 2 ÷ 4 can also be written as 0.5. A decimal is a small number less than 1 which is written after a 'decimal point'."

"So 10 ÷ 4 = 2.5! That means I can give each boyfriend two and a half presents, right? Thank you so much, Constable!"

"What an odd girl." Tamizo muttered when Ohana was out of earshot. "I wonder how she plans to give each of her boyfriends half a present!"

"You got me," replied Kogoro. "Anyway, it's time we headed back to headquarters, don't you think?"

"Sounds good."

On the way back, Tamizo resumed his questioning of Kogoro about numbers. "Well," said Kogoro, "what do you think happened when they added fractions and decimals to the mix?"

"Uh, I suppose they divided the scale on that number line into even smaller sections."

"Couldn't have said it better myself. All of these numbers put together are called 'rational numbers'."

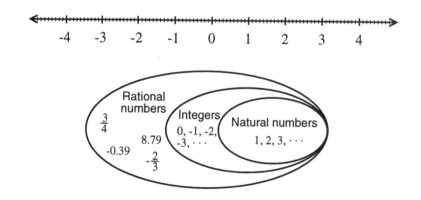

"Boy, this number universe just keeps expanding, doesn't it.

"And that's not the end of it. I know of at least one other type of number. And there might be more, for all I know."

"What? Even more numbers?! You're joking!"

"Remember our talk about exponents yesterday?"

"Oh yeah, $2 \times 2 \times 2 = 2^3$ and all that."

"Right. Okay, when we have 2^2, what is it that's being multiplied by itself?"

"Why, 2, of course!"

"Okay, then, what is it that's multiplied by itself to get 2?"

"You got me. Maybe 1/2?"

"No, $1/2 \times 1/2 = 1/4$."

"Then I have no idea."

"The answers are the numbers called the 'square roots' of 2, written $\pm\sqrt{2}$."

"No kidding! So if you have $\sqrt{10}$, then $\sqrt{10} \times \sqrt{10} = 10$?"

"Hey, not bad! And if we have a number that's multiplied by itself **three** times to get 10, we write it as $\sqrt[3]{10}$. The only time we leave off the superscript to the left of the $\sqrt{\ }$ sign (called a 'radical sign') is for $\sqrt[2]{\ }$, which we write simply as $\sqrt{\ }$. Otherwise we always include a superscript: $\sqrt[3]{5}$, $\sqrt[5]{2}$, and so on."

"Those are some weird numbers you've got there!"

Numbers like this, which can't be expressed as fractions, are called 'irrational numbers'. And all the rational numbers and irrational numbers put together are called 'real numbers'."

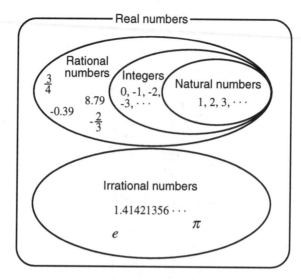

"Hm? So *e* and *π* are irrational numbers too, eh? Now what's this about 'real' numbers – does that just mean all numbers that really exist?"

"I suppose ... though it seems to me there ought to be some other type of number opposed to the real numbers."

Before they knew it, Kogoro and Tamizo had arrived at the Magistrate's office.

The Magistrate was waiting for them. "Any new leads, men?"

"Well, not exactly, sir," replied Kogoro. "But we learned how people created and expanded the world of numbers."

"That sounds potentially useful. How about you, Tamizo?"

"Yessir, I learned that whenever people needed numbers for some purpose, they just put their heads together and invented them. I thought that was interesting."
"Indeed. Whenever we run into obstacles, we need to put our heads together and solve our problems one by one."

Kogoro nodded gravely. "Looking at how numbers were created made me realize that people came up with language in much the same way."

"Well, you two certainly learned a lot in one day! Go on, get some rest."

"Thank you, sir!"

12. Solving *i*

Kogoro and Tamizo walked into the guard room and sat down. Sergeant Tobei and Constable Konoshin were already there. Tobei was pouring hot water from a kettle hanging over the fire.

"Kogoro, Tamizo! How'd it go? Here, have some tea."

"Well, while Tamizo and I were talking, something occurred to me."

"Oh? What is that?"

"If there are real numbers, it seems to me that there must be other numbers that <u>aren't</u> real to balance things out."

"I suppose you're right – after all, if there's reality, there must be unreality too!"

Tamizo broke in. "Say, when we were talking about roots back there, I was wondering – how do you express the square root of a number like -1?"

"The square root of -1?!"

Everyone was stumped. The square root of 1 is $\sqrt{1}$. But what do you do with a number like -1?

At that moment Dr. Fu hurried in. "Listen, everyone! I know what *i* is now!"

"Would it by any chance be $\sqrt{-1}$?" inquired Sergeant Tobei.

"What?! How did you know that?" cried the Doctor. "You're absolutely right. The radical sign ($\sqrt{}$) indicates what number you get when you multiply a number by itself. It's impossible to get -1 that way, because multiplying any number by itself always yields a positive number – whether the original number is positive or negative. So we say that *i* is a number which gives us -1 when squared."

"Aha! So $i^2 = -1$!" said Sergeant Tobei. "But Dr. Fu, how did you crack the riddle of *i*, anyway?"

"Actually, I just happened to run across *i* in a foreign mathematics text."

"So what does '*i*' stand for, anyway?" asked Constable Fuminojo.

"It's short for 'imaginary number'," replied the Doctor.

"Oh, because it's a number that exists only in people's imaginations, is that it?"

Just then the Magistrate entered the room. "It appears you've figured out *i*, am I right?"

"Yes, Your Honor, it's a very strange number which, if squared, gives you -1!" Constable Fuminojo eagerly explained.

"So can we put this *i* to use right away?"

"Not yet, sir," Constable Konoshin replied. "To get results, I believe we must first take a planar approach to the problem."

"Well, let's think about what it means to change signs along a real number axis." As he spoke, Konoshin drew a number line.

"If we multiply -1 by +2, we get -2, correct?," said the Magistrate.

Upon hearing this, Dr. Fu slapped his knee. "But of course! We can think of multiplication by -1 like this!" He drew some arrows around the axis.

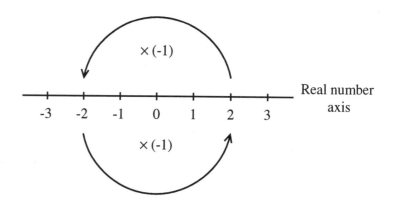

Now it was Constable Fuminojo's turn. "So multiplication by -1 is like rotating 180° around 0 at the center!"
"Then, can we say that multiplication by *i* is the same as rotating 90° around 0?" asked Sergeant Tatsuemon.

"Precisely!" answered Constable Konoshin. "But to do that, we need a vertical axis for imaginary numbers in addition to our horizontal axis for real numbers."

Note

$$i^2 = i \times i = -1$$

In other words, multiplying *i* twice gives us −1, which can be expressed as a rotation of 180°. So it follows that multiplying *i* once can be expressed as a rotation of 90°.

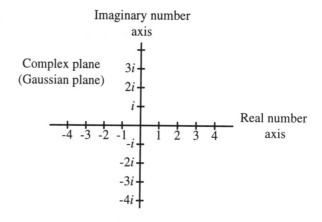

"The two-dimensional space formed by these axes is called the 'complex plane', or the 'Gaussian plane'."

Dr. Fu joined in. "The use of this plane allows us to express two utterly different items – such as a real number and an imaginary number – as one point. Let me show you an example."

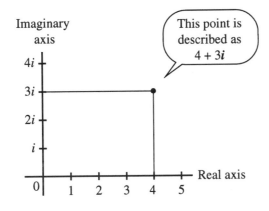

"So one of the numbers we normally use – 100, say – would be expressed on this plane as 100 + 0*i*, I take it?" said the Magistrate.

Constable Kogoro was flushed with excitement. "With the addition of these imaginary numbers, the world of numbers is complete, isn't it!"

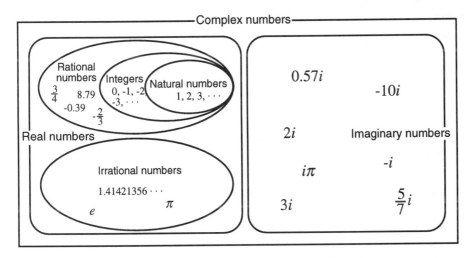

"Well, I'll be!" exclaimed Tamizo. "Put imaginary and real numbers together and you get something called complex numbers, do you?"

Even the Magistrate could not contain his surprise. "Looks like this diagram includes all the numbers we've ever heard of!"

Suddenly the gateman appeared at the door. "This note was thrown over the wall, sir!"

The Magistrate took the note and read it aloud.

> Well done, my friends.
> My compliments on your
> identification of *i* ! It is indeed
> the square root of -1.
>
> *The Non-Periodic Kid*

Sergeant Tobei slammed his fist on the desk and shouted, "That insolent scoundrel! 'My compliments,' my eye! I won't stand for any more of these insults!"

"Not only that, but he must be outside the gate at this very moment!" cried an agitated Fuminojo. "We should go out and catch him right now!"

But the Magistrate responded coolly. "Quiet down and listen to me, men. There's no point in raising a ruckus. We have already obtained two priceless clues:

$$e = \lim_{t \to 0} (1 + t)^{\frac{1}{t}} = 2.71828182 \cdots$$
$$i^2 = -1$$

"But this is only the first step on a long, long road. These numbers *e* and *i* are only clues, and nothing more. We still have to figure out how to use them to solve this case. Instead of getting all worked up over nothing, I'd rather you saved your energy for the work that lies ahead."

"You can count on us, Your Honor! We're with you all the way, come hell or high water!" At Sergeant Tatsuemon's words, everyone bowed deeply toward the Magistrate.

"Good! With that kind of team spirit, we should have no trouble tracking down the Non-Periodic Kid."

The sun had set and the Magistrate's garden was growing dark. Dr. Fu and the Magistrate sat on some rocks and sipped saké.

"Without your help, Doctor, we never could have come as far as we have. Thank you for everything."

"Oh, I'm sure that even without me, the enthusiasm of your men would have carried the day."

Thunder rumbled in the distance. "Sounds like rain coming."

"Why don't we go inside, Doctor, and have some dinner with our saké?"

"It would be a pleasure, Your Honor!"

By the last light of evening, the azaleas in the garden glistened in the rain, as if to augur a happy ending to the quest of the Magistrate and his men.

– fin –

Chapter 10

Euler's Formula

*In this chapter we'll acquire yet another weapon – Euler's (pronounced "Oiler's") formula. This weapon will provide us with a new way to describe sine and cosine functions, using the **e** and **i** we picked up in the previous chapter. But just what is this "Euler's formula" that the great physicist Richard Feynman himself praised as "our jewel"?*

1. Putting *e* and *i* to Work

1. 1 Using *i* to Find Numbers on the Gaussian Plane

What kind of number is *i*?
$$i = \sqrt{-1}$$
In other words,
$$i^2 = -1.$$

Let's start by reviewing what sort of number *i* is. We'll refer to the Gaussian plane we encountered in Chapter 9 to refresh our memory.

As you may recall, the Gaussian plane is a coordinate plane that has real numbers on its horizontal axis and imaginary numbers on its vertical axis. It looks like this:

The Gaussian plane is also called the complex plane.

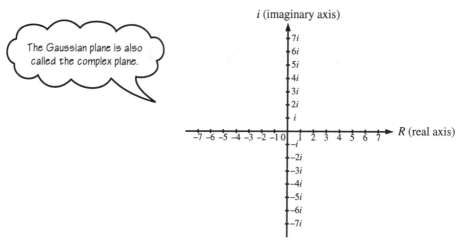

Let's try placing a variety of numbers on this plane.

To find a point on this plane, look for the value of "*a*" on the *R* axis, and the value of "*b*" on the *i* axis.

The "*a*" term is called the "real part" of the number, and the "*b*" term is called the "imaginary part." Together they are called a "complex number."

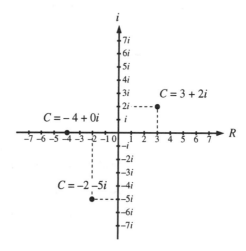

Notice that the numbers on the Gaussian plane can all be expressed in the format $C = a + bi$.

1. 2 Using Functions on the Gaussian Plane

Now we're going to use the Gaussian plane and the format $C = a + bi$ to try something a little different.

Suppose the "*a*" and "*b*" in $C = a + bi$ are both numbers determined by the value of another number *x*. What values will "*a*" and "*b*" display on the Gaussian plane?

If the numbers "*a*" and "*b*" are determined by a number *x*, that means they are functions of *x*. Until now we have expressed functions of *x* like this:

$$f(x)$$

But if both "*a*" and "*b*" are functions of *x*, we can't refer to them both as $f(x)$. To avoid confusing the two, we will call "*a*" the function $a(x)$ and "*b*" the function $b(x)$:

$$a = a(x)$$
$$b = b(x)$$

Then our original format $C = a + bi$ becomes:

$$C(x) = a(x) + b(x)i$$

Now suppose we substitute specific expressions for $a(x)$ and $b(x)$. We'll replace $a(x)$ with x, and $b(x)$ with $1/x$:

$$a(x) = x$$
$$b(x) = \frac{1}{x}$$

That gives us:

$$C(x) = a(x) + b(x)i$$
$$= x + \frac{1}{x}\,i$$

Let's see what happens to these values on the Gaussian plane. First, we'll draw up a table of values:

x	$a(x)$	$b(x)$
3	3	1/3
2	2	1/2
1	1	1
1/2	1/2	2
1/3	1/3	3
0	0	/
−1/3	−1/3	−3
−1/2	−1/2	−2
−1	−1	−1
−2	−2	−1/2
−3	−3	−1/3
⋮	⋮	⋮

This table lists values of x in the range from –3 to 3. Now we're ready to plot these values on the Gaussian plane:

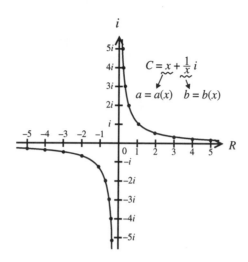

What we get are two curves whose points are symmetric around the origin 0. The curves are asymptotic to the two axes, meaning that the distance between axis and curve approaches 0 the further they get from the origin. Now we know that we can find the values of functions such as $a(x)$ and $b(x)$ on the Gaussian plane.

Next, we want to take the opposite approach – to look at a graph on the Gaussian plane and figure out the functions $a(x)$ and $b(x)$ that describe it. Since the graph itself is a function plotted on the Gaussian plane, it can be written

$$C(x) = a(x) + b(x)i$$

Our graph will be a circle of radius 1 described on the Gaussian plane. What are the values of its functions $a(x)$ and $b(x)$?

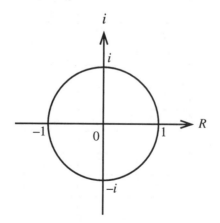

First let's try to figure out what sort of function $a(x)$ is for this graph. Function $a(x)$ is the real part of the graph formula. That means we need to look at how values on the circle change along the real axis of the Gaussian plane to see what happens to $a(x)$.

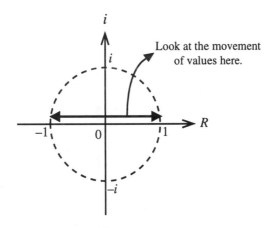

Relative to the real axis, values on the circle move from 1 through 0 to –1, then back through 0 to 1 again as they make a single rotation around the circle. Does this remind you of something? It should!

Let's plot a graph of this change in values along the real axis.

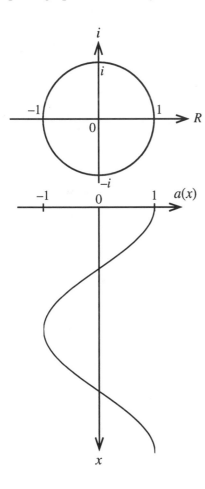

The result is the graph on the left. Looks familiar, doesn't it? That's right, it's our old friend the cosine wave! In other words, values change along the horizontal axis – i.e., the real axis – in the same manner as the values that form a cosine wave. We wanted to know what sort of function $a(x)$ was, and now we have our answer:

$$a(x) = \cos x$$

So it turns out that the mysterious function $a(x)$ has a familiar face: $\cos x$. As a matter of fact, we can substitute $\cos x$ for $a(x)$ in the formula $C(x) = a(x) + b(x)i$. That gives us

$$C(x) = \cos x + b(x)i$$

Now let's turn our attention to the function $b(x)$. We can take the same approach we took to find $a(x)$. This time, however, we have to look at how values on the circle change along the imaginary axis instead of the real axis, since $b(x)$ is the imaginary part of the formula.

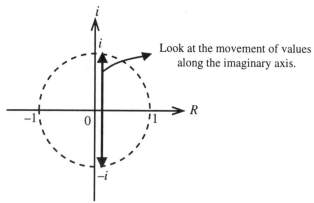

Look at the movement of values along the imaginary axis.

Values move along the imaginary axis from 0 to i, then all the way down to $-i$, and finally back up to 0 as they make a single rotation around the circle. Below is a graph of this change in values along the imaginary axis.

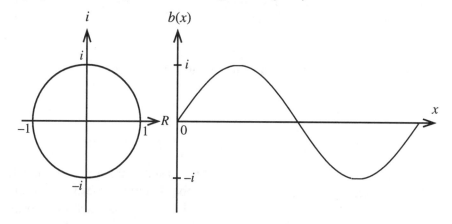

This one looks familiar too. And indeed, it's another old crony of ours – the sine wave. In other words, values change along the vertical axis – i.e., the imaginary axis – in the same manner as the values of a sine wave. Now we know what the function $b(x)$ is:

$$b(x) = \sin x$$

So $a(x)$ is $\cos x$, and $b(x)$ is $\sin x$. When we substitute $\cos x$ for $a(x)$ and $\sin x$ for $b(x)$ in $C(x) = a(x) + b(x)i$, we get:

$$C(x) = \cos x + \sin x \cdot i$$

...To avoid confusing i with the angular velocity of sin, we move i to the front.

$$= \cos x + i \sin x$$

And there we have it – a function that describes a circle of radius 1 on the Gaussian plane:

$$C(x) = \cos x + i \sin x$$

This is an intriguing result: the function for a circle on the Gaussian plane turns out to be a combination of the same sine and cosine functions that we keep running across in our adventures with Fourier.

However, the number $C(x)$ itself can be expressed as a function as well. This will be explained in detail in the second section of this chapter, "Maclaurin's Expansion." Meanwhile, there are some preliminary steps we must take before we can find the value of $C(x)$.

1. 3 What is e?

To find the value of $C(x)$, we first need to reacquaint ourselves with the number e, which we encountered in the previous chapter, "e and i."

As you may recall, e turned out to be the number 2.718281828... We learned that if you raise e to the xth power (e^x) and differentiate the result, you get the same value e^x:

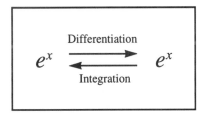

How did we find a value for e that produces the same value when differentiated? By substituting various values for "a" in the number a^x and differentiating them, remember? Let's refresh our memories by looking at the graph below.

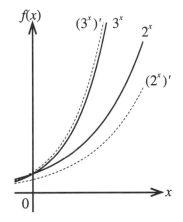

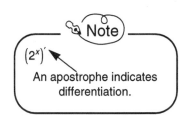

An apostrophe indicates differentiation.

In the graph, the dotted curves represent the results of differentiating 2^x and 3^x. Two things are apparent about the differentiated values that make up these curves:

> When $a = 2$, the differentiated curve is **below** the original curve.
> When $a = 3$, the differentiated curve is **above** the original curve.

That means the value of "a" we are searching for – the one that produces no change when a^x is differentiated – must be greater than 2 but less than 3. In the previous chapter, this approach eventually led us to the following value for e:

$$e = 2.718281828...$$

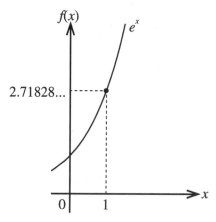

1. 4 Differentiating e^{ax}

Now let's consider what will happen if we differentiate $y = e^{ax}$.

This time, instead of raising e to the xth power, we are raising it to the axth power. Will this turn out the same way as the differentiation of e^x?

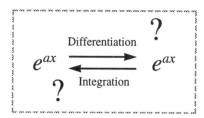

First, let's see what kind of graphs we get for different values of "a" in e^{ax}. We'll compare the graph of e^x with the graphs of e^{ax} when "a" is 2 and 1/2 respectively.

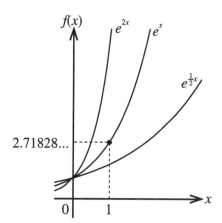

It's clear that e^{ax} produces curves that differ from the curve of e^x. The fact that the curves are different suggests that when differentiated, they will not produce the same values as the original curve.

Let's go ahead and differentiate e^{ax}.

Differentiation of $y = e^{ax}$

First stage: $$y + \Delta y = e^{a(x + \Delta x)}$$

> Find the value of a number greater than x by the amount Δx.

Second stage: $$\Delta y = e^{a(x + \Delta x)} - e^{ax}$$
$$= e^{ax + a\Delta x} - e^{ax}$$

> $ax = A$, and $a\Delta x = \Delta A$

$$= e^{A + \Delta A} - e^{A}$$

> Find the difference between that number and the original number.

Third stage: $$\frac{\Delta y}{\Delta x} = \frac{e^{A + \Delta A} - e^{A}}{\Delta x}$$

> Find the slope from the formula vertical/horizontal.

$$= \frac{e^{A + \Delta A} - e^{A}}{\Delta x} \frac{\Delta A}{\Delta A}$$

$$= \frac{e^{A + \Delta A} - e^{A}}{\Delta A} \left(\frac{\Delta A}{\Delta x} \right)$$

$$= \frac{e^{A + \Delta A} - e^{A}}{\Delta A} a$$

> Calculate this part.
> Since $\Delta A = a\Delta x$, we get:
> $$\Delta A = a\Delta x$$
> $$\frac{\Delta A}{\Delta x} = \frac{a\Delta x}{\Delta x} = a$$

Fourth stage: $$\frac{dy}{dx} = \lim_{\Delta x \to 0} \left(\frac{e^{A + \Delta A} - e^{A}}{\Delta A} a \right)$$

> Find the instantaneous slope as Δx approaches 0 (*i.e.*, the limit).

In this case the limit is found for Δx; "a" is not affected. Therefore we can place "a" in front of $\lim_{\Delta t \to 0}$.

$$= a \left(\lim_{\Delta x \to 0} \frac{e^{A + \Delta A} - e^{A}}{\Delta A} \right)$$

> Pay attention to this part.

Did you notice that this part takes the same form as the result of differentiating e^x (shown on the right)? Although Δx may appear to differ from ΔA, we know that $\Delta A = a\Delta x$, so $\Delta x \to 0$ means $\Delta A \to 0$ as well.

In other words, this part consists of the differentiation of e^A. And since the result of differentiating e^A is e^A again, the above formula is

> ── Differentiation of e^x ──
> $$\lim_{\Delta x \to 0} \frac{e^{(x + \Delta x)} - e^x}{\Delta x}$$
> For details see Chapter 9, "e and i."

$$= a \, e^A$$

– which, since $A = a \cdot x$, is

$$= a \, e^{ax}$$

This is the result of differentiating e^{ax}.

$$\boxed{\left(e^{ax} \right)' = a \, e^{ax}}$$

> 🖋 **Note**
> $$\left(e^{ax} \right)'$$
> One apostrophe indicates first-order differentiation.

The result of differentiating e^{ax} was $a \cdot e^{ax}$. Now let's look at the e^{2x} and $e^{1/2x}$ we saw on the graph a few moments ago.

$$\left(e^{2x}\right)' = 2\, e^{2x}$$

$$\left(e^{\frac{1}{2}x}\right)' = \frac{1}{2}\, e^{\frac{1}{2}x}$$

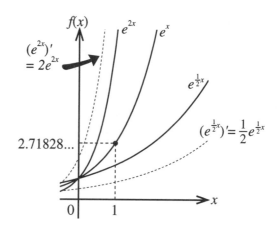

So it's clear that the slopes of these differentiated curves differ from the original curves by the amount "a" shown in the formula

$$\left(e^{ax}\right)' = a\, e^{ax}$$

Next, let's see what happens when we differentiate e^{ax} several times in succession. First we want to see the result of differentiating e^{ax} twice; this is called second-order differentiation. Second-order differentiation means that the result of differentiating e^{ax} is itself differentiated again.

In this case, that means differentiating $a \cdot e^{ax}$.

$$\left(e^{ax}\right)'' = \left(a\, e^{ax}\right)' = ?$$

When differentiating $a \cdot e^{ax}$, we can leave "a" alone because it has no relationship to x. All we have to do is differentiate what's left, which is e^{ax}.

$$\left(e^{ax}\right)'' = \left(a\, e^{ax}\right)' = a\left(e^{ax}\right)' = ?$$

We've already differentiated e^{ax}, so we can just insert the result here:

$$\left(e^{ax}\right)'' = \left(a\, e^{ax}\right)' = a\left(e^{ax}\right)' = a \cdot a \cdot e^{ax}$$

In other words, the second-order differentiation of e^{ax} yields:

$$\left(e^{ax}\right)'' = a \cdot a \cdot e^{ax} = \underline{a^2\, e^{ax}}$$

Note

$\left(e^{2x}\right)''$

Two apostrophes indicates second-order differentiation.

Why stop there? Let's see what the third-order differentiation of e^{ax} produces. That means differentiating the result we just got from second-order differentiation, which was $a^2 \cdot e^{ax}$.

$$\left(e^{ax}\right)''' = \left(a^2\, e^{ax}\right)' = ?$$

Leaving the "a"s alone as before, we get:

$$\left(e^{ax}\right)''' = \left(a^2\, e^{ax}\right)' = a^2\left(e^{ax}\right)'$$
$$= a^2\, a \cdot e^{ax}$$
$$= a^3\, e^{ax}$$

So the third-order differentiation of e^{ax} yields:

$$\left(e^{ax}\right)''' = \underline{a^3\, e^{ax}}$$

If you've begun to suspect that the fourth-order differentiation of e^{ax} might look like this...

$$\left(e^{ax}\right)^{(4)} = a^4\, e^{ax}$$

...you're absolutely right! In a nutshell, the nth-order differentiation of e^{ax} is always:

$$\left(e^{ax}\right)^{(n)} = a^n\, e^{ax}$$

Let's list our results so far.

The nth-order differentiation of $f(x) = e^{ax}$

$$f'(x) \;=\; \left(e^{ax}\right)' \;=\; a\, e^{ax} \quad \text{... First-order differentiation}$$

$$f''(x) \;=\; \left(e^{ax}\right)'' \;=\; a^2\, e^{ax} \quad \text{... Second-order differentiation}$$

$$f'''(x) \;=\; \left(e^{ax}\right)''' \;=\; a^3\, e^{ax} \quad \text{... Third-order differentiation}$$

$$f^{(4)}(x) \;=\; \left(e^{ax}\right)^{(4)} \;=\; a^4\, e^{ax} \quad \text{... Fourth-order differentiation}$$

$$\vdots$$

$$f^{(n)}(x) \;=\; \left(e^{ax}\right)^{(n)} \;=\; a^n\, e^{ax} \quad \text{.... nth-order differentiation}$$

Arabic numerals are used to indicate anything above three orders of differentiation.

Now it's time to consider e together with the number i, which we studied in the first half of this section. We can do this by inserting i into the expression e^{ax}.

1. 5 Differentiating e^{ix}

For our present purposes we'll insert i into e^{ax} by letting $a = i$:

$$e^{ax} \longrightarrow e^{ix}$$
$$a = i$$

Next, we want to perform nth-order differentiation on e^{ix}. All we need to do is substitute i for "a" where it appeared in the differentiation of e^{ax}.

$$f(x) = e^{ax} \quad \Rightarrow \quad f(x) = e^{ix}$$
$$f'(x) = a\,e^{ax} \quad \Rightarrow \quad f'(x) = i\,e^{ix}$$
$$f''(x) = a^2\,e^{ax} \quad \Rightarrow \quad f''(x) = i^2\,e^{ix}$$

Let's pause for a moment and recall what sort of number i is: $i^2 = -1$, remember? In other words,

$$f''(x) = i^2\,e^{ix} = (-1)e^{ix} = -e^{ix}$$

So the third and subsequent orders of differentiation will look like this:

$$f'''(x) = a^3\,e^{ax} \Rightarrow f'''(x) = i^3 \cdot e^{ix} = -i\,e^{ix}$$
$$f^{(4)}(x) = a^4\,e^{ax} \Rightarrow f^{(4)}(x) = i^4 \cdot e^{ix} = (-1)^2\,e^{ix} = e^{ix}$$
$$f^{(5)}(x) = a^5\,e^{ax} \Rightarrow f^{(5)}(x) = i^5 \cdot e^{ix} = i\,e^{ix}$$

What's this? When we perform fourth-order differentiation, it returns us to the original number e^{ix}. Summarizing our results:

The nth–order differentiation of $f(x) = e^{ix}$

$$f(x) = e^{ix}$$
$$f'(x) = i\,e^{ix}$$
$$f''(x) = -e^{ix}$$
$$f'''(x) = -i\,e^{ix}$$
$$f^{(4)}(x) = e^{ix}$$
$$\vdots$$

So now we know that the fourth-order differentiation of e^{ix} yields the original e^{ix}.

In this section we have looked at two different expressions: e^{ix} and $C(x) = \cos x + i \sin x$. In the second section of this chapter, "Maclaurin's Expansion," we will examine the relationship between the two.

2. Maclaurin's Expansion

Earlier we learned that the function for a circle on the Gaussian plane is $\cos x + i \sin x$. However, there is another function that also describes a circle on the Gaussian plane. These two functions can therefore be considered equal.

Gaussian Plane

$$\cos x + i \sin x = ?$$

What we intend to do next is find this other function of x from $\cos x + i \sin x$. We can do this by using a process called "Maclaurin's expansion." As you might have guessed, e and i play crucial roles in this process.

We'll begin with the obvious question: just what is Maclaurin's expansion?

2. 1 What is Maclaurin's Expansion?

Take a look at the formula below.

$$f(x) = a_0 + a_1 x + a_2 x^2 + a_3 x^3 + a_4 x^4 + a_5 x^5 + \cdots \qquad \text{(Formula } X\text{)}$$

Looks a lot like a Fourier series, wouldn't you say? Formula X is what's known as an infinite series expansion formula. This is a formula that consists of the sum of an infinite number of terms of the 0 degree, 1st degree, 2nd degree, and so on up to the nth degree. The remarkable thing about it is that any function can be expressed in this format.

> What's a "1st degree" and a "2nd degree"?
>
> The degree of a term is the power to which x is raised in the term.
> $y = x^2 \rightarrow$ 2nd-degree function

"You're joking!"

No, we're not. Here, we'll give you an example.

Suppose you want to convert this formula to Formula X:

$$y = 3x^3 + 5x^2 + 7$$

Here's how it's done:

$$f(x) = 7 + 0x + 5x^2 + 3x^3 + 0x^4 + 0x^5 + \cdots$$

In other words, you can use Formula X to express any function –and plot it on a graph – as long as you can find the coefficients a_0 through a_n. This discovery was made by the Scottish mathematician Colin Maclaurin.

> What's a coefficient?
>
> The number in a term that precedes x, by which x is multiplied – a_1, a_2, and so on.

However, not all formulas can be readily converted to Formula X. When we want to convert a formula whose coefficients are unknown, we use **Maclaurin's expansion formula** to find those coefficients.

Let's start by trying to find the various coefficients of Formula X.

2. 2 The Road to Maclaurin

$$f(x) = a_0 + a_1x + a_2x^2 + a_3x^3 + a_4x^4 + \cdots \qquad \text{(Formula } X\text{)}$$

We shall now use Formula X to derive each coefficient in turn.

«Finding a_0»

How do we go about determining a_0? If you look carefully at Formula X, you'll notice that all terms from a_1 on are multiplied by x. If x is 0, all terms except a_0 will disappear. So let's do exactly that – substitute 0 for x in $f(x)$.

$$f(0) = a_0 + a_1 0 + a_2 0 + a_3 0 + a_4 0 + \cdots$$
$$f(0) = a_0$$

"No kidding!"

To find a_0, substitute 0 for x in $f(x)$ $\qquad a_0 = f(0)$

«Finding a_1»

We want to find a_1, but x is in the way. To "eliminate x, let's do a first-order differentiation on x for the entire formula."

$$f'(x) = \left(a_0\right)' + \left(a_1x\right)' + \left(a_2x^2\right)' + \left(a_3x^3\right)' + \cdots$$

First off, we have to deal with $(a_0)'$. This will be easier to understand if we look at a graph.

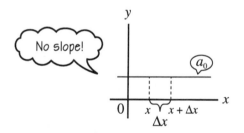

This graph is of $y = a_0$.

When we add $x+\Delta x$, a_0 doesn't change. Therefore:

$$\left(a_0\right)' = 0$$

Next, what about $(a_1x)'$?

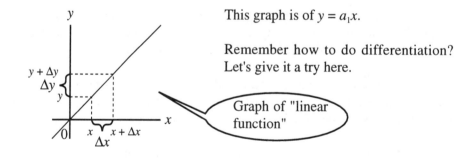

This graph is of $y = a_1x$.

Remember how to do differentiation? Let's give it a try here.

Graph of "linear function"

What's a_0?

Just like the a_0 we found in the Fourier series, this one shows how far the entire function is displaced above or below 0.

Let $x = 0$ in the function $f(x) = 3x^3 + 5x^2 + 7$, which we used as an example above.

Then
$$f(0) = 3 \cdot 0 + 5 \cdot 0 + 7,$$
$$\text{so } f(0) = 7.$$
$$\text{Thus } \boldsymbol{a_0 = 7.}$$

$$y = a_1 x$$

$$y + \Delta y = a_1(x + \Delta x)$$

$$y + \Delta y - y = a_1(x + \Delta x) - a_1 x$$

$$\Delta y = a_1 \Delta x$$

$$\frac{\Delta y}{\Delta x} = \frac{a_1 \cancel{\Delta x}}{\cancel{\Delta x}}$$

$$\lim_{\Delta x \to 0} \frac{\Delta y}{\Delta x} = a_1$$

$$\frac{dy}{dx} = a_1$$

$$\boxed{\left(a_1 x\right)' = a_1}$$

For those of you that have forgotten how to do a differentiation, refer back to Chapter 5.

Is it all coming back to you now? Let's keep going! On to $(a_2 x^2)'$:

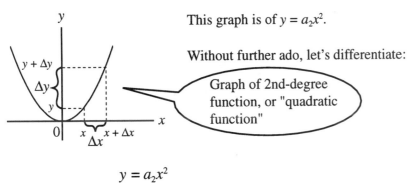

This graph is of $y = a_2 x^2$.

Without further ado, let's differentiate:

Graph of 2nd-degree function, or "quadratic function"

$$y = a_2 x^2$$

$$y + \Delta y = a_2(x + \Delta x)^2$$

$$y + \Delta y - y = a_2(x + \Delta x)^2 - a_2 x^2$$

$$\Delta y = \cancel{a_2 x^2} + 2a_2 x \Delta x + a_2 \Delta x^2 - \cancel{a_2 x^2}$$

$$\frac{\Delta y}{\Delta x} = \frac{2a_2 x \cancel{\Delta x} + a_2 \Delta x^{\cancel{2}}}{\cancel{\Delta x}}$$

$$\lim_{\Delta x \to 0} \frac{\Delta y}{\Delta x} = \lim_{\Delta x \to 0} 2a_2 x + a_2 \Delta x$$

$$\frac{dy}{dx} = 2a_2 x$$

$$\boxed{\left(a_2 x^2\right)' = 2a_2 x}$$

One more to go: $(a_3x^3)'$:

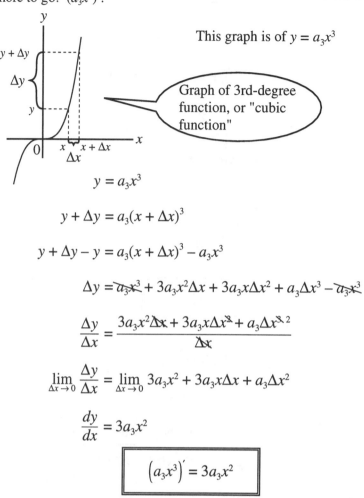

This graph is of $y = a_3x^3$

Graph of 3rd-degree function, or "cubic function"

$$y = a_3x^3$$

$$y + \Delta y = a_3(x + \Delta x)^3$$

$$y + \Delta y - y = a_3(x + \Delta x)^3 - a_3x^3$$

$$\Delta y = a_3x^3 + 3a_3x^2\Delta x + 3a_3x\Delta x^2 + a_3\Delta x^3 - a_3x^3$$

$$\frac{\Delta y}{\Delta x} = \frac{3a_3x^2\Delta x + 3a_3x\Delta x^2 + a_3\Delta x^3}{\Delta x}$$

$$\lim_{\Delta x \to 0}\frac{\Delta y}{\Delta x} = \lim_{\Delta x \to 0} 3a_3x^2 + 3a_3x\Delta x + a_3\Delta x^2$$

$$\frac{dy}{dx} = 3a_3x^2$$

$$\boxed{\left(a_3x^3\right)' = 3a_3x^2}$$

Are you starting to detect a pattern? What do you think the next one will look like?

"$(a_4x^4)'$? Let's see... I bet it's $4a_4x^3$!!"

Bravo! How did you arrive at that?

"Well, I moved the number in the exponent down to the front of the term, and subtracted 1 from the exponent."

Like this:

$$\left(a_4x^{\textcircled{4}}\right)'$$
$$= 4 \cdot a_4x^{(4-1)}$$
$$= 4 \cdot a_4x^3$$

Excellent! We call this formal differentiation. Try to memorize this trick, because it will come in handy.

Key point

$$\boxed{(a_nx^n)' = n\,a_nx^{(n-1)}}$$

This certainly makes things easy! Now all we have to do is string together the results we've obtained so far from first-order differentiation...

$$f'(x) = 0 + a_1 + 2a_2x + 3a_3x^2 + 4a_4x^3 + \cdots$$

Since we want to find a_1 here, we can eliminate all the other terms by substituting 0 for x in $f'(x)$. That gives us:

$$f'(0) = 0 + a_1 + 2a_2 0 + 3a_3 0 + 4a_4 0 + \cdots$$
$$= a_1$$

That was a rather lengthy process, so let's take a moment to summarize it:

To find a_1, perform first-order differentiation on $f(x)$, then substitute 0 for x in $f'(x)$.

$$a_1 = f'(0)$$

«Finding a_2»

To find a_2, we'll want to perform differentiation again. That's because x is attached to a_2, just as it was to a_1.

From which we get:

$$f''(x) = \left(a_1\right)' + \left(2a_2x\right)' + \left(3a_3x^2\right)' + \left(4a_4x^3\right)' + \cdots$$
$$\downarrow \qquad \downarrow \qquad \downarrow \qquad \downarrow$$
$$0 \qquad 2 \cdot 1 \cdot a_2 x^0 \qquad 3 \cdot 2 \cdot a_3 x^1 \qquad 4 \cdot 3 \cdot a_4 x^2$$

> This time we differentiate the formula we got by performing first-order differentiation to find a_1. When we differentiate a function twice, it's called second-order differentiation.

> This is differentiation for x, but there's no x attached to a_1, so $(a_1)' = 0$.

> Any number raised to the 0 power is 1, so $x^0 = 1$.

We want to find a_2, so we substitute 0 for x in $f''(x)$ to eliminate the other terms.

$$f''(0) = 0 + 2 \cdot 1 \cdot a_2 + 3 \cdot 2 \cdot a_3 \cdot 0 + 4 \cdot 3 \cdot a_4 \cdot 0 + \cdots$$
$$= 2 \cdot 1 \cdot a_2$$

But we still need to take one more step to find a_2 – divide both sides of the equation by $2 \cdot 1$.

$$a_2 = \frac{1}{2 \cdot 1} f''(0)$$

> Why is it written "$2 \cdot 1 \cdot a_2$"? Since $2 \cdot 1 = 2$, why not just write "$2a_2$"? Stay tuned and you'll find out.

That was fast! A bit of an improvement over a_1, wouldn't you say?

To find a_2, perform second-order differentiation on $f(x)$, substitute 0 for x in $f''(x)$, and divide both sides by $2 \cdot 1$.

$$a_2 = \frac{1}{2 \cdot 1} f''(0)$$

«Finding a_3»

To find a_3, we'll perform differentiation once again.

From which we get:

$$f'''(x) = (2 \cdot 1 \cdot a_2)' + (3 \cdot 2 \cdot a_3 x)' + (4 \cdot 3 \cdot a_4 x^2)' + \cdots$$

$$\downarrow \qquad\qquad \downarrow \qquad\qquad \downarrow$$

$$0 \qquad\quad 3 \cdot 2 \cdot 1 \cdot a_3 x^0 \quad 4 \cdot 3 \cdot 2 \cdot a_4 x^1$$

Let's see... to find a_3, we substitute 0 for x...

$$f'''(0) = 0 + 3 \cdot 2 \cdot 1 \cdot a_3 + 4 \cdot 3 \cdot 2 \cdot a_4 \cdot 0 + \cdots$$
$$= 3 \cdot 2 \cdot 1 \cdot a_3$$

Then divide both sides of the equation by $3 \cdot 2 \cdot 1$.

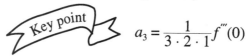 **Key point** $\qquad a_3 = \dfrac{1}{3 \cdot 2 \cdot 1} f'''(0)$

"Hmmm..."

To find a_3, perform third-order differentiation on $f(x)$, substitute 0 for x in $f'''(x)$, and divide both sides by $3 \cdot 2 \cdot 1$.

$$a_3 = \frac{1}{3 \cdot 2 \cdot 1} f'''(0)$$

Looks good. But hang on! Have you noticed a curious pattern here? So far we've found a_0, a_1, a_2, and a_3. In each case the same numbers seem to keep popping up – ones for a_1, twos for a_2, and so on. Do you suppose that means anything?

$$a_3 = \frac{1}{3 \cdot 2 \cdot 1} f'''(0)$$

"I see! For a_3, everything is in threes – third-order differentiation, three apostrophes in $f'''(x)$, dividing by $3 \cdot 2 \cdot 1$."

What we're really talking about is the "n" in $a_n x^n$. To find a_n, we have to perform nth-order differentiation, divide by $n \cdots 3 \cdot 2 \cdot 1$, and so on. We can therefore predict the following:

$$a_4 = \frac{1}{4 \cdot 3 \cdot 2 \cdot 1} f^{(4)}(0) \qquad \text{...and}$$

$$a_5 = \frac{1}{5 \cdot 4 \cdot 3 \cdot 2 \cdot 1} f^{(5)}(0) \quad \text{as well.}$$

But what happens when the denominator keeps getting bigger and bigger Fortunately, there is a convenient symbol for writing terms of this sort:

THE FACTORIAL (!)

It's the ever-popular "!" ♥♥

A number followed by the factorial sign (!) represents the product of all the numbers starting from the indicated number down to 1. Here are some examples.

$$3! = 3 \times 2 \times 1 = 6$$
$$5! = 5 \times 4 \times 3 \times 2 \times 1 = 120$$
$$10! = 10 \times 9 \times \cdots \times 2 \times 1 = 3628800$$
$$50! = 50 \times 49 \times 48 \times \cdots \times 2 \times 1 = 3.0414093 \times 10^{64}$$

As you can see, the factorial of even a small number produces an extremely large number. It seems that the exclamation mark was chosen to represent factorials to reflect this surprising result! Apparently, numbers like 70! and beyond are so large that even electronic calculators can't handle them.

There is one more peculiarity we should note about factorials:

$$1! = 1$$
$$0! = 1$$

While 1! = 1 certainly makes sense, 0! = 1 probably has you scratching your head. There's little point in puzzling over it, however, because that's just the way it is. If you absolutely insist on an explanation, take a look at the Special Bulletin to the right. If we use factorials to summarize our results so far, we get:

Special Bulletin

Having a hard time accepting that 0! = 1? Okay, we'll try to ease the pain. Take a look at this example:

$$(3-1)! = 2! = \frac{1 \cdot 2 \cdot 3}{3} = 2$$

$$(3-2)! = 1! = \frac{1 \cdot 2 \cdot 3}{2 \cdot 3} = 1$$

$$(3-3)! = \frac{1 \cdot 2 \cdot 3}{1 \cdot 2 \cdot 3} = 1$$

...which means

$$(3-3)! = 0! = 1.$$

There, does that help? (Be aware that this is not a rigorous proof of 0! = 1.)

$$a_0 = 1 \cdot f(0) \qquad\qquad a_0 = \frac{1}{0!} f(0)$$

$$a_1 = 1 \cdot f'(0) \qquad\qquad a_1 = \frac{1}{1!} f'(0)$$

$$a_2 = \frac{1}{2 \cdot 1} f''(0) \qquad\qquad a_2 = \frac{1}{2!} f''(0))$$

$$a_3 = \frac{1}{3 \cdot 2 \cdot 1} f'''(0) \qquad\qquad a_3 = \frac{1}{3!} f'''(0)$$

$$a_4 = \frac{1}{4 \cdot 3 \cdot 2 \cdot 1} f^{(4)}(0) \qquad\qquad a_4 = \frac{1}{4!} f^{(4)}(0)$$

$$\vdots \qquad\qquad\qquad\qquad \vdots$$

Nice and orderly!

It's easy to predict what comes next in the sequence.

The superscript (n) represents a symbol for nth-order differentiation.

Now let's try to make a general definition of this pattern using "n".

$$a_n = \frac{1}{n!}f^{(n)}(0)$$

This is the formula used by Maclaurin's expansion to find coefficients. Looks a lot like Fourier coefficients, doesn't it!

You can use this formula to find all the coefficients you are looking for. Maclaurin's expansion is the process of converting a function into an infinite series expansion formula by inserting these coefficients into each term of the formula.

Maclaurin's expansion is an extremely useful mathematical tool for **expressing a complicated function as the sum of simple functions.** It plays a major role in the world of physics as well.

"Hey, that sounds just like Fourier coefficients!"

Now, suppose we rewrite Formula X using Σ:

Quite so!

$$f(x) = a_0 + a_1x + a_2x^2 + a_3x^3 + a_4x^4 + a_5x^5 + \cdots \qquad \text{(Formula } X\text{)}$$

$$f(x) = \sum_{n=0}^{\infty} a_n x^n$$

Then, if we replace a_n in this formula with $\frac{1}{n!}f^{(n)}(0)$, we get:

Key point

$$f(x) = \sum_{n=0}^{\infty} \frac{1}{n!}f^{(n)}(0)x^n$$

This is **Maclaurin's expansion formula**.

Now, at long last, we're ready to perform Maclaurin's expansion on sin x and cos x! Whatever it turns out to be, the result should be interesting...

2. 3 Maclaurin's Expansion of $f(x) = \sin x$

We are on the verge of performing Maclaurin's expansion on the sine and cosine functions. But we can't do so right away. Maclaurin's expansion involves differentiation. Therefore, we first need to know what happens when we differentiate a sine or cosine function.

«Differentiating $f(x) = \sin x$»

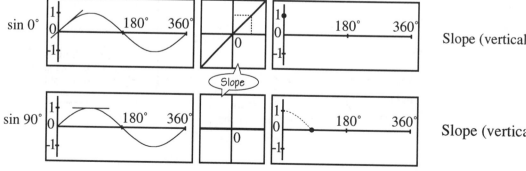

$\sin 0°$ Slope (vertical/horizontal) = 1

$\sin 90°$ Slope (vertical/horizontal) = 0

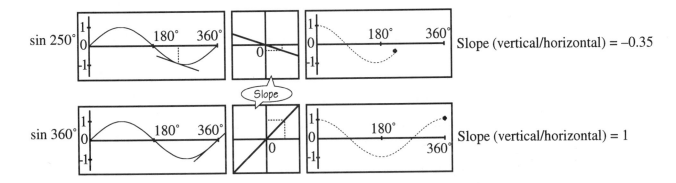

Slope (vertical/horizontal) = –0.35

Slope (vertical/horizontal) = 1

So when we differentiate sin x, we get cos x. In other words, the first-order differentiation of $f(x) = \sin x$ gives us $f'(x) = \cos x$. Second-order differentiation gives us $f''(x) = -\sin x$, and third-order differentiation gives us $f'''(x) = -\cos x$. Now we'll use Maclaurin's expansion to find the coefficients for this function. We substitute 0 for x in each function $f(x)$, remember?

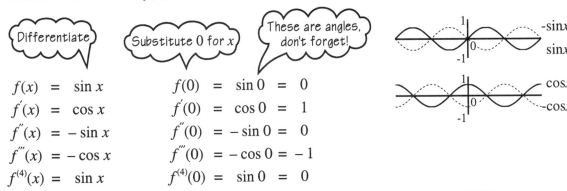

$$f(x) = \sin x$$
$$f'(x) = \cos x$$
$$f''(x) = -\sin x$$
$$f'''(x) = -\cos x$$
$$f^{(4)}(x) = \sin x$$

$$f(0) = \sin 0 = 0$$
$$f'(0) = \cos 0 = 1$$
$$f''(0) = -\sin 0 = 0$$
$$f'''(0) = -\cos 0 = -1$$
$$f^{(4)}(0) = \sin 0 = 0$$

We've made an important discovery: when you perform fourth-order differentiation on sin x, it returns to the original function! Now let's generate our coefficients by inserting each value of $f^{(n)}(0)$ in the formula

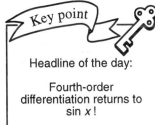

Key point

Headline of the day:

Fourth-order differentiation returns to sin x!

$$a_n = \frac{1}{n!} f^{(n)}(0)$$

$$a_0 = \frac{1}{0!} f(0) = \frac{1}{0!} \cdot 0 = 0$$

$$a_1 = \frac{1}{1!} f'(0) = \frac{1}{1!} \cdot 1 = 1$$

$$a_2 = \frac{1}{2!} f''(0) = \frac{1}{2!} \cdot 0 = 0$$

$$a_3 = \frac{1}{3!} f'''(0) = \frac{1}{3!} \cdot (-1) = -\frac{1}{3!}$$

$$a_4 = \frac{1}{4!} f^{(4)}(0) = \frac{1}{4!} \cdot 0 = 0$$

$\vdots$

Plugging these coefficients in and adding the terms together, we get:

$$f(x) = a_0 + a_1 x + a_2 x^2 + a_3 x^3 + a_4 x^4 + \cdots \qquad \text{(Formula X)}$$

$$f(x) = a_0 + a_1 x + a_2 x^2 + a_3 x^3 + a_4 x^4 + \cdots \qquad \text{(Formula } X)$$

$$\sin x = 0 + x + 0x^2 - \frac{1}{3!}x^3 + 0x^4 + \frac{1}{5!}x^5 + 0x^6 - \frac{1}{7!}x^7 + 0x^8 \cdots$$

Ordinarily we add up the terms in sequence — 0 degree, 1st degree, 2nd degree, and so on. But in this case there's no point in adding the even-numbered terms (2nd, 4th, 6th degree, etc.), since they're all 0.

What's this? Every other term becomes 0! Better check this out!

This is Maclaurin's expansion formula for sin x. Let's see if adding up the terms really gives us a sine wave.

——— This line indicates the term we're currently calculating.

·········· This line indicates previously calculated terms.

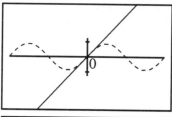

$$\sin x \approx 0 + x$$

The 1st-degree term is a straight line!

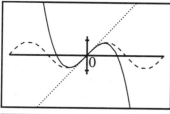

$$\sin x \approx 0 + x + 0x^2 - \frac{1}{3!}x^3$$

By the time we add on the 3rd-degree term, we're getting very close to the sine wave.

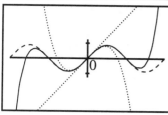

$$\sin \approx 0 + x + 0x^2 - \frac{1}{3!}x^3 + 0x^4 + \frac{1}{5!}x^5 + 0x^6 - \frac{1}{7!}x^7 + 0x^8 + \frac{1}{9!}x^9$$

We've made it to the 9th-degree term. Just a little farther...

Hang in there!

$$\sin x \approx 0 + x + 0x^2 - \frac{1}{3!}x^3 + 0x^4 + \frac{1}{5!}x^5 + 0x^6$$

$$- \frac{1}{7!}x^7 + 0x^8 + \frac{1}{9!}x^9 + \cdots + 0x^{16} + \frac{1}{17!}x^{17}$$

The 17th-degree term! Now we have a curve that perfectly coincides with the sine wave for two periods!

Beautiful!

2. 4 Maclaurin's Expansion of $f(x) = \cos x$

Next let's try our hand at Maclaurin's expansion of cos x.

The first step in Maclaurin's expansion is to differentiate, so we begin by differentiating cos x. The first-order differentiation of cos x gives us $-\sin x$. Second-order differentiation gives us $-\cos x$. Whoa! This is just like what happened when we differentiated sin x! Let's get it down on paper so we can see what's going on:

Differentiate	Substitute 0 for x

$$f(x) = \cos x \qquad f(0) = \cos 0 = 1$$
$$f'(x) = -\sin x \qquad f'(0) = -\sin 0 = 0$$
$$f''(x) = -\cos x \qquad f''(0) = -\cos 0 = -1$$
$$f'''(x) = \sin x \qquad f'''(0) = \sin 0 = 0$$
$$f^{(4)}(x) = \cos x \qquad f^{(4)}(0) = \cos 0 = 1$$

So fourth-order differentiation of cos x returns us to the original function, just as it did with sin x!  Key point

Now let's substitute the values we obtained for $f^{(n)}(0)$ in the formula

$$a_n = \frac{1}{n!} f^{(n)}(0)$$

$$a_0 = \frac{1}{0!} f(0) = \frac{1}{0!} \cdot 1 = 1$$

$$a_1 = \frac{1}{1!} f'(0) = \frac{1}{1!} \cdot 0 = 0$$

$$a_2 = \frac{1}{2!} f''(0) = \frac{1}{2!} \cdot (-1) = -\frac{1}{2!}$$

$$a_3 = \frac{1}{3!} f'''(0) = \frac{1}{3!} \cdot 0 = 0$$

$$a_4 = \frac{1}{4!} f^{(4)}(0) = \frac{1}{4!} \cdot 1 = \frac{1}{4!}$$

$$\vdots \qquad \vdots$$

Plugging in the coefficients and adding up the terms:

$$\cos x = 1 + 0x - \frac{1}{2!}x^2 + 0x^3 + \frac{1}{4!}x^4 + 0x^5 - \frac{1}{6!}x^6 + 0x^7 + \cdots$$

Go ahead and calculate this out the way you did for sin x.

A function like sin x or cos x continues on to infinity. Therefore, adding up an infinite number of terms brings us infinitely close to the original wave. Infinity?

So what was it we wanted to do in the first place?

$$\cos x + i \sin x = ?$$

That's right, we wanted to convert $\cos x + i \sin x$ into the elusive Formula X. We thought we might be able to do this by performing Maclaurin's expansion on $\sin x$ and $\cos x$. Let's add up the terms we obtained.

	a_0	a_1	a_2	a_3	a_4	a_5
$i \sin x$	$0 \times \dfrac{1}{0!}$	$1 \times i \times \dfrac{1}{1!}$	$0 \times \dfrac{1}{2!}$	$-1 \times i \times \dfrac{1}{3!}$	$0 \times \dfrac{1}{4!}$	$1 \times i \times \dfrac{1}{5!}$
$\cos x$	$1 \times \dfrac{1}{0!}$	$0 \times \dfrac{1}{1!}$	$-1 \times \dfrac{1}{2!}$	$0 \times \dfrac{1}{3!}$	$1 \times \dfrac{1}{4!}$	$0 \times \dfrac{1}{5!}$
$i \sin x + \cos x$	$1 \times \dfrac{1}{0!}$	$i \times \dfrac{1}{1!}$	$-1 \times \dfrac{1}{2!}$	$-i \times \dfrac{1}{3!}$	$1 \times \dfrac{1}{4!}$	$i \times \dfrac{1}{5!}$

Uh-oh! We've forgotten something very important. There's an i attached to $\sin x$ in our original formula $\cos x + i \sin x$. That means i must appear in every term where $\sin x$ is not equal to 0.

By the way, did you notice anything about the combination of $\sin x$ and $\cos x$ formulas in each column?

"Hmm... Well, the coefficient of every other term is 0 for both $\sin x$ and $\cos x$. What's more, the terms that have 0 as their coefficient are the opposite of each other in the two functions. The coefficients of even number terms (a_0, a_2, etc.) are 0 for $\sin x$, but the coefficients of odd-numbered terms (a_1, a_3, etc.) are 0 for $\cos x$!"

Indeed they are. Very interesting! **This orderly alternation of "0" coefficients is definitely a key point!**

Now it's time for the great unveiling. What exactly do we have there in the $i \sin x + \cos x$ column of our table?

The $f^{(n)}(0)$ part of the formula $a_n = \dfrac{1}{n!} f^{(n)}(0)$ (omitting the $1/n!$ part) repeats the pattern $1, i, -1, -i$, over and over.

	$f(0)$	$f'(0)$	$f''(0)$	$f'''(0)$	$f^{(4)}(0)$	$f^{(5)}(0)$
$i \sin x + \cos x$	1	i	-1	$-i$	1	i

For the $f(0)$ shown here, we substituted 0 for x in the original function $f(x)$, and got 1. So here's our problem: what sort of function $f(x)$ gives us 1 when we substitute 0 for x?

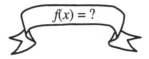

$$f(x) = ?$$

"How about $1 + x$?" $f(x) = 1 + x$

"Or an exponent to the power of 0?" $f(x) = a^x$

"The cosine function would work too." $f(x) = \cos x$

All right, let's try all of the above. We'll substitute 0 and see what happens.

$$f(x) = 1 + x \quad \rightarrow \quad f(0) = 1 + 0 \quad = 1$$
$$f(x) = a^x \quad \rightarrow \quad f(0) = a^0 \quad = 1$$
$$f(x) = \cos x \quad \rightarrow \quad f(0) = \cos 0 \quad = 1$$

What do you know? For all three, $f(0) = 1$. But not so fast – the next function in the sequence is $f'(0) = i$. That means we need a formula that contains i. Otherwise i won't appear when we perform first-order differentiation. Not only that, but i keeps popping up every other time we differentiate. We'd better put $f(x)$ aside for a moment and look at $f'(x)$.

So here's our next problem: what sort of function contains i?

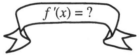

$$f'(x) = ?$$

Let's try appending i to the formulas we came up with for $f(x)$.

$$f(x) = 1 + ix$$
$$f'(0) = i$$

This one gives us i the first time we differentiate it. But if we substitute 0 for x in the second-order differentiation, we get 0...NO GOOD!

$$f(x) = i \cos x$$
$$f'(x) = - i \sin x$$
$$f'(0) = - i \sin 0$$
$$f'(0) = 0$$

This one gives us 0 the first time...NO GOOD!

$$f(x) = a^{ix}$$
$$f'(x) = i \cdot a^{ix} \times \log_e a$$
$$f'(0) = i \cdot a^{i\,0} \times \underline{\log_e a}$$
$$f'(0) = i \cdot 1$$
$$f'(0) = i$$

We want this to be 1, right?
The logarithm is indeed 1 if **a = e.**

Differentiation of $f(x) = a^{ix}$

To simplify the equation,
let's replace $f(x)$ with y.

$$y + \Delta y = a^{i(x + \Delta x)}$$

$$\Delta y = a^{i(x + \Delta x)} - a^{ix}$$

(Now $ix = z$, $i\Delta x = \Delta z$, then)

$$\Delta y = a^{(z + \Delta z)} - a^z$$

$$\frac{\Delta y}{\Delta x} = \frac{a^{(z + \Delta z)} - a^z}{\Delta x}$$

$$= \frac{a^{(z + \Delta z)} - a^z}{\Delta z} \cdot \frac{\Delta z}{\Delta x}$$

$$= \frac{a^{(z + \Delta z)} - a^z}{\Delta z} \cdot i$$

$$\lim_{\Delta x \to 0} \frac{\Delta y}{\Delta x} = \lim_{\Delta x \to 0} \frac{a^{(z + \Delta z)} - a^z}{\Delta z} \cdot i$$

$$= i \cdot \lim_{\Delta z \to 0} \frac{a^{(z + \Delta z)} - a^z}{\Delta z}$$

$$= i \cdot (a^z)'$$

$$= i \cdot \log_e a \cdot a^z \quad \text{(see p.313)}$$

$$= i \cdot \log_e a \cdot a^{ix}$$

$$(a^{ix})' = i \cdot a^{ix} \times \log_e a$$

If $a = e$, then $\log_e e = 1$,
remember ?

That means **$a^{ix} = e^{ix}$**, giving us the following formula for $f(x)$:

$$f(x) = e^{ix}$$

So at long last, after much time and effort, we have our formula. Let's take a look again at the $i \sin x + \cos x$ column of the table. You saw an interesting pattern there, didn't you?

	$f(0)$	$f'(0)$	$f''(0)$	$f'''(0)$	$f^{(4)}(0)$	$f^{(5)}(0)$
$i \sin x + \cos x$	1	i	-1	$-i$	1	i

"Uh, yeah – the function returns to its original value every four times!"

That's right! We saw that both the sine and cosine functions shared this characteristic of <u>returning to the original value every four times</u> (that is, when we perform fourth-order differentiation). But didn't we run across yet another function with this same characteristic?

"Yes! That other one we worked on, e^{ix}!"

Key point

$$(e^{ix}) \to e^{i\,0} = 1$$
$$(e^{ix})' = i \cdot e^{ix} \to i$$
$$(e^{ix})'' = i \cdot i \cdot e^{ix} = -1 \cdot e^{ix} \to -1$$
$$(e^{ix})''' = i \cdot i \cdot i \cdot e^{ix} = -i \cdot e^{ix} \to -i$$
$$(e^{ix})^{(4)} = i \cdot i \cdot i \cdot i \cdot e^{ix} = -1 \cdot -1 \cdot e^{ix} \to 1$$

Don't forget to substitute 0 for x.

Remember this? Not only does it return to its original value with fourth-order differentiation, but the resulting values are the same ones we just saw:

$1, i, -1, -i, ...!$

...Which means that $i \sin x + \cos x$ is just another name for e^{ix}, does it not? While we're at it, let's line up Maclaurin's expansion of e^{ix} alongside $i \sin x$ and $\cos x$:

$$i \sin x = 0 + i \cdot x + 0x^2 - i \cdot \frac{1}{3!}x^3 + 0x^4 + i \cdot \frac{1}{5!}x^5 + 0x^6 - i \cdot \frac{1}{7!}x^7 + 0x^8 + \cdots$$

$$\cos x = 1 + 0x - \frac{1}{2!}x^2 + 0x^3 + \frac{1}{4!}x^4 + 0x^5 - \frac{1}{6!}x^6 + 0x^7 + \frac{1}{8!}x^8 + \cdots$$

$$e^{ix} = 1 + i \cdot x - \frac{1}{2!}x^2 - i \cdot \frac{1}{3!}x^3 + \frac{1}{4!}x^4 + i \cdot \frac{1}{5!}x^5 - \frac{1}{6!}x^6 - i \cdot \frac{1}{7!}x^7 + \frac{1}{8!}x^8 + \cdots$$

A perfect fit! What could be more elegant than mathematics?

Big point

$$e^{ix} = \cos x + i \sin x$$

There's our answer! We did it!!

And that, friends, is **Euler's formula**.

This formula appears frequently in physics books, as well as in lectures at the College of Lex. By becoming acquainted with Euler's formula, we have all gotten a little closer to the essence of mathematics and physics.

The late American physicist Richard Feynman said of Euler's formula: "It is the most remarkable formula in mathematics. This is our jewel."

Now let's see what happens when we plot Euler's formula on the Gaussian plane...

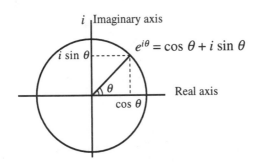

"Hey, wait a minute. Why did you change x to θ ?"

Just think back a bit. Suppose we substitute sin 0 for sin x. That simply means the value of the sine wave at 0 degrees. In other words, x is an angle, so we can replace it with θ, the symbol for an angle.

Ready to call it a day?
Hang on just a bit longer – we're not quite done yet. In our adventures with Fourier so far we've been using sin θ and cos θ, not $e^{i\theta}$. But now we want to be able to write these functions in a new way. To do this we need to find a formula that can express sin θ using $e^{i\theta}$, and another one that can express cos θ using $e^{i\theta}$.

Although there is only one Euler's formula, it has different versions depending on whether θ is $-\theta$ or $+\theta$. We can arrive at formulas that use $e^{i\theta}$ to express sin θ and cos θ by finding the solution to simultaneous equations using these two versions of the formula.

Here we go!
We already know what our function looks like when θ is positive. But what happens when θ is negative?

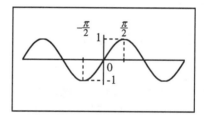

When θ is $\pi/2$ or $-(\pi/2)$ for a sine wave, the sine is 1 or -1 respectively. Therefore we write θ and $-\theta$ separately for sine waves

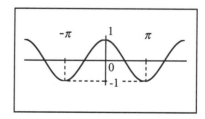

When θ is π or $-\pi$ for a cosine wave, the cosine is -1 in both cases. Therefore we can write θ the same way for cosine waves.

This difference gives us two formulas:

$$
\begin{aligned}
e^{i\theta} &= \cos\theta + i\sin\theta \\
e^{-i\theta} &= \cos(-\theta) + i\sin(-\theta) \\
&= \cos\theta - i\sin\theta
\end{aligned}
$$

To express $\sin\theta$ and $\cos\theta$ individually using e and i, we will treat the two formulas above as simultaneous equations. First, let's add the two equations together:

$$
\begin{aligned}
e^{i\theta} &= \cos\theta + i\sin\theta \\
+\,)\,e^{-i\theta} &= \cos\theta - i\sin\theta \\
\hline
e^{i\theta} + e^{-i\theta} &= 2\cos\theta \\
\cos\theta &= \frac{e^{i\theta} + e^{-i\theta}}{2}
\end{aligned}
$$

Next, we'll subtract the bottom equation from the top one:

$$
\begin{aligned}
e^{i\theta} &= \cos\theta + i\sin\theta \\
-\,)\,e^{-i\theta} &= \cos\theta - i\sin\theta \\
\hline
e^{i\theta} - e^{-i\theta} &= 2i\sin\theta \\
\sin\theta &= \frac{e^{i\theta} - e^{-i\theta}}{2i}
\end{aligned}
$$

And voilà! We now have separate formulas that express $\sin\theta$ and $\cos\theta$ using the same terms.

$$
\begin{aligned}
\cos\theta &= \frac{e^{i\theta} + e^{-i\theta}}{2} \\
\sin\theta &= \frac{e^{i\theta} - e^{-i\theta}}{2i}
\end{aligned}
$$

These two equations will provide us with more powerful forms of the Fourier series and Fourier coefficients formulas. We'll find that Euler's formula ($e^{i\theta} = \cos\theta + i\sin\theta$) plays a pivotal role in our upcoming adventures with Fourier, as well as in the realm of natural science, which we have yet to explore. It's up to you to make Euler's formula *your* formula.

Complex number representation and Fourier transforms await you!

¡ Vamonos !

$e^{i\theta} = \cos\theta + i\sin\theta$

Finding the Value of e with Maclaurin's Expansion

Maclaurin's expansion is an extremely useful mathematical formula that is used to transform various formulas used in physics. It is easy to find the value of e using Maclaurin's expansion.

The function e^x remains unchanged, as e^x, whether it is differentiated or integrated. This can be expressed as $(e^x)' = e^x$. Let's take advantage of this characteristic of the function and try Maclaurin's expansion on e^x.

If $f(x) = e^x$ and we want to find a_0:

$$a_0 = \frac{1}{0!}f(0) = \frac{1}{1}e^0$$

Any number raised to the 0 power is 1, so:

$$a_0 = \frac{1}{0!}f(0) = \frac{1}{1}e^0 = 1$$

Thus a_0 is 1.

Next, we'll try a_1...

$$a_1 = \frac{1}{1!}f(0) = \frac{1}{1!}e^0 = 1$$

And a_2:

$$a_2 = \frac{1}{2!}f(0) = \frac{1}{2!}e^0 = \frac{1}{2!}$$

For a_3 and beyond, we get...

$$a_3 = \frac{1}{3!}f(0) = \frac{1}{3!}e^0 = \frac{1}{3!}$$

$$a_4 = \frac{1}{4!}f(0) = \frac{1}{4!}e^0 = \frac{1}{4!}$$

$$a_5 = \frac{1}{5!}f(0) = \frac{1}{5!}e^0 = \frac{1}{5!}$$

$$\vdots \qquad \vdots \qquad \vdots$$

$$a_n = \frac{1}{n!}f(0) = \frac{1}{n!}e^0 = \frac{1}{n!}$$

Inserting all of these values into the expansion formula for the original function $f(x)$, we get:

$$f(x) = 1 + 1 \cdot x + \frac{1}{2!}x^2 + \frac{1}{3!}x^3 + \frac{1}{4!}x^4 + \frac{1}{5!}x^5 + \cdots$$

And there we have Maclaurin's expansion of e^x. Now, suppose $x = 1$ in $f(x)$:

$$f(1) = 1 + 1 + \frac{1}{2!}1^2 + \frac{1}{3!}1^3 + \cdots + \frac{1}{n!}1^n$$

In other words, the number e is:

$$e = 1 + 1 + \frac{1}{2} + \frac{1}{6} + \frac{1}{24} + \frac{1}{120} + \frac{1}{720} + \cdots$$

...a number that is added up infinitely. If we use a calculator to add together as many of these terms as possible, we find that the answer steadily approaches

$$e = 2.7182818284...$$

Chapter 11

Complex Number Representation of Fourier Series and Fourier Coefficients

*In this chapter we'll learn how to use **e**, **i**, and Euler's formula to rewrite the Fourier series and Fourier coefficients. This will allow us to express both the sine and cosine functions in a single term. Finally, we'll convert the Fourier series and Fourier coefficients into one simple formula for each.*

As you can tell from the chapter title, we are at long last going to be discussing Fourier series and Fourier coefficients again. Over the last two chapters we've referred to Fourier only occasionally; mostly we've been doing things that weren't directly related to the Fourier formulas:

• ***e* and *i***

• **Maclaurin's expansion**

• **Euler's formula**

But once we found Euler's formula, we realized something: by using *e* and *i*, we could express the sin and cos terms!

You'll remember that we derived two versions of Euler's formula:

$$e^{i\theta} = \cos\theta + i\sin\theta$$
$$e^{-i\theta} = \cos\theta - i\sin\theta$$

Then we rewrote these formulas for the sine and cosine functions:

$$\cos\theta = \frac{1}{2}(e^{i\theta} + e^{-i\theta})$$
$$\sin\theta = \frac{1}{2i}(e^{i\theta} - e^{-i\theta})$$

The reason we went to all that trouble to learn about *e*, *i*, and Maclaurin's expansion in the first place was to come up with these formulas. Thanks to *e* and *i*, we now have another way of expressing cos and sin, whereas before we had to express them separately.

This time our goal is to use Euler's formulas to rewrite the formulas we have for Fourier series and Fourier coefficients. These formulas are already elegant and complete in their present format. They cannot be broken down into anything simpler, and they tell us what we want to know. What more could we ask? Since these wonderful formulas consist of cos and sin, rewriting them should be easy; all we have to do is use *e* and *i*. That may not sound like it's worth the trouble, but simply rewriting them is not the point. Our real challenge is to see if we can turn these formulas into something even more elegant.

The upcoming transformation of Fourier series and coefficients formulas should be exciting enough. But, even more exciting, in the process of rewriting these formulas, the writers discovered the real beauty and meaning of mathematics; we would like to share this with you as well.

Fourier

So away we go! To make the formula rewriting process easier to follow, we've broken it down into four steps:

1. Review the original Fourier series and Fourier coefficients formulas

2. Rewrite the formulas with *e* and *i* by substituting Euler's formulas

3. Create new formulas using $e^{i\theta}$ and $e^{-i\theta}$

4. Combine the formulas using $e^{i\theta}$

On page 368 you will find a blank table. As we go through each step, it's up to you to fill in the table with the formulas we come up with. For your convenience, we've numbered each formula where it appears in the text. Write in the appropriate formula next to each number in the table; it should help you keep track of what's going on.

1. Review the original Fourier series and Fourier coefficients formulas

Fourier series:

$$f(t) = a_0 + \sum_{n=1}^{\infty} (a_n \cos n\omega t + b_n \sin n\omega t) \qquad \text{............} \quad (1)$$

Fourier coefficients :

$$a_0 = \frac{1}{T}\int_0^T f(t)\, dt \qquad \text{............} \quad (2)$$

$$a_n = \frac{2}{T}\int_0^T f(t) \cos n\omega t\, dt \qquad \text{............} \quad (3)$$

$$b_n = \frac{2}{T}\int_0^T f(t) \sin n\omega t\, dt \qquad \text{............} \quad (4)$$

Kind of takes you back, doesn't it? It's been a while since we used these formulas, so you're forgiven if you've forgotten them. Go ahead, write them into the table on the top row. Much as we'd like to push on to step 2, we should pause for a moment here to review what these old formulas mean. Otherwise we may get needlessly confused later on.

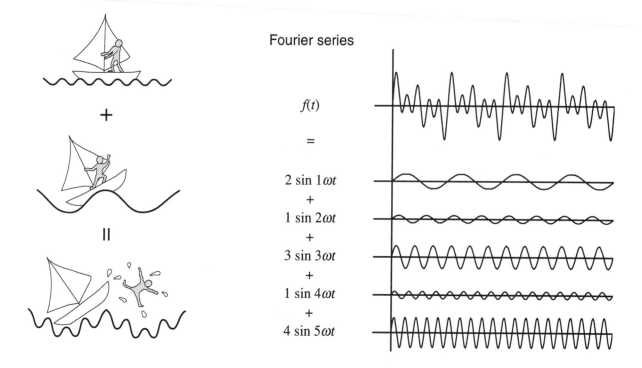

Fourier series

$f(t)$

$=$

$2 \sin 1\omega t$

$+$

$1 \sin 2\omega t$

$+$

$3 \sin 3\omega t$

$+$

$1 \sin 4\omega t$

$+$

$4 \sin 5\omega t$

Periodic complicated wave $f(t)$ can be expressed as the sum of simple waves. There are three types of simple wave – sine, cosine, and a_0. Wave a_0 is a straight wave that indicates how far the entire complicated wave is displaced above or below 0. The periods of the sine and cosine waves are integral multiples of the period of $f(t)$. Amplitudes a_n and b_n show how much of each sine and cosine wave the complicated wave contains.

Fourier coefficients

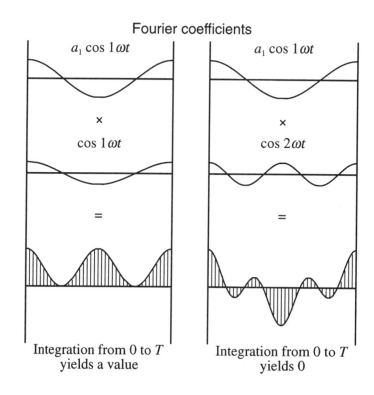

$a_1 \cos 1\omega t$ $a_1 \cos 1\omega t$

$\times$ $\times$

$\cos 1\omega t$ $\cos 2\omega t$

$=$ $=$

Integration from 0 to T Integration from 0 to T
yields a value   yields 0

Fourier coefficients formulas are used in finding the amplitudes a_0, a_n, and b_n, which indicate the "quantity" of each cosine wave and sine wave in wave $f(t)$. To find a_1, for example, we used the formulas of the Fourier coefficients.

$$a_1 = \frac{2}{T}\int_0^T f(t)\cos 1\omega t\, dt$$

Remember, however, that $f(t)$ was expressed by the sum of terms that went on indefinitely like this:

$$f(t) = a_0 + a_1 \cos 1\omega t + b_1 \sin 1\omega t$$
$$+ a_2 \cos 2\omega t + b_2 \sin 2\omega t$$
$$+ \cdots$$

We tried multiplying each of these terms by $\cos 1\omega t$ and integrating it from 0 to T. And we made a startling discovery: for every term but one, the result of integration was zero. The exception was the term $a_1 \cos 1\omega t$ multiplied by $\cos 1\omega t$. That's the great thing about Fourier coefficients – it leaves us with the term containing the amplitude we're looking for, and only that term.

There, does your memory feel somewhat refreshed?

2. Rewrite the formulas with e and i by substituting Euler's formulas

Now that we've gone back over the Fourier series and coefficients formulas, let's substitute Euler's formulas in them. First, we should review what those formulas are. For our present purposes, we'll let

$$\theta = n\omega t.$$

Don't let it throw you; they're really the same thing. That gives us:

$$e^{in\omega t} = \cos n\omega t + i \sin n\omega t$$
$$e^{-in\omega t} = \cos n\omega t - i \sin n\omega t$$
$$\cos n\omega t = \frac{1}{2}(e^{in\omega t} + e^{-in\omega t})$$
$$\sin n\omega t = \frac{1}{2i}(e^{in\omega t} - e^{-in\omega t})$$

Enough review! Let's get down to some serious rewriting!
Rewrite $\sin n\omega t$ and $\cos n\omega t$.

$$f(t) = a_0 + \sum_{n=1}^{\infty} \left\{ \frac{a_n}{2}(e^{in\omega t} + e^{-in\omega t}) + \frac{b_n}{2i}(e^{in\omega t} - e^{-in\omega t}) \right\} \quad \cdots\cdots (5)$$

$$a_0 = \frac{1}{T}\int_0^T f(t)dt \quad \cdots\cdots (6)$$

$$a_n = \frac{2}{T}\int_0^T f(t)\frac{1}{2}(e^{in\omega t} + e^{-in\omega t})dt \quad \cdots\cdots (7)$$

$$b_n = \frac{2}{T}\int_0^T f(t)\frac{1}{2i}(e^{in\omega t} - e^{-in\omega t})dt \quad \cdots\cdots (8)$$

We've substituted Euler's formulas for cos and sin, and nothing more. Write the formulas into the table, and you'll be done with step 2. The formulas are getting more and more complicated, but bear with us: all we have to do next is break them apart and put them together again. Relax! It's not that hard!

3 Create new formulas using $e^{in\omega t}$ and $e^{-in\omega t}$

Now that we've substituted Euler's formulas, cos and sin have disappeared from the original formulas. But all we've done so far is substitute; these formulas aren't yet in a usable format. What we have to do next is break the formulas apart, then put them together again using $e^{in\omega t}$ and $e^{-in\omega t}$. We'll start with the Fourier series formula:

Fourier Series

$$f(t) = a_0 + \sum_{n=1}^{\infty} \left\{ \frac{a_n}{2}(e^{in\omega t} + e^{-in\omega t}) + \frac{b_n}{2i}(e^{in\omega t} - e^{-in\omega t}) \right\}$$

Expand the terms in parentheses ( ).

$$f(t) = a_0 + \sum_{n=1}^{\infty} \left(\frac{a_n}{2}e^{in\omega t} + \frac{a_n}{2}e^{-in\omega t} + \frac{b_n}{2i}e^{in\omega t} - \frac{b_n}{2i}e^{-in\omega t} \right)$$

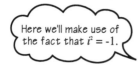

We want to combine the terms that contain $e^{in\omega t}$ and those that contain $e^{-in\omega t}$ – that is, parts A and B – respectively. To do this, we need to make the denominators of all these terms the same. Two of the terms have denominators that contain i, so we'll multiply each of these terms by i/i. Since $i/i = 1$, it doesn't affect the value of the term.

Here we'll make use of the fact that $i^2 = -1$.

$$f(t) = a_0 + \sum_{n=1}^{\infty} \left(\frac{a_n}{2}e^{in\omega t} + \frac{a_n}{2}e^{-in\omega t} + \frac{ib_n}{2i^2}e^{in\omega t} - \frac{ib_n}{2i^2}e^{-in\omega t} \right)$$

$$= a_0 + \sum_{n=1}^{\infty} \left(\frac{a_n}{2}e^{in\omega t} + \frac{a_n}{2}e^{-in\omega t} - \frac{ib_n}{2}e^{in\omega t} + \frac{ib_n}{2}e^{-in\omega t} \right)$$

Now that the terms all have the same denominator, we can combine parts A and B:

$$f(t) = a_0 + \sum_{n=1}^{\infty} \left\{ \frac{1}{2}(a_n - ib_n)e^{in\omega t} + \frac{1}{2}(a_n + ib_n)e^{-in\omega t} \right\} \quad \text{...............} (9)$$

So now we have a Fourier series formula with separate terms for $e^{in\omega t}$ and $e^{-in\omega t}$. Let's write the formula into our table.

Next...

Fourier coefficients

$$a_0 = \frac{1}{T}\int_0^T f(t)dt \qquad \text{.............. (10)}$$

This formula is fine as is, since it doesn't contain either *e* or *i*. Let's stick it in the table.

$$a_n = \frac{2}{T}\int_0^T f(t)\frac{1}{2}(e^{in\omega t} + e^{-in\omega t})dt$$

For this one, we should move the constant (1/2) outside the integral sign, then expand the terms in parentheses.

$$a_n = \frac{1}{2}\cdot\frac{2}{T}\int_0^T f(t)\Big(e^{in\omega t} + e^{-in\omega t}\Big)dt$$
$$= \frac{1}{T}\int_0^T \Big\{f(t)e^{in\omega t} + f(t)e^{-in\omega t}\Big\}dt$$

> Since the value 1/2 doesn't change when *t* is integrated, it is a constant. The result will be the same whether you first multiply by 1/2 and then integrate, or move 1/2 to the left and multiply by it after you integrate.

Take a look at the formula above. The part of the formula that is being integrated consists of the sum of two functions. This is where the following rule applies:

"When integrating two functions over the same range, the result is the same whether you first add the functions, then integrate the sum, or first integrate each function, then add the results."

This may sound confusing, but if we illustrate it on a graph, you'll see what we're talking about.

> Integration means finding the area of the space between a function and the *t* axis.
>
> Area = height × width
>
> If the range of the two functions is the same, their width is the same. Therefore, you can find the total area by multiplying their heights, *i.e.* the values $A(t)$ and $B(t)$. You can add $A(t)$ to $B(t)$ first, or not; it doesn't matter.

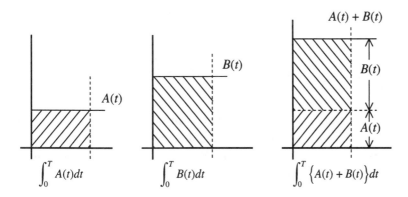

Get it? If you don't, never mind; for the time being, just accept it as the way things are. We're going to use this fact to further rewrite the formula. Let's look again at what we have so far:

$$a_n = \frac{1}{T}\int_0^T \Big\{f(t)e^{in\omega t} + f(t)e^{-in\omega t}\Big\}dt$$

$$a_n = \frac{1}{T}\int_0^T f(t)e^{in\omega t}dt + \frac{1}{T}\int_0^T f(t)e^{-in\omega t}dt$$

For now, let's leave the formula for a_n as it stands and turn our attention to b_n. We can treat this one the same way, except that it contains i, which requires a little more effort.

$$b_n = \frac{2}{T}\int_0^T f(t)\frac{1}{2i}(e^{in\omega t} - e^{-in\omega t})dt$$

Move the constant outside the integral, expand the terms in ( ), and rewrite the formula as the sum of two integrated terms:

$$b_n = \frac{1}{2i}\cdot\frac{2}{T}\int_0^T f(t)\left(e^{in\omega t} - e^{-in\omega t}\right)dt$$

$$= \frac{1}{i}\left\{\frac{1}{T}\int_0^T f(t)e^{in\omega t}dt - \frac{1}{T}\int_0^T f(t)e^{-in\omega t}dt\right\}$$

The only problem is this $1/i$. Let's eliminate it from the right side of the equation by multiplying both sides by i:

$$ib_n = i\frac{1}{i}\left\{\frac{1}{T}\int_0^T f(t)e^{in\omega t}dt - \frac{1}{T}\int_0^T f(t)e^{-in\omega t}dt\right\}$$

$$= \frac{1}{T}\int_0^T f(t)e^{in\omega t}dt - \frac{1}{T}\int_0^T f(t)e^{-in\omega t}dt$$

So now we have two similar formulas for b_n and a_n. Let's line them up:

$$a_n = \frac{1}{T}\int_0^T f(t)e^{in\omega t}dt + \frac{1}{T}\int_0^T f(t)e^{-in\omega t}dt$$

$$ib_n = \frac{1}{T}\int_0^T f(t)e^{in\omega t}dt - \frac{1}{T}\int_0^T f(t)e^{-in\omega t}dt$$

The only difference between the two is in whether the right side is added or subtracted. The goal of step 3 here is to express each Fourier coefficients formula as either an $e^{in\omega t}$ term or $e^{-in\omega t}$ term. We can use the simultaneous equation method to do this.

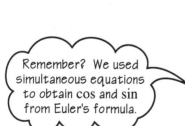

Remember? We used simultaneous equations to obtain cos and sin from Euler's formula.

$$A = X + Y$$
$$+\,)B = X - Y$$
$$A + B = 2X$$
$$\therefore \frac{1}{2}(A + B) = X$$

$$A = X + Y$$
$$-\,)B = X - Y$$
$$A - B = 2Y$$
$$\therefore \frac{1}{2}(A - B) = Y$$

To use this method, we'll define our terms as follows:

$$A = a_n \qquad X = \frac{1}{T}\int_0^T f(t)e^{in\omega t}dt$$

$$B = ib_n \qquad Y = \frac{1}{T}\int_0^T f(t)e^{-in\omega t}dt$$

The results are:

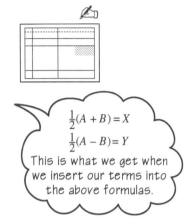

$$\frac{1}{2}(a_n - ib_n) = \frac{1}{T}\int_0^T f(t)e^{-in\omega t}dt \qquad \text{............... (11)}$$

$$\frac{1}{2}(a_n + ib_n) = \frac{1}{T}\int_0^T f(t)e^{in\omega t}dt \qquad \text{............... (12)}$$

$$\frac{1}{2}(A + B) = X$$
$$\frac{1}{2}(A - B) = Y$$
This is what we get when we insert our terms into the above formulas.

Let's write these new formulas into the table. Now is a good time to take a look at what we have in the table so far. Run your eyes across the top row of step 3 – see anything that these formulas have in common? That's right! The left side terms of formulas (11) and (12) appear in formula (9)! Now, suppose we rename these terms A_n and B_n respectively:

$$\frac{1}{2}(a_n - ib_n) = A_n$$

$$\frac{1}{2}(a_n + ib_n) = B_n$$

Then we can rewrite formulas (9), (11), and (12) like this:

$$f(t) = a_0 + \sum_{n=1}^{\infty}\left(A_n e^{in\omega t} + B_n e^{-in\omega t}\right) \qquad \text{............... (13)}$$

$$A_n = \frac{1}{T}\int_0^T f(t)e^{-in\omega t}dt \qquad \text{............... (14)}$$

$$B_n = \frac{1}{T}\int_0^T f(t)e^{in\omega t}dt \qquad \text{............... (15)}$$

You can write these three formulas into the table too.

We now have a set of formulas that are elegantly expressed using $e^{in\omega t}$ and $e^{-in\omega t}$. Our table is nearly filled; just one more step and we'll be done.

4. Combine the formulas using $e^{in\omega t}$

Except for the sign attached to the exponent, $e^{in\omega t}$ and $e^{-in\omega t}$ are identical. That means we should be able to combine our formulas further into formulas that use only $e^{in\omega t}$.

You may be asking yourself: why bother? After all, the formulas we have in hand are certainly elegant enough.

But it's this next step in the rewriting process that is going to be the most interesting. Why? Because instead of playing around with symbols and whatnot, we're going to examine what these formulas actually say from an entirely different point of view. A new perspective, we hope, will give us a new way of writing them. If anything, this is a more truly mathematical approach than simply doing calculations, don't you think? Anyway, it can't hurt us to try...

First let's take another look at the formula for a_0, which we've left alone all this time. There must be some way to combine this with the others. Let's start by expanding the part of Fourier series formula (13) that's in parentheses:

$$f(t) = a_0 + \sum_{n=1}^{\infty} A_n e^{in\omega t} + \sum_{n=1}^{\infty} B_n e^{-in\omega t}$$

For the term containing $e^{in\omega t}$, the range of n is from 1 to infinity. Let's see what happens when $n = 0$ instead. Substituting 0 for n, we get:

$$A_0 \, e^{i0\omega t} = A_0 \, e^0$$

$$A_0 = \frac{1}{T} \int_0^T f(t)e^0 \, dt$$

$$= \frac{1}{T} \int_0^T f(t)dt$$

$$= a_0$$

So when $n = 0$ for $A_n e^{in\omega t}$, the result is a_0. That means we can include a_0 in the $e^{in\omega t}$ term by expanding the range of Σ for that term:

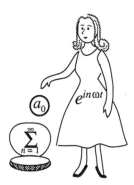

$$f(t) = \sum_{n=0}^{\infty} A_n e^{in\omega t} + \sum_{n=1}^{\infty} B_n e^{-in\omega t}$$

Now we want to combine these two terms together somehow $-e^{in\omega t}$ and $e^{-in\omega t}$. If we can convert the negative sign of the latter's exponent to a positive sign, we should be on our way. But we need to be careful; if we just change the sign arbitrarily, it will alter the meaning of the entire formula. How are we going to do this right?

Well, there is a way. It's a trick called "balancing accounts" using the range of Σ. Here's how it works. Within the exponent "$-in\omega t$" the n itself does not have any special meaning, in the sense that ω or t does. The n is simply a variable representing the numbers that are substituted one after another in the range of Σ. There is a way to change this n to $-n$ without affecting the results of any calculations. Look at the formula below:

$$\sum_{n=1}^{3} 2^n = 2^1 + 2^2 + 2^3$$

If we change **n** to **–n** in this formula and alter the range of Σ appropriately, it won't affect the results we get. Look at this:

$$\sum_{n=-1}^{-3} 2^{-n} = 2^{-(-1)} + 2^{-(-2)} + 2^{-(-3)}$$
$$= 2^1 + 2^2 + 2^3$$

Voilà! If we add a negative sign to the range of Σ, we get the same results! Let's try changing the sign of **n** in the $e^{-in\omega t}$ term:

$$\sum_{n=1}^{\infty} B_n e^{-in\omega t} = \sum_{n=-1}^{-\infty} B_{(-n)} e^{-i(-n)\omega t}$$
$$= \sum_{n=-1}^{-\infty} B_{(-n)} e^{in\omega t}$$

We did it; we came up with $e^{in\omega t}$! Notice that we changed the range of Σ to $-1 \to -\infty$. Now let's write out our entire formula:

$$f(t) = \sum_{n=0}^{\infty} A_n e^{in\omega t} + \sum_{n=-1}^{-\infty} B_{(-n)} e^{in\omega t}$$

So the range of Σ is $0 \to \infty$ for term A_n, and $-1 \to -\infty$ for term $B_{(-n)}$. Thus by altering our perspective a bit, we've been able to rewrite our formula. In the term $B_{(-n)}$, the **n** of $e^{in\omega t}$ has the range $-1 \to -\infty$. That means Σ now has a range all the way from $-\infty$ to ∞.

Now let's try to combine these terms into one term with $e^{in\omega t}$. Take a look again at formula (15) in our table:

$$B_n = \frac{1}{T}\int_0^T f(t) e^{in\omega t} dt$$

That was B_n. What happens when we try to figure out $B_{(-n)}$ instead?

$$B_{(-n)} = \frac{1}{T}\int_0^T f(t) e^{i(-n)\omega t} dt$$
$$= \frac{1}{T}\int_0^T f(t) e^{-in\omega t} dt$$
$$= A_n$$

What's this?! We get A_n! Well, that's not so surprising, since the coefficient of $e^{in\omega t}$ was A_n, after all. In any case, we'll have no problem combining the two terms into one.

So let's do it. We could leave the coefficient of $e^{in\omega t}$ as A_n, but this new A_n has to include a_0 and B_n within a broader range of Σ. Therefore we'll use a new name, C_n, for this coefficient. However, the actual formulas are exactly the same as they were for A_n:

Complex number representation of Fourier series

$$f(t) = \sum_{n=-\infty}^{\infty} C_n e^{in\omega t}$$

············· (16)

Complex number representation of Fourier coefficients

$$C_n = \frac{1}{T} \int_0^T f(t) e^{-in\omega t} dt \qquad \cdots\cdots\cdots (17)$$

At last! These are the formulas we've been struggling to find all along. Compact and elegant, wouldn't you say? Without further ado, let's write them into our table. With that, the table is complete.

Our original formula for the Fourier series consisted of the sum of three terms for a_0, cos $n\omega t$, and sin $n\omega t$ respectively. And Fourier coefficients consisted of three different formulas! Yet by substituting Euler's formulas and doing some rewriting, we've come up with a single formula for the Fourier series and a single formula for Fourier coefficients. Not only that, the two formulas are simple and relate to each other. Simply rewriting the formulas for sine and cosine functions (by performing MacLaurin's expansion, for example) leaves us with some very long formulas and not much else. But by using *e* and *i*, we've now acquired two formulas that are truly short and sweet.

Since all we did to our original formulas was rewrite them in a different format, their meaning hasn't changed. Throughout steps 1 through 4, the Fourier series and Fourier coefficients formulas have always formed a unified set.

There's only one loose end left to tie up. In the complex number representation of the Fourier coefficients formula, *f(t)* is multiplied by $e^{-in\omega t}$ to find C_n. When we found Fourier coefficients using the old formulas, we multiplied *f(t)* by the wave that had the amplitude we wanted to find. But to find C_n, we are multiplying *f(t)* by something other than a wave of the desired amplitude. Does this new formula really match the old ones? To check and see, let's try finding C_m.

$$C_m = \frac{1}{T} \int_0^T f(t) e^{-im\omega t} dt$$

$$= \frac{1}{T} \int_0^T \sum_{n=-\infty}^{\infty} C_n e^{in\omega t} \cdot e^{-im\omega t} dt$$

Here we can apply the integration rule of addition (or subtraction) and move Σ and C_n outside the integrated portion:

$$C_m = \frac{1}{T} \sum_{n=-\infty}^{\infty} C_n \int_0^T e^{in\omega t} \cdot e^{-im\omega t} dt$$

Take a look at this part. ⟶

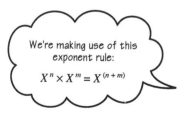

We're making use of this exponent rule:

$$X^n \times X^m = X^{(n+m)}$$

As ***n*** changes from $-\infty$ to ∞, $n = m$ only once. At all other times, $n \neq m$. So what happens when $n \neq m$?

$$\int_0^T e^{(in\omega t - im\omega t)} dt = \int_0^T e^{i(n-m)\omega t} dt$$

In other words, what happens when we integrate $e^{i(n-m)\omega t}$ from 0 to *T*, i.e., for a single period? Recalling Euler's formula, we can write this in the form of cosine and sine functions:

$$e^{i(n-m)\omega t} = \cos (n-m)\omega t + i \sin (n-m)\omega t$$

And when we integrate cos and sin from 0 to T, we get zero for both of them, remember?

$$\int_0^T e^{i(n-m)\omega t} dt = 0 + i \cdot 0 = 0$$

So when $n \neq m$, the result is always 0. Next, let's see what happens when $n = m$:

$$\int_0^T e^{i(n-m)\omega t} dt = \int_0^T e^{i0\omega t} dt$$

$$= \int_0^T e^0 dt = \int_0^T 1 dt = T$$

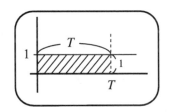

Going back to our initial formula, $C_n = C_m$, so:

$$C_m = \frac{1}{T} C_n T = C_n = C_m$$

This may seem a little unconvincing, but you may rest assured that we were able to find C_m without too much trouble. We now know we can find the coefficient C_n using the complex number representation of Fourier coefficients just as we could with the old formulas.

There is, however, something we should take note of in the calculations we just did:

"The important thing about Fourier coefficients formula is to leave only the term you want to find, and make all other terms become zero."

Up until now, we'd assumed that the important thing was to multiply $f(t)$ by the wave that had the amplitude we wanted to find. What we didn't realize from the old formulas was that the real point is to **retain only the term you want to find**. It doesn't matter what value we actually multiply the function by, as long as we achieve that result.

Another point of interest is that we found C_n directly from $f(t)$. As you wrote all those formulas into the table, you no doubt noticed that we found the formula for C_n simply by rewriting the Fourier coefficients formulas. In other words, C_n is derived from a_0, a_n, and b_n. Yet C_n is not calculated by first finding a_n, b_n and so on; rather, we can calculate it directly from $f(t)$. This may seem obvious, but it's a tremendous accomplishment. Here is a short formula that not only expresses a_0, a_n, and b_n all together, but is also quick to calculate. Furthermore, when we use this formula to search for coefficients, our calculations consist of multiplying exponential terms that have e as their base, so all we have to do is add up the exponents. Simple, compact, and elegant – what more could we want?

We have succeeded in deriving complex number representations of the Fourier series and Fourier coefficients formulas. Not only that, we have learned what the most important aspect of Fourier coefficients formula is. Now we'd like to talk a bit more about some things we, the writers, learned about mathematics during this process.

	Fourier series	Fourier coefficients		
Original formulas	(1)	(2)	(3)	(4)
Rewrite formulas with e and i	(5)	(6)	(7)	(8)
Create new formulas using $e^{in\alpha x}$ and $e^{-in\alpha x}$	(9) (13)	(10)	(11) (12) (14)	(15)
Combine formulas using $e^{in\alpha x}$	(16)	(17)		

☞ see 'Answer Page'

First, let's take another, more objective look at C_n. You may well be wondering – how exactly does one use these complex number formulas to find an actual value for C_n?

Remember that C_n is actually A_n, and our formula for A_n looks like this:

$$A_n = \frac{1}{2}(a_n - i\, b_n)$$

We tried to calculate the value of C_n for an actual wave, but the integration process was too complicated; eventually we gave up, we're ashamed to say.

So it appears as if we can't really find this value without knowing the values of a_n and b_n. The formula for C_n makes it look simple enough to calculate, but when push comes to shove, it doesn't do us any good. Here we've gone to all this trouble to combine sin and cos together, and what have we got to show for it? What's going on here?

Thanks to the help of our colleague Saru, we had no trouble grasping the concepts of complex number representation that led up to this point in our adventure. But when we started asking ourselves what good it really did to use complex numbers in these formulas, we began to have doubts. Why bother with e and i? we wondered. What's so great about them? How are they more convenient than the old way of writing the formulas?

Saru is the nickname of our esteemed complex number group leader, Keiko Sawatari.

By using another function instead of sin or cos in our Fourier series and coefficients formulas, we can express them in a more mathematically elegant manner. We knew that already, and no doubt it's a good thing. But these same elegant formulas make it harder than ever to actually calculate values! However pretty they may be, it seems ridiculous to spend all this time devising formulas that are even more difficult to compute than the old ones.

We tried to figure out what advantages the C_n formulas might have. We racked our brains, we really did, but we came up with zip. As near as we could tell, converting the old formulas to complex number representation might save paper, and that was about it. As a matter of fact, you won't encounter a truly useful rewriting of these formulas until we introduce you to the Fourier transform formulas in the next chapter.

In our darker moments we started referring to complex number representation as the dregs of the Fourier project.

But in the course of our desperate search for the merits of complex number representation, we came to some valuable realizations:

- We finally understood what it means for a formula to be "mathematically elegant."

- We learned that it can be very important to rewrite formulas without there being any "advantage" to it whatsoever.

Say what?

We'd forgotten something we supposedly knew already: mathematics is not just for the purpose of calculating values. The real challenge of math is...
"To find relationships among things and express them as simply as possible."

That's what math is really all about! Take Euler's formula, for example:

$$e^{in\omega t} = \cos n\omega t + i \sin n\omega t$$

This formula employs e and i to express the relationship between cos and sin very concisely. That's what we mean by mathematically elegant! To be "mathematical" doesn't mean making calculations more convenient; it means expressing relationships elegantly. We've been throwing the word "mathematics" around throughout this book as if we knew what it meant. Now, perhaps, we really do.

Complex number representation is the same. We didn't rewrite our formulas in this manner to make them easier to calculate. Rather, we wanted to express them more concisely using the relationships discovered by Euler. That's more important than ease of calculations. And that's why rewriting the formulas didn't yield any particular advantage. Instead, we succeeded in expressing the same thing in a more elegant way, and that's what really counts.

In a nutshell, C_n may be utterly useless for actual calculations, unlike a_n or b_n. But it is a graceful expression of a relationship, and in making its acquaintance we have deepened our understanding of the language of Fourier mathematics.

What we've taken three chapters to show you (not to mention the notebooks we filled with our notes) took Dr. Richard Feynman only three lines to describe in his chapter about Fourier analysis. We've barely scratched the surface, but we've caught a glimpse of the beauty of mathematics. Our vision should broaden as we venture further into the world of Fourier in the next chapter.

C_n concisely expresses the relationship between a complicated wave $f(t)$ and its simple waves.

Chapter 12

The Fourier Transform and the Uncertainty of Waves

And now, what we've all been waiting for – a formula that we can apply to non-periodic waves! In this chapter we're going to produce just such a formula – the "Fourier transform" – from the complex number representation we developed in Chapter 11. We'll do this by applying our complex number formulas to period $T \to \infty$. But at the same time, we're going to find ourselves running into an unforeseen obstacle: the fact that it is impossible to know the characteristics of a wave with complete certainty. What does this mean? Be patient and you'll see; this chapter is the culmination of everything we've studied so far.

1. The Fourier Transform

So how have your adventures with Fourier been so far? Not always smooth sailing, eh? Still, you've made it this far, and that makes you eminently qualified to meet our next challenge: the Fourier transform.

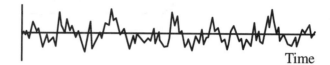

Time

Whoa! What have we here? A very odd-looking radio wave was just picked up on our monitors. This is a waveform unlike any we've seen before.

That's one ugly waveform! Let's try subduing it with a little Fourier coefficient formulating. First, we determine period T... Hmm... Where does this wave repeat itself, anyway? Could it be that it doesn't? Could this be...

THE DREADED NON-PERIODIC WAVE ?!!

Come to think of it, we armed ourselves with the weapons e and i precisely to slay this particular dragon. But are e and i really powerful enough to do the job? Relax, relax. Think: aren't there any examples of non-periodic waves close to home? Sit still for a moment and concentrate. What's that? The beating of your heart? Yes! Your heartbeat is the perfect example! Have you ever seen an electrocardiogram at a hospital? It's simply a waveform generated on a machine just like the FFT analyzer.

In its normal state, the heartbeat repeats itself something like this:

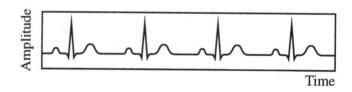

Normal heart rate: 60 to 70 times per minute
Frequency: 60 to 70 times per 60 seconds = 1 to 1.2 Hz
Period: 60 seconds ÷ 60 to 70 = 0.86 to 1 sec

If we extract the waveform for 1 second, we see:

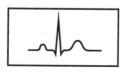

Wait, isn't that a period? Well, of course; we extracted one period's worth of the wave, so what we got was a period.

But suppose you didn't have a copy of the entire EKG waveform we first saw. How would you know this little waveform here was exactly one period? The answer is, you wouldn't. To recognize a period, we need to look at a longer version of the wave.

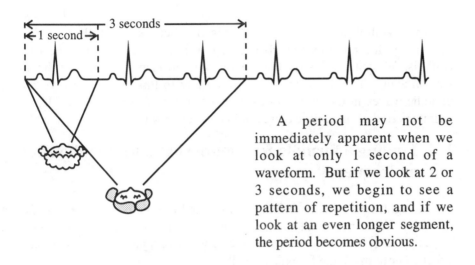

A period may not be immediately apparent when we look at only 1 second of a waveform. But if we look at 2 or 3 seconds, we begin to see a pattern of repetition, and if we look at an even longer segment, the period becomes obvious.

Now, suppose we were to take this to its logical extreme and look at a <u>really</u> long EKG – a 100 year long one, say. Suppose we were able to see this entire waveform in one glance...

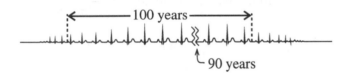

We'd see that the waveform doesn't really repeat itself indefinitely.

Just because people arbitrarily pick out a pattern in a wave and say "this is a period," it doesn't necessarily mean the wave repeats that pattern on into infinity. We tend to assume that it does, but in fact there's no guarantee. Consequently, if you consider any wave in its infinite form – whether it's a non-periodic wave like the one above, or a periodic wave like the ones we studied earlier in this book – you can never be certain whether it has a period or not.

If you could really view a wave over an infinite period of time, perhaps you could determine its period. Unfortunately you can't. But as long as we don't know when a wave repeats itself, why can't we think of it as a wave that repeats over an infinite period of time? That could apply to either a wave that appears to be periodic, or a wave that appears to be non-periodic. Both possibilities fit the definition of a wave that "repeats itself over an infinite period of time."

We already know a symbol that represents an infinite length (in this case, of time):

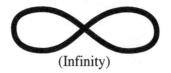

(Infinity)

This symbol doesn't represent a big number like 10 billion or even 10 quintillion. It represents a number so huge we don't have any idea how large it really is. We can use this symbol to write our period as $T \to \infty$. And that means we can apply the Fourier coefficient procedure to this wave, as we've done to periodic waves in the past. By assuming that this wave repeats itself over an infinite period of time, we can treat it like the other waves.

1. 1 Finding a formula for non-periodic waves: the effect on frequency

All right, let's take the infinity symbol and rewrite our Fourier coefficients formula. What that really means is we're going to redefine the period as "infinity." But it's not quite that simple; if we have a period $T \to \infty$, it may well affect other terms in the formula as well.

First of all, let's look at the relationship between the period and the fundamental frequency:

> **Note**
>
> Usually, 'frequency' is represented by symbol ' f ', but here the interval between frequencies (the fundamental frequency) on a spectrum is represented by Δf.

$$\Delta f(\text{fundamental frequency}) = \frac{1}{T(\text{period})}$$

If we have $T \to \infty$, then:

$$\Delta f = \frac{1}{T} \to \frac{1}{\infty}$$

If the wave takes infinite time to advance through one period, then its frequency (the number of periods per second) is extremely close to 0, since the wave passes through only the tiniest fraction of its period in one second. When the fundamental frequency approaches 0, what happens to the spectrum of the wave? The spectrum only shows integral multiples of the fundamental frequency, so that as frequency approaches 0, the interval between frequencies on the spectrum grows narrower and narrower:

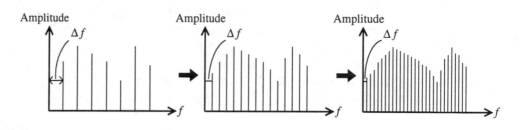

In other words, the longer the period is, the shorter the interval is between spectrum frequencies. Eventually, when the period reaches infinity, the spectrum becomes a continuum with no gap between frequencies. Thus, all frequencies become known when the period is infinity, even those that weren't apparent through Fourier coefficients formula.

1. 2 Rewriting the formula

Now let's rewrite our Fourier coefficients formula.

To start with, here's the complex number formula for Fourier coefficients we picked up in Chapter 11:

$$C_n = \frac{1}{T}\int_0^T g(t)\, e^{-in\omega t}\,dt$$

> Since we'll be using the symbol f to represent frequency in these formulas, we'll rewrite our usual wave function $f(t)$ with the letter "**g**" to avoid confusion: $g(t)$.

> It still means exactly the same thing!

To prepare for making $T \to \infty$, let's change this formula around a bit:

$$C_n = \Delta f \int_{-\frac{T}{2}}^{\frac{T}{2}} g(t)\, e^{-i2\pi f_n t}\,dt \;\cdots\cdots\; ①$$

> $1/T$ is Δf

> We can write the range of one period from 0 to T as being from $-(T/2)$ to $(T/2)$ instead. All we're doing is shifting the position of the entire period to the left by $T/2$.

> Since $\omega = 2\pi f$, we can write $2\pi f_n$ in place of $n\omega$ here. The value of frequency f is an integral multiple (n times) of the fundamental frequency, with n representing the multiple for that particular frequency. Thus the first frequency is written f_1, the second frequency f_2, and so on up to the nth frequency f_n.

Now we're ready to get serious. If we insert $T \to \infty$ into this formula, we'll be able to find the Fourier coefficients formula on a non-periodic wave (i.e. on any wave at all). To make T approach ∞, we'll use the same limit concept (lim) we've used before in differentiation and integration. Let's see what happens:

$$C_n = \lim_{T \to \infty} \Delta f \int_{-\frac{T}{2}}^{\frac{T}{2}} g(t)\, e^{-i2\pi f_n t}\,dt$$

However, a problem immediately arises here. As T approaches ∞, the relationship between the period and the frequency causes f to approach 0. (For the formula above, this would be written $\Delta f \to 0$.) But if Δf becomes 0, the value of the entire formula becomes 0, rendering it meaningless! As things stand, it doesn't look like we can produce a formula that applies to non-periodic waves from the Fourier coefficients formula alone.

But we still have the Fourier series! Let's see if that will help. The complex number representation of the Fourier series is:

$$g(t) = \sum_{n=-\infty}^{\infty} C_n\, e^{in\omega t}$$

> Once again, we've rewritten $f(t)$ as $g(t)$.

Now let's change this formula a bit, just as we did with the Fourier coefficients formula.

$$g(t) = \sum_{n=-\infty}^{\infty} C_n\, e^{i2\pi f_n t}$$

> Since $\omega = 2\pi f$, $n\omega = 2\pi f_n$.

Here's where we play our trump card -- we'll replace C_n in the Fourier series formula with the entire Fourier coefficients formula ①! Now watch what happens...

Fourier coefficients formula
$$C_n = \Delta f \int_{-\frac{T}{2}}^{\frac{T}{2}} g(t)\, e^{-i2\pi f_n t}\, dt$$

> Substitute all of this for C_n in the series formula.

Fourier series formula
$$g(t) = \sum_{n=-\infty}^{\infty} C_n\, e^{i2\pi f_n t}$$

$$g(t) = \sum_{n=-\infty}^{\infty} \left\{ \Delta f \int_{-\frac{T}{2}}^{\frac{T}{2}} g(t)\, e^{-i2\pi f_n t}\, dt \right\} e^{i2\pi f_n t}$$

Now we'll try inserting $T \to \infty$ here.

$$g(t) = \lim_{T \to \infty} \sum_{n=-\infty}^{\infty} \left\{ \int_{-\frac{T}{2}}^{\frac{T}{2}} g(t)\, e^{-i2\pi f_n t}\, dt \right\} e^{i2\pi f_n t} \cdot \Delta f \quad \cdots \cdots ②$$

> Since Δf is being multiplied, it doesn't matter where it's placed. We'll stick it on the end here.

This makes it possible to completely rewrite the formula like this:

$$= \int_{-\infty}^{\infty} \left\{ \int_{-\infty}^{\infty} g(t)\, e^{-i2\pi f t}\, dt \right\} e^{i2\pi f t}\, df \quad \cdots \cdots ③$$

where the inner integral is marked *1 and the whole braced expression with outer factor is marked *2.

How did we do that?! First, take a look at the combination of $\lim_{T \to \infty}$, $\sum_{n=-\infty}^{\infty}$, and Δf in formula ②, and the underlined section *1 in formula ③. As T approaches ∞, Δf approaches 0, just as it did when we added $T \to \infty$ to the Fourier coefficients formula. In the earlier formula, Δf eventually became 0, but here we have $\sum_{n=-\infty}^{\infty}$. That's where the secret of our success lies, in fact. Thanks to this combination and section *1, we can completely transform the formula without worrying about Δf becoming 0.

Now let's look at section *1. Before rewriting the formula, we had:

$$\int_{-\frac{T}{2}}^{\frac{T}{2}} g(t)\, e^{-i2\pi f_n t} dt$$

But now, because $T \to \infty$, the range of integration indicated by the integral sign $\int$ has changed from $\int_{-\frac{T}{2}}^{\frac{T}{2}}$ to $\int_{-\infty}^{\infty}$ (infinity divided by 2 is still infinity).

Notice, too, that f_n is now simply f. Before, the values f_n jumped from frequency to frequency. But now that $T \to \infty$, these values are continuous, leaving us with f without the n. (This applies to the term $e^{i2\pi f_n t}$ that appears to the right of section *2 as well.) All of this means we can change the formula to the configuration that appears in section *1. However, we still have to determine what sort of function section *1 is.

The term $e^{-i2\pi f t}$ to the right of $g(t)$ is a function of f and t. In our new formula we are multiplying this term by $g(t)$ and integrating it for t from $-\infty$ to ∞. When we integrate for t from $-\infty$ to ∞, however, the value of t becomes fixed. So the resulting function is one that changes according to the value of f. In other words, section *1 is a function of f.

Now we can also think of section *2 (section *1 multiplied by $e^{i2\pi f t}$) as a function of f. We then see that according to the entire formula, the values of this function are multiplied by the width Δf and added together from $-\infty$ to ∞. Since Δf approaches 0 as T approaches ∞, the width of each "strip" approaches infinitely close to 0, and these strips are all added together -- integration plain and simple. (We did this in Chapter 8, remember?)

So it wasn't enough to change the Fourier coefficients formula alone. But by combining the coefficients formula with the Fourier series formula, we have come up with an elegant solution, where section *1 is a function of f enclosed by $\lim_{T \to \infty} \sum_{n=-\infty}^{\infty}$ on one side and Δf on the other.

1. 3 Fourier transform and inverse transform

Now let's turn formula ③ back into the two formulas from whence it came. Section *1, which started out as a Fourier coefficients formula, has now become a function of f. So if we rename it $G(f)$, we get:

$$G(f) = \int_{-\infty}^{\infty} g(t)e^{-i2\pi f t} dt$$

This is none other than the formula for Fourier coefficients of any wave, including non-periodic waves, that we were seeking in the first place! We call this formula the **Fourier transform**.

This new formula in turn provides us with a new version of the Fourier series formula as well. Replacing section *1 with $G(f)$, we get:

$$g(t) = \int_{-\infty}^{\infty} G(f)\, e^{i2\pi ft} df$$

This formula is called the **inverse Fourier transform.**

When you line these two formulas up next to each other, they form a very symmetric and elegant pair indeed:

Fourier transform	**Inverse Fourier transform**
$G(f) = \int_{-\infty}^{\infty} g(t)e^{-i2\pi ft} dt$	$g(t) = \int_{-\infty}^{\infty} G(f)\, e^{i2\pi ft} df$

At last! We now have the tools with which to take any wave, however complicated -- periodic or non-periodic, it doesn't matter -- break it down into simple waves, and calculate its components.

2. The Uncertainty of Waves

2. 1 The truth about the Fourier transform $G(f)$

Well, we can pat ourselves on the back – we got the Fourier transform formulas we wanted. Now we want to calculate an actual value for $G(f)$, using an actual wave just like we did with integration, discrete Fourier expansion and so on. But first, we need to take another, closer look at our Fourier transform formula for $G(f)$.

The Fourier transform suddenly materialized when we took the Fourier coefficients formula and altered it by declaring the period of the wave to be infinite. Our objective was to improve the Fourier coefficients process by making it applicable to any wave, periodic or not. But let's compare these Fourier coefficients and Fourier transform formulas for a moment:

Fourier coefficients $\qquad C_n = \dfrac{1}{T}\int_0^T f(t)e^{-i2\pi f_n t} dt$

Fourier transform $\qquad G(f) = \int_{-\infty}^{\infty} g(t)e^{-i2\pi ft} dt$

What do you know? They have virtually the same format, except the Fourier transform lacks the $1/T$ term that's attached to the Fourier coefficients formula.

Just what was $1/T$, anyway? In Fourier coefficients formula, we multiplied complicated wave $f(t)$ by a wave of the same frequency as the component wave whose amplitude we wanted to find. Next we found the area of the resulting wave, and finally, we divided this result by the period T to get the desired amplitude. In the Fourier transform, the "divide by period T" part of the operation is missing. In other words, the Fourier transform does not give us the amplitude of the wave!

So where did $1/T$ disappear to?

$$g(t) = \sum_{n=-\infty}^{\infty} \left\{ \left(\frac{1}{T}\right)\int_{-\frac{T}{2}}^{\frac{T}{2}} g(t)e^{-i2\pi ft}dt \right\} e^{i2\pi ft}$$

(Fourier series and coefficients)

$$g(t) = \int_{-\infty}^{\infty} \left\{ \int_{-\infty}^{\infty} g(t)e^{-i2\pi ft}dt \right\} e^{i2\pi ft}df$$

(Fourier transform and inverse transform)

$$G(f) = \int_{-\infty}^{\infty} g(t)e^{-i2\pi ft}dt$$

(Fourier transform)

$$g(t) = \int_{-\infty}^{\infty} G(f)e^{i2\pi ft}df$$

(Inverse Fourier transform)

To come up with the Fourier transform formula, we had to combine the Fourier series and coefficients formulas into one, then break the result down into two new formulas – the Fourier transform and inverse Fourier transform. In the process, we didn't notice that $1/T$ had attached itself to the inverse Fourier transform.

In declaring the period to be infinite, we substituted ∞ for period T. To avoid ending up with $1/\infty$, we declared that $1/T = \Delta f$, from which we got df. That little sleight of hand gave us a nice integration formula in place of Σ. Finally, when we broke this formula down into the Fourier transform and inverse Fourier transform, $1/T$ ended up with the inverse transform. Taken together, then, the two transform formulas make a complete whole, with no loose ends left over.

If we compare only the Fourier coefficients and Fourier transform formulas with one another, they obviously differ. But that is because each is really part of a pair – the Fourier coefficients with the Fourier series, and the Fourier transform with the inverse Fourier transform. As a unit, each pair of formulas actually says exactly the same thing.

So what does the Fourier transform formula really mean?

Since the formula for finding $G(f)$ does not have a "divide by T" part, it finds the area of the wave, and that's it. What do we get when we find the area of a wave?

We need to go back to Chapter 3, "Discrete Fourier Expansion," and review how we performed the Fourier coefficients calculations for a real wave. The wave we used had a period (T) of 10 seconds. Therefore, whenever we calculated the amplitude of its components a_1, a_2, b_1, b_2, and so on, we always ended up dividing the area by $2/T$ – i.e., we divided by 10 and multiplied by 2. In Fourier coefficients, period T is always fixed, so we always divide by the same number in the end. Thus as long as you know the area of each component wave, you don't really have to calculate their respective amplitudes. The relative amplitude of a wave compared to any other wave is always the same. Simply by comparing their areas, you can tell right away that the amplitude of C_1 is twice that of C_2, say, or that C_3 and C_4 have the same amplitude. Since the Fourier transform doesn't include $1/T$, it doesn't provide us with the actual amplitudes expressed in the Fourier series. However, it does provide us with the <u>relationship</u> among the amplitudes of the component waves.

After going to all that trouble to find the Fourier transform formula, it may be a bit of a letdown to find that it doesn't tell us the amplitude of each wave. But as long as we know the relationship among these amplitudes, we have all the information we need about the characteristics of the waves. For example, suppose we find the Fourier coefficients for two versions of the sound AH, one loud and one soft, spoken by the same person. The two sounds will have different spectra, as we can see from the graphs below. But the ratios among their respective component waves are the same – $C_1 : C_2 : C_3 : C_4... = 5 : 6 : 4 : 3...$

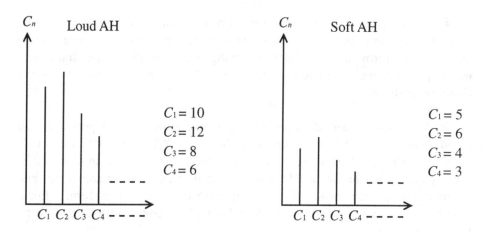

So it's not the amplitudes themselves, but the ratios among the amplitudes that are characteristic of AH.

Harking back to our old analogy of the vegetable juices, it doesn't matter whether you have 200 ml or 500 ml of tomato in a given juice; as long as the tomato is in the same proportion to the other vegetables, the overall flavor of the juice will be the same. But if you have tomato, celery, and carrot in the ratio $5 : 1 : 2$ in one juice, and the same vegetables in the ratio $3 : 2 : 3$ in another juice, then the two juices will taste different. The important thing is the ratio.

The spectrum provided by the Fourier transform is not merely a continuous version of the Fourier coefficients spectrum, but in the end, either spectrum can show us the characteristics of a wave.

2. 2 How to calculate a wave of period $T \to \infty$

Now that we know what the Fourier transform formula really means, we can use it to do some calculations. First we must decide what sort of wave we wish to subject to Fourier transformation. But we immediately run into a problem here. Since the Fourier transform presumes that period T is infinity, whatever wave we choose to calculate will have to be observed over an infinite period of time. Otherwise we won't be able to do any calculations for this wave. But how can we continuously watch the same wave forever? Are we going to monitor it until we die, then bequeath the job to our children, who will have to pass the torch to their children? Nonsense! This job is too big even for Superman!

Even if our wave has an infinite period, it's clear that we can only observe it over a finite period of time. Does that mean we can't do our calculations...?

Hang on! Don't give up so easily. We have one more trick up our sleeve: we can define a limited range of time to look at, Δt.

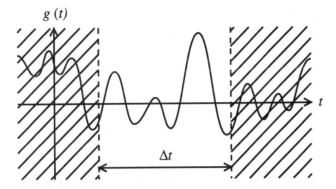

But isn't that just the same as defining period T? The answer is no! Range Δt is not period T; it's something completely different! The period is infinite, so we can't even begin to deal with it. Instead, we're going to look at a finite portion of the period and try to figure out the characteristics of the entire wave from that one piece. Will that work? Can we get an accurate view of the wave that way? Won't the value of $G(f)$ vary depending on which chunk of time we select as Δt?

Well, we won't know unless we try. Having come this far to get hold of the Fourier transform, we might as well put it to use. And perhaps in the process of using the Fourier transform to calculate $G(f)$ we'll find the answers to our questions.

2. 3 Calculation time!

To keep things simple, let's consider the wave below.

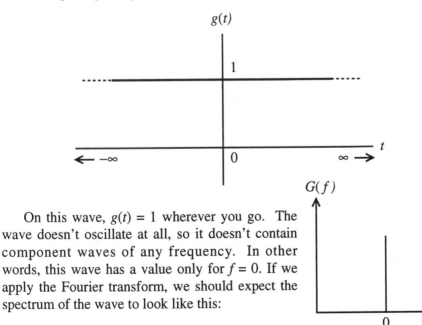

On this wave, $g(t) = 1$ wherever you go. The wave doesn't oscillate at all, so it doesn't contain component waves of any frequency. In other words, this wave has a value only for $f = 0$. If we apply the Fourier transform, we should expect the spectrum of the wave to look like this:

All right, let's verify that with some calculations. First, we'll define time Δt. Again, we'll keep it simple by using an interval that has $t = 0$ at its center:

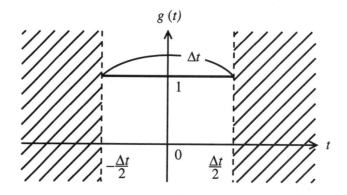

For the duration of Δt, $g(t) = 1$. We can't even see the rest of the wave outside Δt, so we'll just say that $g(t) = 0$ everywhere else.

$$\text{When } -\frac{\Delta t}{2} \leq t \leq \frac{\Delta t}{2} \rightarrow g(t) = 1$$
$$\text{When } t < -\frac{\Delta t}{2}, t > \frac{\Delta t}{2} \rightarrow g(t) = 0$$

Here's how this would look on a graph:

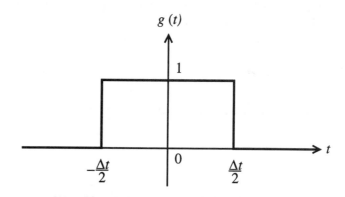

The Fourier transform formula, remember, is:

$$G(f) = \int_{-\infty}^{\infty} g(t)e^{-i2\pi ft}dt$$

If we integrate any section of the wave where $g(t) = 0$, the result will always be 0. So we only need to concern ourselves with integrating the section between $-(\Delta t/2)$ and $\Delta t/2$.

Since $g(t) = 1$, we get:

$$G(f) = \int_{-\frac{\Delta t}{2}}^{\frac{\Delta t}{2}} 1 \cdot e^{-i2\pi ft}dt$$

In short, all we have to do is integrate $e^{-i2\pi ft}$. And don't forget, we can integrate any expression by figuring out what we would have to differentiate to produce that expression. Since e has an exponent, we can also take advantage of certain special characteristics of e – remember what they were?

$$e^x \xrightarrow{\text{differentiation}} e^x, \text{ so}$$
$$e^{ax} \xrightarrow{\text{differentiation}} a \cdot e^{ax}.$$

In this case we're integrating over time t. All the exponential terms in front of t, $-i2\pi f$, are merely coefficients, so they are the same as "a" in the formula above. Therefore, if we differentiate $e^{-i2\pi ft}$, we get:

$$e^{-i2\pi ft} \xrightarrow{\text{differentiation}} -i2\pi f \cdot e^{-i2\pi ft}$$

Now the $-i2\pi f$ in front of e is superfluous, so if we divide our original expression by this amount in advance, we get:

$$\frac{-1}{i2\pi f} \cdot e^{-i2\pi ft} \xrightarrow{\text{differentiation}} e^{-i2\pi ft}$$

Look! Now we know what to differentiate to produce $e^{-i2\pi ft}$!

Our range of integration was from $-(\Delta t/2)$ to $\Delta t/2$, which gives us:

$$G(f) = \left[\frac{-1}{i2\pi f} \cdot e^{-i2\pi ft} \right]_{-\frac{\Delta t}{2}}^{\frac{\Delta t}{2}}$$

If you're having a hard time following this, go back and reread Chapter 7, "Integration." (Hey, we're the writers, and <u>we</u> don't remember this stuff!)

Now we want to subtract one range number from the other. Since $-1/(i2\pi f)$ is irrelevant to t, we can put it outside the brackets.

$$G(f) = \frac{-1}{i2\pi f}\left(e^{-i2\pi f\frac{\Delta t}{2}} - e^{-i2\pi f\frac{-\Delta t}{2}} \right)$$

Next we'll get rid of the -1 outside the brackets by multiplying it by the two terms inside the brackets, which changes their signs. Also, the 2 and the 1/2 cancel each other out in the exponent of e. That leaves us with:

$$G(f) = \frac{1}{i2\pi f}(e^{i\pi f\Delta t} - e^{-i\pi f\Delta t})$$

Does this format ring a bell? No? Well, it should!

It's a trick we learned in Chapter 10 – how to express the sine and cosine functions using e and i.

$$\frac{e^{i\theta} - e^{-i\theta}}{2i} = \sin\theta$$

Just think of $\pi f \Delta t$ as θ.

$$G(f) = \frac{e^{i\pi f \Delta t} - e^{-i\pi f \Delta t}}{2i} \cdot \frac{1}{\pi f} = \frac{1}{\pi f}\sin\pi f \Delta t$$

We've done it! We can use this formula to apply the Fourier transform to the wave $g(t) = 1$! Well, not quite, actually. It turns out we'll run into some problems when we try substituting bona fide values for f and Δt. Look closely at the formula for $G(f)$. There's an "f" in the denominator, right? If we try to do calculations for $f = 0$, which is what we wanted to do all along, the denominator will become 0. Since you can't divide by 0, that will leave us with no answer at all.

Therefore we'll change the form of the equation by multiplying it by $\Delta t/\Delta t$ (which is 1, so it won't affect our answer).

$$G(f) = \frac{\sin\pi f \Delta t}{\pi f \Delta t} \cdot \Delta t$$

With this formula, we can calculate with impunity! Why? Because of one more little trick we had up our sleeve:

$$\lim_{\theta \to 0} \frac{\sin\theta}{\theta} = 1$$

Putting Δt in the denominator gave us $\pi f \Delta t$, which is the same as θ. That means we can find a value for $G(f)$ when $f = 0$. When $\theta = \pi f \Delta t$ approaches infinitely close to 0, $G(f) = 1 \cdot \Delta t$, so:

When $f = 0$, $G(f) = \Delta t$

2. 4 Let's get graphic

So now we have our formula for $G(f)$. Let's stick some numbers in it and plot a graph. First we have to decide on the range of Δt we want to observe. We're not sure what a good range would be for our purposes. But for the moment, let's try computing the formula with three different range values – $\Delta t = 1$, 2, and 5 – and make a graph for each of them.

Specifically, we're going to substitute 1, 2, and 5 in turn for Δt in the formula below, then substitute different values for frequency f from one end of the graph to the other.

$$G(f) = \frac{\sin\pi f \Delta t}{\pi f \Delta t} \cdot \Delta t$$

Since we can't calculate the value of sin θ ($\theta = -i2\pi ft$) on our own, we'll rely on a function calculator to do the work for us (a real pro would use a computer). Or, if you like, you can refer to the trigonometric tables in the back of your math textbook and make your own calculations. Go for it!

And here are our graphs! Very interesting... they look quite different for each value of range Δt.

This is the graph we predicted we'd get. But instead...

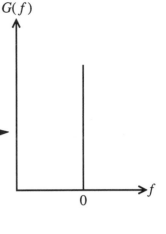

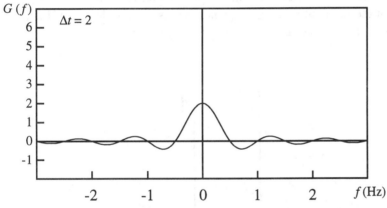

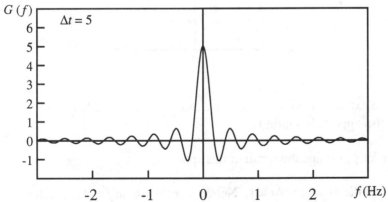

So you wanna do your own calculations, and plot your own graphs??

You know that $\theta = \pi f\Delta t$, $\pi = 3.14$, and Δt is the time range over which you are observing the wave (which can be any value you want). That leaves only f as a variable.

All you have to do now is substitute values for f from one end of the graph to the other. (In this example, we've made $f = 0$ the center of our range, so you might want to plot f from -10 Hz to 10 Hz, say.) The closer together the values you substitute are, the more accurate your graph will be.

Now that you've plotted one graph, change the value of Δt and try plotting a few more!

Hmm. These are not exactly what we expected. It's true, the value at $f = 0$ is the highest point on every graph. But why do they look so different from our prediction? All we did was apply the Fourier transform to the same wave...

Here comes the good part; we're finally getting down to the nitty-gritty of this chapter.

Supposedly, there are no values for $G(f)$ except for $f = 0$, because the wave doesn't oscillate at all within the range we are viewing.

BUT –

We know nothing about the part of the wave we can't see, so we don't clearly know the characteristics of the entire wave. This lack of precise knowledge of the wave is reflected by the graphs in the mysterious manner we see above.

There is a technical term for this lack of precision: "uncertainty"!

Let's give these graphs another look.

The wider the range we assign to Δt – i.e., the longer the period of time over which we observe the wave – the higher the graph rises at $f = 0$. That is to say, the more closely it resembles the graph we predicted in the first place. The height of the graph at a given frequency represents the degree of likelihood that the wave contains a component wave of that frequency.

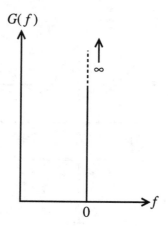

As we extend our view of the wave out to infinity, the height of the "spike" at $f = 0$ also approaches infinity.

Now let's examine the width of this spike.

Look at the graph for $\Delta t = 1$. Notice that the rise at $f = 0$ is much wider than in the other two graphs. This is because the range of time is so short that it is impossible to declare with any certainty, "This wave has a frequency of 0." The graph therefore reflects the inclusion of many other waves with frequencies near 0, such as 0.5 Hz, –0.3 Hz, and the like.

As we extend time Δt to 2 or 5, the rise progressively narrows to a spike, as it becomes increasingly probable that the frequency of the wave is indeed 0. In other words, the width of the spike is proportional to the **uncertainty** of the wave's frequency. We can tell how uncertain this value is by measuring the width of the spike.

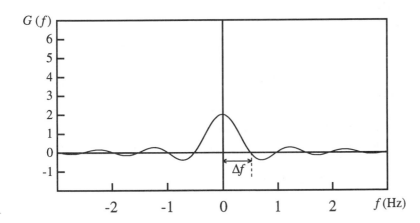

Suppose we assign the name Δf to the width of the spike, i.e., the degree of uncertainty. We can then observe an interesting relationship between Δf and the range of time Δt. The larger Δt gets, the smaller Δf gets, and the smaller Δt gets, the larger Δf gets.

Thus the relationship $\Delta t \times \Delta f$ is always constant. And if it is constant, then however large or small Δt may be, this value can never be 0; there is always some degree of uncertainty. But what if Δt were 0? you may ask. Since Δt is the period of observation, $\Delta t = 0$ would mean we weren't viewing the wave for any time at all, which would be meaningless for our purposes. Conversely, $\Delta t = \infty$ would appear to eliminate the width of our "spike of uncertainty," but since we can't possibly view the wave over an infinite period of time, this too is an untenable proposition. And as long as we are observing the wave for a finite time, we can't possibly bring this uncertainty down to zero.

If you're feeling uncertain about this entire explanation, take another look at the three graphs above. Roughly speaking, at least, we can say that all three graphs are similarly shaped. So even when we can only view a wave over a very short time, we can still get some notion of its characteristics. Even with a large degree of uncertainty thrown in, the general outline of the wave is available for us to see.

The Fourier transform merely permits us to break a complicated wave – any complicated wave, even a non-periodic one – down into simple waves. It also expresses the degree of uncertainty in this breakdown – i.e., how sure we can be of the components of a wave based on a given period of observation. Even if we can't be sure of the details, we can still determine the overall shape of the wave by viewing just a part of it. That is, after all, precisely how human beings acquire most of their perceptions.

No doubt about it: the Fourier transform is a formidable weapon!

2. 5 More thoughts on uncertainty

We'd like to take a moment to consider the relationship between the concept of uncertainty and the behavior of human beings. For example, the authors of this chapter were working against a deadline – i.e., we had a finite period of time in which to write this. And to be honest, we still don't completely understand what "uncertainty" is. What you've just read is the extent to which we understand it at this point in time. But does the human mind ever completely understand things at any given time? Our normal learning experience suggests that we often think we understand something, only to realize much later that our understanding has further improved with the passage of time. The more time goes by, the more our understanding deepens.

Just like the Fourier transform, the human mode of understanding is to acknowledge an element of uncertainty while trying to grasp the big picture Then, as time passes, we whittle away at the uncertainty as we improve our understanding of the details. The Fourier transform works the same way. Indeed, it might be more accurate to say that the Fourier transform works this way precisely because that is how human understanding works.

Fourier analysis is used in many areas of modern physics, but it plays a particularly essential role in the field known as quantum mechanics. Quantum mechanics describes the ultra-microscopic world of atoms, electrons and other subatomic particles. This description works only because it takes into account the concept of uncertainty.

According to quantum mechanics, the elemental particles known as quanta (which include electrons and photons) can also be thought of as waves. If they behave like waves, Fourier mathematics can be used to describe them. But as waves, they are also subject to the uncertainty that applies to all waves, which we discovered in this chapter. In the subatomic world, nothing is certain. Phenomena at this level can only be described within a range of precision that allows for the uncertainty of waves.

This principle is known as the Uncertainty Principle. It was first formulated by Werner Heisenberg, author of the book **Physics and Beyond**.

We embarked on our adventures with Fourier because we wanted to examine the waves of the human voice. First we discovered the Fourier series, which allowed us to describe any periodic wave, however complicated, as the sum of simple waves. After picking up many keys and unlocking many doors, we finally unearthed the ultimate treasure: the Fourier transform, which can describe any wave at all, periodic or not. And we made a bonus discovery, something we hadn't been looking for at all – the uncertainty principle. We learned that as human beings, we are unable to view waves over an infinite period of time; consequently, we can never be 100% certain of the characteristics of a given wave.

If anything, we've learned that, formulas or no formulas, humans cannot perform superhuman feats. For those of us who always assumed that the world of mathematics was one of absolute truths where x is always x and y is always y, this encounter with uncertainty has been a bit of an eye-opener.

But it shouldn't come as such a surprise that formulas cannot extend our perceptions to the superhuman. After all, formulas exist only because we devise them to describe the natural phenomena we humans see around us.

Our study of the Fourier transform and the uncertainty of waves reminded us once again that, indeed, formulas are a type of language.

Memo

The FFT Method

We conclude our Fourier adventures with an explanation of the Fast Fourier Transform (FFT), a method of calculation that is essential to the analysis of voice waves. The FFT is capable of performing instantaneous Fourier transformation on any wave whatsoever. How does it manage to do all those calculations so quickly? You'll be amazed at the FFT's remarkable ability to drastically reduce the number of calculations required.

Introduction

We've studied waves from a variety of angles. The Fourier series showed us how to view complicated, periodic waves as the sum of simple waves. Fourier coefficients showed us how to calculate the frequency components of these waves. We picked up several valuable weapons – Σ, e, i – along the way. But we originally set out on our Fourier quest because we wanted to learn how the FFT analyzer was able to generate the spectra of human voice waves. Over the course of our journey we have encountered and overcome many obstacles. Now we would like to reap the benefits of all the experience and knowledge we've acquired as we take up the challenge of the voice one last time.

1. The Challenge of the Voice

Before going any further, we have to answer this question: What exactly is a voice wave? Since it's the job of the FFT analyzer to display voice waves, let's take a good look at the output of this machine.

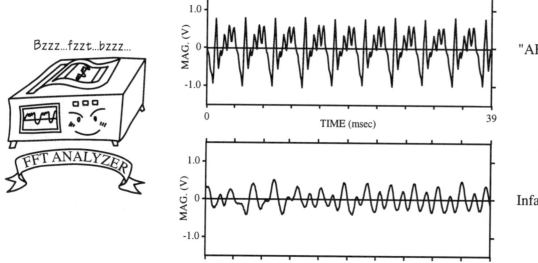

The FFT analyzer has kindly presented us with the two waves shown above. The pattern of repetition in the adult's voice wave is obvious, but the baby's voice wave seems to wander all over the place; it's not clear if it repeats itself at all. This could be significant!

Next question: How do we come up with the spectrum of a voice wave? A spectrum, you may remember, is a graph showing which frequencies make up a wave, and in what quantity. To produce a spectrum, in other words, you have to find the frequency components of the wave.

To find frequency components → Fourier coefficients

So all we need to do is find the Fourier coefficients of the wave, right? Not so fast; first we'd better review what Fourier coefficients are all about. Fourier coefficients formulas calculate the components of a periodic wave by extracting a single period of the wave and finding the area of that period for a given frequency, one frequency at a time. Consequently, it's crucial to clearly identify the period of the wave. Since the regular repetitions of the adult's voice wave are so obvious, it should easily lend itself to Fourier coefficients. But the same cannot be said of the baby's voice; Fourier coefficients would appear to be impossible for an irregular wave of this sort.

> **Secrets of the FFT analyzer**
>
> We've tended to think of the FFT analyzer as a machine that can do anything. But in fact there's one thing it can't do – extract a single period from a wave. That's why it makes perfect sense for the analyzer to use the Fourier transform, which treats the entire wave as a single period.

Now, how was it that we vanquished the dreaded non-periodic wave? That's right! We defined the entire wave as a single period, then used the Fourier transform on it. And this is precisely what the FFT analyzer does: it subjects a voice wave to the Fourier transform to produce its spectrum.

2. Using the Fourier transform on a voice wave

Remember the Fourier transform formula:

$$G(f) = \int_{-\infty}^{\infty} g(t)e^{-i2\pi ft}dt$$

The Fourier transform seems like something that could only exist in the world of mathematics. In the real world, it's absurd to even contemplate viewing an entire wave out to infinity. How are we supposed to apply the abstract notions of the Fourier transform to a real voice wave?

In the Fourier transform formula, $G(f)$ represents a frequency component. The integral sign $\int$ and dt represent integration – i.e., the calculation of area. And $g(t)$ is the name of the complicated wave. Come to think of it, we have no idea what this name $g(t)$ really represents. And if we don't know what $g(t)$ is, this formula won't do us any good. We need to come up with a name that more accurately describes $g(t)$.

In the course of our adventures, we must have picked up some clues as to how to do this. Let's see... $g(t)$ must be a function. If it's a function, we can illustrate it with a graph like the one we drew for the ricecake robot back in Chapter 1. If we put time on the horizontal axis and the value of the function on the vertical axis, we should be able to plot the graph of a complicated wave such as that of the human voice. Let's try it and see.

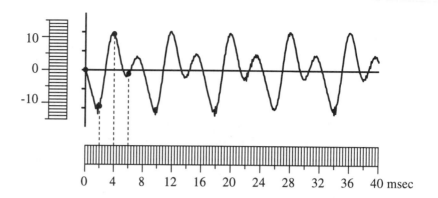

This is the wave of the vowel sound EE spoken by an adult male. For our graph scale, we borrowed the ruler provided by our friend the FFT analyzer in Chapter 2. Let's write down the value of the wave at every 2 msec. At 0 msec, the value of the wave is 0. We can write this as $g(0) = 0$. Here's a table of values at subsequent points on the scale.

$g(0)$	$g(2)$	$g(4)$	$g(6)$	$g(8)$	$g(10)$	$g(12)$	$g(14)$	$g(16)$	• • • • • • • • • • • •	$g(40)$
0	–11	11	–1	–1.5	–11	9	–1.5	–1	• • • • • • • • • • •	3

Secrets of the FFT analyzer

We arbitrarily read values from this wave at 2 msec intervals, for a total of 21 values over 40 msec. The FFT analyzer would read far more values than that – 512 or 1024, for example – from the same wave.

These values are all we've managed to obtain from the voice wave so far. We don't have any record of what's between these points. We've been using "$g(t)$" to describe the wave, but instead of time t, it might be more accurate to say that this is a function of discrete <u>points</u> of time – point 1, point 2, and so on. We'll use the letter k to represent the "place" (1st, 2nd, 3rd and so on) of each of these points.

Since this wave is a time function, we can multiply k by the interval at which these values were read – 2 msec in this case. The time at which each value is read can thus be expressed as $2k$. We usually represent an interval at which values are read by the Greek letter tau (τ). In other words, $g(t) = g(k\tau) = g(2k)$. Now we have a name that accurately describes our wave.

k = the place of each value in the series (1st, 2nd, 3rd, etc.)

Now let's consider the range of integration defined by the Fourier transform formula. The range is infinity, remember? But we could spend our whole lives looking at this wave, and we still wouldn't be able to see an infinite range. Even if we could, we'd be long dead before a voice spectrum could be generated from the wave. So instead, let's be content with finding the area for the length of the wave we have in front of us.

Furthermore, we can't really perform integration on this wave because we've only read values from it at sporadic intervals. So we'll try to calculate the area by performing a multiplication that will leave us with a specific frequency component of the spectrum.

3. Finding the area

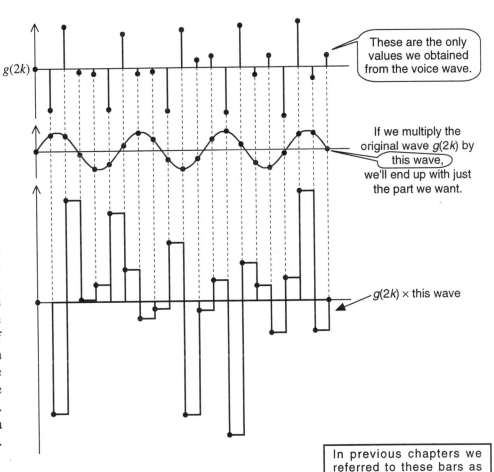

"Calculate the area," we said, but what area are we actually trying to find?

We obtained formula $g(2k)$ by reading a series of values off a voice wave.

We want to multiply the values of $g(2k)$ by a wave that will leave us with only the part of $g(2k)$ we want. The area we're going to find is the area of the wave resulting from that multiplication. Since $g(2k)$ consists of discrete values, so will our result. We'll calculate the area from those discrete values.

The graph of the result of multiplying the two waves looks like a bar graph, doesn't it? Though it will take a while, we know we can find the total area by calculating the area of each bar, one at a time, then adding them all together. Shall we give it a try? For our first value, the product is 0, so there's no area. We find the area of each bar (or "strip") by multiplying its height by its width, remember? Since we initially read these values in 2 msec intervals, width = 2. The height is the product of multiplying the two waves. If we look at the Fourier transform formula, we see that the wave by which we multiplied wave $g(2k)$ is none other than $e^{-i2\pi ft}$. And since $t = 2k$, we can call it $e^{-i2\pi f 2k}$. Thus height = $g(2k) \cdot e^{-i2\pi f 2k}$.

$$\text{Area of strip} = 2 \cdot g(2k)e^{-i2\pi f 2k}$$

Now we know how to find the area of each strip – but we still have to add all these strips together. How do we go about adding many terms together in a series? That's right, we use summation (Σ). But first we have to know how many of these strips there are, and how to represent them in a formula. Once we get started, it's immediately obvious that if we take N values from the wave, there will be N strips. So we know how many strips we have to add up.

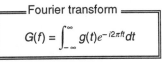

Fourier transform

$$G(f) = \int_{-\infty}^{\infty} g(t)e^{-i2\pi ft}dt$$

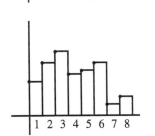

$N = 8$

N = number of values
or
N = number of strips

Here's our formula:

> The number of values is N, but the first value is at point 0, so the last value is called $N-1$.

$$\text{Area} = \sum_{k=0}^{N-1} \left\{ 2 \cdot g(2k)e^{-i2\pi f 2k} \right\}$$

> If k represents the number of a given value in the series, why do we start with 0? Because k is related to time, and the time starts at 0.

Fourier transform

$$G(f) = \int_{-\infty}^{\infty} g(t)e^{-i2\pi ft}dt$$

To find the period, multiply the number of values N by their interval 2.
Period = time taken up by the wave
Frequency = 1/period

k = the place order of each value
τ = the interval between values read
N = the total number of values read

Just when you thought you finally had a formula, there's always one more thing! This one concerns the f in $e^{-i2\pi f 2k}$, which stands for frequency. In the Fourier transform, the period was set at infinity, so f became continuous. But we've decided to treat the finite image of the wave we see here as one period. Consequently, we should be able to tell from the outset what the frequency is for each wave contained in the original wave.

Since the period of our original wave is $2N$, its fundamental frequency is $1/(2N)$. Then we can write its component frequencies, which are integral multiples of the fundamental frequency, as $n/(2N)$. Here n represents an integral multiple of the fundamental frequency. So we can complete our formula by replacing the f with $n/(2N)$:

$$G\left(\frac{n}{2N}\right) = \sum_{k=0}^{N-1} \left\{ 2 \cdot f(2k)e^{-i2\pi 2k\frac{n}{2N}} \right\}$$

Looks complicated, but don't panic! Remember, we arbitrarily chose 2 msec as the interval between values to get this formula in the first place. Although we read our values every 2 msec, someone else might have chosen values at shorter intervals, or longer ones for that matter. We want a formula that will work for anyone. No problem! All we need to do is insert symbols that will allow other people to substitute any value they want in place of our interval of 2 msec. Here goes:

$$G(\frac{n}{\tau N}) = \sum_{k=0}^{N-1} \left\{ \tau \cdot g(k\tau)e^{-i2\pi\tau k\frac{n}{\tau N}} \right\} \quad \text{— Cancel the } \tau\text{'s}$$

$$\boxed{G(\frac{n}{\tau N}) = \sum_{k=0}^{N-1} \left\{ \tau \cdot g(k\tau)e^{-i2\pi k\frac{n}{N}} \right\}}$$

At last, a formula with which we can find the spectrum of a voice wave! Since we extracted discrete values from the Fourier transform formula to get this formula, we call it the **discrete Fourier transform**.

Can we really use the discrete Fourier transform to calculate the spectrum of a voice wave? Only one way to find out! But hang on a minute – our friend the FFT analyzer is buzzing and whirring impatiently. It seems he has something to tell us...

"I'd like to explain to you how I, the FFT analyzer, decide how many values to read from a voice wave. You folks started out by arbitrarily picking 2 msec as the interval between values. Actually, there's a more sensible way of choosing the number of values to read.

Take a look at this!

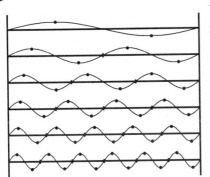

What's the least number of points we need to tell that a wave is oscillating once? You're right if you guessed two. Okay, how many to tell that it's oscillating twice? You've got it – four.

1 oscillation   → 2 points
2 oscillations   → 4 points
3 oscillations   → 6 points
4 oscillations   → 8 points
5 oscillations   → 10 points
6 oscillations   → 12 points

In other words, if you have *N* points, you can plot a wave that oscillates *N/2* times.

"What I'm trying to say is, if you know how many oscillations of the wave you want to look at, you can tell how many points you'll have to find on the wave. So when you want to obtain the spectrum of a human voice wave, all you need is a general idea of the highest frequency it contains. That automatically determines how many points you need to find on the wave. In my experience, an adult's voice can go up to around 4000 Hz. That means a wave that oscillates 4000 times a second. If the wave oscillates 4000 times, you need to extract 8000 points from it. So if you want to view the human voice up to 4000 Hz, you'll have to read values at 8000 points. That's 8000 points in one second. The wave you read your values from a few minutes ago was 40 msec long. There's 1000 msec in 1 second, so multiply 8000 points by 40/1000. That gives you 320. Earlier you folks found values at only 21 points, but if you want to get the spectrum of a wave up to 4000 Hz, you'll need to read 320 points. This is called **sampling theory**. It's a very important part of wave analysis."

Oscillation

The number of times a wave oscillates in 1 second is its frequency, remember? Frequency determines how high-pitched a voice is, and it is measured in Hertz (Hz).

What was that about the FFT analyzer reading 512 or 1024 points? Now you're only talking about 320. What gives?

Fine, we'll try reading 320 points. But 320 points in 40 msec means we'll have to read values at eight points from within the smallest scale marks on our ruler! How can we possibly do that? And suppose, just for the sake of argument, we actually do manage to read all 320 points. Next we have to multiply every one of those values in turn to find the height of each strip. Then we have to multiply each height by the width of the strip to get its area. And finally, we have to add up all 320 areas. Those are the calculations required for just one frequency, and we have to repeat the whole process 160 times!

What's this about 160? We're not talking about a wave that oscillates only 160 times! This one oscillates 4000 times, doesn't it? Hey analyzer, what's the deal here?

"Relax. The wave oscillates 4000 times in 1 second. But how many seconds long is this wave you're looking at? 40 msec, right? If you only need to see 40 msec of a wave that oscillates 4000 times a second, that's only 160 times in all."

1000 msec   →   4000 times
40 msec   →   ? times
$4000 \times 40/1000 = 160$

N number of values → *N/2* oscillations

Therefore, 320 points → 160 oscillations;
320 points lets us see up to 160 oscillations of the wave, so we only need to do our calculations 160 times.

Okay, 160 times it is. What was it again that we have to do 160 times? We were trying to figure out the actual calculations we'll have to perform when we read values from 320 points on a wave. To recap: multiply all 320 values, one at a time, to find the height of each strip; multiply each of these by the width of the interval between values to find the area of each strip; and add up all 320 areas. Repeat this entire process 160 times.

For example:

$$(2 \times 3) \times 2 = 12$$
$$(4 \times 5) \times 2 = 40$$
$$(6 \times 7) \times 2 = 84$$
$$\underline{+)\ (7 \times 8) \times 2 = \underline{+)\ 112}}$$
$$124 \times 2 = 248$$

We can save time by multiplying the width only once at the end, and the addition shouldn't present much of a problem. What is a problem is having to multiply each and every value for all 320 points. That's 320 calculations repeated 160 times, for a total of:

$$320 \times 160 = 51{,}200$$

Perform multiplication 51,200 times....?! All that for just one spectrum? Isn't there an easier way to come up with a spectrum? If this is what you have to do to find just one, we may as well give up right now on our study of voice waves. Even assuming a machine can do it faster than we can, that's an awful lot of calculations....

"Don't be so pessimistic. Trust me, you've picked up plenty of clues during your adventures to help you out. Think for a moment – what can you afford to eliminate from these calculations?"

Hmm. Let's see. The worst part of these calculations is having to multiply every value, one at a time. It'd be nice if we could cut down on the number of multiplication operations . . . but how? We can't reduce the number of values, can we? Plenty of clues, eh? Easy for you to say!

The Fourier series doesn't involve the multiplication of waves. Fourier coefficients do, but we didn't try any real calculations until we got to discrete Fourier expansion. If you remember, we came across the same result over and over, or the results repeated themselves every few values. . . Aha! If we know in advance where the results are going to be identical, we can use those results instead of doing the actual calculations. Let's review what we did with discrete Fourier expansion.

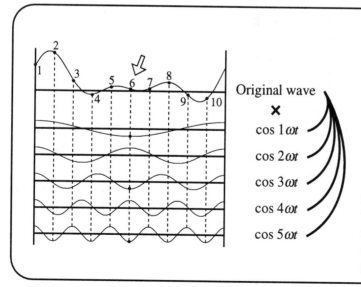

Original wave

×

cos $1\omega t$

cos $2\omega t$

cos $3\omega t$

cos $4\omega t$

cos $5\omega t$

With discrete Fourier expansion, we multiplied the original complicated wave by cos $1\omega t$ when we wanted to find a_1, cos $2\omega t$ to find a_2, cos $3\omega t$ to find a_3, and so on. As you can see from the waves in the chart, the results are the same when the value of point 6 is multiplied by cos $1\omega t$, cos $3\omega t$, or cos $5\omega t$. So we only need to perform multiplication once to get the results for these three waves. As the number of points increases, the number of waves we have to multiply by those values automatically increases too. And many of those results will be the same. We can use this fact to reduce the number of times we have to perform multiplication.

We've tried all kinds of tricks to get the Fourier transform into a format we can actually use. Just when we thought we had one, it turns out to require an interminable amount of time just to come up with a single spectrum. We can produce a spectrum with the discrete Fourier transform, but we still need a faster method than that. Our next step, with the help of the FFT analyzer, will be to figure out a way to generate spectra quickly by reducing the number of times we have to multiply.

4. Cutting Down on Calculations

To reduce the number of multiplication operations, let's think about how to rewrite the discrete Fourier transform formula in a simpler form, with fewer numbers N.

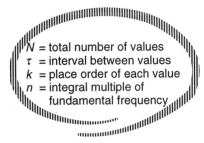

N = total number of values
τ = interval between values
k = place order of each value
n = integral multiple of fundamental frequency

Discrete Fourier transform

$$G(\frac{n}{\tau N}) = \sum_{k=0}^{N-1} \left\{ \tau \cdot g(k\tau) \cdot e^{-i2\pi k \frac{n}{N}} \right\}$$

First of all, what can we do to simplify the discrete Fourier transform? The formula contains one item we can choose on our own: tau (τ). Earlier we decided to read values at intervals of 2 msec, but we can simplify the formula by setting τ at 1 second ($\tau = 1$). Here's what happens to the formula then:

$$G(n/N) = \sum_{k=0}^{N-1} g(k)e^{-i2\pi k \frac{n}{N}}$$

Let's use this formula to do some real calculations. First we have to decide how many points to read off the wave. The FFT analyzer tells us that $N = 8$ is a good number, so let's use eight points. As soon as we define N, the value of $e^{-i2\pi/N}$ is automatically defined as well. This is a pain to write out, so let's just call the whole thing "W":

$$e^{-\frac{i2\pi}{N}} = W$$

This value W is known to mathematicians as a rotation operator. The rotation operator is an extremely convenient tool that gets plenty of use in the world of math.

$$G(n/N) = \sum_{k=0}^{N-1} g(k)W^{nk}$$

Now for some calculations! Since $N = 8$, we get:

$$G(n/8) = \sum_{k=0}^{7} g(k)W^{nk}$$

First let's calculate the value for the constant component of the wave, *i.e.*, when $n = 0$:

$$G(0/8) = \sum_{k=0}^{7} g(k)W^0$$

This formula doesn't help us much, so let's write out the terms to be added up according to Σ:

$$
\begin{aligned}
G(0/8) \ &= g(0)W^0 + g(1)W^0 + g(2)W^0 + g(3)W^0 + g(4)W^0 \\
&+ g(5)W^0 + g(6)W^0 + g(7)W^0
\end{aligned}
$$

Since we've read values from eight points, we should be able to view a wave of up to four oscillations – up to $n = 4$, in other words. Suppose we write them all out:

$$G(0/8) = g(0)W^0 + g(1)W^0 + g(2)W^0 + g(3)W^0 + g(4)W^0 + g(5)W^0 + g(6)W^0 + g(7)W^0$$
$$G(1/8) = g(0)W^0 + g(1)W^1 + g(2)W^2 + g(3)W^3 + g(4)W^4 + g(5)W^5 + g(6)W^6 + g(7)W^7$$
$$G(2/8) = g(0)W^0 + g(1)W^2 + g(2)W^4 + g(3)W^6 + g(4)W^8 + g(5)W^{10} + g(6)W^{12} + g(7)W^{14}$$
$$G(3/8) = g(0)W^0 + g(1)W^3 + g(2)W^6 + g(3)W^9 + g(4)W^{12} + g(5)W^{15} + g(6)W^{18} + g(7)W^{21}$$
$$G(4/8) = g(0)W^0 + g(1)W^4 + g(2)W^8 + g(3)W^{12} + g(4)W^{16} + g(5)W^{20} + g(6)W^{24} + g(7)W^{28}$$
$$G(5/8) = g(0)W^0 + g(1)W^5 + g(2)W^{10} + g(3)W^{15} + g(4)W^{20} + g(5)W^{25} + g(6)W^{30} + g(7)W^{35}$$
$$G(6/8) = g(0)W^0 + g(1)W^6 + g(2)W^{12} + g(3)W^{18} + g(4)W^{24} + g(5)W^{30} + g(6)W^{36} + g(7)W^{42}$$
$$G(7/8) = g(0)W^0 + g(1)W^7 + g(2)W^{14} + g(3)W^{21} + g(4)W^{28} + g(5)W^{35} + g(6)W^{42} + g(7)W^{49}$$

> Remember, each instance of $g(k)W^{nk}$ represents the area of a single strip.

But if $n = 4$, why did we write out eight formulas, up to $n = 7$? Because the FFT analyzer recommended that we write eight formulas. We're not sure why, but we figured we should follow his advice...

Before we go any further, however, we want to reduce the number of multiplications! How many of these operations are there, anyway? Let's count 'em up. Each formula has eight multiplication operations, and there are eight formulas, so $8 \times 8 = 64$.

> Number of first-step multiplications: 64

We want to use these eight formulas, but only if we can do something that reduces the number of operations they require. Just lining them up like that doesn't help make sense of them, though. Isn't there a more sensible way to arrange them? The exponent of W changes in a regular fashion, but it's hard to see how we can take advantage of that. The value of k in $g(k)$ stays the same for each vertical column. That gives us an idea of how to arrange everything in a table:

	$g(0)$	$g(1)$	$g(2)$	$g(3)$	$g(4)$	$g(5)$	$g(6)$	$g(7)$
$G(0/8)$	W^0	W^0	W^0	W^0	W^0	W^0	W^0	W^0
$G(1/8)$	W^0	W^1	W^2	W^3	W^4	W^5	W^6	W^7
$G(2/8)$	W^0	W^2	W^4	W^6	W^8	W^{10}	W^{12}	W^{14}
$G(3/8)$	W^0	W^3	W^6	W^9	W^{12}	W^{15}	W^{18}	W^{21}
$G(4/8)$	W^0	W^4	W^8	W^{12}	W^{16}	W^{20}	W^{24}	W^{28}
$G(5/8)$	W^0	W^5	W^{10}	W^{15}	W^{20}	W^{25}	W^{30}	W^{35}
$G(6/8)$	W^0	W^6	W^{12}	W^{18}	W^{24}	W^{30}	W^{36}	W^{42}
$G(7/8)$	W^0	W^7	W^{14}	W^{21}	W^{28}	W^{35}	W^{42}	W^{49}

Now we have a table full of W's with different exponents. If we can somehow group some of these exponents together, that would reduce the number of times we have to perform multiplication. Let's think about what these W's really stand for.

2π radians = 360°
N = total number of values
n = integral multiple of fundamental frequency
k = the place order of each value

Remember, W stands for $e^{-(i2\pi)/N}$. Back in Chapter 10, we learned that e can be expressed by i sin and cos. And if W can be expressed by i sin and cos, that means it will appear on a graph as a circle. In other words, the graph of W rotates repeatedly over the same course. Let's see what this means when $N = 8$.

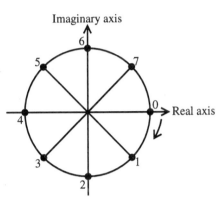

Imaginary axis

Real axis

If $N = 8$ in $e^{-(i2\pi)/N}$, that gives us $2\pi/8$, which simply means we're dividing 360° by 8 ($2\pi = 360°$, remember?). The minus sign in $e^{-(i2\pi)/N}$ means the graph rotates in the negative direction, *i.e.* clockwise. Now, our formula says W^{nk}. The n in the exponent indicates how many times the graph has rotated through the circle. The time it takes to rotate once is the fundamental period – *i.e.*, a single period of the original complicated wave. And if we assign a number to each point read as we rotate through a single period, k represents that number.

How can we put this graph of W to use? Well, if it rotates repeatedly over the same course, that means the same values are repeated over and over. So just as 0° and 360° are the same, $W^0 = W^8$, $W^1 = W^9$, and so on. No matter how large the exponent of W gets, it is still rotating through the same circle, so it can always be expressed by one of the exponents $W^{0, 1, 2, 3, 4, 5, 6, 7}$. That's why W is called a rotation operator and why it is so popular among mathematicians.

This should help simplify our table of W's. Let's see how it looks when we rewrite all these exponents.

	$g(0)$	$g(1)$	$g(2)$	$g(3)$	$g(4)$	$g(5)$	$g(6)$	$g(7)$
$G(0/8)$	W^0	W^0	W^0	W^0	W^0	W^0	W^0	W^0
$G(1/8)$	W^0	W^1	W^2	W^3	W^4	W^5	W^6	W^7
$G(2/8)$	W^0	W^2	W^4	W^6	W^0	W^2	W^4	W^6
$G(3/8)$	W^0	W^3	W^6	W^1	W^4	W^7	W^2	W^5
$G(4/8)$	W^0	W^4	W^0	W^4	W^0	W^4	W^0	W^4
$G(5/8)$	W^0	W^5	W^2	W^7	W^4	W^1	W^6	W^3
$G(6/8)$	W^0	W^6	W^4	W^2	W^0	W^6	W^4	W^2
$G(7/8)$	W^0	W^7	W^6	W^5	W^4	W^3	W^2	W^1

Well, that's certainly an improvement. All those exponents can now be broken down into only eight groups – the numbers from 0 to 7. It seems that this should certainly reduce the number of multiplication operations. But where do we go from here? What do we actually do with these eight groups?

Hint:

Odd and even numbers

The FFT Analyzer

k = the place order of each value

n = integral multiple of fundamental frequency

What's this? A hint from our friend the analyzer! But what does it mean? The table contains three kinds of numbers: k, n, and the exponent of W. Dividing the W exponents into odd and even numbers doesn't seem like it would make much of a difference. Nor would dividing the table into odd and even values of n, which represents frequencies; we wouldn't expect that to have much effect on the number of multiplication operations.

That leaves us with k. If we divide the table into odd and even values of k, what happens to the exponents of W? Let's check it out. When k is 0, 2, 4, or 6, the exponent of W is one of only four even values: 0, 2, 4, or 6!

What about when k is 1, 3, 5, or 7? This time the exponents include all the numbers from 0 through 7. Although the results are hardly symmetrical, dividing k into odd and even values looks to be the most promising of the options available to us.

Even

	$g(0)$	$g(2)$	$g(4)$	$g(6)$
$G(0/8)$	W^0	W^0	W^0	W^0
$G(1/8)$	W^0	W^2	W^4	W^6
$G(2/8)$	W^0	W^4	W^0	W^4
$G(3/8)$	W^0	W^6	W^4	W^2
$G(4/8)$	W^0	W^0	W^0	W^0
$G(5/8)$	W^0	W^2	W^4	W^6
$G(6/8)$	W^0	W^4	W^0	W^4
$G(7/8)$	W^0	W^6	W^4	W^2

Odd

	$g(1)$	$g(3)$	$g(5)$	$g(7)$
$G(0/8)$	W^0	W^0	W^0	W^0
$G(1/8)$	W^1	W^3	W^5	W^7
$G(2/8)$	W^2	W^6	W^2	W^6
$G(3/8)$	W^3	W^1	W^7	W^5
$G(4/8)$	W^4	W^4	W^4	W^4
$G(5/8)$	W^5	W^7	W^1	W^3
$G(6/8)$	W^6	W^2	W^6	W^2
$G(7/8)$	W^7	W^5	W^3	W^1

$$G(n/N) = \sum_{k=0}^{N-1} g(k) W^{nk}$$

Still, it's not clear how this is going to do us any good. Now if the W exponents in the odd group and even group matched up perfectly with each other, we could cut the number of multiplications in half. . . But they don't, so we can't. Take a look at the even side, though – it's very symmetrical! In fact, the top half and bottom half are identical! If there were something we could do to match the odd side up with the even side, we'd be in business. But how can we do that? Well, to begin with, let's try creating a formula to express this division into odd and even numbers.

The number being divided into odd and even values is k, so

Even numbers $\rightarrow 2k$ $(k = 0, 1, 2, 3\ldots)$
Odd numbers $\rightarrow 2k + 1$ $(k = 0, 1, 2, 3\ldots)$

$$G(n/8) = \sum_{k=0}^{N-1} g(k)W^{nk}$$

$$= \sum_{k=0}^{\frac{N}{2}-1} g(2k)W^{n2k} + \sum_{k=0}^{\frac{N}{2}-1} g(2k+1)W^{n(2k+1)}$$

Since it would be cumbersome to use $f(2k)$ and $f(2k+1)$ in our calculations, let's call them something simpler:

Even group $= g(2k) = p(k)$
Odd group $= g(2k + 1) = q(k)$

$$G(n/8) = \sum_{k=0}^{\frac{N}{2}-1} p(k)W^{2nk} + \sum_{k=0}^{\frac{N}{2}-1} q(k)W^{2nk+n}$$

$$= \sum_{k=0}^{\frac{N}{2}-1} p(k)W^{2nk} + \sum_{k=0}^{\frac{N}{2}-1} q(k)W^{2nk} \cdot W^{n}$$

$$= \sum_{k=0}^{\frac{N}{2}-1} p(k)W^{2nk} + W^{n} \cdot \sum_{k=0}^{\frac{N}{2}-1} q(k)W^{2nk}$$

> We can write W^{2nk+n} as $W^{2nk} \cdot W^{n}$. Since n does not change with Σ, we can move n outside Σ.
>
> Example:
> $$2^{2+3} = 2^5 = 32$$
> $$2^2 \cdot 3^3 = 4 \cdot 8 = 32$$

So there's our formula. It looks a bit different from the results we got by merely dividing the W values into two tables. The tables didn't reflect the existence of this W^n which now sits outside the Σ. And W^n is important; by moving it outside the Σ, we wind up with the same value, W^{2nk}, for both the even and odd numbers. If we can remove W^n from the odd table in the same way, maybe the odd number group will come out looking the same as the even number group. But how do we do this to the table? To move W^n outside the table as we moved it outside Σ, we can subtract n from the exponent of each W in the table. Let's try it and see.

> Hey, that looks familiar! Let's place the even table next to it!

> $g(0)\ g(2)\ g(4)\ g(6)$
> $= p(0)\ p(1)\ p(2)\ p(3)$

W^n

Odd group

	$q(0)$	$q(1)$	$q(2)$	$q(3)$
$G(0/8)$	W^0	W^0	W^0	W^0
$G(1/8)$	W^0	W^2	W^4	W^6
$G(2/8)$	W^0	W^4	W^0	W^4
$G(3/8)$	W^0	W^6	W^4	W^2
$G(4/8)$	W^0	W^0	W^0	W^0
$G(5/8)$	W^0	W^2	W^4	W^6
$G(6/8)$	W^0	W^4	W^0	W^4
$G(7/8)$	W^0	W^6	W^4	W^2

Even group

	$p(0)$	$p(1)$	$p(2)$	$p(3)$
$G(0/8)$	W^0	W^0	W^0	W^0
$G(1/8)$	W^0	W^2	W^4	W^6
$G(2/8)$	W^0	W^4	W^0	W^4
$G(3/8)$	W^0	W^6	W^4	W^2
$G(4/8)$	W^0	W^0	W^0	W^0
$G(5/8)$	W^0	W^2	W^4	W^6
$G(6/8)$	W^0	W^4	W^0	W^4
$G(7/8)$	W^0	W^6	W^4	W^2

The even and odd groups now look identical, and their top and bottom halves are identical too. Now all we need to do is multiply the top half, and use the answers for the bottom half as well. Looks like we finally managed to reduce the number of multiplications! Let's see how many operations actually remain now:

> Even group: 16 operations
> Odd group: +) 16 operations + 4 (no. of times W^n is multiplied)
>   36 operations

We've reduced the number of multiplication operations from 64 to 36!

What does this mean in terms of waves?

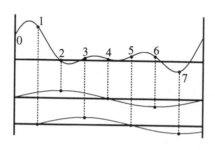

> W^n is not just an ordinary number; it can be expressed by something known as a diagonal matrix. That means you only need to perform one calculation for each horizontal row. And since the top and bottom halves of the W tables are identical, you can omit half the calculations. In all, you only need to multiply W^n four times.

How were we able to come up with these waves? By subtracting n from the exponents of W, that's how. For the waves we drew here, $n = 1$, so when we subtract 1 from the exponent of W, the wave begins at 0. Thus we can multiply the odd number group by exactly the same wave values as the even number group.

Going back to the formula, you'll notice that the value of the W exponent is different from that which is expressed in the tables. When we wrote up the tables, it was W^{nk}, but the new formula says W^{2nk}. It was using W^{2nk} that allowed us to express both the even and odd numbers the same way.

$$W^{nk} = e^{(-\frac{i2\pi}{N})nk}$$
$$W^{2nk} = e^{2(-\frac{i2\pi}{N})nk}$$
$$= e^{\left\{\frac{-i2\pi}{\frac{N}{2}}\right\}nk}$$

These formulas show that W^{2nk} is really just W^{nk} with the N in the exponent of e divided by 2. With W^{nk}, the circle on the graph was divided into eight equal parts; W^{2nk} means it is now divided into four equal parts instead.

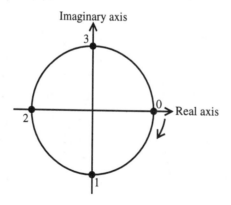

When we used W^{nk}, there were eight different values for k. But if we use W^{2nk}, only four values can be used for k. This is the same as shifting the start of the circle by 45°, the same shift we saw when we drew the waves above. Now, in place of the 0, 2, 4, and 6 that appeared on the circle for W, we have 0, 1, 2, and 3. This is possible because we replaced f with p and q, and replaced W^{nk} with W^{2nk}

By dividing the table once into odd and even numbers, we were able to reduce the number of multiplications from 64 to 36. Now we can divide the values of k in $p(k)$ and $q(k)$ into odd and even as well. Who knows, that might cut the number of multiplications even further!

	$p(0)$	$p(2)$	$p(1)$	$p(3)$
$G(0/8)$	W'^0	W'^0	W'^0	W'^0
$G(1/8)$	W'^0	W'^2	W'^1	W'^3
$G(2/8)$	W'^0	W'^0	W'^2	W'^2
$G(3/8)$	W'^0	W'^2	W'^3	W'^1
$G(4/8)$	W'^0	W'^0	W'^0	W'^0
$G(5/8)$	W'^0	W'^2	W'^1	W'^3
$G(6/8)$	W'^0	W'^0	W'^2	W'^2
$G(7/8)$	W'^0	W'^2	W'^3	W'^1

W^n

	$q(0)$	$q(2)$	$q(1)$	$q(3)$
$G(0/8)$	W'^0	W'^0	W'^0	W'^0
$G(1/8)$	W'^0	W'^2	W'^1	W'^3
$G(2/8)$	W'^0	W'^0	W'^2	W'^2
$G(3/8)$	W'^0	W'^2	W'^3	W'^1
$G(4/8)$	W'^0	W'^0	W'^0	W'^0
$G(5/8)$	W'^0	W'^2	W'^1	W'^3
$G(6/8)$	W'^0	W'^0	W'^2	W'^2
$G(7/8)$	W'^0	W'^2	W'^3	W'^1

Turning the tables into a formula worked for us before. Let's try it again:

$$G(n/8) = \sum_{k=0}^{N-1} g(k)W^{nk}$$

$$= \sum_{k=0}^{\frac{N}{2}-1} p(k)W^{2nk} + W^n \cdot \sum_{k=0}^{\frac{N}{2}-1} q(k)W^{2nk}$$

Here W^{nk} has become W^{2nk}.
☞ see p.403

$$= \sum_{k=0}^{\frac{N}{2}-1} p(k)W'^{nk} + W^n \cdot \sum_{k=0}^{\frac{N}{2}-1} q(k)W'^{nk}$$

The 2 in the exponent just gets in the way, so we've written W^{2nk} as W'^{nk} instead.

$$W^{2nk} = W'^{nk}$$

Thus to write W', we have to divide our original exponent nk by 2.

$$= \sum_{k=0}^{\frac{N}{4}-1} p(2k)W'^{n2k} + \sum_{k=0}^{\frac{N}{4}-1} p(2k+1)W'^{n(2k+1)}$$

$$+ W^n \left\{ \sum_{k=0}^{\frac{N}{4}-1} q(2k)W'^{n2k} + \sum_{k=0}^{\frac{N}{4}-1} q(2k+1)W'^{n(2k+1)} \right\}$$

As before, $W'^{2nk+n} = W'^{2nk} \cdot W'^n$

$$= \sum_{k=0}^{\frac{N}{4}-1} a(k)W'^{2nk} + W'^n \sum_{k=0}^{\frac{N}{4}-1} b(k)W'^{2nk}$$

$$+ W^n \left\{ \sum_{k=0}^{\frac{N}{4}-1} c(k)W'^{2nk} + W'^n \sum_{k=0}^{\frac{N}{4}-1} d(k)W'^{2nk} \right\}$$

We'll assign these functions easier names:
$p(2k) = a(k)$
$p(2k + 1) = b(k)$
$q(2k) = c(k)$
$q(2k + 1) = d(k)$

Now that looks nice and orderly, doesn't it? Once again, how would we apply these changes to a table? Since W'^n has been moved outside Σ, we can subtract n from the exponent of each W' in the table, just like before.

	$a(0)$	$a(1)$	W'^n	$b(0)$	$b(1)$	W^n		$c(0)$	$c(1)$	W'^n	$d(0)$	$d(1)$
$G(0/8)$	W'^0	W'^0		W'^0	W'^0		$G(0/8)$	W'^0	W'^0		W'^0	W'^0
$G(1/8)$	W'^0	W'^2		W'^0	W'^2		$G(1/8)$	W'^0	W'^2		W'^0	W'^2
$G(2/8)$	W'^0	W'^0		W'^0	W'^0		$G(2/8)$	W'^0	W'^0		W'^0	W'^0
$G(3/8)$	W'^0	W'^2		W'^0	W'^2		$G(3/8)$	W'^0	W'^2		W'^0	W'^2
$G(4/8)$	W'^0	W'^0		W'^0	W'^0		$G(4/8)$	W'^0	W'^0		W'^0	W'^0
$G(5/8)$	W'^0	W'^2		W'^0	W'^2		$G(5/8)$	W'^0	W'^2		W'^0	W'^2
$G(6/8)$	W'^0	W'^0		W'^0	W'^0		$G(6/8)$	W'^0	W'^0		W'^0	W'^0
$G(7/8)$	W'^0	W'^2		W'^0	W'^2		$G(7/8)$	W'^0	W'^2		W'^0	W'^2

Now the top and bottom halves are identical in every column. This should really cut down on the multiplications we have to perform.

Let's see what's happened to the waves and to the circular graph of W. Since it's hard to keep track of what a, b, c, and d mean, let's trace them back to what they originally were in terms of f.

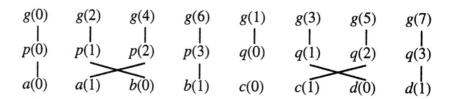

Originally, $b(0)$ and $b(1)$ were $g(2)$ and $g(6)$. They are multiplied by W'^n, meaning that 1 is subtracted on the circle of W', representing a shift of 90°.

Originally, $d(0)$ and $d(1)$ were $g(3)$ and $g(7)$. They are multiplied by both W^n and W'^n, representing a shift of 45°, then 90°.

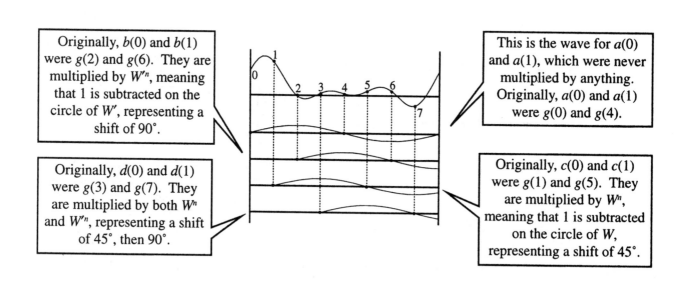

This is the wave for $a(0)$ and $a(1)$, which were never multiplied by anything. Originally, $a(0)$ and $a(1)$ were $g(0)$ and $g(4)$.

Originally, $c(0)$ and $c(1)$ were $g(1)$ and $g(5)$. They are multiplied by W^n, meaning that 1 is subtracted on the circle of W, representing a shift of 45°.

Thus we reduce the number of multiplications by shifting the waves. The operation that returns the shifted amount is represented by the W^n or W'^n that appears in front of the Σ.

Thinking in terms of the circle of W, we were able to make all parts of the table identical this time by using W'^{2nk}. W'^{2nk} actually means:

$$W'^{2nk} = e^{2\left\{-\frac{i2\pi}{\frac{N}{2}}\right\}nk}$$
$$= e^{\left\{-\frac{i2\pi}{\frac{N}{4}}\right\}nk}$$

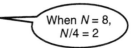

$$W' = e^{-\left(\frac{i2\pi}{\frac{N}{2}}\right)}$$

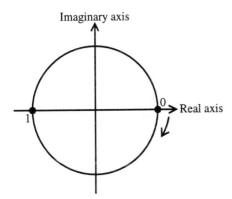

Imaginary axis

Real axis

Since $N = 8$, we can divide the circle into two equal parts this time. Dividing the circle into 8, 4, or 2 parts indicates that we only need to multiply that many values. To sum up, we started out having to perform multiplication on the values of all eight points, and ended up only having to multiply two points.

When $N = 8$, $N/4 = 2$

Let's get back to our table. The top and bottom halves are now identical all the way across. We must have even fewer multiplications to perform at this point. Let's count them up:

$a(0), a(1)$ → **4 operations**
$W'^n(b(0), b(1))$ → **4 operations + 2 (no. of times W'^n is multiplied)**
$W^n (c(0), c(1))$ → **4 operations + 2 (no. of times W^n is multiplied)**
$W^n[W'^n\{d(0), d(1)\}]$ → **4 operations + 2 (no. of times W'^n is multiplied)**
+ 2 (no. of times W^n is multiplied)

24 operations

So we've knocked 64 multiplication operations down to 24. Actually, it would be more accurate to say that while we've reduced the number of times we have to perform multiplication, the number of actual operations hasn't changed at all. The only difference is that now we can take the answers from one set of operations and use them for all the others.

By repeatedly halving the number of values we must calculate, we've been able to dramatically lower the total number of calculations required. What do we call a number that we can halve repeatedly like this? An even number? Well, try 100. Halving it once gives us 50. Halve that, and we get 25. Halve 25, and we get... never mind. Just being an even number is obviously not enough. A number that can be repeatedly divided by 2 is a number that was produced by repeatedly multiplying by 2, right? We can express such a number as 2^n (2 to the nth power). So a number that can be repeatedly halved must be 2^n.

The FFT analyzer informed us that the human voice has a frequency of 4000 Hz, and that we would therefore need to read 320 points on a wave of 40 msec. But we were also told that the FFT analyzer actually reads more – 512 or 1024 points, for example. Why read so many more than 320? Because 512 and 1024 are 2^n numbers, and the FFT analyzer can generate a spectrum from 2^n points much faster than it could by using the discrete Fourier transform on 320 points.

$$512 = 2^9 = 2 \times 2 \times 2 \times 2 \times 2 \times 2 \times 2 \times 2 \times 2$$
$$1024 = 2^{10} = 2 \times 2 \times 2 \times 2 \times 2 \times 2 \times 2 \times 2 \times 2 \times 2$$

$8 = 2^3$

That's why the FFT analyzer suggested we make $N = 8$, and write out eight formulas.

And that's how the FFT analyzer manages to generate spectra so quickly. This is the universal method we've been talking about – the Fast Fourier Transform (FFT). Let's take a look at a spectrum generated by the analyzer using this method:

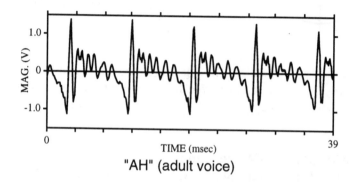

"AH" (adult voice)

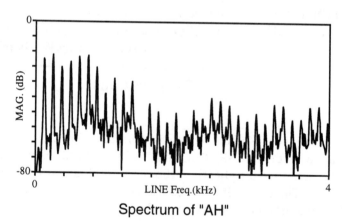

Spectrum of "AH"

As you can see, the actual spectrum does not take the form of a bar graph. That's because the FFT analyzer cannot extract a single period of the wave. Instead, it treats the entire wave (to be precise, the entire image of the wave provided to it) as one period. The rest of the wave outside of this range is treated as 0. The result? The uncertainty that comes from being unable to view the wave to infinity is reflected in the width of each frequency spike shown in the spectrum. What do you know! What we assumed was a purely mathematical concept actually becomes visible to the eye when we try to divide the human voice into its individual components.

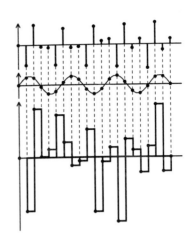

One more thing. Earlier we calculated the area by multiplying values read at 2 msec intervals on the wave. You'll recall that we wound up with strips having both positive and negative values (see the chart on the right). While we didn't come up with an exact value for the area, we know that it would certainly be possible for the total area to have a negative value. However, we don't need to worry about the possibility of a negative area in the FFT calculations. That's because the analyzer always squares the value of total area before generating the height (i.e. amplitude) of each spike in the spectrum.

Conclusion

It's been a long journey. We weren't satisfied with the mathematical elegance of the Fourier transform formula; we wanted to be able to use it to produce actual voice spectra, and fast. When we found the Fourier transform wouldn't do us any good in its existing form, we converted it to the discrete Fourier transform, and decided to treat whatever image we had of the wave as its period. It might have seemed like we were putting these formulas through some rather forced contortions to get what we wanted. But in math as in life, talk is cheap, and converting words to action takes a lot more effort.

The upshot was that we were able to slash the number of multiplication operations, of which there would have been 51,200 if we had relied on the discrete Fourier transform. Reading values from eight points on the wave required 64 operations, which we knocked down to 24. That may not seem like a big difference, but that's because we were reading only eight points. If we wanted to read 1024 points, for example, this same procedure would reduce the number of multiplications from 1,048,576 to 10,240! If we had to do them manually, even 10,240 calculations would take us a long time, but that's what we have the FFT analyzer for. This machine cuts the number of calculations required to the bare minimum, producing a wave spectrum in no time at all.

☞ see p. 398

Thanks to this last big adventure, we now know how the FFT analyzer generates a spectrum from a voice wave. No doubt there's plenty we still <u>don't</u> know about the FFT analyzer, but we'll save that for another adventure.

Memo

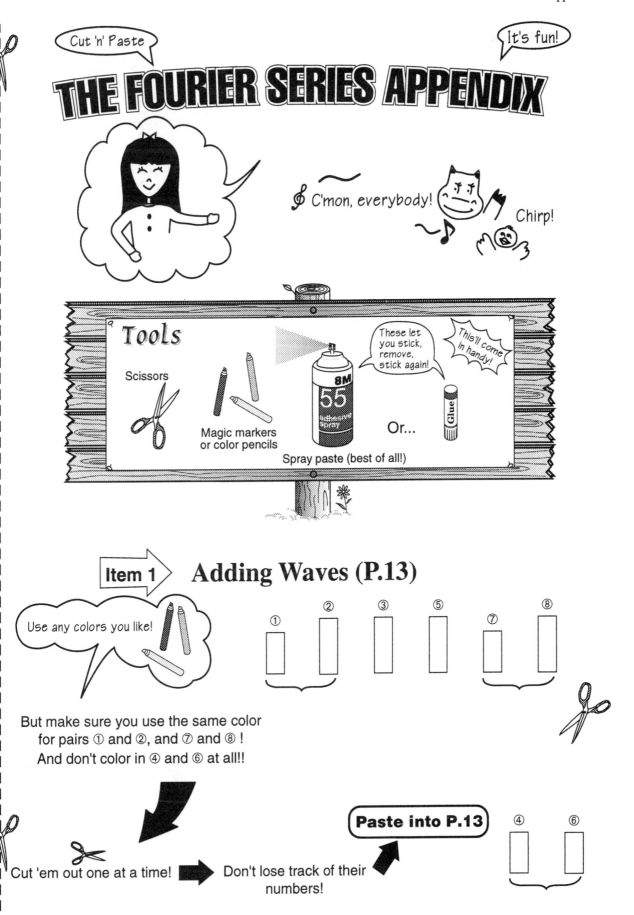

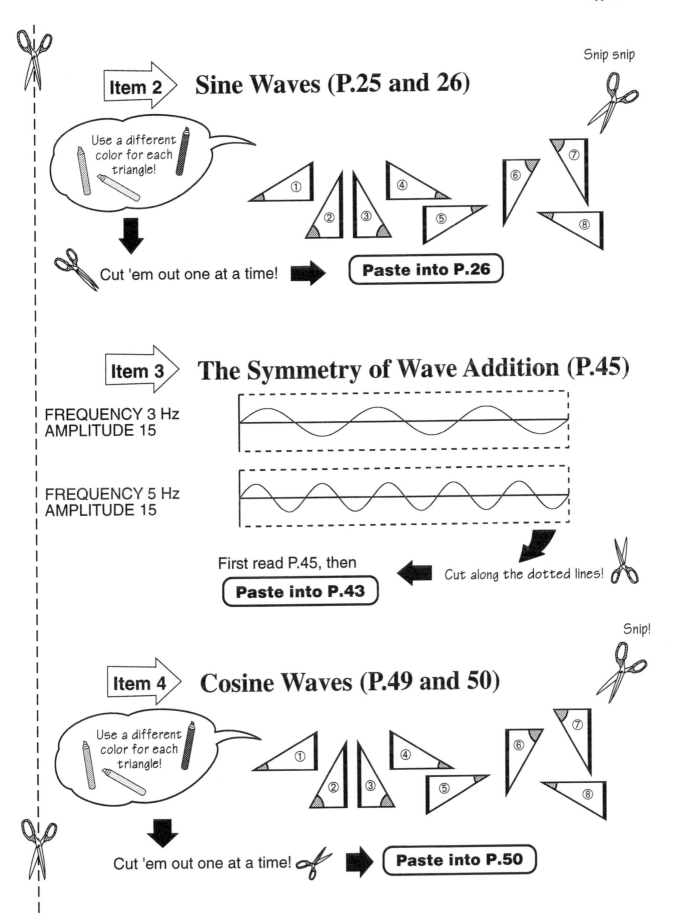

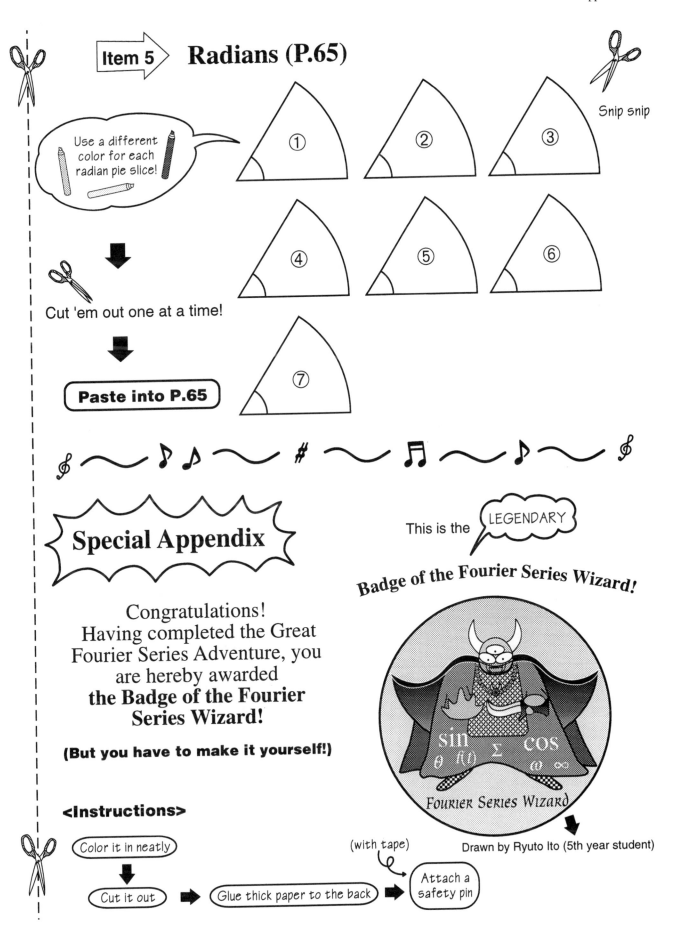

Item 5 ▷ **Radians (P.65)**

Use a different color for each radian pie slice!

① ② ③

Snip snip

④ ⑤ ⑥

Cut 'em out one at a time!

Paste into P.65

⑦

Special Appendix

Congratulations!
Having completed the Great Fourier Series Adventure, you are hereby awarded **the Badge of the Fourier Series Wizard!**

(But you have to make it yourself!)

This is the LEGENDARY

Badge of the Fourier Series Wizard!

sin θ f(t) Σ cos ω ∞

FOURIER SERIES WIZARD

Drawn by Ryuto Ito (5th year student)

<Instructions>

Color it in neatly → Cut it out ▶ Glue thick paper to the back ▶ Attach a safety pin

(with tape)

The Zero-Area Series, No. 1

<Appendix items 6 - 10>

How to use Items 6 - 10

① Use any color you want. (Note: Use the same color for all of Item 6, the same one for all of Item 7, etc. It'll look better if each Item is in a different color.)

② Cut along the solid lines and remove the pieces of the wave.

③ Spray paste onto the back.

④ Paste the pieces into the plus part of the wave on the indicated page. (They should make a perfect fit!)

⑤ Now remove the pieces and paste them into the minus part. (Again, they should fit perfectly.)

That means "Area = 0".

Item 6
P.84

Item 7
P.92

Item 8
P.93

Item 9
P.94

Item 10
P.95

The $a_n \times \dfrac{T}{2}$ Rectangle Series   <Appendix items 11 - 14>

How to use Items 11 - 14

Steps ① through ③ are the same as for Item 6 - 10.

④ Paste in the pieces so they fill in the curves of the wave on the indicated page. They should form a rectangle measuring $a_n \times \dfrac{T}{2}$ – a perfect fit!

Snip snip

The Zero-Area Series, No. 2   <Appendix items 15 - 16>

How to use Items 15 - 16

Steps ① through ③ are the same as for Items 6 - 10.

④ Paste the pieces into the minus part of the wave on the indicated page.

⑤ Now fit the pieces into the plus part of the same wave. Everything should fit!

The $b_n \times \dfrac{T}{2}$ Rectangle Series   <Appendix items 17 - 20>

How to use Items 17 - 20

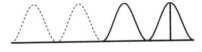
Item 17
P.105

Steps ① through ③ are the same as for Items 6 - 10.

Item 18
P.106

④ Paste in the pieces so they fill in the curves of the wave on the indicated page. They should form a rectangle measuring $b_n \times \dfrac{T}{2}$

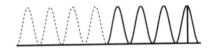
Item 19
P.106

Item 20
P.106

APPENDIX TO THE APPENDIX

Students of the Transnational College of LEX

Answer page

Chapter 1 (p. 18)

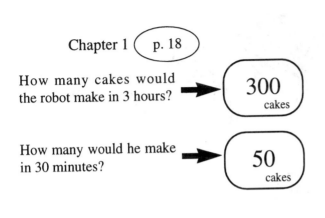

How many cakes would the robot make in 3 hours? ➤ **300** cakes

How many would he make in 30 minutes? ➤ **50** cakes

Chapter 1 (p. 34)

t	⑤ $\frac{1}{3}$	⑧ $\frac{1}{2}$	① 1	③ 2	⑩ 3
f	⑥ 3	⑦ 2	② 1	④ $\frac{1}{2}$	⑨ $\frac{1}{3}$

Chapter 1 (p. 35)

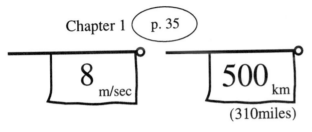

8 m/sec

500 km

(310miles)

Chapter 1 (p. 36)

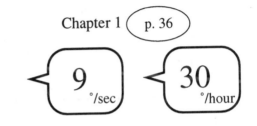

9 °/sec

30 °/hour

Chapter 1 (p. 37)

ω \ t	1 sec	2 sec	3 sec	4 sec	5 sec
90°/sec θ	90°	180°	270°	360°	450°
180°/sec θ	180°	360°	540°	720°	900°
360°/sec θ	360°	720°	1080°	1440°	1800°

Chapter 1 (p. 39)

t (sec)	$\frac{1}{4}$	⑤ $\frac{1}{3}$	$\frac{1}{2}$	① 1	③ 2	3
f (HZ)	4	3	⑦ 2	1	$\frac{1}{2}$	⑨ $\frac{1}{3}$
ω (°/sec)	1440	⑥ 1080	⑧ 720	② 360	④ 180	⑩ 120

Chapter 1 (p. 41)

Wave $A \rightarrow f_A(t) = 20 \sin 360t$

Wave $B \rightarrow f_B(t) = 25 \sin 720t$

Wave $C \rightarrow f_C(t) = 13 \sin 1440t$

Wave $D \rightarrow f_D(t) = 16 \sin 2880t$

Chirrrp!

Chapter 1 (p. 57)

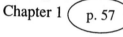

Chapter 1 (p. 62)

① $A = (W - 1) + (W - 2) + (W - 3)$

$\downarrow$

$A = \boxed{\displaystyle\sum_{n=1}^{3} (W - n)}$

③ $C = (1 \times 5) + (2 \times 5) + (3 \times 5)$

$\downarrow$

$C = \boxed{\displaystyle\sum_{n=1}^{3} (n \times 5) \text{ or } \sum_{n=1}^{3} 5n}$

② $B = (Z + 1) + (2Z + 2) + (3Z + 3)$

$\downarrow$

$B = \boxed{\displaystyle\sum_{n=1}^{3} (nZ + n) \text{ or } \sum_{n=1}^{3} n(Z + 1)}$

$f(t) = a_0 + a_1 \cos \omega t + b_1 \sin \omega t$
$\qquad + a_2 \cos 2\omega t + b_2 \sin 2\omega t$
$\qquad + a_3 \cos 3\omega t + b_3 \sin 3\omega t$
$\qquad + \cdots \cdots \cdots \cdots \cdots$

$\downarrow$

$f(t) = \boxed{a_0 + \displaystyle\sum_{n=1}^{\infty} (a_n \cos n\omega t + b_n \sin n\omega t)}$

Chapter 3 (p. 134)

n	a_n	0	1	2	3	4	5	6	7	8	9
0	8	8	8	8	8	8	8	8	8	8	8
1	3	3	2.43	0.93	-0.93	-2.43	-3	-2.43	-0.93	0.93	2.43
2	2	2	0.62	-1.62	-1.62	0.62	2	0.62	-1.62	-1.62	0.62
3	1	1	-0.31	-0.81	0.81	0.31	-1	0.31	0.81	-0.81	-0.31
4	0	0	0	0	0	0	0	0	0	0	0
5	0	0	0	0	0	0	0	0	0	0	0

n	b_n										
1	2	0	1.18	1.90	1.90	1.18	0	-1.18	-1.90	-1.90	-1.18
2	4	0	3.80	2.35	-2.35	-3.80	0	3.80	2.35	-2.35	-3.80
3	3	0	2.85	-1.76	-1.76	2.85	0	-2.85	1.76	1.76	-2.85
4	0	0	0	0	0	0	0	0	0	0	0
5	0	0	0	0	0	0	0	0	0	0	0

$f(t)$	14	18.6	8.99	4.05	6.73	6	6.27	8.47	4.01	2.91

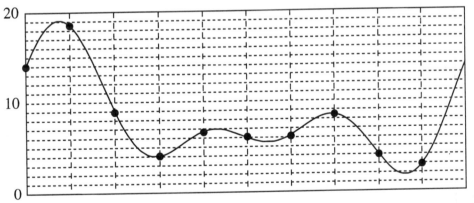

10 sec

Chapter 7 (p. 227)

Height	Width	Area
4.9	0.5	2.45
9.8	0.5	4.9
14.7	0.5	7.35
19.6	0.5	9.8
24.5	0.5	12.25
29.4	0.5	14.7
34.3	0.5	17.1
39.2	0.5	19.6
	Total strip area	88.2

Chapter 7 (p. 228)

Height	Width	Area
2.45	0.25	0.6125
4.9	0.25	1.225
7.35	0.25	18.375
9.8	0.25	2.45
12.25	0.25	3.5625
14.7	0.25	3.675
17.15	0.25	4.2875
19.6	0.25	4.9
22.05	0.25	5.5125
24.5	0.25	6.125
26.95	0.25	6.7375
29.4	0.25	7.35
31.85	0.25	7.9625
34.3	0.25	8.575
36.75	0.25	9.1875
39.2	0.25	9.8
	Total strip area	83.3

Chapter 11   p. 368

	Fourier series	Fourier coefficients
① Original formulas	(1) $f(t) = a_0 + \sum_{n=1}^{\infty}(a_n \cos n\omega t + b_n \sin n\omega t)$	(2) $a_0 = \frac{1}{T}\int_0^T f(t)dt$ (3) $a_n = \frac{2}{T}\int_0^T f(t)\cos n\omega t\, dt$ (4) $b_n = \frac{2}{T}\int_0^T f(t)\sin n\omega t\, dt$
② Rewrite formulas with e and i	(5) $f(t) = a_0 + \sum_{n=1}^{\infty}\left\{\frac{a_n}{2}(e^{in\omega t} + e^{-in\omega t}) + \frac{b_n}{2i}(e^{in\omega t} - e^{-in\omega t})\right\}$	(6) $a_0 = \frac{1}{T}\int_0^T f(t)dt$ (7) $a_n = \frac{2}{T}\int_0^T f(t)\frac{1}{2}(e^{in\omega t} + e^{-in\omega t})dt$ (8) $b_n = \frac{2}{T}\int_0^T f(t)\frac{1}{2i}(e^{in\omega t} - e^{-in\omega t})dt$
③ Create new formulas using $e^{in\omega t}$ and $e^{-in\omega t}$	(9) $f(t) = a_0 + \sum_{n=1}^{\infty}\left\{\frac{1}{2}(a_n - ib_n)e^{in\omega t} + \frac{1}{2}(a_n + ib_n)e^{-in\omega t}\right\}$ (13) $f(t) = a_0 + \sum_{n=1}^{\infty}\left(A_n e^{in\omega t} + B_n e^{-in\omega t}\right)$	(10) $a_0 = \frac{1}{T}\int_0^T f(t)dt$ (11) $\frac{1}{2}(a_n - ib_n) = \frac{1}{T}\int_0^T f(t)e^{-in\omega t}dt$ (12) $\frac{1}{2}(a_n + ib_n) = \frac{1}{T}\int_0^T f(t)e^{in\omega t}dt$ (14) $A_n = \frac{1}{T}\int_0^T f(t)e^{-in\omega t}dt$ (15) $B_n = \frac{1}{T}\int_0^T f(t)e^{in\omega t}dt$
④ Combine formulas using $e^{in\omega t}$	(16) $f(t) = \sum_{n=-\infty}^{\infty} C_n e^{in\omega t}$	(17) $C_n = \frac{1}{T}\int_0^T f(t)e^{-in\omega t}dt$

AFTERWORD

From the original Japanese-language edition

The Fourier Instructors

We completed our first edition of <u>The Fourier Adventure</u> in September 1987, together with a formula software program that allows viewers to understand mathematical formulas with ease. This book is the second, revised edition of that original manuscript.

We believe that learning the language of mathematics has dramatically enhanced our understanding of the natural world, and we want others to share our experience. When we finished the first edition of this book, however, we worried that the individual reader, working his or her way through the book alone, might not experience the fun we had in exploring the world of formulas and physics. Here at the Transnational College of LEX (TCL), some of us were more familiar with mathematics than others. But we all benefited by comparing notes as we inched our way, step by step, toward a mastery of this new language: the language of formulas.

So we decided to improve the user-friendliness of our book by holding a series of test lectures on <u>The Fourier Adventure</u>. We gathered members of the Hippo Family Club together and had them listen and critique as the TCL students who wrote this book tried to teach them Fourier mathematics in the same way we had learned it. We also had them try out our computer program. The Hippo "monitors" consisted of 50 people, male and female, from middle school age on up. Most of them had little if any experience with mathematics, to say nothing of Fourier analysis.

The lecturers were to be TCL students, with one instructor assigned to each chapter of the book.

Forty students – nearly the entire college – volunteered to lecture on at least one of the chapters. Some of the more ambitious candidates vowed to master the concepts in every chapter for good measure. As a result, we had as many as three or four students vying for the honor of lecturing on some chapters. We set up an instructor selection committee, but its members couldn't bring themselves to dash the hopes of so many eager candidates, and wound up unable to make any choices at all.

Yet we still needed to select a single instructor for each lecture. In the end, we decided to let the candidates for each chapter meet and practice lecturing together, with someone familiar with the concepts in that particular chapter serving as group leader. After working together in this manner, the members of each group would have to choose the official lecturer from among themselves. If they couldn't, the job of lecturer would fall to the group leader by default. That would be extremely embarrassing for the students as well as their group leader, so everyone involved had a vested interest in training hard to make sure this didn't happen.

Some groups were able to choose their instructor after only a few practice sessions. Others barely made their decision in time for the lecture itself, with rehearsals continuing up to the last possible minute. Some students gave as many as seven practice lectures. Others gave up less than ten minutes into their first attempt, laying down the chalk with tears in their eyes. The practice sessions had their share of heartbreaking moments, but in the end everyone benefited from the experience. Students who started out comprehending nothing about Fourier gradually increased their understanding through the mock lecture process. Eventually everyone had mastered the material and could share in the pleasure of discussing the concepts they had studied together. No one dropped out part way through the practice sessions. Regardless of who was finally chosen as lecturer, every group displayed tremendous team spirit and continued meeting right up to the big day. Nobody sulked because they couldn't be instructor; everyone took pride in their chosen teammate's successful performance.

The Lectures Begin

On the day of the first lecture, the Tokyo classroom of the TCL was packed with a capacity crowd of nearly 100. Everyone was extremely nervous – group leaders, instructors, and the students in the test audience. At last the lecture got underway. Initially, whenever the instructor asked a question, the students sat petrified in silence, or, if called upon, stuttered their answers with great trepidation. But the audience greeted each answer with cheers and applause, and eventually even the most timid students were raising their hands to volunteer answers. In the beginning, more than a few participants would have admitted to having a phobia about mathematics, of getting chills up their spine at the very sight of a formula. Some appeared totally lost during the first part of the lecture. But by the time it was over, the unanimous verdict of the monitors was, "It all made sense!" One even added, "I can't believe I really understand it as well as it feels like I do. Maybe I just think I understand it."

Every listener was touched in a different way. One was a mother who hadn't gone near math since her high school days. Another was a father who had excelled at the subject, but said he'd never had so much fun with it as now. A primary school student said the lectures got him more interested not just in arithmetic, but in social studies and other school subjects as well. A high school student astonished her teacher by delivering a LEX-style lecture to her biology class as part of a lab project. Those of us who were giving the lectures were deeply affected by the unexpected impact they seemed to be having on the audience.

Our monitors were all supposed to be of middle school age or older. But since the lectures were being held at night, some parents, not wishing to leave their younger children at home, brought them along as well. Thus the audience included several entire families. The presence of primary school and even pre-school kids took our adventures with Fourier in some unforeseen directions. As one would expect, the youngsters spent their time running around the room, throwing cushions, and generally ignoring the lectures. Yet to hear the mothers tell it, something strange was happening to their kids.

One second-grader, upon seeing her arithmetic teacher draw a right triangle on the blackboard, said to him, "That angle's called theta!" After class she went up to the teacher and declared, "I knew everything you were talking about today. Studying's fun!" At the next parent-teacher conference, the dumbfounded teacher asked the little girl's parents if they could explain this remarkable behavior.

A three-year-old toddler, who attended the lectures every week with her parents and one-year-old brother, was apparently affected by hearing the constant talk about "Fourier." She learned the word by heart, and could be heard haranguing her friends in the sandbox, "Do you know about Fourier? I'm gonna go to school with Mama and Papa today!"

It's a sight that is all too rare these days. Families learning together. People of all ages – even the youngest children – having fun studying something like Fourier mathematics. Families can have the same fun with languages, listening to tapes together or playing word games around the dinner table. When a family studies together, it creates an opportunity for discoveries one person would never make alone. Parents attending the Fourier lectures gave us glowing accounts of lively conversations with their children about wave phenomena during the ride home. As stories like these proliferated in our monitor audience, it was only a matter of time before everyone began referring to our weekly gathering as the "Fourier Family."

A short time later, the Tokyo Fourier Family was joined by families in the cities of Nagoya and Osaka as well. Most of these participants were indeed families; after hearing about the lectures in Tokyo, they assumed that family participation was part of the experience. One mother and her second-grader son made the journey from Tsu to Nagoya (a three-hour round trip from another prefecture) every week for ten weeks without missing a single lecture. A mother who always brought her three- and five-year-olds had to miss one lecture when the younger one got sick. To make up for their absence, she and the older son spent the day talking about Fourier. At dinner that night the boy said, "Let's eat Fourier-style!" Drawing a picture of some waves, he added, "I wish I could've gone tonight to hear about Fourier. Even though they don't have any pictures, it's fun!" Families who were already having fun working on seven languages together seemed to have added an eighth to their repertoire – the language of mathematics.

The first series of Fourier Family lectures ended in March 1988. The main objective of the monitoring process was to improve the book and the accompanying computer program. The result of these lectures and their audience's response is this new edition of The Fourier Adventure. We can hardly wait to reconvene the Fourier Family to go over this version too!

About the Manuscript

Our members actually wrote at least three times as many manuscripts as you will find in this book. Not only that, all were handwritten and extremely individualistic. Many, like Junko Nakamura's "Fourier for Grandma," were so delightful that a reader would easily forget he was reading a math text.

With several authors for every chapter, and every manuscript unique, it was impossible to rank one over another. Our original plan was to compile all the manuscripts together. But in the interests of making this book as easy as possible to read and use as a classroom text, we reluctantly decided to settle on one manuscript for each chapter.

However, we want our readers to know that there were many wonderful Fourier stories that we couldn't include in these pages.

WHAT NEXT?

Most of the students at the Transnational College of LEX who wrote this book had never heard of Fourier when they first entered the college. But in the course of chatting with their classmates about it, listening to others explain it, and trying to explain it themselves, comprehension gradually set in. Eventually they found themselves standing in front of a crowd, lecturing about Fourier to other members of the Fourier Family. Students who started out as silent listeners have now become instructors. Hippo families all over Japan are embarking upon a whole new series of Fourier adventures. Who knows, someone somewhere may be writing their own sequel to The Fourier Adventure at this very moment!

April 1989
Transnational College of LEX

Bibliography

Agui, T. and Nakajima, M. 安居院 猛／中嶋 正之 電子科学シリーズ91 FFTの使い方, Kouseido-Sanpo Pub. Co., 1981.

Feynman, R. **The Feynman Lectures on Physics vol. I,II,III**, Addison-Wesley, 1965

Feynman, R. ファインマン物理学(全 5 巻)(**The Feynman Lectures on Physics**), Iwanami Book Co, 1967

Heisenberg, W. **Physics and Beyond**, Harper & Row, 1972

Heisenberg, W. 山崎 和夫 訳 部分と全体(**Physics and Beyond**), Misuzu Book Co., 1974

Hino, M. 日野 幹夫 スペクトル解析, Asakura Book Co., 1977

Nakajima, S. 中嶋 貞雄 物理入門コース5 量子力学 I , Iwanami Book Co., 1983

Sakakibara, Y. 榊原 陽 ことばを歌え！こどもたち, Chikuma Book Co., 1985

Spiegel, M. R. 数学公式・数表ハンドブック(**Mathematical Handbook of Formulas and Tables**), McGraw-Hill Book, 1984

Strang, G. 線形代数とその応用(**Linear Algebra and its Applications**), Sangyo-tosyo Co., 1978

Toda, M. 戸田 盛和 物理入門コース1 力学, Iwanami Book Co., 1982

Wadachi, M. 和達 三樹 物理入門コース10 物理のための数学, Iwanami Book Co., 1983

Wylie, C. R. Jr. 富久 泰明訳 微分積分学(**Calculus**), Burein Book Pub. Co., 1980

Transnational College of LEX **ARTCL '84-'87 (Annual Report of TCL)**, Transnational College of LEX, 1985-1988

Princeton University Store, NJ
Sat 13 July 1996 ~ $24.95+ 1.50 tax

Princeton University Store, NJ
Sat 13 July 1996 ~ $24.95+ 1.50 tax